D0991036

THE GEORGE GUND FOUNDATION
IMPRINT IN AFRICAN AMERICAN STUDIES

The George Gund Foundation has endowed
this imprint to advance understanding of
the history, culture, and current issues
of African Americans.

The publisher gratefully acknowledges the generous support of the African American Studies Endowment Fund of the University of California Press Foundation, which was established by a major gift from the George Gund Foundation.

Digging

MUSIC OF THE AFRICAN DIASPORA

Samuel A. Floyd, Jr., Editor Emeritus

Guthrie P. Ramsey, Jr., Editor

Digging

*The Afro-American Soul
of American Classical Music*

Amiri Baraka

UNIVERSITY OF CALIFORNIA PRESS
Berkeley · Los Angeles · London

University of California Press, one of the most
distinguished university presses in the United States,
enriches lives around the world by advancing scholarship in the humanities, social sciences, and natural
sciences. Its activities are supported by the UC Press
Foundation and by philanthropic contributions from
individuals and institutions. For more information,
visit www.ucpress.edu.

University of California Press
Berkeley and Los Angeles, California

University of California Press, Ltd.
London, England

Library of Congress Cataloging-in-Publication Data

Baraka, Imamu Amiri, 1934–
    Digging : the Afro-American soul of American
classical music / Amiri Baraka.
        p.   cm.—(Music of the African diaspora ; 13)
    ISBN 978-0-520-25715-3 (cloth : alk. paper)
    1. African Americans—Music—History
and criticism.   2. Music—History
and criticism.   3. African American
musicians.   I. Title.
    ML3556.B1612   2009
    780.89'96073—dc22   2008025976

Manufactured in the United States of America

18   17   16   15   14   13   12   11   10   09
10   9   8   7   6   5   4   3   2   1

The paper used in this publication meets the
minimum requirements of ANSI/NISO Z39.48–1992
(R 1997) (Permanence of Paper).

Little of beauty has America given the world save the rude grandeur God himself stamped on her bosom: the human spirit in this new world has expressed itself in vigor and ingenuity rather than in beauty. And so by fateful chance the Negro folk-song—the rhythmic cry of the slave—stands today not simply as the sole American music, but as the most beautiful expression of human experience born this side the seas. It has been neglected, it has been, and is, half despised, and above all it has been persistently mistaken and misunderstood; but notwithstanding, it still remains as the singular spiritual heritage of the nation and the greatest gift of the Negro people.

W. E. B. DuBois, "Of the Sorrow Songs,"
in *The Souls of Black Folk*

Contents

Introduction

A great song arose, the loveliest thing born this side of the
seas. It was a new song. It did not come from Africa, though
the dark throb and beat of that Ancient of Days was in it
and through it. It did not come from white America—never
from so pale and hard and thin a thing, however deep these
vulgar and surrounding tones had driven. Not the Indies nor
the hot South, the cold East or heavy West made this music.
It was a new song and its deep and plaintive beauty, its great
cadences and wild appeal wailed, throbbed and thundered
on the world's ear with a message seldom voiced by man. It
swelled and blossomed like incense, improvised and born
anew out of an age long past, and weaving into its texture
the old and new melodies in word and in thought.

W. E. B. DuBois

One of the most beautiful explications, as analysis and history, of
"the Music" comes from Du Bois, in his grandest work, *Black Reconstruction in America*. So, because the good Dr. combines the material
social world with and as the origins of Art. The Earth & the Sky.

So *Digging* means to present, perhaps arbitrarily, varied paradigms
of this essentially Afro-American art. The common predicate, myself,
the Digger. One who gets down, with the down, always looking above
to see what is going out, and so check *Digitaria,* as the Dogon say,
necessary if you are to dig the fartherest Star, *Serious.*

So this book is a microscope, a telescope, and being Black, a peri-
scope. All to dig what is deeply serious. From a variety of places, reviews, liner notes, live checking, merely reflecting, the intention is to
provide some theoretical and observed practice of the historical essence
of what is clearly American Classical Music, no matter the various
names it, and we, have been called.

The sun is what keeps this planet alive, including the Music, like we
say, the Soul of which is Black.

Essays

CHAPTER I

Griot/Djali

Poetry, Music, History, Message

Griot has grown in significance in the U.S., essentially because of the burgeoning perception here, now, that Afro-America is inextricably bound not only to Africa, but to the U.S., Pan-America (the Western Hemisphere, the actual "Western World"), and, through its Pan-African diaspora (pre & post and always, right now, modern), international culture too.

So the word *Griot,* the poet, musician, historian, story teller, is getting known all over the world. Though "French" as transmitted "symbol," it is the best-known term for the West African *Djali* (or *Djeli,* but *Djeli ya* also means the Djali's act, his "getting down" to take us up and out), the Central and South African *Imbongi,* the East African *Mshairi* or *Ngombe* (rapper), the Yoruba *Iiala,* all carry the same general meaning, though altered somewhat by the detail of history of the specific culture they come out of, Africa is a continent, there are many cultures, from West to Central to East as from South to Central to North. To say African anything is like saying European anything. Where you talking about? . . . the question.

Griot, with its "French" vibration, from the colonial "gift" the northerners imposed on their piece of the West African pie, yet carries with it the insistence of "Cry." As in Cry Out? From tears, or in the essentially secular remonstrance of "Town Crier," as it was used in the North, Europe. (There is also, with that, the inference, in the word, of "Gray," as in *Gris,* so that the Gray is being cried away, or there is some presence bursting out of the grayness. The fact that "gris-gris" is a "fetish," i.e., carrier of, or celebrator of, or homage to, whatever power kept us cool, kept the gray away. (You mean "Grays," like we used to call "white" people? If African "Lucy" is human #1, how does "white" get in it, unless you from outside the Van Allen belt?)

What is important about this is that if you look at the Masks of Drama, you see the geography and philosophical aesthetic of the world. The smile at the bottom of the world, sided by the frown at the top. It means that the southerners', the Africans', highest point of revelation was the unbridled joy that we still find in Black U.S. churches, or now, with more "integration," in Rock concerts everywhere. Those old women screaming in church on Sundays, "getting happy," the Gospel (God Spell). Going up and outta here to receive the soul's revelation! Another name for the Djali is the *Gleeman*! Dig it? Is that why we called "Shine," cause we be gleeman? (One Greek philosopher hated us because, he said, we be smilin all the time. Yeh? Well, not no more!) So it could be "Cry" as in the southern "Shouts" and "Hollers" and in them churches they was sure hollerin.

In the north, they taught us in school, tragedy is the highest revelation of humanity, hence the frown. In Ency. Brit, they say they yet do not understand the purpose of laughter! and describe it as a concatenation of physical connections!! (Oh, yeh!). So that the dude who iced his ol man, slept with his mommy, and put out his own eyes so he could go colonial and not have to dig it is a paradigm of northern revelation, like Nietzche said, Emotion interferes with my thinking!

Djali is more to the point, though *Griot* is its translatable quantum. Like Rock & Roll means R&B. But *Griot* is specific enough, until you get under the word, and understand that the Djali was to *raise* us, with the poetry, the music, the history, the message, to take us up and out, not to drag us. (That's why we still call dumb stuff "a drag," you know, like the Klan is a drag. That's why we call "Squares"—which the Egyptians said was the angle of failure, while the pyramid is the angle of "Success"—those who are "Lame," like the first Crazy Eddie, Eddie Pus.)

The Djali is not a "Town Crier," he is a Town Laugher. We were not screaming when Trane blew because we were sad, were dragged, Trane had got down and went out and took us up with him! Up up and away, beyond the squares. He had got ON (like the African city named so because it was precisely constructed under the Sun to dig the biggest

Sol we know). The original meaning of "Comedy" is "together or to gather in Joy" not "Slap Stick" (ow!).

So the Djali, in his revelation of the "everywhere allways." The "message" is not just "Six O'Clock and All's Well," it might be Gylan Kain saying, "You shdda cut the mf, made him bleed. You shdda made it personal!" It could be Amus Mor saying, "Who are we, where are we going?" It could be Larry Neal saying, "Don't Say Goodbye to the Pork Pie Hat." It could be Margaret Walker saying, "For my people, everywhere. . . . " You know.

The misunderstanding that many of us have, even those who style themselves "Afrocentric," is that we don't understand that Africa colors everything that exists! In the Western Hemisphere, we are a combination of African, European, Native (Asian). That is the culture and the people, what ain't that ain't here, except on paper, or as paper. The reciting of poetry with music, recycled in the '50s by Langston Hughes, etc., and which received such ignorant response (both pro and con), was not new, it was the basis of what poetry (musical speech) has always been. Just as the talking heads of European theater, which got, after the Victorians and the modern Imp of colonialism, less integrated with music and dance, as ignorant supremacy, the devil's brew, took over the world's mind, and convinced people they didn't exist and nobody else did either, Never did! Otherwise yall wouldn't be laughing and still in chains.

Poetry is music! Read Du Bois's *Black Reconstruction,* a history book could move you as a poem. The African, whose early society was communal, and woman dominated, created, from the beginning (*art* means "exist," e.g., "and thou art with me"), social expression that replicated the structure and nature of that society. Mother Africa, the Mother Land. Not "the Father Land." "The spirit will not descend without song!" Equiano tells us. When "Blue was our favorite color," before we got so nutty we sold our selves to the junkman, took a really bad trip, and wound up cross the sea with the Blues, another story.

Rap, for instance, is as old as the African tree, upon which we rapped, and told our story, which later was *Ngoma,* the drum. The Pygmies were here before God, or the drum! A log, the semen tells us (how're you spelling that?) to record, the rap. The best, of our heart, why we under On to dig, the BE and where it's AT. Spirit is literally Breath, inspire expire. Space, as it is specific to we, and us, & I (means Black), becomes speech. What Air is that (you mean Song, son? Or

Sangre, Blood? or the hotness with which you blue, blew, singed you, didn't it).

Speech is the oldest carrier of human life. Song, from Sun (where the Sol gives you Soul), dig? Get down. Find Out! The body of happiness (Funk). Everything we carried, from watermelons to boogalooing in the end zone after the t.d., was carried. Where would it go? U.S. culture is a pyramid of African, European, Asian (Native). So that it is not a matter of "African Survivals." To be an "American," north, south, or central, is to be that as well.

The Griot has always been with us, even in the U.S., listen to Lightnin Hopkins, Bessie Smith, Louis Armstrong ("What Did I Do, to Be So Black & Blue?"), or Al Hibbler flying in his Dukeplane, or Billie, God knows, or Larry Darnell, "Why you fool, you poor sad worthless, foolish fool!" Or Stevie, Aretha, Abbey, Sun Ra. You wants some Djali, and the Djeli Ya, the get down, like we say. Well, begin with Djeli Roll Morton, who invented Jazz (you mean "I AM!" the come music? JA ZZ). He said that? Or Dinah and Ella singing (getting hot as the sun), "It must be Djeli, cause Jam don't shake like that!"

Jam? You mean Jamaa, the family? Like a Jam Session? Or Ujamaa, the communal society. Is you all in all them colors (many stories, co lores) because you communal, like Max Roach said, our Music always is. My man call it polyrhythmic, polyphonic. When the priest (before the is, and digging, prying into it) calls and we respond (come back), we together many, this connection opens us as Gates. You straight, Gate? Or the *Imbongi*, you mean you can drum *(Ngombe)* your way inside us? Be at the where we is under standing, so get ON?

That's why it's *Mshairi,* you communal on us again. In the U.S., We is a bunch of I's without the logical connection. The rap for your cap to wake you from your nap, or wake you to your naps. Ba, Ba, Black Sheep, they asked, have you any wool? Yeh, a whole head full! (Wisdom, the Sufi said. That's our bag.)

That is, let the story of the Griot get you Djali, make you understand you is as old as you is new. And what you don't know is how you blow. It's why we Blue, because we blew. But then get down with the Djali, Mr. B. say, "Djeli Djeli Djeli," what is needed is what the Griot/Djali provided, information, inspiration, reformation, and self-determination! Mama Sky, we cried, hook us up with the Electricity. Turn us ON. That city of our deep desire.

6/19/96

CHAPTER 2

Miles Later

The fact that Miles Davis is a great African American cultural figure, a musician, composer, more impacting and influential than most, should never be in contention. The work is there. Its history and its shaping force are as obvious as anything in the world of art and social life.

I can speak, for instance, from my own experience, my own life, having come upon Miles when he was first standing up with Charlie Parker, part of the transforming force of the music called BeBop. Part of that music but also a bearer, in whatever specific identification, of that philosophy, both musical and social. Because BeBop, the music, was both the expression of African American life and itself part of the philosophy developed with that life, as history and as art.

Miles Davis was a middle-class black youth from East St. Louis come to New York seeking high art. His transitions and travails are well known, however twisted by white supremacy as incident and report- age. The drug addiction, the rise to grand expression as a sidekick of the great Bird. Miles was a musician whose music carried the message of himself and a whole generation, both in transition, both defining and constantly redefined. By the world and their own consciousness and reaction to that world.

The Miles of the '40s, the young wild Miles who was so hip that even his regular "fluffs" on the Bird sides were taken as gospel. The small cracked lyrical tone we all wanted to emulate. And then when he came out of the era of conk and drape (conked hair and zoot suit type pants) and began to look like the hip gray flannel suit styled '50s we were there too.

Miles had a demeanor about him that we liked. He was serious, he was "clean," and he could play. He was one of our priests from that beginning. He was one of the sound scientists who had ushered in the new learning of BeBop from the black laboratories of Minton's and the all-night jam sessions that rescued black expression from the grim mediocrity of commercial big band chartism the corporate media sacrilegiously called "swing." Like Bird, and Monk, and Max, and Klook, and Dizzy in the first rank, Miles was a young master, a young prince, a black prince, whose very demeanor and voice was the essence of what was *hip*.

And this must be understood, that Miles Davis was what hip *meant*. Bird was God and Dizzy his frantic herald. Monk was the High Priest of weird (though Monk's weirdness was the measure of all things for me personally) but Miles was hip. He looked hip, he dressed hip, he talked hip, and he played . . . shit, he was what hip sounded like.

Miles was the measure then of the '50s to be sure. He wore the uniform of the gray flannel suit, as we were wont to do then. A black neo-ivy, neo-english garb, rhythmed into higher being by the paisleys, the turn of color we wore to keep us connected with our mother (Africa). He talked in the language of the new learning, post Pres, who gave us a language of words, and a language of cool 8th notes and thoughtful languor that meant we were with it but not so yokelish as to be on top of a beat cause nobody knew where it was going or if it was even gonna be there given the few turns we'd seen under the sun.

So from the beginning Miles was also *cool*. He carried that with him a direct gift from the President of what it is. And we valued that, that coolness, that refusal to be committed to any of this workaday dumbness we grew up in the middle of. If the world of white supremacy, mediocrity, and useless effort were square (the angle of pain and failure according to the ancient Egyptians) then the pyramid of our constancy was to be cool.

But it was always a coolness like the Congolese described, a fire hotter than heat. A fire too serious to use up its being with being hot. Its hotness was in its self-defined expression, if you looked at it, it might seem like dancing blue ice, edged with reds and yellows barely, but a cold blue, except when you touched it, it was extremely hot. So its speech could burn the world down, could burn you down if you stumbled into it, like some abusive geometry.

Miles's history is a history of constant changing, to be sure, like so many of us. And like so many of us Miles's changes are predictable to a certain extent, if we are familiar with the subject and its object. Miles in the BeBop world was young Miles, learning to be Miles. But BeBop was not itself cool, the fact that it had to express what was basic, the blues, improvisation, polyrhythms against the context of the dead trying to kill the living, gave it a fundamental hotness, a heat of life exploding into being.

Miles explains this by saying that Bird was playing too fast. It was over so quickly, this heated expression. Miles needed a bottom, he called it. Some connection with the given, the firmament of the other world. Not just the heat of his own being, and the justification of his own consciousness. This was Miles's *Americanness* it seems to me. His bridge of relationship with the "other." So that BeBop for Miles, though he was one of its most princely practitioners, was a transitional theme sounded in search of his own whole.

The "coolness" that Miles carried was expressed on his own with the *Birth of the Cool* sides. There were not only some of the boppers on these sides but hip white musicians like Lee Konitz, Gerry Mulligan, some Gil Evans arrangements. And even though Miles's coolness to me was the hippest of the cool, the so-called "West Coast" jazz these sides were harbingers of was in the main a kind of white mood music which commercially sprang from Bop like commercial swing leaped off of the backs of the hot big bands of Ellington and Basie.

The main black voice reshaped the music with the Hard Bop re-expression. Max and Brownie, Horace Silver and Art Blakey and the Jazz Messengers, Sonny Rollins, brought the black church directly into the fray, and "funk" became the call for a hotter expression as statement of a fundamentally black aesthetic and social development.

But Miles became a master of this statement as well. His sides with Jackie McLean and Rollins. And finally the classic quintet with John Coltrane and Cannonball Adderly, Philly Joe Jones and Paul Chambers attests to this with much power.

This '50s juncture coincided with the upsurge of the civil rights movement, which marks a qualitative social development as well as just the pile-on of more events. The coolness of Miles in a sense reflected the pre–civil rights demeanor of a generation, not a quietism per se, but an introspective turn, an inside reflection that for some was enough in terms of dealing with a hostile outside world. But the hostility can never be kept "outside." The gray flannel suiting had come off many of that generation and was scoffed at by the generation coming up, the sit-inners, and young militants and soi-disant revolutionaries. The cool was something one burst loose from to confront the enemy openly.

The woman attacking Clay in *Dutchman,* my 1963 one-act, taunts him by saying, among other things, "Be Cool, Be Cool . . . that's all you know. . . . " Yet finally he does burst loose to confront the antagonist, and the whole of a hostile environment.

Miles's bursting loose was always personal, though as a celebrity it could never remain that way. It was symbolic or apocryphal. Miles's reputation for "being nasty" to people, though finally overblown, was in reality merely one aspect of his personality being fitted to a time. His stage demeanor, long controversial, where he turned his back to the audience or left the stage, was taken as the elitist permissiveness of the western artist model. It could also, if placed into the context of dealing with "white people," be justified as a kind of micro-revolt against the proprieties of "the good negro."

As far as the art tip, BeBop, the fundamental African American modernism, carried a revolutionary impact and philosophy socially and as art. It was, aside from its musical content, the music that served as a transitional form of African American culture placing itself openly in the context of American expression. It was the music that clearly attested to the historical phenomenon that black American music was also American Classical music. From the time of the emergence of "the Street," 52nd Street, as an American cultural mecca, and with the subsequent appearance of BeBop's various musical children, the music would never again be relegated strictly to the African American community. By the time World War Two was over African American music was international.

The import of this is that now "integration" as a social context for this black expression could make it "art," not just the functional expressionism of the African American people (which is also art, but chained to denigration by white supremacy). Many of the early BeBop groups were integrated, and integration in a segregated society is progressive, where it means a genuine multinationality of purpose and not just the false integration of big commerce ripping off black art for white money.

Rock & Roll, a '50s phenomenon, signals this integrated American cultural development, when white players can now cover black music as well as substitute a style of their own creation. Though Rock & Roll is still basically black music played by white people. But the venues are closer than they were. There is still Race music, like the records the companies issued to get in on the blues craze of the '20s. Now it's called Soul. You see the two charts in the newspapers. A Pop chart and a Soul chart. But then they got to keep the music lovers somewhat segregated or the black art might infect white America so thoroughly that what the art wants the whole people want and the society is forced to change.

Miles is the quintessential American voice, so moving and penetrating because he carries the whole weathervane of this society's expression. Miles is a black musician, and the greater part of the music he has made, and which he will be remembered for, is classic African American art. Yet Miles is also the American, in an ironic sense, and one cannot know America, one cannot express the whole of America, without at least having an inside tip on the black question!

Since the '50s most American art is one-sided and shallow because it cannot convey the emotional life of the force which turns this society forward. Clearly that is black life, not as a nationalist anthem, but as an analytical précis as to what is the sharpest and largest contradiction between what we produce and who we are.

It is so much clearer because it is so much starker. In the 1850s the slave narratives told the underside of the American Dream even before it got spoken. But that black life was not completely part of American life, though American life was shaped by it to a much larger extent than even American historians perceive. The U.S. is not Europe, it never has been. It is a multicultural post-European society with a multinational social base.

The United States since BeBop and Rock & Roll is an obviously multicultural society and it is impossible to tell about it unless one is sensitive to this fact as a living context. The enormously successful recordings Miles made with Gil Evans, *Sketches of Spain, Porgy & Bess, Miles Ahead,* all speak directly to this phenomenon. While the "blacker" Miles is "Jazz" or more clearly African American, the Evans sides are a seamless American music into which Miles has brought the black feeling empowering the harmonies and melodies of American middle-class modern.

The American context must be raised as say Duke Ellington does so that the jazz and the American music are so integrated as to pay homage to one another rather than one ride the other. But this is not simply double-think because the Jazz is the music of Americans who were not allowed to be Americans, and while there is an American music possible without African American expression, since the middle of the 20th century such expression has not been very serious or important.

Miles entered the '60s with the baddest band of the age. It was the '50s hard bop, but now carrying a thoughtful lyricism to it, as well as an expanding expressionism. Coltrane is the expressionist, Cannonball the lyrical soul miniaturist. These are the two aspects of Miles's thinking. And even today those two elements dominate most of the Jazz, whether the avant-garde direction of the expressionist, Trane, or the fusion, i.e., the mix of blues bottom and melodic ready-mades on top.

So that of the two trends of Jazz Miles has had an important impact on both. That great band sent vibrations both musical and human in all directions. The most "important" of the fusion musicians are Miles sent, and the most important of the expressionists, whether mainstream or experimental, are also Miles influenced.

Since the '70s Miles's music has grown increasingly more overtly weighted toward the fusion sound, though the actual sound of his horn in and underneath the tons of electricity played by whiter and whiter bands still sounds like Miles and occasionally (hear *Tutu*) like vintage Miles. But the bottom Miles sought, that clear connection with the given, which made his voice so American and his music like a weather-vane of American musical elementals, has shown signs of dominating the eerie blue gorgeousness of his negritude. If only from the demands of commerce.

Because, for certain, Miles is always, and congratulatorily so, aware of where the bux is going and what pays and what don't, so to speak. Though he never had to sweat that, his natural expression as a mature composer/musician has been so reflective of the crisscross of American life that it is like a national sound, funky and lyrical at the same time. Hot and cool. Still and moving.

But I cannot dismiss the music Miles is making today like some so-called purists who seek the impossible dream of purity when such a boogie man never existed. We can agree that Miles has made more beautiful and more expressive music, though we should never even try to wave our hands at Miles because that would be like playing Beethoven cheap. ("Well you didn't like the 4th Symphony, well I heard he's writing a 5th, and got plans for a 6th, 7th, 8th, and 9th . . .")

And there is still, even under the klaxon and turgid electronics, the Milesian heart cool and afire, lyrical and throaty, telling us something. Yet what he wants to tell now seems submerged by how he has chosen to keep his footlight presence formidable. We are shocked for instance at what Miles wears! That's wild ain't it, but form and content, appearance and substance often are confirming presences.

Often he looks like the wackiest of Rock stars, with long coats and spangles and superbejewelled, boots, leggings, multicolored horns. Though we do not reject this on R&B musicians, but that is not exactly true since most R&B musicians do not get that far into the waygone-sphere, unlike Kiss and the Rocks, who search for being in appearance since meaning is not their intention.

Perhaps it's that we look for the valorization of Jazz musicians in their music, in the content of their expression, though we have been overjoyed at a Monkian hat, a Dizzy horn, the strangeness of a Bud, or even the otherworld garb of a Sun Ra. But these have seemed much more expressive of the musician's personality than the co-signing of some jittery commercial trendiness. With Miles it seems like he means to be a Rock musician, like he's no longer being agented as a jazz act but a pop/rock act, we feel this as a kind of estrangement from the first estate. Where soul seems an excuse for exclusiveness and elitism rather than the fundamental all-inclusiveness of feeling.

But then look around you, that's what's out here. But we keep look-ing deeper, and for deeper confirmation of life, if we are to live at all. It is as if Miles in being the American expression of our blackness emerges as the black expression of our Americanness. The Buppies for instance (black upwardly mobile professionals) claim a neutrality of culture as American ethos. They claim to be the all of America in this part of the 20th century, their breath and reason coming from all parts of the society. Except the gloss they do on the black side is commercial through and through. A use they carry as vitas for new employment, the disguise which permits a somewhat heftier and more hauntingly tear-stained paycheck.

Except one part of America is rotten and dying, this should be clear. And that part which is living and wants to live must constantly struggle to extricate itself from the dead thing's bowels, and fearfully oppose being absorbed by the dead thing's mind.

When Europeans ask us, "Is Miles Davis still the voice of Black people? And if so, why do white people admire him so much?" It is simply that our NATO allies are sure enough of themselves, not only having grown up on U.S. culture, as Occupier and Nourisher, but now they have gotten emotion specific as to which one of the States of this emotional union they are in tune with and which they reject.

What is not understood with this question is that Europe is now cul-turally influenced by America on the real side even more than America is influenced by Europe. Though the dead still speak of English Departments and American Studies is tiny and Black Studies imperiled by reaction. The power of the U.S. is in its multicultural force, that recycling of international perceptions and lives in this "local" social space. Plus the impact this local has on the international, like a replaying, a retuning, from where it came from through the American transducer on out to reinfluence the world. The African of Stevie Wonder is African Americaned back out into the world as American. So that even the Africans want to sound like Stevie or James Brown, when they were the first Stevies and Godfathers of Soul!

Miles is loved as American expression but valorized, given philosophical profundity, as "black," i.e., African American. Miles's very "rebelliousness," e.g., his much-publicized run-ins with racist American police, is part of the general story of African American Liberation. A slave narrative. Yet Miles wants to exist as post-slave, as a well-to-do American, traveled, suave, sophisticated. But at one point, one cannot be both those things in peace. The producer is not in charge yet of those definitions, they are empowered by the merchant and merchandising.

The slave makes slave music, it can be covered or improved or rendered more profound by merchants and merchandising. But it can never be suave, sophisticated, etc. In order for Miles to be Miles he must be black and yet not black. In order for the new middle classes outside the U.S. or even inside it to appreciate his "blackness" they must deprecate his Americanness, and in order for them to be consoled by his Americanness they must deprecate his blackness.

But there is still another, heavier factor, that being, Miles's music still carries the seed of more innovation, not just the present commercial treadwater. In *Tutu, Human Nature, Something on Your Mind,* and some others the specter of what an actually new Miles music would be can sometimes be glimpsed. If that were B. B. King, Little Milton, Jr. Walker, say, playing with Miles or musicians of that stature rather than barren Rockers, that mix Miles gets would be mind-bending, funkily terrifying, not to mention lyrically transporting. I still hold out for that eventuality myself. We'd really see some shonuff fusion then, nuclear not con.

Miles's status with white middle-class internationalia is problematical for all of us and it is historic. When the black anything gets accepted by white society, they then put it down, to maintain white supremacy. Though all expression coming as fresh is assaulted by the disgust of familiarity, which means that now the commercial world can reproduce that expression so it no longer has to be courted or held up as unique or important. That is the evil of mass production outside of mass control. The expendability and spendability of life itself. Since money is the only real sacrament. Neither art nor feeling can ever be, except temporarily and superficially.

When speaking about Europe, specifically about "white" petty bourgeois Europe, not the thousands of Pan-Africans and Asians that live there as well, perception and rationale about Miles, like the music, have undergone some fundamental change since the earlier halcyon days of mostly uninformed Gee Whizism.

However, European scholars and musicians did show a sincere appreciation for the music, some transcending white supremacy if only to understand that African American music was not European music and it had its own standards and geniuses. Ansermet on Bechet, Horowitz on Tatum, Stravinsky on Ellington would be good opening references. Such serious discussion in Europe goes back to Brahms, Martin Williams tells us.

But since those times Europeans, like white Americans, no longer qualify as a passive audience for the music. Now there are European jazz players so ubiquitous as to make it even more difficult for African American players to get as much play in Europe as before. Just as in the United States, often it would seem that Jazz and Blues are European and Euro-American inventions. Racist media and anti-scholars are working feverishly on such a klannish historical genocide.

These trends also uncolor much of the perception and rationale about Miles Davis. Of the still living superstars of Jazz, Miles Davis must be among the most, if not the most, prominent. Obviously, it ought to be Dizzy Gillespie from the BeBop years, he was held as co-author of the genre, but Miles has always carried, as Dizzy says, "an aura" to him, which his constant changes render as mystery, and translate into commercial "excitement."

So Miles has been part of Europe and white America's portrait of "them," i.e., Black folks, for as long as they can remember. He is held both guru and thug, artist and tough guy. The racist imbecile Chambers, in his ugly chauvinist tome on Miles, even implied Miles was a pimp. That would tie the little gruesome picture he wears inside his head about black people with the proper bow.

But while there is some obvious valorization and legitimization of Miles among this crowd, even a grudging admiration for his "wildness, etc.," the very familiarity with Miles, the "knowing about him," must strip him of anything ultimately important. Only mystery is ranked close to money as something to be revered by the Christian West. That and the dead.

As jazz has entered via the '50s white rock revelation closer to the mainstream because that mainstream now was more admittably "chocolatey," with the concomitant rise of the African American petty bourgeoisie and their neocolonial brothers and sisters in the Pan-African world, so Miles has had to be "explained" at least as thoroughly as white supremacy and the negro middle class think they need. With the accuracy of a prophylactic.

Being a commodity while yet alive means that one can be covered with paid-for contempt. Petty bourgeois whites now think of themselves as "hipper," whiter, for being less white (in this post–civil rights age). It is a coarse self-aggrandizement at best. Claiming to be knowledgeable by disparaging what is known. Part of that empty pseudo-hipness would be to treat Miles Davis as a part of the Buppie trend. He has certainly, with his image and attitudes, become a father figure to them. The Yuppies as well. But as "Bupped up" as Miles might be, he is, as I opened, much much more than that.

So in the zeitgeist of the dying beast prosperous yet, the ritual of king murder while chanting Long Live the King still goes on. The final murder will be themselves, we hope and must act to see that this act is neither genocidal nor planetcidal (or is that a word yet?).

Meanwhile, Miles is as Miles does. But he is already one of the "immortals," clay feet and all.

6/4/89

CHAPTER 3

The "Blues Aesthetic" and the "Black Aesthetic"

Aesthetics as the Continuing
Political History of a Culture

The term *Blues Aesthetic,* which has been put forward by certain academics recently, is useful only if it is not depoliticization of reference. So we can claim an aesthetic for Blues but at the same time disconnect the historical continuum of the blues from its national and international source, the lives and history of the African, Pan-African, and specifically Afro-American people.

The Blues Aesthetic is one aspect of the overall African American aesthetic. This seems obvious because the blues is one vector expressing the material historical and psychological source.

Culture is the result of "a common psychological development." But the common psychological development is based on experiencing common material conditions which are defined, ultimately, politically and economically.

The African American culture comes to exist as the living historical experience and development of the African American people, a Western Hemisphere people(!) whose history and heritage are African and the Americas.

By the nineteenth century, this new people had become consolidated and "Back to Africa" no longer represented the escape of captives and was replaced by either the psychological and political submission of a small sector of that people or the mass mainstream ideology of "Stay and Fight."

The Blues arises as a late nineteenth-century/early twentieth-century secular thrust of the African American musical culture, whose oldest musical and lyrical heritage was Africa but whose changing contemporary expression summed up their lives and history in the West!

The Blues reflects earlier developments of an African American speech and continuing musical experience now given new forms as reflection of the post–Civil War African American culture that was no longer limited as severely to religious reference or the social restraints of slavery.

The Blues is secular, it is also post chattel slavery. The drumless African choir sound of the Sorrow Songs (much like Black Ladysmith Mambazo) gives way to a sassier actually "more" African and more contemporary American. The later Gospel style reflects this as well.

By the nineteenth century the diverse Africans had become African Americans, and the Blues, from spiritual and work song through Hollers and Shouts and Arwhoolies, jumped out to celebrate black entrance into a less repressive, less specialized world, less harsh, more uncertain, but still tragic and depriving in too many ways.

The blues as a verse and musical form is one thing, but what needs to be gotten to here is the whole, the aesthetic overview, the cultural matrix that the Blues is but one expression of. Particularly the Blues is African American secular—country or city. The former is older, relating even into chattel slave society. The various city and other urban forms reflect that social and historical motion. Black people first moving from plantations to southern cities from the Civil War on and then by the late 1880s beginning to go up north, fleeing the destroyed reconstruction, the KKK, and looking for the new world.

The Blues aesthetic must emotionally and historically carry the heart and soul of the African Antiquity, but it is also a *Western Aesthetic*, i.e., *expressing* a western people, though African American. (Finally, Europe is not the West, the Americas are! Head west from Europe you come to Jersey! West of the Americas is the East!)

So the Blues itself must express the human revelation of life outside, or "post" the plantation—though I guess we ain't got very much "post" that bad boy yet! It is regional, or southern, or urban, etc. It's instrumentation changes to reflect the level of the people's productive forces and the social, political, and economic structure of those people's lives.

But that is the particularized yet constantly altering changing form of the Blues qua blues. Yet it is deeper and older than itself as this self.

If we study Equiano, DuBois, Douglass, Diop, Robert Thompson, and LeRoi Jones we will see that the single yet endlessly diverse African cultural matrix is the basis not only of what's called the Blues Aesthetic but any Black Aesthetic.

First, the Africans are the oldest humans on the planet, and all aesthetics on the planet, relating to human society, must use them at least as a point of departure!

Even the European so-called Apollonian Aesthetic mode (formalism and restraint) that characterized the Athenian Attic culture is so significant because it emerges not only in contradiction to the older, once world-dominating Dionysian (expressionist, emotion characterized humanistic) philosophical and aesthetic mode.

It is a redivision of human sensibilities and priorities as epoch creating as the flood that divided the world as the Mediterranean. We are still dominated by those tribes that emerged north of this biblically referenced waterway.

In capsule, the African Aesthetic, in its seemingly most ancient projection, first is an expression of the *Animist* worldview of our earliest ancestors. That is, to the classic African sensibility, everything in the world was alive, but even more important, everything that exists (as present—because both the past and the future only exist in the present and as speculative continuum of the is—the African "Goddess" Is/Is) is part of, connected as, the same thing!

Everything is one thing, one living thing. In this case you can see how even so-called *Monotheism* is like "Rock & Roll" (my term for the Bourgeois culture north of the middle of the world). The ideas of "One God" is already jive decrepitude of the philosophy of the antiquity. It is not "One God" as opposed to many, the qualification for savagery—but that every thing is one—All is All—everything is everything! *Allah* means literally All—everything is part of the same thing. Like the donut and the hole are *both space*!

So the continuity, the endlessness, the myriad multiformed expressiveness of "the One"—what is. is/is.

The continuity of even later African religion carried a fundamental relationship as in its continuing Call and Response form. That is, Priest to Congregation. The One and the Many are one thing. Like the heartbeat—beating is sound and not sound (where *be* is *at*—at least now then, when) they are not disconnectable as existent.

Evidence, Monk says (scat) the African celebrates. His life is meant, consciously, as evidence—it is in that sense *material*. (E.g., natural evidence—like it is, rather than artifactions, i.e., formalism.) Everything is in it, can be used, is, then, *equal*—reflecting the earliest economic and social form, *communalism*.

Above the Mediterranean what it *looked like* was more important than what it was or what it did. In the Southern Cradle what it did, its practice, its *content* was principal.

The African religion (see DuBois's "The Sorrow Songs" and "The Faith of the Fathers" in *The Souls of Black Folk*) had their Priest and Congregation as Call and Response ("Two is One" says Monk and Marx) . . . Dialectical character of what is, negation of the negation, the unity of opposites. The religion must also have music. Since "The spirit could not descend without song."

Spirit is literally "breath," as in in/spire or ex. Where you aspire is where you (go be at) headed, like the church spire. No breath, no life. But the drum replicating the first human instrument keeps life, the sun, replicating itself inside us. Its beat. Night and Day. In and out, the breath. Coming and Going, the everything. The Pulse, the flow, the rhythm carrier. (Time is formal, it is the reverse of expressionist sensibility, i.e., *emit* vs. *time*.)

So, as DuBois explains, Priest, Congregation, Music; which brings the Spirit down (from where? the soul is the invisible influence of the Solar—what life means, the smallest I, the largest Eye).

It is the *Frenzy*, the soul possession, that the African thought scientifically, and as a result of historical cultural perception, rationale, and use, the recombining of the two (the single with the all), the atonement, the Gettin Happy, which is the music's *use*. A way into consciousness of the whole, transcending the partial understanding of the single self.

The ecstasy is the being, the is/life. So Jazz is Jism, Come music, creatinging music. Coming is the spiritual presence of the all-existent one focused, we can see, inhaling.

The northern aesthetic has never assimilated sexuality, to it sex is dirty or embarrassing. But the sexual experience is as explicit a reflection of the "One is Two" dialectic as well. This is also a reflection of the overthrow of Mother right (the matrilineal social relations of ancient Africa) and the enslaving of women. The anti-woman character of the northern cradle, whether Salem witch burning (specifically to totally eliminate Dionysian survivals) or anti-ERA, is historically consistent.

So the revelation, the Going out, quality of African American culture as music or anything else is constant and evident. From religion to social relations.

The polyrhythms of African music are a further reflection of this animist base of the culture. But not only music, but in the clothes, body or hair adornment, graphic or verbal arts of the people, as a consistent means of characterizing the Pan-African culture and its international significance.

The bright colors of the Pan-African culture are reflection of those same polyrhythms. Acknowledgment of several levels or sectors or "places" of life *existing simultaneously.*

So the historically traceable *Cosmopolitanism* of the African people. Open and welcoming, intrigued by diversity and the "other." Ironically, in this sense, Diop points out the essentially non-African essence of Nationalism. Again, the recognition of all as All—everything is everything.

The attempt to denigrate Pan-African people with the stereotypes of racialism by claiming that the only things Pan-Africans can do are sing and dance (OK w/ me—just let us be in charge of it! How many people can we house and educate just with Michael J's 93,000,000 albums sold?). Equiano points out in his narrative, "We are almost a nation of singers and dancers." The socialization of the people was song and dance. As expressions of being. On all occasions. (Like America's stereotype as sports fans.) The Africans were socialized around song and dance and the participation, contribution by everyone in that. Art itself was a collective and communal expression. It was also functional and social.

Even the Blue, the color, from our own proto-Krishna faces, so black they blue. Diop says people in Southern India are the blackest people on the planet—like Krishna they blue. But also Equiano tells us that "Blue"—that beautiful Guinea Blue—was "our favorite color."

The Italians, though dark, didn't like to be called Black Slaves. We, of course, are the *real* Guineas, our head was on the English gold coin of that name gotten from the old "Gold" or Guinea Coast.

The Blues as the expression of sorrow should be obvious, a reference to our sad African slave lives here as well. It is also, after Black Mama is/night a sign that the sun gonna be at our door directly. So a poem of mine says, "Blues came / even before Day / Got here."

So the Blues Aesthetic is not only historical and carrying all the qualities that characterize the African American people but social in the same way. It must be how and what Black life is and how it reflects on itself. It is style and form, but it is the continuum of the content, the ideas, the feelings' articulation that is critical as well as the how of the form. Yet form and content are expressions of each other.

As verse form, the typical AAB Blues form is, by its structure and dynamic, given to emphasis (repeated first lines) as well as change and balance (the new rhyme line, the AA BB rhyme scheme).

The flatted thirds and fifths, the slurs or bending of notes of singer or instrumentalist, is the Kamite antiquity cultural character and summation of reality. KAM or HAM means change (the changes, the chemistry—the Chemists or Kamists). Hamites were the first chemists. The change from one quality or element to another. The dialectic of life itself. One is two, as Lenin said, explaining the dialectic in *The Philosophical Notebooks*. Everything is itself and something else at the same time, i.e., what is or becoming.

Twelve bars are the four quarters of the 360 (four arcs, i.e., seasons) of the trinity—past-present-future—the pyramid of dimension and motion itself, rhythm, *not* time—dancing, *not* those Arthur Murray footprints which is advertising finally and money, not dancing at all.

And the blues is not even twelve necessarily, the insistence on that form is formalism (as say Martin Smithsonian is guilty of when he says that Billie Holiday wasn't a blues singer because her songs weren't twelve bars!).

But Blues is first a feeling, a sense-Knowledge. A being, not a theory—the feeling is the form and vice versa.

John Coltrane could turn Julie Andrews's "My Favorite Things" into our real lives. The CAMIST—going through changes—rhythm & changes rhythm and blues—about feeling, not counting. (Goin thru Changes is the Blues.)

Roll over, Beethoven, we cry and relate it to us over and under any way. We blues or jazz up, syncopate any and every. We are incumaters and syncopaters. One is Two. One Breaks into Two.

The Black woman is everyone's mother and the domesticator of the human being from the animal, the black man is the second domesticated animal. His wife done it!

The key to the distortion of the so-called xtian trinity is there is no woman in it, so it is a cross sign. The ankh in-dicates. The head and nuts are missing from the christian cross, hence neither reproduction or creativity—a death sign.

So the northern culture hangs on to the memory of the old blue black church with fragments of the black madonna. But Roman church is rock and roll. Jesus (Jesse—"I am") evolves (Christ), crosses to higher ground, rebirth or continuum of human development.

"I am hip" is what Jesus Christ means—I am become Hip. As Fred said, "No progress without struggle." It is not the flattened distortion of Betty Wright and Negro politicians, "No pain no gain." It is not *pain* indicated but *struggle*. As in "The sun's gonna shine in my back door one day."

The past (black night's your mother) is also the future (what is *nigh* is coming—*Eve* before *Am*). The Present was here before it was the past and after it was the future.

The world is a tragedy, i.e., it is a carrying, the weight, the changes—not time, rhythm, not counting, feeling.

Any and Every—All are related as the *one*, part of a whole, whole of a part. The hole and what goes in and out, the creatinginginging (as it was in the beginning and ever shall be, world without end, etc.). What is *funky* is history, what comes goes.

The Blues is the first come from Black—Red, the last, going out to re-come. The cycle the circle. The Red what reading did re adding reproducing revolution, red, old going out into black and coming back through blue Mood Indigo.

So blues is the past, the blown all what got blew; the expressive, i.e., the blowing; the loss, the blown, the blowing. The known gone, the unknown coming all the non-time.

We are sad about what was that is not and about what is that should not. And we are glad just to be feeling. G the name of expression, LA the sixth birth joy the reaffirmation, and are is out is D is worth what everything exists as a whole holy.

Being and Changes Coming and Going Happy and Sad. It is life's feeling, and the rising restay of revelation, evolution, raise on up, rah rah rah we say to our sol above the first cheer leader Rah Rah Rah alive is holy the consciousness which ultimately combines KNOW & HOW is Conscience perception, rationale, use, as Mao laid out, explicating the Marxist theory of knowledge.

Love ultimately we feel (the upgrading of the fuck mode—Anglo-Saxon word *fuck* means "to hit," imagine then what "fucked up," i.e., pregnant, implies for this culture). Love is the necessity even as sex for our continuation. When Love is the Law and the Consciousness—the Holy Family will be what it is anyway like Every thing is Every thing.

The Holy Family of the human world, not exclusive but inclusive no separation, e.g., form and content or form and feeling. Hamlet is the northern opposite, to be or not—the liberal—not even sure life is worthwhile.

We seek Wholeness. Atonement.

Not Nietzsche saying feeling made it hard for him to think. For us what cannot feel cannot think. They say Dr. J, Magic, Michael Air are "instinctive." Boston Larry B, etc., intelligent. The highest intelligence is dancing, not the Arthur Murray footsteps advertising! The highest Thought is a doing, a being, not an abstraction.

Hence the *improvised*, the spontaneous, the intuitive, the felt are so valued, like the B line AAB—that rising B is the recognition of form but the primacy of content *B*. Like the revealed ecstasy of the congregation, enraptured, gettin happy, funky, high, moved, what is and what will, what was . . . is where we coming from, our story, our tail just like that snake crawling into its own mouth.

Calling our selves' tale we can admit of no Blues aesthetic that tries to hide from the politics of wholeness like the recent retrograde trend of Buppie/Yuppie trying to cop the "style" of Black without the substance, struggle, the changes. As Fred said, "They want the sea without its awful roar." And for the Negro who is using this to sidestep the politics of liberation for the economic and social advancement of the Pimp. The people who make the authentic Blues *have* the blues, it is not something out of a schoolbook—the vicious and laid-back pimps of dawning compradorism can tout to enrich without endarkening.

It is Black life historically, politically, and socially, the form and content of the Blues, as Langston says, the *signifying* is what revealed us as higher forms of animal, and yet as we were the *first* to raise up off all fours, it appears humanity is still some ways off. But without the signification, the meaning, the tale to swing, the story of the seeds, where we come from and where we going loses its significance. The signification is what makes the monkey man. Remove the words (past, pass that baton runner, run it, beat it out on wood or skin, even your own, rapper), the signs Breath and Change, and everything is a design without a key the Man Key he opened it up.

There is a current retrograde trend of black artists who see black life as caricature, there is another part of the same trend, the so-called "new black aesthetic," which tries to disconnect black art from black life and make it simply "a style" (e.g., the *Village Voice* coven of young Negroes [sic]), but this is certainly not the mainstream currently or historically. The black aesthetic is drawn from black life in the real world, just as any so-called blues aesthetic would necessarily be as well.

Held in the forms and content of the black aesthetic, in any of its cultural or historical elements, there is the will the desire the evoked "name" of *freedom*. What Monk was talking about. Freedom! Bird.

Trane. On Higher Ground. Duke. Count. Lady. Sassy. Bessie. Monk, etc. etc.

The retrograde Bup/Yup trend can't handle the African American Aesthetic because it signifies, it "talks shit" from Rap to Rap, from Fred to Big Red. The Black Aesthetic, as communal, revelational, and ecstatic, expressionistic, content focused, first signifier signifies freedom (new life, revelation, evolution, revolution) always. Songs, dances, clothes. Freedom Now, Freedom Suite, Free Jazz!, etc. etc. Asked about Jazz, Monk said, "It's about Freedom, more than that is complicated."

It cannot be an authentic reflection of the main thrust of the African American aesthetic without dealing with the Question of Freedom. As person or as part of the One.

Its Afro-American symbols contain the freedom expression, whether Brer Rabbit, who *laid on symbol* and got over through guile (showing in American culture as Bugs Bunny), or the other side of the dialectic, e.g., Stagolee or John Henry or Jimmy Brown, who dealt with force and power. Our history is full of such dialectically contradictory heroes and heroines.

To depoliticize the African American Aesthetic is to disconnect it from the real lives of the Afro-American people and instead make an offering to the seizers, that is—we must understand that not only our history aesthetically is contradictory to the so-called Northern cradle, but certainly as slaves and now an oppressed nation, the slave/slave master contradiction is the most serious of all.

Without the dissent, the struggle, the outside of the inside, the aesthetic is neither genuinely Black nor Blue—but the aesthetic of submission—whether for pay or out of ignorance or ideological turpitude.

90/91

BLUES PEOPLE ADDENDUM

1. Actually, in deepening an understanding of American culture (really Pan American culture), Bruce Franklin's observation "African American culture is central to American culture, not peripheral to it" is a key element.

When I talked (in *Blues People*) about surviving Africanisms in Afro-American culture I did not take into consideration that *American culture itself* is historically partially constructed of continuing and thematic Africanisms!

CHAPTER 4

Blues People

Looking Both Ways

Blues People has always meant a great deal to me. It was a dramatic self-confirmation, as an intellectual and artistic "presence" the expression of a set of ideas and measures that were to last me for many years. Most, until today.

First, the book had a presence, even in my own head, of weightiness, that is, it meant a great deal to me as it emerged and certainly when completed, in the sense that I was "shooting from the hip," though like Billy the Kid said once, I had been aiming a long time before I reached for the machine. But it was a thrill to see my own ideas roll out, not always "precise," but forceful enough to convince me that I did know something about this music I have loved all my life.

It confirmed ideas that had been rolling around in my head for years, that now, given the opportunity, flashed out upon the page with a stunning self-exhilaration. The book, from its opening words, got me high. It made me reach for more and more and more of what I had carried for years. How to measure this world we find ourselves not at all happy with, but able to understand, and hopefully one day to completely transform. How to measure my own learning and experience and to set out a system of evaluation of weights and meaning.

It was Sterling Brown who first hipped A.B. Spellman and me to the fact that the music was our history. In our English 212 class, lolling around like the classic submature campus hipsters we were, those who would be down. Amidst Sterling's heavy lectures on Shakespeare (which are still incredible in their spotlight on what that all is, i.e., that Willie S was the antifeudal revolutionary, in whose work all the problems of capitalism were first exposed to the quick, dig the evil Richard the 3 or Macbeth the nut, or Othello on racism, the Merchant on anti-Semitism, Shrew on Women's Oppression, Hamlet on the Liberal, the various monstrous kings and rulers of that dying feudal age).

Sterling signified to A. B. & me one day that we wasn't quite as hip as we thunk, since we were young boppers probably quite nasty in our altogether ignorant pseudo-wisdomic stancing. Oh yeh, we was hip to Bird and Diz and Monk, you dig. Though we was in a Dave Brubeck, Paul Desmond, Gerry Mulligan period right then, thanks to Miles's *Birth of the Cool,* which we swore was the big number!

I imagine this must have incited Sterling to grasp us lovingly and metaphorically by the scruffs of our conceits and invite us to his crib. Man, there in a center room was a wall completely wrapped around our unknowing, of all the music from the spasm bands and arwhoolies and hollers, through Bessie and Jelly Roll and Louis and Duke, you know? And we watched ourselves from that vantage point of the albums staring haughtily at us, with that tcch tchh sound such revelations are armed with.

The albums, Folkways and Commodores, Bluebirds and even a Gennet or three, stared at us with our own lives spelled out in formal expression. "This is the history. This is your history, my history, the history of the Negro people." That was the phrase that lifted me, both I'd say, since A. B.'s "Three Lives in the BeBop Business" was another formidable thrust from that encounter.

Later, Sterling began to give a few informal talks on this history as Black music, in the lounge of the old then new Cook Hall, and we sat, very literally, at his feet, taking those priceless teachings in. The Music, the Music, this is our history.

But that sat, of course, for years. I had heard this and it dug a hole in my static absolutes, but then it had dropped down inside to foam and bubble and give off ideational vapors that blinked endless analogies and revelations into my perceptions and rationales throughout the years.

So even as I began *Blues People,* that idea, now a fundamental philosophical feature of my seeing and understanding, was not at the tip of my focus. What was, was the first essay I wrote for publication, "Black Music White Critics." The first title I gave the book was *Blues, Black and White America.* It was the contrasting aspect of the theme that first superficially captured me. That there was a body of music that came to exist from a people who were brought to this side as slaves and that throughout that music's development had had to expand and reorganize and continue and express itself as the fragile property of a powerless and oppressed people.

How did it do this? What was so powerful and desperate in this music that guaranteed its existence? (As long as its creators existed!) This is what pushed me. But as I began to get into the history of the music, I found that this was impossible without, at the same time, getting deeper into the history of the people. That it was the history of the Afro-American people as text, as tale, as story, as exposition, or what have you, that the music was the score, the actually expressed creative orchestration, of Afro-American life, our words the libretto to those actual lived lives. That the music was an orchestrated, vocalized, hummed, chanted, blown, beaten, corollary confirmation of the history. And that one could go from one to the other, actually, from the inside to the outside, or reverse, and be talking about the same things. That the music was explaining the history as the history was explaining the music. And that both were expressions of and reflections of the people.

So that moving from the middle passage forward, as Roumaine said, from that railroad of human bones at the bottom of the Atlantic Ocean, one traced the very path and life and development, tragedy and triumph of Black people. How they had come from Africa and had been transformed by the passage and by their lives in the west into a Western people. So that by the beginning of the nineteenth century, the great majority of us were "Americans."

And at each juncture, twist, and turn, as Black people were transformed so was their characteristic music, to reflect the "new" them, the changing same, yet the continually contrasting contexts of their actual lives. My deep concentration on the continuing evidence of Africanisms and the parallels between African customs and philosophies and the Afro-American continuum were to teach myself, and whoever, that Black people did not drop out of the sky, although fo sho, we were the "band of angels."

But for all the syncretic representation and continuation of African mores and beliefs even under the hideous wrap of chattel slavery— many have suffered as much as Black people, said DuBois, but none of them were "real estate"—I have learned one thing that I feel is a critical new emphasis to the original text. And that is that *the Africanisms are not just limited to Black people, but indeed, American Culture itself is an expression of many Africanisms. So that the American culture in the real world is a composite of African, European, and Native or Akwesasne cultures, history, and people!* (So that both the Ebonics and Standard English arguments are one-sided and paltry. . . . Try to go someplace in California, for instance, without speaking Spanish! Or someplace in South Carolina without speaking a Bantu language. Or someplace, anywhere, in the U.S. without speaking a Native tongue.)

Actually, *Blues People* is a beginning text. There is yet much work to be done to properly bring the music into the open light of international understanding for all the commercial exploitation, and proof that there is, as *Jazz Times* recently proclaimed, "An International Business of Jazz." The scholarly and artistic institutionalization of the music is almost nonexistent. Not only to further illuminate the obscured history but to bring all the voices, the contributors, the pioneers, the innovators, the unknown and little known facts and people, up front where they belong. The actual strains of the music's development, how and where and why and by whom and the historical impact, must be reconstructed. The music of the various cities and regions has to be really studied with the social economic institutional stability with which European concert music is studied. Particularly since Blues and Jazz are constantly developing and changing, like every living organism, while European "classical" music (as contrasted to the myriad folk forms) seems, for the most part, to be fixed by a bourgeois tradition of formalism and elitism.

In addition, independent venues, networks, publications, festivals, orchestras, scholarship must be created by the diggers to expand and magnify the impact of the music as well as preserve it with all the sanctity of the Museum of Natural History's ancient artifacts or MOMA's great works. That, and to reach the new generations and the great sections of the population still unhip, perhaps even prove an effective antidote to the shabby exploitative commercialism of U.S. artificial "popular culture."

As for my own contributions, I have several books to release if I can find a publisher. Books on Trane, Monk, Duke, Miles, a new book of essays called *Digging*. Plus, here in Newark, we have initiated the Newark Music Project, as part of a national program called Lost Jazz Shrines, to archive, record, perform, and create indigenous institutions and programs to reconstruct and present all the music produced in the city of Newark. This is a project I hope many other cities will take up.

This project has been replaced by the Lincoln Park Coast Cultural District (LPCCD) organization, which is trying to build a Museum of Afro-American Music in association with the Smithsonian Museum.

CHAPTER 5

Rhythm

Rhythm is the natural motion of matter. What exists presented to us by our sense organs. Though the very understanding of just what sense organs exist is still only primitively partial. "Physical," for instance, cannot be defined simply as a known paradigm, if we understand dialectical materialism. The contrasting motions of matter, the continuous development as change, understood, perceived, by us (any thing—Consciously), cannot limit what actually exists. Our knowledge limits us, not what exists.

Our approach to truth is always partial, advancing in stages (some regard as "Gaps"). Motion is and isn't what is moving. Yet the oneness of matter exists because of its twoness, which is motion. A thing is it and not it at the same time (i.e., it is what it is and what it is becoming) as a property of motion. The present is a connector of the past and future. Yet it is more transient than either, but always remains what exists. What exists as "truth" is also matter in motion and also a reflection of that Being (process) wherever it is expressed, as what it means.

African Religion sought to discover the human relationship to what exists *always* by "tuning" in to it, and becoming, at whatever level, at one, cognizant, conscious, "with knowing," be possessed, by it, as the direct expression of the whole, and as a direct experience. This is the "Holiness" (Whole/ness, at/one), the revelation.

The Joy that animates the African, "the laughter at the bottom of the world," because Ecstasy is the motion, the livingness of the motion.

Jazz is literally I AM! (JA IS!). The IS NESS of AM. I, I, Aye, Eye, Si, IS—ING (I SING). Conscious Come! Creating the Semen of Consciousness, JISM'S mind. The G, sensuous life. With the circle, existence as motion, energy. GO. To be it must be dialectical as well, which is its expression as Dimension. GO—OD. Like BE—AT, it is expressed as rhythm—matter in motion. What is "dead," nonexistent, the lie, delusion, is irrational. Reality cannot "die"—What R(AM) I.

Consciousness is degree, stage, motion, speed, intensity. So Rhythm, from the meaning of the alphabet signs themselves: R for "Exist"; H for "Develop" or "Build" (from the German *Bild*, picture, image); Y for "Split" (Quest, mitosis, or Elegba, the crossroads); T for "Rest at"; H for "Build"; M for "Move."

The composite rhythm of everything is everywhere. The whole life (Time, Place, and Condition) shapes the rhythm, the where you be at (Bloods say). And it is a physical/mental construct. Finally it is deeper because it goes deeper. Will grow deeper, i.e., the perception of the finest(?) particular (of a) rhythm accesses properties in the perceiver (or confirms them). Rhythm's infinite "circles" of transformation, in modes and forms and directions we do not even know exist.

The whole of what we, as matter in motion, are, in whatever degree of particularity, are connected as part of "Nature's" rhythm. It is entirely possible to "trace" all the whatevers of whatever as a specific (compound complex) network of sense, at whatever level, able to be understood by its rhythm (or its sound, smell, etc.). What the physical, social, etc. reality of the world is, we are part of, as rhythm. Our closeness, our distance, our awareness—the heart speeds up, in relation to what? Color is the same reference. Number, Letter, Sign, Symbol or Cymbal. The actuality of our total objective relationship to whatever forms of motion and mode of matter we are and in and part of is us.

Africans used rhythm to speak and sing, to dance—to communicate over long distances with each other and to the forces of the universe. This ancient grasp of rhythm's relationship to everything is a feature of the "Primitive Communist" (Engels) social organization of that epoch. The Call and Response, Preacher-to-Congregation forms call spirit through rhythm, enforced as dance and song, as music, the drum, the voices, the flutes and whistles, rattles, balaphones, choruses, athletes, poets, actors, call the spirit and from the place of our regular selves we are *moved*, until we rise to "frenzy" as Du Bois called it *(Souls of Black Folk)*.

We rise like the Black Bird (BA, the Phoenix, the Soul). We reach for intuitive meaning and understanding of Existence, of what exists forever! Which is the ultimate Goodness. Like a temperature rising, the possession by and as, the spirit (that hot breath . . . lives "before" with "after" us as us in us in whatever form "continues"). Who thinks this is 1996 is the Johnny-Come-Lately of Civilization. The "Going Out," the Trance, Trans, Cross into another consciousness. Go inside the Known outside the seen. This is the spiritual form. To know the Beyond!

"Divine" means to know the future, not "GOD." The degeneration of the ancient religion into Deism reaches its extreme with Egypt and the Pharaohs becoming "God," though not apparently Good. The creation of God must coincide with the ending of the communal societies and the emergence of slavery.

Awareness, i.e., the degree of Consciousness, is a sensitivity to what exists. The rhythms of Africa are so deep a human characteristic, as history and presence and an aspect of the Black aesthetic anywhere. Five hundred years of African slavery, yet their rhythms dominate most of the world, even while its creators are in chains. One reason, because the ancient drum so basically replicates our hearts and the changes everything is, goes through. Day/Night, Good/Bad, Wet/Dry, Past/Present/Future, the endless beat of breath and life.

Using rhythm and vocal verbal tonal expressions, as MUSIC (you could DANCE!), but as a *technology* of communication! So the political opposition to the drum in the U.S. and western slave kingdoms. It was Seized! Censored! So is the European minimalization of the drum political or aesthetic?

The communication of the drum was political and musical. By its conception. So the aesthetic functionalism as emotional expression of consciousness. Djali (Griot). History as Poetry-Music. The rhythms of the African are alive, living as part of the world. Not removed as "ART" in the bourgeois Western sense, though Art it certainly is. But not alienated from the pulse of the greater mass world. Not exclusive, abstract, not as design or utilitarian but as recondite predicated on willful obscurity. Reducing "understanding" to the biosubjective arbitrariness of "the Pose" of distance from real life!

What is expressed from the old communist reflection of the connected world of essence and effect. The masks of the theater outline, as geography and aesthetic, the South and the North, the Woman and the Man, HotCold, ValleyMountain, SmileFrown. One noted Greek philosopher spoke of his disgust with the constantly "smiling Africans." They laugh too much. So in slavery, this feature is turned into an expression of ignorance. So too, the dancing and singing that have registered the history of the human world.

The geoclimatic character of Africa, its natural richness, was especially suited to support the "natural economy" of the early Communist cultures. The communal nature of the southern culture, as a result of the relative ease with which the natural economy supplied most needs, could be maintained for a long period. This is in sharp contrast to the frozen inhospitable unproductive north, which likewise put an indelible stamp on the cultures that came out of there.

The Afro-American use of African rhythm is obvious, but finally more "integrated" with European musical conventions than most of the other African-based musics of the world. (Except the creation of Rock & Roll, the "slavemaster" of Black-White social Slave/Master relations!)

The Afro-American drum is a machine, "the Set." It is an industrial product, as reflection of U.S. industrial capitalist culture. "The Set" is descended, says Max Roach, from the "One-Man Bands" that arose after the Civil War. The singer performer covered with a snarl of instruments, some of his own invention—bells, cymbals, whistles, horns, drums, wood blocks, might have a harmonica in a hookup on a bass drum, sumpin might have wheels on it. . . .

The reintroduction of the word into the very body of the music will come again. It is the very levels of the advanced corporate imperialist social economic technology that are and will be absorbed into the speech and rhythm of the Afro-American use and response to the rhythm of time, place, and condition.

Rhythm is in the essence of what exists and we are expressions of rhythm as are described by our lives (time, place, condition). The Afro-American flows from Africa to cross where and become themselves or that experience dissociated from the African past. Yet that passage is a historic documented rhythm. The speech of real life expressed like the heart does, from the life the heart keeps alive.

All life is rhythm in that sense and expressed, registered as such. Afro-American rhythm is African West as slave and victim, as pre- and post-U.S.; American and to that extent individualistic, yet Eastern and Collective, Communistic. Existential as Improvised and Spontaneous. Experimental and deeply Traditional.

It is the speech of those who yet have not become what their words know is absolutely real. The Drum is real, like the heart of a living being. The soul is the heat and birth and ejaculation—to express the *Material Life Force* ("God's," i.e., "the Creator's," obvious residence).

I AM is what "God," the creature created by a slave culture (when nothing can say that always but what will always exists), says. JA, the Hebrew G., Shango's twin lightning bolts. JAZZ! AM (The motion of the "I" = Eye, Sun, Son, etc.). But it is everything real which is the real exclaimer, and we respond, like the music, screaming YEH! YEH! JA! (RA) ZZ!

The communal improvised Blues (bending light) history, memory, feelings, vision, etc., are old and visible as the seasons. Which rhythm we are part of as much as sea and moon. Or the schedule of the radio station—History's self-portrait as human feeling and communication. Wherefrom within we make the self-entering arc of reflection as it is as live report we register with our senses (on up to *Use*).

Where we are as to the newspapers' description of "where we're at" is a song and a story, a dance, part of the whole music of the Here. Even as Style and who digs it! Rhythm, on the other hand, does have the truth of science. Even to explain why we are where we are (physically or mentally).

Monk or the Osmonds? TV Commercials. The Catholic Church offices are connected to us as part of what we are receiving and broadcasting as the world.

Death is a rhythm, and terror, Fascism, just as Beauty or Ugly as objective descriptions of who is describing.

The social life of the rhythm's "other" visibility, expresses culture, class, even nationality, perhaps gender, philosophy, etc.

What Black Rhythm (ridm, ritm) worldwide and historically is is "The Call of the Living," and as such it describes and fuels a real world other than itself to exist. Communication includes Desire. Even Hope—Expectation. Confirmation, Identification, History.

The Rhythm connects nature to itself as material self-consciousness and expression. We create the feeling we can feel and what we think is therefore matter's. Reality's Self-Confirmation. And it draws to it what it expresses and sends out what it is.

CHAPTER 6

The American Popular Song

"The Great American Song Book"

American culture itself is still unbelievably "abstract" to Americans themselves; at the same time it cannot possibly be, since it is their day-to-day lives and expression. "Abstract" only in the sense that Americans do not really understand their culture.

For one thing, American culture is much broader, much deeper, much darker, than official commentators of the social status quo allow. For another, when these same unworthies talk about Western Culture, relating it principally to Europe, they infer the lie that makes for the abstraction, since the "Western Culture" is the Americas. America is the west, the Pan-American experience is the American Experience, El Mundo Nuevo, the New World.

If we look a little deeper we will quickly understand that behind all this "Western World equals Europe" misgeographic claptrap is simply colonialism and white supremacy, with an overlay of Eurocentricity.

In a recent poem of mine I say of this phenomenon, "Leave England headed West / you arrive / in Newark." The whole of the Pan-American hemisphere and experience constitute "Western Culture." What the Eurocentric worship that identifies the essence of official American Culture guarantees is that the European powers can step off at the top of the standard of living, while most of the Pan-American countries are in a state of neo-, or some in straight-out, colonialism.

Say all that to say, that in a concept of something like "the American Popular Song," we will see that historically, the peoples that "discovered and settled" (a dubious labeling of colonialism) the Americas from Europe brought with them their own culture, i.e., their history and experience, the art and philosophy, but this underwent continuous change under the whole weight of the new culture they entered into and helped shape in many ways. But we know the native peoples were in this hemisphere by the millions before the Europeans arrived (Leif Ericson notwithstanding) and that the Africans—witness the Afro cultures ubiquitous throughout the whole of Pan-America, e.g., the striking heads on the west coast of Mexico near Acapulco—were familiar with the Pan-American world centuries before.

But the English (and Irish, Welsh, Scotch, etc.), French, Spanish, Portuguese did bring both living culture and artifacts and machines to this side; the Dutch, Germans, even the Danes all came this way. In the U.S. we can see historical evidence of English, French, and Spanish in the main as the primary European settlers, before the doors of the 19th century really swung the New World open to the German, Italian, and Irish masses. And with them came the working class and small and middle peasant culture as well: their folk and traditional songs and dances, the history of experience and manners through which a people express their consciousness.

But from the Native American cultures that greeted the Europeans when they arrived, there had already been a particularity of "Americanness," what existed as history and artifact, institution and culture; but the English hymns and plainsongs, the chansons and arias and jigs and lieder came with the whole of the European migration.

Slavery and the Indian wars, the wars of conquest between the various European conquerors, served to keep the new world a spread and multiple dotting of "sub-cultures" held in the contrasting quilt of what had already existed in these lands previous to the conquest. The formation of the nation-state at the end of the 18th century made the nation a Eurocentric political construct sewn out of diverse cultural fragments, the most numerous always the non-European, native American, and African pieces.

Part of the anti-democratic corruption at the core of the U.S. nation-state has always been the political betrayal of the American revolution and its continuing colonial epoch connection to Europe as "a white child." This is done, at base, for purposes of exploitation and super-profit, in whatever their forms. But it has also served to make the general citizenry of the place less intelligent than necessary.

The apparent separateness, yet confluence of diverse sources that make up modern American culture, in this case North American, U.S., culture, are brought together, ironically, by the underpinning, the slave (and colonial) base of the society. As a fixed social base for a society stridently calling for social development, it meant that there was a cultural reference as well, a "bottom" like a bass line to the whole.

It is here important to make a distinction between the *popular* and the *commercial*. Sidney Finklestein in *Jazz, A People's Music* (Citadel), says much to the point, "Commercialism should be restricted, as a term, to what is really destructive in culture; the taking over of an art, in this case popular music, by business, and the rise of business to so powerful a force in the making of the music that there was no longer a free market for musicians. Instead of distribution serving the musician, distribution, where the money was invested, became the dominating force, dictating both the form and content of the music."

This period does not happen in the U.S. until the 20th century, and it is probably the late 19th century that there is even any sign that such a phenomenon could occur. The end of slavery, which signifies the end of competitive capitalism and the beginning of monopoly capitalism/ imperialism, is what ushers in this ongoing period of commercial control of the arts.

But popular music arises as the confirmation of the living culture of the people. The African culture transformed by chattel slavery and the totality of the Pan-American cultural experience has been, since its introduction in the West, a binding and all-pervading influence on the whole of the American culture, not only in most of the Americas, where the colonizers were always a minority, but even in the U.S., where the African and Afro-American slaves were a minority.

You can hear the influence of the Spirituals on the so-called Barbershop quartets or vocal music of the U.S. 19th century. In the South that influence, particularly in the church music and the plantation and slave labor system, was almost immediately reflected.

White southern religious music, country and western music are deeply and very clearly influenced by Afro-American musical culture. In every venue where black labor was utilized, sailor songs, cowpoke songs, soldier songs, miner songs, lumber-camp songs, jail-house songs, broadening as slavery first put slaves into work alongside "free" white workers, and then when it was overthrown an even broader and deeper influence resulted. But even in the 1880s and '90s Ragtime and what was called "Barrel House" and "Honkey Tonk" had already brought black influence into the mainstream culture. The field shouts and work songs and even the street cries go back to the 17th century. By the 18th century, there had already developed a tradition of Afro-American Whistling (like the chilly home boy with the boom box) evidenced in the American colonies.

The ending of chattel slavery and the gradual releasing of Afro-Americans from its extreme restrictions was, of course, the stream of cultural renewal that has ultimately transformed the whole of U.S. culture, so that now it has a clearly Afro-American aspect.

The biggest impact on U.S. musical culture in the 20th century was the urban coalescence and explosion that marked New Orleans. The entrance of the black rural and slave elements into the urban and highly sophisticated context of New Orleans produced an urbane though seemingly ingenuous expression that summed up the post-slavery U.S.

The creation of New Orleans Jazz and the urbanized blues it came out of were developments of world-shaking immensity. European observers and critics as early as Brahms and later Ernest Ansermet attest to the impact of this music as a musical culture upon world culture.

On one hand, anyone who has ever seriously contemplated the longevity of the African culture will understand the profound reach the continuing elements of that culture have. Certainly, there has been quite a bit written about the musical and graphic aspects of it. But the New Orleans development showed that the ancient aspect that could be carried (e.g., voice oriented, call and response, percussive and poly-rhythmic, polyphonic, importance of improvisation, "possession" by the music, i.e., what DuBois called the "Frenzy") could be raised again within the new impressions of the chattel, and could be raised yet again in the still newer context of the post-slave southern city to express a staggeringly precise aspect of a U.S. multicultural experience.

Certainly, Afro-American culture is "open," by history and social circumstance, to the broadest array of influences. Black people have never hesitated to borrow and add to their own stash of expression whatever interested them, no matter what the source.

New Orleans was truly a gathering focus of African and Afro-American, Caribbean, Latin-American, French, Spanish, English, Italian, and Native American and the so-called "Creoles" or Afro-Whatever cultural elements through a historical process that crystallized in that 19th-century urban venue to produce a high and sophisticated artistic culture.

There was minstrelsy and blackface in the 19th century, largely coming out of the South. But by the end of the century, the black minstrel circuits would begin to follow the rush of black people out of the South, as an addition to that circuit. (Though even with all the out-migration there were still more Afro-Americans in the Black Belt South than anywhere else in the country, and by the 1970s the largest migration of blacks was back into the South!)

Jazz and blues were coming out of the South even ahead of the masses of black people, to the extent that there were several white bands who had picked up the music, white singers, who had even earlier picked up on the blues or some other variant of African American musical culture, and who were carrying them, at first as novelties, to broader venues.

But the emergence of Jazz and "Classical" Blues coincides and gives substance to the early part of the 20th century in the U.S., called "the Jazz Age." And it is the spread of thousands of black people out of the South into the northern and midwestern cities that brings the heart of the black southern culture across the U.S.

This large migration out of the South helped transform the Afro-American people from largely southern, rural, and agricultural to a people located in large numbers in the North and Midwest, mainly urban and industrial workers.

One measure of the impact of Black culture on the U.S. and the world during this period is what we have called "the Harlem Renaissance" (though the U.S. and Harlem are simply the most visible expressions of what is actually a worldwide anti-imperialist movement, the 1917 Russian Revolution is one indication). *Negritude* from African and West Indian students in Europe touched Africa, and the West Indies *Negrissmo* in Latin America, *Indigisme* in Haiti, are similar cultural expressions of what is essentially an international "Black Consciousness Movement."

The title "the Jazz Age" certainly sums up the great impact Afro-American culture had on the U.S. and the world. It is now necessary to use Jazz as the musical background for anything focusing on the early 20th-century U.S., "the Roaring '20s."

When Mamie Smith (one of the famous and unrelated "Smith Sisters," with Trixie and the great Bessie) replaced Sophie Tucker and sang "Crazy Blues" (1920), it became a national hit, selling 8,000 records a week for a year. It meant that Afro-American popular music could be widely distributed throughout the U.S. Sophie Tucker was herself a "cover" for Black female blues singers, just as the Original Dixieland Jazz Band, New Orleans Rhythm Kings, and later Paul

Whiteman and Bix Beiderbecke were used to cover Louis Armstrong, Oliver, Morton, Bechet, and the rest of the early jazz giants. But the "covers" themselves were conduits disseminating the music even deeper into the mainstream U.S. culture, even though created as an expression of political and socio-economic domination.

The historic basis and continuing reference of African and Afro-American music is the voice. And always, not just the sound of the voice, but the *spoken* word is the communicating expression. Even in the drum, the percussive form was a mouth, which *talked*. Blues, Jazz, maintain the word as, Pres said, "a story," being told.

Louis Armstrong and Bessie Smith were the most influential singers in U.S. popular culture of the early part of the 20th century (just as Michael Jackson and Whitney Houston are today, though now these two are even more dominating because they are probably freer socially). Of course, Louis Armstrong was also the greatest instrumental influence the music has seen.

Both Bessie and Louis are classic Blues artists and setters of the standard of how the Blues voice, now multi-instrumentalized, is drawn into the Jazz expression. They are the double barrels of Afro-American musical culture blasting across the early U.S. (and international) '20s.

Naming black artists and white artists shaped by these Two, singularly or together, is itself the subject of yet another long essay, though there have been hundreds already.

The fact of U.S. segregation and discrimination, the national oppression that followed slavery, meant that one of the most definitive and shaping aspects of U.S. culture, Afro-American culture, would be a ubiquitous emotional and stylish model or mode of American cultural expression, but the social repression of the Afro-American people, ironically, *limited* the extent to which the whole essence and body of that culture could be stunted (as *expression*) by U.S. commercialism.

As Finklestein states in *Jazz,* Commercialism "tended to force the musician into the status of a hired craftsman whose work was not supposed to bear his own individuality, free thought and exploitation of the art, but was made to order, to a standardized pattern."

The irony is that the post-slavery Afro-American people were excluded from the mainstream of U.S. socio-economic organization. The marginalized existence of a people segregated from that mainstream, socio-economically discriminated against, as aspects of national oppression, was made more blatant because of its distinct racial character.

Afro-American music, because of its exclusion as a social product yet ultimate exploitation as a commercial object, could influence the whole of the musical (and social and aesthetic) culture of the U.S. and even be subjected to mind-boggling dilutions and obscene distortions, yet the source, the Afro-American people, could be spared the full "embrace" of commercial American absorption because of their marginalized existence as Americans. This is reflected, as well, *in* the music, which is an expression of Afro-American life, hence a registration itself of the pain and struggle that it exists as the expression of, as that beauty continuing to exist and be seen even more stunningly because of the ugliness which surrounds and limits it.

Armstrong influenced trumpet players, singers, drummers, saxophone players, etc. etc. Bing Crosby spoke often of his debt to Armstrong! (See the film *New Orleans,* where Bing plays the leader of "the best hot white band in New Orleans.") Billie Holiday tells us she was shaped by Bessie and Louis, listening to their records in a Ho Ho Ho house.

Frank Sinatra sings a song "Lady Day" and has often spoken of his debt to Billie Holiday. The whole panorama of U.S. musical culture, if we look at each of its "white stars" of popular music, shows that the general or even specific personal impetus is Afro-American music.

In the '20s, Finklestein says, "The beloved American popular music of song and dance is a certain first of the Negro people, and then of the Jewish, Irish, Italian and other minority peoples."

The history of American popular music since the 19th century has moved on the impact and influence of Afro-American music and its songs and singers. Increasingly, into the 20th century, as imperialism and monopoly control of the music business intensified, many of the newer immigrants, the Jews, Italians, and Irish, who, as Finklestein says, were stalwart contributors to American popular music, which increasingly carried a blues and jazz sound, were nevertheless pulled further into American commercialism at the expense of their art.

It was the price for assimilation into America, to give up that part of you that was "un-American," especially that part that included the dissent of the first generations of struggling Jewish, Italian, and Irish immigrants.

Just as James Weldon Johnson's hero in *Autobiography of an Ex-Colored Man* says at the tragic denouement of the novel in which he is "passing" for white, "I have given up my heritage for a mess of pottage."

From the Jazz Age onward, and certainly today, there has been a significant change from what had been before, in minstrelsy and the caricatures of Chandler Harris and the like, primarily a ridicule of the Afro-American people and culture. For instance, there are thousands of artifacts, tea pots, salt and pepper shakers, flour labels, all kinds of products, Uncle This, Aunt That, that still bear this legacy of racist ridicule of black people as their forms. This kind of poison continues as D. W. Griffith or Eddie Cantor and Al Jolson.

But then Jolson becomes, not just a blackface mammy yodeler, but "the Jazz Singer," Benny Goodman the "King of Swing," Elvis Presley "the King," Bruce Springsteen "the Boss," and the Rolling Stones "the Best Rock & Roll Band in the World!"

The 20th century saw minstrelsy "change into" a white style! Afro-American culture was now sufficiently accessible "within" the mainstream (or visible at its margins because it had so long been pimped and caricatured and imitated). From NORK and ODJB through Beiderbecke and the so-called "Chicago Style," "Dixieland," there arose a "white style." Actually, it was a re-Americanization of Afro-American musical culture, that usually diluted and distorted it, depending on the performers.

By the late '30s there were white swing bands to cover the Ellingtons, Basies, Henderson, Luncefords, as a "white style" of jazz, etc., no longer minstrelsy. Except the racial exclusion and repression of the black originals makes the white styles bloodless replicas because there is no sharp dialectical flow of equally responding registration, only drop and cop.

But by the same token there was still a genuinely engaging and meaningful cultural product created by the "re-Americanization" process. Certainly the most interesting handling of Blues and Jazz by other than the original creators can be seen in American popular music.

We cannot be speaking of the present 1990s plundering of the '60s Motown treasure chest to plagiarize real lives in order to justify the nothingness of racist intellectual pretension and falsity. This is no better than open pimping by the corporations, using everything from the Supremes to Smoky Robinson to sell their soap.

But the Irving Berlins, Johnny Mercers, George Gershwins, Harold Arlens, Leonard Bernsteins, etc., etc., and Jerome Kerns, Cole Porters, etc., etc., have created a creditable body of Blues and Jazz-derived American Popular music, which especially when rekindled by the Blues and Jazz players themselves, becomes pure gold. A Classical American Music. Just think of the American Popular song in the hands of the

Blues and Jazz players historically, from Louis Armstrong to Duke Ellington to Billie Holiday to Charlie Parker to John Coltrane. (Dig, for instance, the trip Trane takes "My Favorite Things" on. Miles Davis would take it right to the fringes of sanity with stuff like "Surrey with the Fringe on Top!")

So that American popular music was exemplified by its obvious popularity (discounting the commercialism which seeks to reduce any art to a packaged predictability of painless profit), from the '20s white jazz popularizers to the white pop composers of the '30s and '40s until the second explosion in "white" American culture of the '50s, Rock & Roll and the coronation of the new white "King" Elvis Presley; not only had minstrelsy become a white style, but whites now could pretend to be the original creators. (But even in the 1950s, Metronome's All Stars were almost all white!)

And today "Hip Hop" with its Vanilla Ices, Young Black Teenagers (Yes, Virginia, they're all white too!), etc., or the Madonnas and Michael Bolton, but only a little more so than the Beatles, Stones, Osmonds, Chet Bakers, or Barbra Streisands for Aretha, oh yeh! shows how the same trend goes on.

The musical culture of the whole American people becomes by open affirmation (exploitation, imitation, deception aside) at base in large part the creation of the Afro-American people. Like Chocolate in a bottle of milk. Yeh, it is still milk, but why is it that color?

CHAPTER 7

Blues Line

In a book of mine, *Blues People,* which appeared in the early '60s, I argued that blues was first a verse form and then an extension of that form into music. Not only some attention to history but any scrutiny of the variety of blues forms will verify this, I think.

Rap, for instance, is a recent co-signature. The music generated by the verse is a panrhythmic explanation of the verse and is intended to expand that verse into a complementary yet dissociative medium.

Yet at the base of "both" is the rhythm which comes out of the makers' lives, concurrent, projective, and memorative. The verse that the rappers create is itself musical, as chant or liturgy, more like the epic toasts that reach back into the tales and ballads of a developing people, and even further back into other languages, pre-American. (See W. E. B. Du Bois's "On the Sorrow Songs" in *Souls of Black Folk*).

But no matter the form of the content or the content of the forms, there should be little doubt that the blues, like any art, reflects the life of its creator, and blues, taken as a broad genre identified at least by the commonality of form and broader conjunction of content, is an "ideological" reflection of human society, particularly that aspect of it the blues makers exist in. The blues reflects the lives of the people who created them.

To try to make these people merely unconnected "individuals" who go around making blues like troubadours from nowhere, without history or description, relating to no social grouping whose "ideas" (if you can stand the idea of blues having—what—ideas!!) exist merely as passive marks in books edited by other people, who have ideas who have history who exist in well-documented social-political groupings, is tiresome and unscholarly. Without mentioning the chauvinistic posturing.

Blues Line is a marvelous book simply because it gives us hundreds of blues lyrics. Like any anthology of poetry, the poets existed in real lives in real cities and countrysides and were subject, as are we all, to the historical development of human society, wherever they were in it, and likewise, the not quite arbitrary dictates of powerful rulers.

It is a fact that the Afro-American people came to the U.S. as chattel slaves, that their lives were both shaped and circumscribed by that reality. The African music, Afro-Anglo (Franco, Luso, Latino, etc., whoever had "cotched" them) work songs, the shouts and Arwhoolies, sorrow songs, that existed during slavery all carried and are carried by what came to exist by the end of slavery, we call the blues.

That whole history and feeling and memory is in this verse, and in the music (as music and as musicked speech). It is impossible to read the verse, or hear it, as speech or music, without being aware of its origins in slavery, pain, tragedy, struggle, including the purest joys of being alive. To deny the blues a human origin is like putting people into ovens while saving, in the name of the grossest of scholarships, their prayers for liberation.

Volumes like *Blues Line* should help some of us realize the poetry of the blues, but if we are not frozen by a need to dehumanize its makers, we will see and understand better the human dimension in this great poetry, and eventually even come to understand the humans themselves, as a part of the whole real lives of human beings on this planet throughout history.

5/7/93

CHAPTER 8

Cosby and the Music

Even when you see Bill Cosby doing a Coke or J-E-L-L-O Pudding commercial, there is a kind of *Dizzy* (Gillespie, that is) quality to his banter with the children in the commercial—his eyes light up, the humor just short of slapstick, but sophisticated because of the obvious brightness of the repartee—not adult to child, but one on one.

I say Dizzy Gillespie, because Cosby is a humorist, in fact one of the few contemporary jokers, who can reach child and adult with nothing lost in translation.

Cosby is known for his family-oriented comedy, whether his triumphantly popular sitcom or the standup monologues we see from time to time on cable or guest shots on Carson. Cosby was also, a long time ago, the ostensible "sidekick" to Robert Culp in the long-lived spy romp *I Spy*. But again, Cosby's ability and persona gave his dubious secret agent a depth of character that made audiences interested past the superficialities of TV formula scripts.

Cosby's humor itself possesses a kind of depth and diversity that reaches an obviously wide audience. He is "clean cut," yet he is wacky. He is irreverent, yet the main themes of his monologues and skits, family life, children, American social illusion, are decidedly "mainstream."

His appeal is not just based on the punch lines or sight gags. Cosby is really talking about things the majority of Americans must be interested in, since most who are married and have families recognize the commonality of his concerns and are even elated that sophisticated adult comedy can take on the day-to-day banalities, mini-tragedies, and mini-victories. On the other hand he makes us understand ourselves, our families, and our society much more profoundly.

But at base we are aware of the "put on," the jiving, the unshakable cool of the casually erudite, and this makes his themes and dialogues even funnier because we can see that as warm and accessible as Cos's various personae are, he is only letting us in on *most* of the facts, there is a deeper side to him we sense, and this is our fascination. It is this chuckling edge to his rap that allows him to deal with themes that in someone else's mouth might be ultramundane.

But like Jazz, Cosby has another beat to his telling, another view. Straight ahead but a little funky, even poignant and usually head clearing. Here in Newark, we can hear Cosby every day, at least a tape of him, "begging" money for this city's 24-hour jazz station, WBGO. The station sent out pledge cards with Cosby's picture. With his longtime celebrity and charisma and the world-shaking ratings dominance of *The Bill Cosby Show* pushing NBC to a ratings victory this year, there are bound to be much heavier returns for the fundraiser (to build a new studio for live sessions).

Throughout the years Cosby has always identified with and been identified with "the Music" (as jazz musicians call it). He's had various stars on his Carson guest host shots: Max Roach, Wynton Marsalis, Joe Williams, among others, have made appearances on *The Bill Cosby Show*. Cosby has a record out right now, with an understated jazzical background, talking to his wife, as they dance after the children are asleep and relive the sounds and dances and romance of their youth.

And no matter what Cosby takes on, though there might be any breadth of appreciation variables given the material and the context, he is usually very good and often quite hip. His performances are always marked by smooth improvisation, face, body, props, voice, stance; there is laughter in it to begin with. The loose flexibility, open to any interesting direction.

This is the Hipster quality—e.g., Monk's personality was a marvelous artifact his music merely confirmed! And Cosby lets us know that there is *fun* to be had about anything. (Specially if you *need* fun!) Yet it is only worthwhile if it is fun in the act of *knowing*.

. . . . .

Talking to Bill between shows at Caesar's Palace, he wants us to know that talking about the music is talking about *me* and *he* and the whole *we* of us who grew up with modern Jazz as our measure, our heart, our teacher and our preacher. His hometown, Philly, has a legendary significance in the music, and the myriad Philly musician-heroes, Trane, Shepp, Philly Joe, a few Philly names and many more, including the ones who never leave the city and who the rest of us will never hear about.

A story Cosby likes to tell gives us some insight. "To talk about me and the music we have to talk about Philly. We used to call record albums 'Jams.' And along with the music itself there was a whole social thing. We used to go to see our girlfriends with a bunch of Jams under our arms. You're riding on the bus and you see three or four cats with an armful of Jams and that cap, 'the Jeff,' cocked to one side, with eight or nine albums under their arms. Then I understood that one reason the girls were seeing us was because of the Jams!"

Like myself, Cosby was of that generation for whom absolute devotion to the music was a given, a fact of nature. Coming up in the '40s in Philly one senses the young Bopper Cosby was and the slightly older one he is now. The music of the '40s was not as esoteric or distant from the people in our neighborhood as some people like to think. People dug that music. They grew up with it.

"I'd go in the record shop and see a new Jam and I had to have it—at least once a month. It was not just following names, but what the music *was*. I had to have it. Prestige, Savoy, Blue Note, Atlantic were some of the biggest names."

Was it the Philly style he dug most, the hard bop–smooth funk of the prototypical Philly-originated contemporary group? "It was East Coast, not just Philly. It was that African drum feeling. That *bottom*. That African sound, I liked!

"People in European culture say, 'I don't like a whole lot of drum solos.' But in the African American culture, people expect that—that African *bottom*, those drums. I think the Cubans and Puerto Ricans collaborated with the African Americans to get those rhythms. That's why you can see dudes on street corners with spoons, pots, knives, gettin it together." He started to laugh.

"That's also why in a few minutes Hollywood would come up with those movies with some wild-looking dudes beating on the bongos. This was the Beatnik period." Cosby's laughter suggests the fact that the music is coming from where it's coming from and it ends up in Beatnik movies!

"But there wasn't nothing Beatnik about us. That was somebody else, we were *clean*!" There is a sensitivity in this to the phenomenon of "covers," as the music business calls them. Black hits hidden by well-advertised commercial usually white versions of whatever. He is likewise sensitive to the various distortions of history that not only cover but deprive many black performers of opportunity. Like most of us, this idea, particularly talking about the music, can make Cosby uproariously ironic or not quite comically profane!

DANCING

"Dancing—the Dancing," Cosby was wowing himself with the image. "See, the dancing was part of it. Yeh. We used to do the *Bop,* the *Strand.* (His telling recalls his recent record.) "Man, we used to dance to Bird's 'Confirmation'? Bird's 'Confirmation,' we'd dance, I mean really get down! We'd dance to all those Jams. And if you weren't from that North Philly community you couldn't do that.

"See, there's a cultural gap in this country. Horace Silver, Art Blakey. Man, you'd grab your girl and do the Bop!"

And except for Bill's North Philly exceptionalism, his memories of "Bopping" to the wildest and hippest of the new sounds animate my own recall of that period. We Bopped in Newark (before Hollywood made it about teenage suburban gangs) to Bird and Diz, Monk and Miles, Bird and Max. Sometimes you can see Cosby bopping on his shows. (All real boppers got to bop till they drop!)

But that is what the music has always been about. African religion, from the first ancestor, is based on the belief in, worship of, and possession by Spirit! The music is always an inextricable part of that ritual and the "Frenzy" of spirit possession the highest realization of that religiosity in African culture.

Music and dance are each other's projections. Dance is what music is in the body world. And the very taste of his memory's image, of us very clean young dudes bopping, being possessed by the spirit of our collective historical profundity, has Bill chuckling again as he recalls how the Jams did cause us to be possessed. And, yes, we did dance Monkishly our wholly Bop, till the spirit receded and the square world proceeded.

That memory and idea that we did dance to the most avant of the avants was what it was to us. It led me to ask Cosby what he thought of the music's development. Its future. "Jazz can reach the mainstream by being something people care about. Not strange, but *a part of your emotions!*

"John Coltrane wasn't just being 'the revolutionary'. What he was doing became part of our emotional life.

"They said, 'Bob Dylan, he's a really revolutionary writer'—but I think one of the greatest records made then was Marvin Gaye's *What's Goin On?* And that comes right out of jazz. It's closely related to Miles, Bird, Diz." The sound and the consciousness.

I wanted to know who were Cos's favorites, his main sources through the years. "To be perfectly frank, *all* of them! Even to the local cats I used to play with in Philadelphia. I remember one set down there with Art Blakey and Tito Puente. Jim "Bird Man" Oliver, Bootsie Barnes. and C Sharpe—who is a great player, quiet as it's kept. There are always a lot of wonderful musicians nobody knows outside of Philly.

"I always get an empty feeling when I think about Bobby Timmons—we went to the same high school. I knew Lee Morgan too. Drugs got in them, turned them into dependents. Then they forgot all the people they learned from!" He went on somberly recounting fragments of the negative that shadows the beautiful sounds.

I wanted to know how Jazz influenced Cosby, particularly his work. I'd perceived it and sketched out a rationale. Cosby confirmed it. "Well, you got a beginning, a middle, and an end to a particular piece. You can blow anything you want as long as you adhere to those changes."

You could hear the improvisational spirit animate his description. "Longer, shorter. You can bring in different characters. When I'm working I'm always looking for something fresh. There's a *freedom* to it. There's also a *fun* to it!"

I asked him was this like the improvisational motif in jazz. "Sure, sure . . . that's it!" More confirmation, as when I told him how I'd hooked him up with Diz.

"Oh, yeh. The cats. The great musicians . . . when you talk to them they can tell you about musicians in ways you never heard before. Like when Diz talks about Miles. It's a different perspective. About what Miles is doing or whatever. And the great ones have no fear of sharing respect.

"Established intellectual cats. If people don't perceive Diz as serious, serious, then they must just be waiting for him to die, so they can celebrate him afterwards!

"And Diz is still doing it! Two years ago Diz was playin with Wynton

Marsalis. Diz played about eight bars. Wynton was supposed to follow up, but Wynton just stood there. He passed it up.

"Moody told me the first time in town, he got up on the bandstand with all kinds of bad cats. Moody said he played and he played, but then he realized he had played everything he knew in the first chorus! Now what?

"Then he started to repeat himself. The old cats said, 'Now you listen we got some stuff to teach you!'"

The old teaching the new. Would the future of the music reflect this? "For me," Cosby considered, "the most positive combination has to be *thinking* and *exploring*. Also educating the public, letting them know what the musicians are doing. But people have got so many toys to play with these days . . .

"But like any art—say like Monet and the cats who were going through the Impressionist period—I mean dudes who were tormented to be different—then those that got accepted could not accept the younger people's work.

"But our music has everything from Kid Ory through Bop. Cool, Progressive, Avant Garde, Fusion close to Rock and Roll, complicated solos. The spiritual people like John Coltrane and Pharoah Sanders. Rahsaan Roland Kirk . . . I really want people to know this music has a *life!*

"There's a wonderful story I like to tell. It's the end of the world—gray, blowing, turbulent—and there's this tombstone that says, 'Jazz: It Broke Even!'

"The music has its highs and lows, but it can never never die!

"I was working before this very large, very middle-income audience, and I thought they might not know anything about the music. So before I introduced Bootsie (Barnes) I began by saying, 'You wouldn't believe this, but in France, in Europe, this music is respected as a complex, classical form. Not Wagner or Liszt. This is the American intellect.

"In Europe, you might see a French gardener. He can tell you Thelonius Monk's whole life story. Or maybe a French landowner and he'll be able to tell you where Dizzy Gillespie was born, where he's played, and the size of his mouthpiece."

Cosby was reflecting how sometimes the more well-to-do the American, the more likely they are to be still organized by 18th-century colonialism. They will usually more readily accept something legitimatized by Europe. "I did all that to bring on Bootsie Barnes."

For certain, we both agreed that the future of the music depends on the strength of the institutions created to sustain it. What about the recent *Downbeat* high school jazz awards, which *all* went to largely white, suburban high school jazz bands? Too often inner-city schools don't have budgets large enough to put together such much-needed units. I was asking Bill what he thought this augured for the future.

"Larry Willis and I are setting up the jazz college championships of the world. It's good the music has got to the suburbs, but I want to hear something other than the California and Arizona sound—those straight up and down 16th notes.

"All some people want to hear are Spyro Gyra and Manhattan Transit. It always happens." It was the Bopper in Bill coming out again. "Like this sad movie where this young boy is in search of the blues . . . so he finds this 94-year-old Black man to teach him. 94!?

"Like Sylvester Stallone keeps distorting history. They have the money and power to do anything. And then when some publication, for instance like the *Village Voice,* gets a few Black writers, every few words are foul, otherwise it looks like there's nothing there but some repeats of Eddie Murphy stories.

"But Claude Brown can tell you" (the author of *Manchild in the Promised Land*), despite the distortions and covers, "There's billions of cats out there who can do anything!"

CHAPTER 9

Nina Returns

In 1984, while I was in Boulder, Colorado, teaching for a week at Naropa Institute, calling home I was told by my wife, Amina, that Nina Simone had suddenly arrived in Newark. In fact she was sitting outside our house in a car driven by a woman named Ja-Neece, who she sent into the house to ask Amina could she use the phone and also could she borrow our car.

Once inside, Nina told Amina she liked our house because it reminded her of Africa. In fact, she ended up staying, telling Amina that she wanted me to do her book.

As surprised as I was by Amina's revelation, it did put me immediately in mind of our last joint encounter with Nina at the West Village's Blue Note cafe. That had been wild enough, but now Amina was asking me what I thought, was it all right for Nina to stay.

As I said, what complicated Nina's appearance somewhat was the way we had gotten together just previously. For quite a few years the "word" on Ms. Simone was that she was at least somewhat difficult to deal with.

Nina's series of misadventures with American promoters and club owners were always widely publicized. The fact that many times she was in the right and was trying to do what most of us would do, defend ourselves, seldom got through.

But then the seemingly relentless negativity of certain critical events and periods in Nina Simone's life, while the subject of usually wildly imprecise rumors as well as the character assassination so popular with members of the "in crowd," to prove they are *in* the know, is notorious. Scandal, for instance, has proven eminently profitable, particularly when it's most bizarre, e.g., in the pages of the *Enquirer,* etc.

However, there was some basis for the continuing story of Nina's "difficult" personality and eccentricities. The real story in a general and psychologically essential way is that Nina has been frustrated with a failed marriage, isolation from family, and finally a career in the U.S. and internationally that once had soared to dramatic and historically significant heights but had "trailed off" and become almost nonexistent as she grew more and more unable to cope with the complex negativities of racism, male chauvinism, the rigors of the performer's life, and personal, romantic, and family frustration.

Amina and I saw Nina one night earlier that summer at a West Village jazz joint in the literally funky tradition of the old "Jazz Corner of the World," Birdland. Nina had already had run-ins with the management about her bread. And she was slapping at the piano every once in a while, almost as an afterthought, but what she did continuously and finally to both audience and management's distraction was *talk.*

Nina complained about her and our lives. She talked about her loneliness, her fears, her needs, her past, her seemingly endless frustrations. And while the most progressive of us wish performers would talk more, to the extent that they utilize their stage to expose the real "causal connections" of society. Nina seemed to talk almost as a defense against performing.

At the completion of the gig, the frustration rose to an even more intense level, as the owners of the club refused to pay Nina, according to Nina, all the money she expected because her "excessive talk," according to them, had driven customers away.

When Amina and I were there, however, the joint was "jammed up," people everywhere. At one point of her talk, Nina was brought the information that my wife and I were in the club. (The last time I had seen her was at Rev. Daughtery's church in Brooklyn, a year or so before, making an appearance during one of the National Black United Front's regular Brooklyn rallies.)

But now she called through the microphone for me to come up to the stage. As I finally moved to go up, it reminded me of the time I heard Jimmy Baldwin went up on the Village Gate stage and sat on the bench with Nina and "steadied her," the tale went (confirmed by Baldwin) through one set, even joining in with her in impromptu "duets" on some of the tunes.

This is essentially what she wanted that night. Someone who would add to her confidence. Who could be a focus for her and the audience's "sounding" (measure, polemic, song). She actually wanted me to sit on the stage with her as she played and sang.

But as her drawn-out introduction and its response subsided and she saw that I had no intention of remaining on the stage, she asked me what song I wanted to hear her perform. I said, almost automatically, "Four Women," the 1960s hit which stirred people with its class-caste analysis of black women's lives historically.

"That's a hard piece," she burred, "Why do you want such a difficult piece?" But I was coming off the stage. She sang the piece very simply, and with almost no elaboration. Very much unlike the intense and dramatic '60s version.

. . . . .

Nina, during this period, did have a tendency to be emotionally demanding even in her slightest relationships. She sometimes attacked people unjustly in conversation or dismissed them. Because she had been exploited, "used," so many times, she adopted a "get you before you get me" attitude.

The camp followers, sycophants, would-be in-crowders, aging groupies, who tail and complicate performers' lives, Nina demanded be *useful* to her, not just the fluorescent gas of the comet's tail.

A woman, alone, on the road, constantly beset by these characters and a few worse beside, can be made deeply self-protective and paranoid. For one thing, Nina feels that she has never really received what she deserves in accolades or wealth from her career, though that career has made her a historically important African American artist, a charismatic institution.

At the same time, the *Streisands, Shores, Ronstadts,* with less talent, have reaped far more benefits. She knows, as does any person really clear about American life, that such injustice is rooted in the racism and class bias of the society's history and development. But many times knowing something does not kill the attendant pain or frustration.

Her greatest hits, i.e., those with deepest hooks in the Black and progressive communities, identify, oppose, ridicule these negative constants of American life. Still, singing or writing poems about ugliness need not necessarily assuage its personal effect on the singer.

. . . . .

Nina Simone lived in Europe almost fifteen years. She refused to live in New York, saying it would kill her. It reminded one of Jimmy Baldwin's consistent identification of the U.S. as a multipersonified menace to one's sanity and actual life. These were a couple of his reasons for becoming an emigré.

Nina had lived in the West Indies, Paris (where she still had an apartment when we hosted her in '84), Switzerland. But now, even though she had come back to the States on tour (which got disrupted) when we talked to her that summer of '84, she was wanting to come home. She was torn between what she knew this infernal society was and her longing to be among even *familiar* evil.

She made phone call after phone call back to Paris, checking on her apartment, making sure the rent was paid, even in her absence. She also called Jamaica, Great Britain, California, North Carolina, and bunches of other people in New York City. She checked on her dog, who was being held in the baggage department of the airline. (The next time she came, it was with another dog, a big blue one. People who bumped into it/us insisted it looked like a pit bull. Nina kept saying, "This is the oldest dog. A royal dog. This dog was bred to kill.")

Nina's presence in Newark early on was related to confrontations of one sort or another, like the blue dog. It was like she had been away and wanted, even she admitted, to come back. But that exile, Europe, and the bitterness it represented made Nina bitter and a bitter experience as well.

Plus, there are aging groupies, constantly auditioning sycophants, who are drawn to celebrities. Some are like deadly weights of unproductive indulgence, to take you out by being excessively at your service. Only, you guessed it, that service is their claim to immortality. And they "charge," in cold ways, as well, though not always coin.

Nina had a comet's tail of these. Odd, slightly deranged "fans," who wanted to live their lives with, or even *as*, Nina. They were a shield to the world, at the same time a substitute for it!

She frequently launched into these poor souls as vent to deeper, more easily definable, frustration.

Nina went through "Out" moments in Newark, alone and abetted by an American spirit that is like Dracula panic stricken at the rumors of daytime!

But the place that this city is as an emotional social connection quickly makes absurd less realistic modes of behavior. (Say What?) The citizens are too advanced for much okie-doke, even the state's!

Nina and Amina have a close emotional relationship. Nina Simone is a great artist. And she needs, more than anything, support and love!

. . . . .

One great night was a party we gave for Abbey Lincoln, who did a benefit for the Newark Jazz Society and Newark jazz radio station WBGO. Amina had pulled all this together and made it work. At our house at the party, Abbey scintillated in her striking beauty, and the two great artists talked and laughed, and Nina's pride finally did give support to Abbey's night. At the Peppermint Lounge in East Orange, Abbey set the place on fire, and Nina was announced and stood and was joyfully welcomed by the grooved-to-be-there-grooving assembly.

To close friends, there were twin notes of cautious friendly respect with more than a flutter of defensive oaths. But in the end the whole night got up and flew!

. . . . .

This summer I thought Amina and us should go to the Hamptons. Nina accompanied us, along with our five children. She was accompanied by a magazine writer who was interviewing her and whom she assumed would make a proper escort. But he got in the wind not long after we "settled" at a cabin in a cut-rate but charming summer tourist site in Quogue.

We all swam, especially Nina, who, complete with scuba-diving paraphernalia, hit the water daily, and repeatedly, from early morning throughout the day. We also found ourselves racing up and down the Long Island shore to get to one Hampton or another. We hung out one day with abstract expressionist painter Ray Parker. Nina went out as passenger with their sons and some young girls as the boys water-skied. Nina claimed to have perceived the remote possibility of a fantasy romantic adventure she wanted to talk about.

Or we would be in Larry Rivers's front room in South Hampton, a pop-deco minimalist rehearsal room. Larry's young lady friend was pregnant. In his studio, he showed me some of the murals and detail drawings for his monumental and extravagantly impressive *History of the Jews*. Later, we ate fresh mussels plucked out of the bay by Buddy Wirtshafter, an old head from the painter-Village '50s and '60s. With Nina restive in the back, Amina and I sailed up and down the dark Long Island roads discussing the world.

Sometimes in the cabin, or at our house in Newark, upstairs on the third floor, Nina would sing. High and lilting, vulnerable as a worn and gorgeous dream. She sang and sang. Especially, when she was happy or lighthearted, she sang, and her song still filled the space with warm perception and the sensitive heart.

But Nina would still show up suddenly with newly turned fans, in this case two white women and the cabin's owner, whom she entertained with accounts of her stardom. In trade for whatever favors and ease of mind could be obtained so casually as conversation would allow. She set up dinners and transatlantic phone calls. Made appointments with real estate brokers to go looking at estates while I got a few hundred dollars for her from an interview for a magazine that I write for.

Nina appreciates personalities like Rivers, himself a legend in the making as well of very personal lifestyle and tastes. The two of them together would make a terrific TV series, with both playing themselves. From famous personalities Nina gets a sense of her own career and what its value should have provided. Alas, but how can Art prosper in a society ruled by the dangerously undeveloped?

· · · · ·

One afternoon we went into Bridgehampton to attend a gallery opening. Ray Parker was to meet us there, he had paintings in the show. When we left the tiny gallery we went up the street to a smooth-looking supper club restaurant with, apparently, I'm told, a famous name. We went in, and the soft dark wood seemed rich, relaxed enough to have a relaxing shot or two. Except there was a gorgeous great grand piano behind the bar, center spot. Nina saw it, and we could not resist.

She made the box sing high and tender. Some of the patrons recognized her. Her brother's "Saratoga" took on the weight of a classic. We shuddered and applauded. One woman bolted out of her seat to shake Nina's hand and beg her to come out to some school there on Long Island for pretty fair money. The bartender told us he recognized her as well. That groovy feeling—the spontaneous grace humans are still capable of.

But then the day manager came up and sez he'll have to ask her not to play the piano. It's against club policy!

Everyone told him, but ignorance is very powerful in America. Yes, we were all crushed. It was like a television drama.

· · · · ·

We left Nina on Long Island, after a few more days, with a poet named Max Schwartz, himself a practiced Nina watcher. But in a few months Nina was back to do a program at Newark's Symphony Hall for school children.

As preface to this, Amina put together a celebration for Nina and newly installed executive superintendent of Newark Schools, an old friend of ours, Eugene Campbell.

This was a wonderful party. Nina singing. Assembled poets calling image Round Robins, singers, hot dancers. There were scores of Newark politicians, education activists, cultural workers, and good party folks of all descriptions. We had a fabulous Chinese supper catered by some very skilled comrades. Several political groups were in evidence. And the talk and laughter rolled around and through Nina. There was an atmosphere of great promise, somehow, and willed accomplishment.

Also, with this set, there was now an obvious trust and closeness between Nina, Amina, and me. Though it is Amina who I think has provided Nina with the strong, responsible, yet compassionate friendship that has quite obviously helped her get adjusted to life in Weimar America.

There was some young guy trying to talk his set of overused adventure propositions. It was funny to practiced observers. We saw her whiz him off protesting that it was he who was the aggressor.

. . . . .

A few months later, Nina returned. This time a name we thought at times a figment of her imagination had formally become her manager. We hosted him and his aide, a black pleasant schoolteacher like an executive officer with a smooth comforting rap.

What was interesting is that the rigorous and consistent work these two offered was something Nina needed and needs. The soft-spoken Italian all-business, middle-aged, white-haired manager and his assistant were offering steady work, fewer hassles, and a more stable situation.

Nina was buying his condo in L.A. and a motor home. Her newest secretary, a lank British actor with a skin of steel.

She did a Lincoln Center appearance for the Kool Jazz festival that observers say was a triumph. There was a cancelled second show at Town Hall because of management's vagaries. But again, the first show was said to be dynamite.

After this program, we went with Nina, her manager, and some other friends to the Angry Squire. Nina was dressed in gold that night, with a gold tiara. We talked electoral politics at the table and the twisted path of political power in South Africa.

. . . . .

When Nina returned on the next trip, she was featured at Hunter College in an anti-apartheid program. Time and again the nostalgic and sophisticated crowd rose to salute her. Her songs spoke of stronger, more conscious times, when people our age thought it might be possible to smash injustice forever within our lifetime. But the songs put us in touch once more with the "sweetness" of struggle, the self-conscious dignity. Digging Nina, then, was really digging all ourselves at perhaps the top of our acts! The crowd rose again and again, celebrating Nina and ourselves.

When she stayed with us this time, she mentioned that ex-*Ebony* writer Phyllis Garland had agreed to do her biography. Originally, she had said that Jimmy (Baldwin) was to do it. But then she said he had said he was too busy. For the last year or so whenever we'd meet she'd persistently ask me to write the book. But I did not think I had the state of mind or the obligatory thickness of skin to prevail in such a project and was not-so-nimbly trying to toe-dance out of any commitment. Now Ms. Garland was being considered.

We went to Newark's classic black watering hole, Carl Jones's Bridge Club on Washington Street, and talked biography writing and writers, while old and young folks flowed by casually and not to pay their homage. One of Nina's deprivations she'd mentioned often, as a result perhaps of living so long in Europe, had been African American cuisine. Amina is a marvelous cook and scholar of dee potz, you can get testimonials from the many grooved palates that have gritted in our digs. And around these parts, next to Amina's and our immediate family's work, the Bridge Club is where it's at as far as top-shelf A-A i.e., soul, food, is concerned. Filmmaker Bill Greaves holds the one-shot eating record here, during a film project in this city—two dinners eaten on the spot, with two desserts, and two dinners to go!

Phyllis did not do the book either.

. . . . .

Nicaraguan cultural attaché Roberto Vargas called for Amina and me to read in Washington, D.C., as part of a celebration for the anniversary of the Nicaraguan revolution. Amina got Nina to go, and Vargas, a longtime U.S. resident, was ecstatic.

Even though one young Trotskyite, part of an American support coalition, embarrassed us and angered Nina by not recognizing her. It is one of the weaknesses of the American Left that they do not even know the people's heroes.

We went to OAS headquarters for a formal banquet and met several exiles from Reagan-harassed Latin America, even Victor Navasky, editor of the *Nation*.

But the "Joint" was later, at an African-owned club called Kilimanjaro, where an overflow crowd roared and screamed and Nina hypnotized us with "I Wish I Knew How It Felt to Be Free!" plus her classic version of Gershwin's "Porgy."

Nicaraguan and Chilean singers and dancers and Vargas himself with a powerful necessarily *engaged* poetry held us up as high as Nina had lifted us. Amina and I also read, and Amina stood the audience up with her Xhosa singing which prefaces her poem "Soweto," as well as a poem about Nicaragua, which ends chanting *No pasaran!* (They will not pass!)—with echoes of the Spanish Civil War, which was the watershed, as a result of the defeat of the Republican government by fascist Franco, of fascism itself! So the Nicaraguan situation, especially seen in an international context, seems like it is being made "an example," in the same way that Republican Spain was, by Reagan's apartheid-supporting government!

The inspiring clarifying cultural program raised the spirit of everyone in the place. It was a celebration, and the people shouted their love at Nina all night.

. . . . .

What is encouraging is how much more realistic and functioning Nina has gotten since visiting with us and waltzing around this scene. A smooth and joyous birthday party for playwright and screenwriter Richard Wesley in Montclair, given by his wife, writer Valery Wesley. Nina sang, shyly and quietly, "Porgy," and people hugged each other, so happy were they to be there.

At another set, this one after the anti-apartheid program, at poet Rashidah Ismaili's Harlem spot. And there, among a significant presence by New York's Black and Latino literateurs, again there was a similar kind of leavening and courageousness, coupled with the warmth of straight-out appreciation, that even South African poet Duma Ndlovu, who arranged the program and party, was filled up with the realization that yes, it is one struggle, and Africa, despite the slave trade and the diaspora, is still "one," in pain, but in motion!

Essence magazine, which had earlier sent poet Alexis Deveaux to interview Nina, sent a chauffeured limousine to bring her to New York

City for photos. They styled her hair African contemporary, which made the photos they took reveal the smoldering sexuality of the singer.

At Hunter, she had finally gathered in the whole audience with her love chants and work songs, her tearful ballads of love requited and un–.

Nina's voice, never overpowering, is an even more fragile instrument. As she works more regularly, which seems now to be the case, she will get stronger and more in control. Still she has a sound and presence that sum up a whole epic of human feeling.

Nina's songs wring feeling from us like the shudder of an authentic tragedy. She digs deeply into herself and so likewise into us. It is as revealing as a biography.

What is it like to be Black and a Woman? A great artist, repressed and *intentionally* obscured by the garbage and venom of the music industry monopolists? Nina gives the impression of wanting to be an artist in the "classic" sense, as related to a vanished mode of production. But the artist is *not* free. The most "successful" artists are co-signers of the social catastrophe. (That is the cost!) As one teacher has written, (the successful artists) are the fortunate whore foot troops of the state!

But Nina, as seemingly exposed as she sometimes seems, is also predictably wise—canny and defensive. She has said she thought "they" wouldn't forgive her for her 1960s consciousness-raising songs, "Four Women," "Mississippi God Damn," "Young, Gifted and Black," as a few for instances, among the myriad other celebrations, exhortations, and common yet unique personal grief.

"But those are the songs the people love you for," Amina was telling her. In opposition, I thought, to the schizophrenia and intimidation of artists by capital. Yet Nina still sings these "redemption songs," as Bob Marley called them. And she is always writing new songs, e.g., "They Have Dust in Their Brains," to fit her continuing experience.

Nina at a party is the stuff of a hipper American musical. The person who is the center of the focus and irritated that that is not happening really enough. Yet someone whose demand for privacy is in her eyes. A round insinuating face, amazed yet passing for cynical. And nervous. Whose constant rap at one party was about various quickly conceived paradises anywhere else in the world, which avoided manifestation only because certain hard-to-find elements were missing. And these elements, "the stuff of dreams," apparently continue to be missing.

At an interview at the cabins in Long Island, she said straightfacedly that she was born in Incarnation, North Carolina, then broke up at the reporter's seriousness at writing this Incarnation down.

She talked about her childhood and early days. How deeply immersed her family was in the church. How her mother, to this day, still would prefer her singing and close to religion.

Nina also painted a striking portrait of her long-passed father, who was central to Nina and apparently her relationship to religion and her family. Without her father, the church was less than magnetic to Nina. Yet its embrace is obvious throughout Nina's music. Her father, according to Nina, is still not too far away, and watching over her.

Nina was raised in and given the dramatic legacy of the Black church. Yet she also was partially molded by the formal musical training she received, piano lessons with concert professionals.

In fact it is perhaps one very critical factor of Nina's life that she began her study of European "classical" music at age four, a "child prodigy." A white woman piano teacher heard Nina playing for the church and asked to train her. She studied with this benefactor five years. Nina calls her the "founder of my career," characterizing the relationship as that of having "two moms . . . one white and one black."

The Eunice Waymon Fund was set up, and with contributions from people in Tryon and Ashville, North Carolina, Nina studied at Julliard in New York City and at the Curtis School of Classical Studies (in Philadelphia) for almost twenty years!

After high school Nina left Tryon for Julliard, then went to Curtis. She says she wanted to be a "black classical pianist." She had her first recital at twelve (Bach, Beethoven, Prokofiev, Chopin, Poulenc, plus "improvisations on classical and pop tunes"). One feature of her programs was to improvise a song named by members of the audience.

The fact that Nina's father was also an entertainer keeps his memory close. He was a singer and dancer before Nina was born. He owned a pressing plant. The Depression ended all this, and for a while he was a gardener and a handyman. Then, according to Nina, "He became a preacher . . . to please Mama, I might add."

Nina was the tenth of twelve children. But four of the children were lost very early. Her mother is an ordained minister in the Methodist church (thirty-four years). At age three, Nina was playing piano. Her favorite song: "God Be with You Till We Meet Again." "In the key of F," she hastens to add.

"I was too poor to know what notes were. I remember when [the

piano] came into our house! It was my favorite toy. I liked F sharp
(G flat), B, and E natural. My favorite keys.

"I wanted to leave Tryon," she smiles, "when I was three or four.
I knew somehow about the racial problem. I knew why my parents
wouldn't talk about it. I knew I wanted to get out of there.

"In school I had my first racial experience. I tried for a scholarship—
and got turned down. I went to the other side of town and got a job
accompanying students who were studying popular tunes.

"The first job I got was playing in Atlantic City. It was a job in a
bar, $90 a week. I played everything I'd learned—Bach, Beethoven,
Spirituals, "My Funny Valentine," "Children, Go Where I Send Thee."

"On the second night, the owner said, 'You want this job, you gotta
sing!' So I began to sing all those tunes I was playing for the kids."

· · · · ·

Nina's first big hit, of course, was Gershwin's "Porgy." She was opening by then at One Fifth Ave and the Village Vanguard. It was at this
time she also begin to release a steady flow of popular albums. She lists
Black Gold, Emergency Ward, Silk & Soul, Nina Simone & Piano, a
solo album (all produced by RCA), and *Fodder in Her Wings* (Carrere,
Fr.) as perhaps the most popular.

Nina, during this time that she crossed Amina's and my paths, was
at a crossroads in her own life. She had been away from home a very
long time. The indignities that had driven her away flowed off her lips
like an injured queen.

· · · · ·

Since she's been back Nina's moved along to a little higher ground
emotionally and in terms of being a trifle more "secure" or at least less
insecure.

But there is still such an intense sense of having been *had* by the
whole of society. Nina will talk bad about both black and white folks at
the same time or one at a time or with both in contradiction and beating each other to death. She hates management and those managed.

Fiercely patriotic (in the sense of love for the African American
people), she is acid critical, and quite regularly so.

She is clearly a person struggling to come to terms with everything,
in no specific order. The wonderful skill coupled with a lifetime of
affront and frustration breeds a hair-trigger paranoia, which, when we

understand American social life and the "madness of crowds," we can see is not just paranoia but a kind of battle fatigue reserved for those in the public eye or ear.

Even in those earlier days of our friendship, when she had just come back to the States, already she had played the Village Gate, Blue Note, Swing Plaza, was talking with Fat Tuesday, Sweet Basil, the Chestnut in Philadelphia. A few minutes later she was in Town Hall, then Lincoln Center. In those days she was searching for a manager, which apparently she found, and times got obviously better, her temperament as well. But would it last?

There is no doubt that Nina's edgy candor throws some people. Her pre-emptive strike demeanor from time to time can put still others to flight.

When I talked to her on Long Island she said she'd come back to see her mother on Mother's Day and her grandchild, whom she'd never seen, who was seven months old at the time. Nina has a daughter who's in the WAFS, stationed in Tucson. Part of her description of self-frustration has to do with the distance, not just geographically, between her and her daughter.

"I don't like the U.S.," she thrusts, ". . . its racial conflicts . . . its politics . . . . the way its hurt me in the past.

"I like its money. I try to collect money owed me. I haven't lived in the U.S. in twenty years. I come back every five years to give a concert, if I can stand it."

The rain was holding off, just above our heads. Quoque was grey and cool.

"I'm never happy here—there's an extraordinary amount of pressure. Plus all the other things we know.

"Was that a sudden decision [to leave]? It took more than twenty years to get out, to make it clear.

"I come back for the money. And the money from pirated albums. You know my albums are *pirated* all over the world. I saw one a couple of weeks ago selling for $40.

"I guess it would be different if I had more friends. [In Europe] it's difficult not seeing any more Black persons than I do." Even now, during the interview, she was wrestling with what she wanted to do.

"I'm trying to live here now for a short time—I'm not giving up my Paris residence. There's a peacefulness there. The people are not crazy. Americans are crazy!"

She speaks of her "sister," singer Miriam Makeba. Nina says that close friendship and twelve years of persuasion are what got her out of the U.S. in the first place.

But since she has "returned," she has compromised perhaps in the sense that indeed she has stayed. She did get the manager she wanted. She did get that California condominium she'd talked about. Her life, with certain qualified exceptions, did get a great deal more stable.

For instance, at the end of the Long Island interview, she gave a list of things she wanted to do—her "in motion" list of life priorities. At the top was her autobiography (or biography). She's tried five or six times, and at this sitting there is no one certain.

She said also she wanted to make a videocassette, find a new manager. She wanted to work in Atlantic City and Vegas and come out with a new album.

The album, *Nina's Back* (VideoMusic), is just out, complete with a picture of Nina in only a wreath of gauze and a flower. Her back is turned toward us. But the album itself is *fantastic*! It is the strongest and most rewarding music she's done in years.

Plus this record, even with no coy punches pulled, is obviously looking for listeners. It has a mature, even spicy balance to it.

There are the R&B-rooted "It's Cold" and "Another Lover" by assistant manager Singleton, nice and pop-funky. Nina's biting and indelible originals, e.g., "I Sing . . . ," which carries a Makeba-like beat and feeling. Or the cold portrait of our entire social persona, "Fodder." Her brother Sam's striking ballad "Saratoga," which always puts me in mind of something old as human compassion.

"Touching & Caring" is the most jazzical piece on the album. It has a swinging, yet touching quality.

But check the new version of "Porgy," with a sample of Nina "talking." She tells you her recent history and perhaps something about African American women that is as poignant in some ways as the recent wave of Black women writers.

There is literally a little something on this album for everyone with ears. And it is more than a "comeback" album, it's a confirmation of Nina's stature as an important artist and I think part of a new blast of positive energy that is swelling perhaps in defense against the radical backwardness of contemporary America.

The album is a sign of health and determination. That Nina Simone is still a talent and mind to be reckoned with.

The last words on the Long Island interview were typical of Nina at the time, when she had not long returned to the States. In telling me her plans, she ended by saying, after laying out the new album she planned to make, "I wanna get married," she was grinning, "and honeymoon in Martinique. Go horseback riding in Galilee. Go on an African safari in Kenya . . . after which we [her proposed new husband and she] will live separately!"

Nina has come some distance since then—Amina and I still see her whenever she comes near bouts. She insists we are her "family." She has even partially adjusted to our CENSORED children, as she calls them. We are still the listeners and furious talkers at whom she screams current events in her cinemascopic expressiveness over the phone. She makes the most demands when she is most agitated.

But then the last time she showed, just before Christmas, the three of us, Amina, Nina, and I, went up to her brother Sam's place in Nyack, New York, near the great Toni Morrison (who was supposed to be there along with director Gil Moses, who is doing her *Dreaming Emmett* at SUNY Albany).

Sam and his co-host, playwright, screen dramatist, novelist, and actor Bill Gunn *(The Black Picture Show)*, presided. Sam Waymon is Bill's musical collaborator. Nina's somewhat younger brother is a singer, pianist, and composer who works frequently in clubs with his own group.

Sam has just received a $2.4 million commitment from backers to make a film, with Bill writing and Sam Waymon's music and topside direction.

Christmas afternoon, 1985, they serve us an exquisite and elegant Afro-American American table. Nina, Amina, and I, Sam's partner in record production, a black CBS cameraman, his wife, and a young woman friend of Bill and Sam's.

An intimate merry occasion in the big wooden elegantly appointed nineteenth-century country house, amidst the beautiful warm functional artifacts Sam and Bill have collected, is a perfect setting for a first hearing of Nina's new record. We all gather, intensely satisfied by good food and potent spirits. Nina will not come into the room as we listen. The record producers with us say this platter can fly if given some media play. But then we all know the game, and the history that surrounds and animates Nina's name. But this work is so hot maybe maybe . . . we hope.

But Nina seems ecstatic in a quiet, even humble way, like an audition sitting outside the room where we listen. In a few minutes she has asked Amina to sit in the other room with her.

On the drive back, my wife supports the idea of me doing Nina's book. And I say, "Okay, let's see if it can happen."

. . . . .

A day or so later, Nina, intensely agitated because there is not enough happening, perhaps, gets her bags together and says she is going to Barbados. There is an ex-prime minister there who wanted to marry her.

She calls back a few times from Accra Beach, she is talking about her book. Then a little later she is back in Los Angeles, we hear from her again. A minute or so later we hear she is in London. But we still think of Nina as having returned!

2/2/86

CHAPTER 10

Jazz Criticism and Its Effect on the Music

The contradiction we are dealing with here, at one level, is expression versus reflection. Though both are interchangeable or co-related to exist at all. The dialectic of their relationship is that expression reflects reflection and reflection (as criticism) is expression!

Criticism, ideally, should be analysis, but also identification and *use!*, based upon the work and its creator's intent and values and their *relationship* to the real world. How exemplarly the work is of this intent and values is what we are analyzing; and what does this mean *practically.* Aim and result. But what is key is that the critic actually understand just what the work intends, i.e., what it means to mean as well as how close it comes to meaning it, i.e., what is it *being,* on the real side.

The critic should attempt to uncover the reality of the work, what it actually is and does, illuminating the creator and his conception together as part of a material world.

But no analysis is valuable without the critic being at least familiar with the premise and presumptions of the work and its creator, as well as the real-life context (multidimensional) it issues from.

But also, given the specific aggregate of values and philosophy which are one dimension of *both* the form and the content of a work, we must know what the work (and the artist) are saying, and their real-life significance, as well as the "grammar" and record-keeping aspect of an art, i.e., identification as to "what genre," artistic school, influences, but even these categorizations are useful in fully explicating any important work and artist.

What *Blues People* raised to a certain extent was the significance of "criticism" issuing from writers and institutions whose values and aesthetic were *antithetical* to the values and aesthetic of the artists themselves, as well as to the essentially Black mass audience for whom the works were created. Basically the contrast of philosophy, values, and aesthetic would be as in opposition as Slave versus Slave Master!

It is so ironic as to elicit continuous at times nigh hysterical laughter. First "They" steal us from our homelands, make us slaves, make generations of the African American people, even now, in closer intimacy with hourly tragedy than almost anyone in North America!

Now they want to "judge" our art. But to the Slave Master, the art of the slaves is first of all *Slave "Art."* What is even displayed of it, the slave master "understands" is done with his *tolerance*. Since Blacks still have no institutions, albeit the church!, the Beggar or White Man's Burden still hangs about the African American people for this reason, in the sense that this makes our economic and political weaknesses as glaring as they are crippling. It is the question DuBois raises in *The Souls of Black Folk*. What is it like to see yourself through the eyes of those who despise you? (That is the Black petty bourgeois self-hatred and defeat, etc., syndrome or "Double Consciousness," which DuBois baits with: How to be Black and American?)

One expression of this conglomerate of oppression-created relationships is the assumption of inferiority (historically moving from a principle of the slaveholding society to its more camouflaged contemporary continuation), to everything African, Black, etc. American society, indeed western capitalism's domination of the world, was fueled *fundamentally* by African Slavery (and the conquest of India)! Black exploitation is one of the most glaring aspects of world capitalism.

So that in the earliest years of Black presence in the New World, Black Art was initially (after the conquest) a *threat*. Since it could fuel and communicate rebellion. The drum was banned, which should draw attention to its *political* nature.

Substitution for the drum brought the steel band in the West Indies, but it also *deepened* and made even more profound the slaves' vocal music.

The rhythmic sophistication of the African was forced into vocal expression which was highly sophisticated from its beginnings, if we are to judge from recordings of the Babenzele Pigmies as well as Leon Thomas's adaptation of their "Hocketing," i.e., yodeling style. Black percussive style was brought into other instruments, any instrument blacks played, fiddle, jawbone, broom, body, feet, sticks, and later to horns, even piano, though by that time the drum was allowed. But to this day, as Max Roach says, "Drums are the niggers of the orchestra."

Just as Black persons were systematically humiliated so that they would submit more easily to chattel slavery, so the slave empire's history writers, philosophers, critics, academics, institutions "inferiorized" African culture. In the chronicle-sized poem of many songs I am writing about African American history called *Y's/Why's/Wise*, the griot tells us in the very first poem:

WISE I
(Nobody Knows the Trouble I Seen)

If you ever find
yourself, some where
lost and surrounded
by enemies
who wont let you
speak in your own language
who destroy your statues
& instruments, who ban
your omm boom ba boom
then you are in trouble
deep trouble
they ban your
omm boom ba boom
you in deep deep
trouble
humph!
probably take you several hundred years
to get
out!

The much-talked-about destruction of African culture was a basic requirement for reducing the new African slaves to unconscious instruments of gain. The slave was, himself, a part of the *means* of production—a tool!

The rewriting of history, DuBois, the father of Black Studies, pointed out, was repeated throughout the slave society's superstructure, to justify and legitimatize Slavery! The same reason Duke Ellington cannot be allowed to be the world-class creator that he is because if Duke is Duke or Zora Neale Zora Neale, what does that do to white supremacy, as an idea?

So if the slave society has to deal with the historical reality and facts of the African people, as the first Humans, the harnessers of fire, the creators of language, song, dance, clothing, art itself, how do we then explain why they now have them clamped in chains?

The main institutions of jazz criticism are like any of the more basic American institutions in relationship to the African American people, white supremacist, fundamentally exploitive, and self-serving.

Earlier, the principal focus of these critical institutions simply dismissed African culture as savage, later nonexistent, as the alien African became the more familiar Negra slave. The only "culture" and art a slave had were, at most, imitative and witless. One has only to read 19th-century observers and "scholars," Krehbiel, Kemble, to understand this.

A relationship based on slavery and repression, like that which defines U.S. society, is likewise based on the "inferiority" of those oppressed, *materially* and *philosophically!*

Ironically, though, African American culture and art and even, finally, political utterance is such a combustible, catalytic substance within the broader American culture that its transforming, *advanced,* and *radical* force (in the context of it being a slave/oppressed projection necessarily in spite of and in opposition to the dominant culture) politically must be "covered." Economically, its covering is the identical social act that distinguished slavery! Minstrelsy, for instance, explains a critical economic relationship as well as a social and political one. It is like wearing the skin of a slain beast!

The "advance" of American society is seen in the fact that now minstrelsy is "respectable" in that it pretends to be *real*, e.g., simply another "style."

Equally masked is the continued and constantly paralleled exploitation of Black Americans! The relationship of America to Black people is generally the same relationship the society has to Black Art and Culture fundamentally.

So that in the same way that the dominant society, through its economic-political repression, social and cultural chauvinism, crushes Black people, so any segment or vector of it has a similar relationship. No less the "official" criticism of Black Music, i.e., that which is best financed, whether "independent," university, or other powerful institutional base; media, government, corporate, are, in their objective effect, parallel to the main focus of the superstructure.

African culture and European and colonial Euro-American cultures were quite different, even before the enforced "intimacy" of the slave trade. In music, for instance, the rhythmic sophistication of the African culture can be contrasted to the harmonically developed European musical aesthetic.

The historically consistent aesthetic of Africa and African American music, DuBois pointed out, was linked directly to the oldest religion, the "faith of our fathers." *Music* itself was indispensable to the worship, likewise the central role of the *priest*. The *call and response* form found in most Black music is the form of dialogue between the shepherd and his flock, and the *frenzy* (Spirit possession) that accompanied these are a basic fabric of the *spirit worship* itself.

"The Spirit will not descend without song," the Africans said. The frenzy, what we called "Gettin Happy" in the Bethany Baptist Church, is the method of communications with and possession by the spirit. It is this spirit possession that is the *highest* religious expression. Becoming animated by the divinity as life force.

This is the religious *content*, its forms exist to obtain or as displayers of this content. Screams, shouts, moans, cries, stomps, tearing the air wildly, staring pop-eyed into space quivering like a cosmic gong.

These are forms of God! World into us as itself and as ourselves in it, of it, unconsciously superconscious of all of it (as Ar[t] against the "not it").

Black music is meant anthrophilosophically, historically, to bring the worshippers into unity with the super-Being (*all* being). With the *Holy Spirit!* "He went Out!" we say, in 1986.

This is the African cultural (art, philosophy, religion, social, etc.) thrust—seen in specific reference to art as an *aesthetic*, or a basic and abiding part of that aesthetic.

The other world-connecting aspects of that aesthetic are the exact condition of the human bearers of this aesthetic and how this is one expression of worldview. Subjective yet reflective of objective existing political and economic existence.

Slavery and the destruction of Africa that was advanced by its removal and degeneration of the continent's productive forces. Its people and its technology. This is also one critical aspect of the African American thematic aesthetic.

Black culture has been a slave of racist America and Black art in chains. The critical establishment erected in the name of and off the backs of Black music is its abusive *overseer*. The commercial and corporate wealth reaped by the exploitation of Black culture is inestimable.

Michael Jackson saved Columbia Records' popular music division before he was near-banished for consorting with Black People (his family) in the act of trying to make $100,000,000, and wanting to celebrate that *Victory* with the infamous nigger promoter of evil bloody boxing, Don King.

The slave versus slave master society still exists as it must, today. The destruction of Stax records, the cooptation and dilution of *Motown*, the reduction of many small black record and production companies to "independent" producers for the big houses are historically classic. Democracy is seen as *competition* in a society where everything is a commodity.

Barbra Streisand is no Aretha Franklin (no one else is either). Cyndi Lauper cannot be either—ask Patti LaBelle. But it is Streisand (or Dinah Shore) who makes the millions, has the TV or movie career. The "cover" was a blind to suck blood. Dracula in blackface, so no one is wise.

But times change. Debussy, Ravel, Ernest Ansermet, Brecht, Stravinsky, Panassie, Berendt, Hodeir, Copeland, Ives, Gershwin, European and white American jazz players, the American theater, the Lost Generation, Langston Hughes, the Harlem Renaissance, Vachel Lindsay, the Beat Generation, the New York School, the Black Mountain School, Picasso, Matisse, German Expressionism, Jackson Pollock, Abstract Expression, Merce Cunningham, Balanchine, Leonard Bernstein, progressive sectors of America and Europe saw to some of that explanation in the mainstream when it was "avant."

The primary creators of the music, largely African American, saw to the expression, the "telling of the story," and the social economic and political conditions of the society and international conditions set the real-life pressures and transformation.

The largely white Critical establishment living off Black music shapes less sophisticated taste. It can create "stars," geniuses, fortunes, and fiction. It can also stop them. Yet historically, the American, essentially white-owned, critical establishment has been the most overtly racist in the world. A slavery, then national oppression, based superstructure made it more difficult to judge Black music as an independent self-determining expression.

The Blues is what Black People are as music. It is what Black life is over in there too. The critical establishment masks its oppressive relationship to Black music and musicians with formalism and distorted history. Formalism normally stresses form over content. The formalism of the jazz critical establishment celebrates form as content and as formal "invention." Craft is exulted and structure, but "objectionable" content is denigrated as having flaws in technique.

But the "story," the content of Black music, tells us of Black life in America. It's all in there. It is itself, the music, definer and resister to the "world of trouble" America has been for the African American nation.

It exists as proof of the lie of the slave society, the hypocrisy of American "civilization." It accuses and denounces and exposes as consistently as it loves and laughs. And it does this as part of the "highest" art this society has produced.

Discuss Langston Hughes and Carlos Williams seriously or Ellington and Stravinsky and you will begin to understand. But Black Culture is radical in overview in the context of the U.S. slavery–based and white supremacy–rooted society, fundamentally, because as a reflection of the African American people it is itself part of the struggle for democracy and self-determination! Therefore, the most advanced projections of that culture carry that life, that focus, that history in varying degrees of consciousness. Cabral said, "The culture of the people is the repository of resistance" to national oppression. The art is the griot's tale of the nation's travail. From the oldest work songs in African languages to the new new music. From gut bucket to avant gut bucket.

The resistance, in turn, of the slave and racist society to black struggle for democracy has been world advertised. The American critical establishment first resisted the idea that African Americans were human beings or could even produce art, that would at least "color" or "uncolor" it, as the case may be.

Once slavery ended, it did not suppress white supremacy, as the destruction of reconstruction and the emergence of "separate but equal" readily attest. The '60s upsurge of Black writers on jazz was at the same time a reflection of the Black masses' cry for self-determination (at its most practical, beginning with *self-definition*).

Objectively, as well, this critical establishment is linked to the powerful corporate and commercial interests of the society upon which it depends for financial support. Whether through advertising, consultancies, foundation grants, corporate gifts, etc.

For this reason the commercial dilutions of the music usually transfer competent white players into stars, geniuses, and innovators while deprecating the Black innovators. Economically, it's obvious that the critical establishment linked directly to the corporate-commercial establishment can make millionaires of white players, while the actual black initiators and innovators of the style, that corporate and critically supported players are replicating, might literally starve to death!

It is the nature (ideologically and culturally) of the corporate owners of the music business to oppose any "radicalism" generally, and to water such expression down for commercial exploitation, regardless of the nationality. (It is "eaten.")

E.g., there is no auto industry—they make cars to make money. Publishing deals with books to make profit . . . films, etc.—with certain clear "ideological" guidelines. "Art" is a snide joke, an obstruction to profit taking, everything is literally reduced to filthy lucre, i.e., *shit.*

It is decaying capitalism, which reduces all its own institutions to money worship and that wants to reduce human transformational experiences to the passage of commodities and the owing and collecting of money. They would reduce the world to a large bank with moneymatic 24-hour pay and grab machines installed in our homes, cars, and clothes.

This is the basis of the establishment "aesthetic" and critical standards. The common assumption that European music is superior to African music is the philosophy and aesthetic analysis of slavery and fascism. It is quite respectable in the U.S., up to the highest-ranked racists in the society (academic, cultural, political, artistic). This view is an expression of white supremacy, the philosophical justification for slavery!

But for the Black artist the existent national oppression of his community produces a *superexploitation.* The robbery and deprival of rights that has categorized Black oppression in society, which is the definition of national oppression, means that not even the ordinary "bourgeois democracy" that exists for working-class whites exists for the Black masses. For instance, 30,000,000 African Americans without *one* U.S. senator to "represent" them.

So that that superexploitation means in the music business hit songs bought for a few pennies, while the corporations made millions. It means heavy-thumbed promoters and agents ripping off Black musicians and music with impunity, as part of the social and economic tradition of white supremacy.

Duke Ellington has songs he had to list exploiting producers as *co-composers!* in order to get the music distributed. Or explain why Duke, Count, Billie, Trane, Monk, Papa Joe, Philly Joe, Mary Lou Williams, Louie are already dead, while their promoters, producers, agents, most around the same age, are alive and well off and still making money off the dead folks' work!

Since the '50s and the emergence of Rock and Roll, what changed significantly was that now there were even more of the white jazz players and blues and black music-influenced white musicians and singers, and more could be celebrated and promoted, made rich, etc.: "the King of Jazz," "the King of Swing," "the Best Rock & Roll Band in The World." (Now they are even calling Bette Midler "the Divine" and Bruce Springsteen "the Boss." There have been movies about Janis Joplin!, Glenn Miller, Benny Goodman, Bix Beiderbecke, Red Nichols, Helen Morgan—like we have films about Graziano and LaMotta, but none about Sugar Ray! Where are the films about Duke, Count, Sassy, Miles, Trane, etc.?) But the "covers" and segregation did not necessitate anything more than patronizing chauvinism towards the Black source from the mainstream critical establishment and corporate music business owners.

However the social progress of Black people domestically and internationally and the more objective analyses of European and non-American critics raised the music to a point of visibility in the U.S. mainstream it had never had *directly* before.

Since the Harlem Renaissance, and its accompanying "Jazz Age" and the arrival of Blues and related Black musics into the big cities of the U.S., Black music and its influence have been more visible.

This visibility and international praise and valorization of the music, plus its deepening influence on U.S. society, especially white youth, made it necessary not only to cover Black musicians and their hits, but since Presley it has been apparent that the critical establishment in collaboration with the corporate owners want now to project Whites as the real innovators and significant stylists of the music! (See "The Great Music Robbery" in my book *The Music,* William Morrow.)

Chauvinist garbage like Len Lyons's *Great Jazz Pianists*, which *excludes* Duke, Monk, Tatum, Waller, Bud, Willie the Lion, James P. Johnson! It includes Joe Zawinul, Jimmy Rowles, Keith Jarrett, Paul Bley, Dave Brubeck, Marian McPartland, George Shearing, Steve Kuhn, Chick Corea, and Ran Blake! The same author's *100 Greatest Jazz Records* is filled with similar twisted racism, e.g., there being more of those "greatest" from Corea and Zawinul than Bud Powell!

The Reagan-led rightward motion of society is clearly duplicated by the steady flow of chauvinist reactionary scribbling passing as commentary or analysis of the music. Jack Chambers's incredibly racist books on Miles Davis, one of the main themes of which is that Miles played his best when he played with white musicians! Or Lincoln Collier, whose various writings about the music give off a distinct aroma of rotting mint julep.

But the older more outrightly racist denunciation of the music has now been succeeded by an equally racist attempt to pirate it. Every major writing job on African American music is held by whites. Most institutions that deal with it are white dominated.

As an entity, the critical institutions related to Black music should at best be secondary and modified adjuncts to an African American and progressive critical institutional process.

Economic development, at one point, is an expression of conscious cultural development. E.g., Black music alone, as a developed industrial, commercial, academic, artistic, and professional complex, could have supported millions of African Americans for performing, editing and writing, scholarship and research, record, video, publishing (music and related literature, e.g., books, periodicals, etc.), audio, technology and electronics, design, maintenance, graphics, management, e.g., booking, clubs, theaters, concert halls, legal, manufacturing and packaging, distribution and sales, mail order, etc., etc. But most of these jobs are held by whites because of the historic exploitative and racist structure of U.S. society.

Most of the individual performers work at laughable wages, though sometimes accompanied by lavish "praise," even elevation to "legend," "genius," etc., status, to mask the normal slave economic condition of these really great artists!

In many cases, though, it was the very hostility of the critical establishment that prevented innovative Black artists from being respected and celebrated in a *real* way, i.e., to make a decent living from their art! *Downbeat*'s attacks on Charlie Parker, Miles Davis, Dizzy Gillespie, and some of the music's great classics when they first appeared could be cited. *Downbeat* re-reviewed the records after they *had* to, when Bird, Diz, and Miles began to be recognized as the great creators they are. The first review gave *no stars*, the second *five*! Hindsight and dishonest critical mutation but neither principle nor intelligent informed analysis.

The attacks on John Coltrane were infamous. His transcendently beautiful sound was called "ugly." A remarkably gentle person, Trane's music was constantly reviewed simply as "angry." I remember one reviewer calling Coltrane's playing "Barbaric yawps." (Check the recorded interview with a Scandinavian journalist on the recently released *Miles Davis and John Coltrane in Sweden* [Dragon]).

Yet Coltrane was a major innovator and artist. His contributions took Black music into another era, literally expanded the perceived range and articulation of the instrument, while reflecting in exact emotional analogy the turbulent period in which he lived.

In this sense the critical establishment, like the society itself, consistently attacks the profoundest advances and innovators in the music and therefore, objectively, aggressively opposes and weakens the music's legitimate historical development. The criticism openly attempts to *retard* the music and make impossible independent development.

But the music, like the people, has its own independent motion, no matter the abusive irrelevance of the critical establishment. It is why, for instance, the styles of black music evolve as open *rebellion* against the aesthetic (and social) dilution of the last style by the corporate deculturization process.

White "Dixieland"'s dilution of New Orleans style was, in one aspect, simply an indication that the most contemporary genre of black music had already *changed!*

When corporate big bands and their hipper arranged non-swing reached their most devastating stage of dilution, the Boppers arrived at Minton's to collectively create a new black musical form, which emerged to refocus on the classic African *polyrhythms,* the historical profundity of the *Blues* and the critical importance of *improvisation: BeBop.*

BeBop was "Monkey Music," "Chinese music," "scandalous," "madness," "crazy," a "con game." One critic even called it "Stalinist"! Yet soon enough, as the style became more familiar and presumably more accessible, the corporations came out with the "West Coast" and "Cool" white commercial styles, as the watery ripoff of the real.

But again, the most advanced stream of African American music had already created an antidote for the commercialism: "Hard Bop." This style went back to the black church, particularly in its gospel voice (the mating of the spiritual with the blues). "Soul," "Funk," the basic historical spirituality of the African American culture was summoned to reclaim the music from white supremacy and commercial destruction.

A little later, the classic Miles Davis group, Sonny Rollins, John Coltrane, brought and inspired new developments, the so-called "New Music" or "Avant Garde" picked up on younger heads, e.g.., Ornette Coleman, Cecil Taylor, Pharoah Sanders, among the leaders.

Yet all these series of important innovators at different points in the music's history were *attacked* by the aggressive, chauvinist critical structure. And this abets the social and economic robbery that the class that "prices" art commits.

To say, e.g., what Whitney Bailliet said in the *New Yorker,* that the major women singers were Bessie, Billie, Ella, Anita O'Day, and that the most influential was *primarily* Ms. Oday, is about chauvinism more than music! That is defining the original by the copy. (Where is Sarah Vaughan?)

Robert Palmer of the *New York Times* (a good ol Ivy-type good ol boy) suggests that pianist Bill Evans was the major stylistic innovator and primary influence on contemporary jazz pianists. In reality, Miles wanted Ahmad Jamal; Evans was one of several pianists who approximated that style.

Plus Evans was given a lot of ink. The white musician who is skilled and plays with the kind of historically important group such as Miles's will receive all the publicity there is. But to say that Evans was the *innovator,* the primary influence on recent jazz musicians, is to reverse Evans's role and to belittle Jamal, not to mention the great and very influential Red Garland and McCoy Tyner, nor does it take into account Cecil Taylor of the Avants. And of Evans's peers, surely Wynton Kelly was one of the pure swingingest mo'fo's on the set, and Tommy Flanagan could match Evans sensitivity for sensitivity of his obvious contemporary peers.

But then there is also, beside the constant and humiliating racism the critical establishment dispenses, the question of this establishment's *aesthetic.* I went into this as far as I could earlier in *Blues People.* Simply that there is, and the white supremacy foundations of the society make it obvious and presumed, a marked and sharp aesthetic contradiction between the creators of the music and the critical establishment erected on its back!

Such aesthetic contrast is the continued reflection and confirmation of basic philosophical "distance." Say, the distance between slave and slave master, between oppressed and oppressor. There is also the aesthetic distance, the philosophical contradiction between Europe and Africa, which stretches back into the mists of history. But people who have lived in the same society ordinarily would have more nearly merged into a newer entity combining both originals. The U.S. melting pot has done this for Europeans here, who are now almost homogenously American. The Africans, however, have not been allowed to melt. Slavery and segregation saw to that, racism and white supremacy see to it continuing.

So that here, white supremacy not simply a philosophy, but an imposed method of *social organization,* because it creates an artificial and tragic social division, maintains an *aesthetic* distance between the African American people and whites.

The post-'50s Rock phenomenon shows how even as the aesthetic distance is broken down, e.g., Rock & Roll is not "influenced" by Rhythm & Blues, it *is* Rhythm & Blues, appropriated by whites. White supremacy, however, makes a wholly "original," wholly "independent" white music with no connections to its obvious parent, or brothers and sisters.

The Euro-American aesthetic uses Europe as its star of faith (even up to and past the Beatles), though "place" identification can be replaced by the dollar. So that the performer with the most platinum or who's had the biggest hit often becomes the "first ancestor" and setter of historic standards for the "business."

But "Europe" means the culture of the free and white, before now. But there is also a class significance to this "whiteness" as well, not just a racial question. The economics are basic, but there is a *class aesthetic* as well (tied to race because who got the money had to be in a position to get it, etc., but now such class attitudes are made more ubiquitous by the advance of technology and even influence players with potentially something much more original to say).

Though a class note can be sounded by just an emotional commitment to the tempered scale, the jig or ditty, European song or dance form, academic formalism (i.e., form celebrated over content); the softened timbres of *well-being* over the desperate screams of those for whom they themselves have said, "Nobody Knows the Trouble I Seen." The use of commercial gimmickry over emotional force. The non-blues blues imitation. Philosophical focus on the socially irrelevant or unimportant, pornography, silliness, devil worship, "out" psychological states, etc. The life and times of white teenager fantasy (as synthesized by adult merchants) and near-real nonbeing.

To be sure, there is really progressive and advanced music created by white musicians, but the society itself demands mediocrity and catatonia from *everybody!* The arrogance and ignorance of America's leaders confirm the common psychological development that defines a common culture. Ronald Reagan is the president of the U.S., that is a grimmer condemnation than I could more abstractly conceive!

Whites, since they are in the main part of the fabric of the decadent imperialist U.S., are connected in a more direct and organic way.

Blacks, on the other hand, have never been admitted. It is that enforced separation that creates despair but at the same time literally holds blacks away from fully embracing the decadent commercialism of U.S. society in its "last days."

It is the classic tension of an art that is *outside* and inside the dominant society at the same time. The same tragedy and bitter irony, national consciousness, humor, self-deprecating rage and human heroics have provided a line of demarcation between Irish and English literature these many years.

From the black religion of the old country (till the present day), passion is not an adjunct but an end. The music is *(about) feeling.* The feeling generated by black life, which is defined by its opposition to the dominant culture. Its most advanced (even its healthiest) existence is in some fashion predicated on resistance. What Cabral meant when he said the culture of the oppressed exists at its most essential as a proof that people have survived and have not been liquidated by imperialism and its cultural aggression and genocide.

In the slave context the slaves' feelings are so important because all else is denied. The slave is property—without history, culture, status, or future. Only his *feelings* deny this slave existence, despite the slave master's view of the world.

The most dangerous thing about the slave's feelings is that they are the deepest source of living resistance to slavery, whether expressed as words or music!

But if the slave's deepest feeling is anti-slavery, slavery's continuing presence is the *essence* of even contemporary U.S. social relations. So that at the level of deepest consciousness, the black liberation movement and its enemies remain in sharp conflict, even in the arts.

However, as the level of *productive forces* (education and social development of black people and technology they have access to) of the African Americans has risen, so too the possibility and eventual creation of black institutions that can objectively analyze and "measure" Black Arts from the general aesthetic (i.e., common psychological development) of African American culture.

Mao Zedong said the area of arts criticism is an area of intense class struggle. The critical "subjugation" of the Black Arts, jazz included, by the racist U.S. critical establishment is just one other aspect of Black national oppression!

CHAPTER II

Not "the Boss"

Bruce Springsteen

What is refreshing and encouraging about Bruce Springsteen is his capacity to translate both the form and some of the content of the country and urban blues. Springsteen is an American shouter, like the black Country Blues shouters, from Lead Belly on, with perhaps an ear on the urban incarnation James Brown and Wilson Pickett represent.

This was clear in *We Are the World*, the style value Springsteen carried, in that context, as well as his overall musicality. The "social consciousness" lyrics to many of his songs, e.g., "Born in the USA," have put yeast in his public and commercial persona. He is the voice of working-class youth, we have heard, and there is much truth in that. Would perhaps that there were more American youth independent of the double maw of working-class economic insecurity and lack of education (hence, often, of political sophistication) to be as clear as Springsteen on what being born in the USA, for instance, yokes a young white (and black) working-class youth to.

Even so, Springsteen himself, as a superstar, must confirm, even as illusion, the upward social mobility obtainable by being Free, White, and 21. His willingness to dispute that in the real America is healthy and important.

What makes it so significant is seen if we contrast what Springsteen is doing as compared to the freak-flesh-devil cult of the dollar sniffers.

What makes Springsteen convincing besides his appropriation of the blues shouter vocal timbre is the focus of his concerns. The often tragic poetry of African American blues is packed with reflections on a brutal, enslaving race empire in which they are slaves or victims or lonely or bereft, certainly broke and many times hungry.

Springsteen's focus on a visible living America and its obvious internationally known flaws, a real world, draws him deserved attention. His American blues appropriation is solid and not given to minstrelsy. The fact of his presentation and its obvious authenticity is in great part due no doubt to an understanding, at some level, of what those blues songs, or Woody Guthrie's for that matter, *mean!*

What is amazing however is the ease with which the commercial media can spread backwardness. The whole "Boss" naming, for instance, creates a relationship to traditional blues players that is false and obviously not even wanted by Springsteen. BS knows he is not Joe Turner, "the Boss of the Blues." He also has demonstrated with the stance of his concerns and political tendencies that he feels closer to the common people than the "bosses."

Springsteen's persona, for instance, the working-class youth checking out reality, would find anathema the individualism as an expression of some would-be (bogus) musical elite, empowered by the big dust of some real economic and trend-making elite, who are the real partners who see money in confusion, which retards all the music lovers, especially separate and unequal as they is.

One wonders though, at the flush of the Springsteen explosion, as witnessed by the recent *Born in the USA* tour, how far can he go in refining and raising and deepening his vision. Has he the resources (consciousness and commitment) to go further or to at least keep on at some important level?

We should know by now that no artist, no matter how popular, can completely buck the forces of commerce, or their career, even their name, will *disappear!* (In some cases their body first!) We have witnessed Stevie replaced by Michael, who for all his Victory still has been swiftly covered for daring to try to make all that money! Prince and Boy George to Commerce's rescue.

There is a crossroads in U.S. society at this moment. The raging energies of traditional enemies are being stoked. The world is in violent flux. What Springsteen has been telling is one path and direction, still more reaction than concrete exhortation or analysis (though one paper, after the Jersey concert, did mention Springsteen's "preaching"!).

These are part of the ingredients of a critically important public drama, here in the USA!!

CHAPTER 12

Wynton Marsalis

Black Codes (from the Underground)

Young Wynton Marsalis is already a kind of touchstone of contemporary jazz. In the sense that whenever his name comes up, "you can tell where people are at by where they coming from on Wynton." And there is a wisdom to it.

Meaning: that Wynton is a *cause celebre* of the music. For one reason is that there are so many reasons! The son of an estimable jazz pianist, in fact, a jazz family, residing, where else? New Orleans, naturally!

But the mythological vibes bouncing off the stereotype reveals it to be, in fact, a prototype—and a very productive one. The father Ellis, a very swinging and thoughtful post-Hines con-blues pianist, who is actually a contemporary of drummer Eddie Blackwell, Ornette's man. He is also a musician linked with the legendary New Orleans clarinetist, Alvin Battiste.

Branford Marsalis, Wynton's older brother, is one of the freshest sounds on tenor come along in quite a few minutes. Right now, he is deep in Wayne Shorter's musical debt, and like most other contemporary tenor players, linked indissoluably to the great new music revolutionary, John Coltrane.

Another important factor in Wynton Marsalis's rise is his virtuosity, instrumental facility and technical skill on the trumpet, a notoriously difficult instrument. When Marsalis won Grammy awards in both Jazz and European classical music as an instrumentalist, the awe that racism breeds suggested that this was such a great feat because blacks of course are too underdeveloped to deal with European concert music.

This chauvinist absurdity is reflected even by certain blacks who still hero worship apparently the racist social relations of big money USA.

Wynton, himself, in conversation told me a year or so ago that since he came to New York, he had come to appreciate in a practical way how there are many seasoned blues and jazz trumpeters who, with a bare few notes, create a hot artifact of undenial skill. A kind of antithesis to Wynton's thousand-note attack.

In published interviews and television programs he has shown himself to be at times both courageous, albeit certainly not errorless, as well as deeply knowledgeable about music—European and African American. With a particular sense of the African American social and aesthetic traditions.

His music, in person, has been stimulating and electric (e.g., Sweet Basil); strangely dispirited (Carnegie Hall), perhaps in reaction to an amazing solo by Jimmy Owens. At another appearance in a west side loft, with Lester Bowie's Brass Fantasy (w/ Olu Dara, &c) he was measured and fresh.

Wynton's playing at its best still obtains its effect mainly by instrumental virtuosity. Sometimes of a very high order. But the worship of formalism aside (commerce's brainchild), Marsalis is still a relatively unseasoned though frequently quite brilliant player. Some people say they have been more impressed with Branford's Trane-Shorter reflections. There is no doubt that both are players of great promise.

Certain critics have categorized Wynton's efforts as "imitations" of Davis, Gillespie, Clifford Brown, perhaps. But Marsalis has rejoindered, and I think rightly so, that if he didn't sound like them dudes, he probably wasn't playing jazz!

The correct and most positive interpretation of this eclectic stylistic tendency is in the player's still rather brief exposure to "the cats." That is, the high level mainstream blues players and jazz innovators to the extent that his own playing wd begin to cull his important and necessary influences into a dominant and distinctive style.

Yet Wynton is an interesting and inventive player. What one wants to hear now is his own, as Pres wd say, *Story*.

This album is mostly middle period Miles sounding. The feeling like that of those records with Miles on flugelhorn. The tendency towards mood-feeling encountered in *Hot House Flowers* is maintained, though at times the "dreaminess" and aural ambience is stung or penetrated by Wynton's moving reflections on the *hot*.

The pieces on this album seem in the main to form part of what feels like a single mood. They are coolish, Milesian to be sure, but with not a little of the Shorter-Blakey collaborative flavor of that period of the Jazz Messengers. The title tune, *Delfeayo's Dilemma,* and *Phryzzinian Man* are linked by this emphasis. What moved me was *Chambers of Tain* which carries both the mood and the funk. A Jackie Mc type move, with most of Wynton's solo highlights, full of that piercing brass heat that Wynton can command, keening and telling the wailer's tale. These kinds of rhythm-fired brass thrusts show the Gillespie Brown appreciation.

But in these pieces there is a decided gesture in the direction of a slightly heavier footed Milesian Mood-a-teria, with a little more contemporary depression. But even these ghosts are relaxed. There is a feeling that Wynton is searching for a signature, a clear & hip persona (*Tain* predicts this). That is the hope, because Wynton, on fire, can be very very hot.

CHAPTER 13

"The International Business of Jazz" and the Need for the Cooperative and Collective Self-Development of an International People's Culture

The title tries to say most of what this essay is about. Yes, there is an international business of jazz, just as there is an international jazz culture. Unfortunately there is not a continuing strengthening of the fundamental source and essential resource of the most profound and important aspect of the music itself, nor of the entire social, political, historical, and aesthetic foundation of that business, and what passes as an international jazz culture is most often mainly a commercial exploitation and diluting of the incredible treasure that the music has provided, as art, social and intellectual development, and economic resource.

What is missing is the element of self-determination, cooperation, and collective focus of our overall effort and productivity. From the diminishing nature of the freely creative input of the musician, which depends not only on the individual skill attained and displayed, and the imaginative projection and endless renewal, but also on the educational source, formal or traditional, the venues where the musicians can play and make a living, the recording and video operations where they can be further projected and remunerated, the institutions (recording companies, TV and movie studios, universities, other educational and cultural entities from the earliest preteens to the free concerts from cities, federal, and other governmental, foundations, corporations, independent organizations, individuals and groups), whatever the identity of those places where musicians can work, get paid, get known, develop, and help the rest of us, by being exposed to revelation, like-

wise develop intellectually and socially. As well, institutions that deal
with the archiving, the history, the representation and reproduction.
Publishing companies, graphics outlets, from posters to calendars to
T-shirts to postcards, to illustrations in books, etc., and art galleries.
Wherever the music can be played, wherever it can be heard. Wherever
that history can be archived and stored and exhibited. Whatever networks and touring circuits are set up. The point is that the music not
only is the expression of a people and the people, a reflection of our
lives on the planet, heightened for self-revelation and social and intellectual growth, but it carries with it all those elements and must be
used to mutually enhance all those people and entities it touches as well
as all those it has been the gift of.

The point is that if the music is to create with its direct beauty the
social economic aesthetic intellectual material reflection of its expressive aesthetic presence then new work has to be done by all of us concerned for one reason or another with that music and its future growth
and existence.

What we must do is begin to understand and utilize every element
and sector of the music's creation, expression, growth, history, distribution, and impact, in new ways that consolidate its strengths, eliminate
its weaknesses, preserve its past, and guarantee its future. In some ways
the tasks that face those of us who, like the Dogon say, are conscious
in ON (the ancient African city where they charted the Sun's hipness),
then we must rise to Digitaria, you dig, then go on out past that, to
Serious. The furthermost visible star in the galaxy. We must begin to
see the Music, not only its fundamental creation, but all the elements,
aspects, individuals and organizations, etc., as part of One thing. Like
the ancients in On, pre the Pharaohs, who did not believe in One God,
but that everything was One Thing. So that we can see the musicians,
the audience, the record companies, the media, the institutions, the
technicians, the logistical and other associated cultural workers and
artists as part of the One, as necessary parts of the Whole Music.

The old and historically obsolete rugged individualism of this society has already passed into the void, though like the Flat Earth Society
there are still those who think they profit by playing sabertooths. The
Russian versus Chinese experience is a useful aside. The attempt by
U.S. and other corporate Conans to absolutize the corporate domination of the USSR has failed utterly. Mixed economy is the growing cry,
even from the hardnoses who give our money to the IMF. China, with
its mixed economy, has a national economy, according to the Thieving

Banshees at the Times Business Section, that is infinitely more stable, and dwarfs the Soviets', basically because it is based on a mixture of government control and the market system. The outcries we hear these days about China are not about their presumed socialist orientation but about the Gigantic Impact the Chinese economy will have on Asia and the rest of the world.

What is the relevance to the music? It is this. The international business of jazz creates its own limitations in market share and revenues and international impact because it is still run like a billion rum joints functioning half legally in the American Medina of jazz creation. The musicians themselves suffer too much from the same philosophy, although their material conditions make them objectively in need more obviously of a collective and cooperative approach to their collective development. This is because the musicians, like most workers in the world, are at the bottom of the social structure of the music which they alone create.

But first, if we are looking with a more sophisticated overview, we will move to help construct a worldwide association for the development of the music, consisting of all the aforementioned parts of it. In every country, in every city, where this is possible. To bring together all concerned to see that there is, at least, a sympathetic and developmentally oriented association of people and institutions that will help in the reorganization of the music as entertainment, education, employment, so that both the new and old musicians of all nationalities will pass through these locations regularly, and perform, teach, delight, and socially and economically enhance all who in some way, not even necessarily directly, are impacted by it.

In the U.S., for instance, there are 27 major cities where the music has deep roots and unlimited audience development potential. Such an association of musicians, club owners, critics, academics, record, TV, radio representatives, union spokespersons, would actively work at setting up a stable network of venues in each of these cities where musicians could tour regularly. Not only clubs, or theaters, but municipal and other public venues and facilities, whether alternating or appearing at a variety of these locations with each contracted program. The recent emergence of city jazz festivals and the continuing presence of university and commercial festivals and extended programs should be expanded.

One certain focus of such efforts would be to organize a major jazz festival in each major city, which combines local players and well-known and little-known musicians from the other cities. This can only be organized by combining both the individual artists and cultural workers, club owners, publications, corporate and private resources of the area with the community, local arts and cultural organizations, city and area entities, such as universities, local school systems, and foundations.

Such an organized network of touring and new venues should obviously be recorded, packaged for television, radio, and other commercial and nonprofit uses, and the resources of such a stabilized and publicly and privately managed programming would strengthen the entire dimension of the music, aesthetically, socially, economically, and educationally. Plus, create an ever-widening audience.

We must also look for new venues for jazz festivals outside of the standard Euro-American mainstream. No one is denigrating the Montreux or Berlin or New York, but we must be innovative and popularly based and flexible enough to create new sites for Jazz Festivals in Johannesburg, Habana, Bei Jing, Zimbabwe, Pyongyang, Hanoi, Goree Island off Dakar, Senegal, new locations throughout the Third World, Scotland, Ireland, Australia, Haiti, Trinidad, Jamaica. The world beckons us, and the music is not bound by the backwardness of U.S. political dementia, that's why Dizzy Gillespie and Louis Armstrong before him were named Ambassadors of the Music by the U.S. State Department.

The history of the music must likewise be archived and made accessible for research and new presentation. Each major city must have an orchestra, such as the Wynton Marsalis–led Lincoln Center Orchestra or the Jon Faddis–led Carnegie Hall Orchestra. In Newark, we have already organized the New Arkestra, which earlier this year did a series of concerts re-presenting the music of the great Willie the Lion Smith, who was raised in Newark, and began playing in the old red-light Coast district of that city.

The New Arkestra, which features musicians, old and young, from the city and the area generally, is already focusing on representing the works of a diversity of its homefolks, e.g., Wayne Shorter, Sarah Vaughan, Babs Gonzalez, James Moody, Woody Shaw, Grachan Moncur III, Hank Mobley, Larry Young, the Savoy Sultans, and the whole host of Newark-sprung creators. This project has emerged from the national project known as Lost Jazz Shrines, which is already focused on New York City.

What will be critical to the success of such a project will be the extent to which an actual cooperative relationship can be created among the elements I named. The economic development will be greatest where the most diverse and necessary aspects of the whole are joined together to contribute to all dimensions of what is created.

Another project of the Newark effort is our continuing focus on rebuilding the old Coast district, one of the four centers for the music in the early 1900s, when the leading Afro American entertainment centers were Hell's Kitchen in NYC . . . this is before Harlem . . . the Levee in Chicago, and the Barbary Coast in San Francisco, along with Newark's Coast, where not only Willie the Lion but the great James P. Johnson reigned, when Newark was called a "Ticklers' Town" because all the great pianists of the time came through to prove themselves, such as Donald Lambert, Duke Ellington, Fats Waller, and so many others.

Not only are we the Newark Music Project (and you'll find our brochures and brand-new arts publication RAZOR with the other items), RAZOR is a bimonthly missile NMP will be publishing, and to which we humbly request you subscribe, give advertising to, send review records and tickets to events, reprint our hip articles and photos, as well as give large donations to help us get up to Sun Ra speed in a New Ark minute.

This publication is also part of my projection today. Not just as an individual voice, but we are calling for a host of new publications on the music, from each city. And we will be looking for correspondents, stringers, distributors in all the cities of the world. And certainly, we promise to do our part to keep on sounding about the need for a new international cooperative organizing and association for the continued development of the music we all claim to love.

Part of the problem with the development of Jazz, Blues, etc., is the social limitations historically of its creators, not only the Afro-American innovators, but most who have taken up the music must also face at least the residue or social distancing which includes economic dislocation that comes with it. It is well known the disparity between the salaries, social status, creative environment, academic prestige of the Jazz player and the European concert musician or Rock and Roll entertainer, for that matter. It is, of course, a hostility carried forward with the debased anti-humanity that chattel slavery imposed on Black people, but it is also a class dissing. That is, who lives better, employed more consistently and in haughtier venues, is celebrated and recognized more ubiquitously, casually given the nom de guerre "artist," etc. Whose art is carried more "universally" both commercially and institutionally, who is given more "ink" and more favorable ink at that, etc. etc. All these are in essence class distinctions, though the racial aspect simply makes the diss easier and able to be carried out from a greater distance and more automatically.

This is one of the reasons that the international jazz community must rely more on cooperation, including cooperative academic, profit-making and nonprofit, public and private efforts. The international community, like any member of a community burdened by excessive and distinct social economic obstruction, must begin to create international relationships that depend on the "internal," if you will, or self-determined self-assertive organization of the international jazz community.

For instance, if a group is coming to a city, cooperative efforts could easily see that that group plays not only at a designated club but in schools or other institutional venues. There are a great many varied locations for groups, solos, lectures, educational appearances, as well as media opportunities, public appearances, programs in widely varied areas of that city and the environs where other potentially valuable venues can be found.

Such a cooperative approach will benefit the group, the individual musicians, at that time and in the future, as far as new connections, and the city itself should experience added social and economic benefits. And there must always be the consistent effort to record, both audio and video, and give further dimension to what can be a formidable tradition of national archiving. There are far too few institutions in this country that are actively working at the scholarly and historically accurate and detailed history, which happens every day, of the music and its multidimensional culture.

Such efforts, again, if they issue from cooperative associational efforts, will bring revenue, which is the bottom line of the international business of jazz, but revenue or economic development is a necessary aspect of all of our lives. We should begin to make certain that our most serious or ultimate intellectual concerns are able to support our material lives.

With the continuing enlarging of the international Corporate "Jaws" across the world, the disappearance of small and medium-sized corporations as one result of the endless mergers and buyouts and takeovers that are the main trend in the domination of the world by a increasingly nongovernmental imperialism, the music is very hard hit, as the smaller record companies are bought up, and a good many of the headquarters of the new Giants are not even in the U.S. anymore. The domination of U.S. popular culture by an outrageously reactionary commercial culture of mindlessness, mediocrity, violence, and pornography means that it is increasingly more difficult for the innovative, serious, genuinely expressive, or authentically popular artist to get the same kind of production as the anti-creative garbage that the corporations thrive on.

Rap is an ugly example of how the corporate co-optation of that genre has replaced, in many of the most ubiquitous cases, a distinctive and powerful mass popular social expression with thuggish sociopathic self-hating exhibitionism or the self-indulgent extremism of the posturing petty bourgeoisie. But Jazz too has been taken on a trip by these same forces. The Ellingtons, Basies, Vaughans, Monks, Coltranes, Holidays, Armstrongs, who only a few years ago we might see on the same night, have been saddled with the killer label of "classic," while the soulless dishwater furniture music called fusion and its elevator buddies in all directions and genres are pushed like Dope and called "Contemporary Jazz." I guess that's why Duke and Max Roach today oppose even the term "Jazz" because once a hollow labeling is given to an artistic genre, the well-organized flyers of the skull and crossbones can sail in and Voila, Paul White Man is the King of Jazz, Benny Good Man is the King of Swing, the Rolling Stones are the Greatest Rock and Roll Band in the World, and Elvis Presley is the King . . . whatever that is he sposed to be King of. But in a poem of mine, "A Low Coup," which is an Afro-American verse form I created, as distinct from the Japanese Haiku, I ask, "If Elvis Presley is / King / Who is James Brown? / God?"

There are piles of media-pushed trash piles advertised everywhere as "Jazz" which have as little to do with the music as Rudy Giuliani's alleged brain. Even those who are mainly committed to the dollar or the mark or the franc or the yen must understand that most of the con and fusion of the trashy commercial culture now inundating us is at base trendy media bric-a-brac with little aesthetic or social value, which will be missing in a very short time. One has but to look in the storerooms of anyplace where there are old commercial records with onetime headliners who are absolutely obscure now, and happily so, whose work on those sides will positively amaze you that it was ever recorded or published at all.

But the dialectic of our focus must be that if there are whole areas of old exquisite expression and new revelations being excluded and left out by the strictly commercial garbage purveyors, then these are areas where fresh really innovative efforts will be viable. These are the areas that our cooperative associations and networks and organizing can expand by such concerns as representing, archiving, preserving the historical dimensions of the music, while clearing the way, creating the necessary environment, and enabling the constant redefining of the music by its creators and the whole superstructural dimension of the music necessary for it to be accessed by a broad international community, at this moment and on into the future. As we try to give our ideas a concrete material base for their existence as a continuum of such expression in the future.

For one thing the entire being of the music and its reflection must be opened up, opened wide, projected worldwide in a more revolutionary democratic way. Again, we go back to our fundamental statement that this can only be done by creating an international community of cooperation and mixed social economic methodology and organization.

Musicians, Club Owners, Union Reps, Critics, Audience, Institutional people, Theater Owners, Media people, Academics can see that the Jazz audience is expanded by expanding the artists' presence throughout the area. From Club, to University to Woman's Group, to Union Meeting. Such a cooperative group would work on opening all schools in the areas to the music, as performance and instruction.

Such a group would see to the organizing of all city jazz bands, named from high school students throughout the city. They would see to establishing jazz festivals and scheduling of seminars, live and in the media. Youth jazz orchestras, such as Newark's rising Baby Legends, the pride of Newark's Sarah Vaughan Arts High School, would be encouraged and given gigs throughout the area, like the Yankees develop a future star third baseman who one day will hit a home run in the big stadium. Even stone-cold business types must see the enhancement of business from such methods of audience organization and artist encouragement and employment.

Such a cooperative would see to the teaching of the music in all the schools, work at getting musicians, whether groups, or solo pianists or singers, whatever, all over the city. In the libraries, small restaurants, and bars where now only grim drunks hum their hopelessness or keening organ trios offer the best of what exists. Musicians can work everywhere. In libraries, churches, haberdasheries, business offices, malls. Such expansion would benefit the entire area in all the ways you can think of.

This is our task, not only because we love the music, and not only because we can see there can be money made, we have also got to understand that the very health and positive context of the culture is strengthened by the reorganization of environment such a cultural focus would produce. Part of the excessive even dangerous commercial-ization of popular culture has been its removal from the people, from the working-class communities. Once the music left the Harlems of the land and went "downtown," not only did the economic landscape of those communities grow bleaker, but too often with the artists' disap-pearance into the commercial circle of venues, not only did the most advanced form of indigenous art disappear, but for many of those com-munities the most ubiquitous role models were no longer the musicians but the drug pusher or pimps. Converting all of the schools in a city to potential arts and culture venues for local audiences would have a salutary effect on the socialization of the youth as well.

The enlarging of the entirety of the music's social economic fabric will have distinct political reform as a concomitant feature. For instance, astonishing and ironic as it sounds, there is now no Afro-American critic or commentator of the music in any of the major U.S. newspa-pers. The critical and academic establishment is still largely non-Black and not altogether cognizant of the state of the art, at any time. There has been a great deal of advance, vis-à-vis the reporting from the major newspapers and journals since the old DB and Met (both of which I used to publish in) gave Bird, Monk, Diz, and the rest no stars and had to re-review the records several years later so they at least could pretend to be in the world. But this exclusiveness, elitism, and outright racializing of the evaluation of what is still, at base, Black Music must be ended if the cooperative relationship of which I speak, and for which I pledge myself to be a partisan, is to come into being.

It is not just that so many of us could use the work, but it is the question of how the very expansion of the international community of the music can be practically encouraged. To think that only white men can have a profound or scholarly or analytical understanding of Afro-American Music is at least as disgusting and ignorant as Hitler. Remember the first one of Hitler's Racial Laws was the Banning of Neger Kultur, as a result of the Ellington '33 tour of Europe.

Even if you mighty mighties must have a white guy's opinion to really feel you know something, there must be somebody Black somewhere who can at least write what they think, the inclusion of contrasting opinions or reviews is certainly not new. You publishers should review your sorry condition and backward practice and end this ruthless seg-regation and discrimination. Can you believe the second essay I had published in the old jazz review said the same thing (1958, "Jazz and the White Critic").

But likewise I am urging the musicians and other progressives to get behind the production of new and alternative publications that give voice to a multinational diversely attitudinal stable of writers and opinions. Like Mao said, "Let a Hundred Flowers Bloom, Let a Hundred Schools of Thought Contend." It can only broaden both the depth of understanding and the length of outreach of the art form itself. It will also enrich the scholarship and authenticity of analysis, which can only benefit the entire international community. At RAZOR we will be sending out an extensive list of exciting and deeply knowledgeable writers on the music, hoping that some of the international media will begin to reprint or rebroadcast this work and expand the collective ear and the collective I that finds its way consistently into print about this music.

In the U.S. specifically, our lack of a social democratic social economic structure such as in Europe and Japan, which is why the musicians have to go to outside the U.S. so often because there are more public funds available than in the U.S., often combinations of public and private and institutional funds that allow them to be employed and even recorded or appear on television, at universities, etc. In the U.S., where the last zombies of "Rugged Individualism" still yowl, not only in the forests of the night, but in Congress and in public life, like the executive of a billion-dollar corporation who told the *Times* he knew Tony Bennett only as the guy who sells stuff in TV commercials. The lack of knowledge about America's richest contribution to world culture is a reflection as well of the deadly ignorance which stalks this country from the New York City Hall to the halls of Congress to the corporate offices to academic classrooms, like a ubiquitous serial killer who murders people by eating their brains. And then passes gas with a sound broadcast everywhere called Kenny G.

A new cooperative self-reorganizing network of relationships and associations with an economic base that is mixed, including private, public, institutional, and cooperative resources is the only method that can build an expansive international jazz community which networks and consolidates both the international business of jazz and the international culture and human dimensions of the music into a newly more self-defining and self-reliant productive artistic and progressive and influential world culture with a fresh and creative entrance into the twenty-first century.

CHAPTER 14

Newark's "Coast" and the Hidden Legacy of Urban Culture

Every city in the world has a legacy, some are known, and if those legacies are known, kept before the peoples of the world, and that legacy is rich with history and culture, the city itself becomes an object of glamour, excitement, and curiosity.

But when the best legacy, the highest level of civilization that city has contributed to, is hidden or forgotten, and the city becomes identified with a set of negative or dangerous characteristics, then it will look like Newark looks after five p.m. on any evening, like a ghost town, or a warehouse for the moneymaking operations of a people that do not live there.

Even the city's residents must leave that city for cosmopolitan entertainment, self-attainment, sophisticated educational endeavors, or even a well-prepared meal. It is not just a psychological damage to the residents that such a condition engenders, it is also a devastating economic effect when the little money the residents make is consistently removed from circulating within that city's limits. Because no matter what sophisticated commodity the residents seek, they cannot find it within the city limits, so that millions of dollars a year disappear in our pursuit of whatever.

The project "Lost Jazz Shrines" is one aspect of urban transformation this city sorely needs. The location of the rich history of Newark as a center for Afro-American music of all genres is by now a somewhat obscure fact. But fact it is. In fact, from the earliest days of the twentieth century, *Newark's Coast* was one of the four centers for Afro-American culture in the United States. The others, *Hell's Kitchen* in New York City (this was after Blacks were driven out of their first community in New York, when it was still New Amsterdam, *Greenwich Village,* the birthplace of Fats Waller, among others, and before the move to Harlem in the 1920s); *the Levee* in South Chicago, and the *Barbary Coast* in San Francisco.

By 1918, New Orleans's French Quarter, one of the key centers for the development of the music called "Jazz," was closed by the authorities, citing corruption (though we know that if that was the case for closing down something, the whole of the U.S. should be closed up by now). And with that closed for entertainers, musicians, dancers, singers, along with the masses of Afro-American people who went north after the destruction of reconstruction, even more got in the wind and headed north. New York City, Chicago (right up to the river) and, for those going West, as far away from the South as San Francisco & L.A.

The Newark settlement, which by the early twentieth century numbered about 10,000 Afro-Americans, meant that here also would develop a Black cultural entertainment district. Every major Black community in the U.S. has also been a key entertainment arts center. (Look at New York City . . . "the Village," "Hell's Kitchen" behind Lincoln Center. The "Jazz Street," 52nd Street, was the road in and out of "the Kitchen," then Harlem.) Remember the great Harlem Renaissance of the '20s and '30s brought to an end by the Depression, Corporate rip-off, Invading Crime Lords, the Government? Look beneath the intentionally or accidentally obscured history of America's major cities and you will find a rich and profound legacy of the Arts.

Newark is so close to New York that it has always been connected to the goings-on in "the Apple" organically. Many of the musicians who made great names in New York lived and were raised in Newark. Every major musical figure who has appeared in New York has played in Newark's once plentiful venues, Six Steps Down, Club Harold, the Adams Theater, Laurel Garden, the Terrace and Wideway Ballrooms, Grand Hotel, Howard Bar, and so many others, carried in song and story.

Not only that, Newark's Coast district was for a long time one of the main centers where people like Willie "the Lion" Smith, James P. Johnson (from New Brunswick), Donald Lambert, Fats Waller, and so many others came to play in that golden age of "the Ticklers," or the greatest piano players of the age. As "the Lion's" autobiography *(Music on My Mind)* attests to, since he was raised on Academy Street. The same street of another notable player, Mayor Ed Koch of New York, who was raised later.

And Newark has a history of great musicians in its borders, not only "the Lion," but the great piano player who emerged in "the Lion's" shadow, Donald Lambert. What about the fabulous Savoy Sultans, the "globetrotters" of music, who developed an approach very common in Afro-American culture of "stunting" with the instruments, doing dances, passing their instruments around from member to member, and a host of deeply entertaining gambits, all while playing the music at a fantastic clip. It is said that the only band the great Duke Ellington "feared" in those constant "battles" the great bands waged in their heyday at Harlem's legendary Savoy Ballroom was the Sultans. Or trumpet star Harold Mitchell, the Savoy Dictators, the master of all piano styles, Robert Banks, Jackie Bland, who, with Nat Phipps, was the teenage BeBop star during the fifties. Classic Blues stylist Ruth Brown ("Teardrops from My Eyes") and Faye Adams ("Shake a Hand"), Jimmy McGriff, or John Patton, Newark is also the Organ funk capital of the universe.

Eddie Platter, Count Basie's straw boss; the real "Divine One," Sarah Vaughan of Avon Avenue; the immortal "Little" Jimmy Scott; Miss Rhapsody, a little-known Brick City treasure; Grachan Moncur III, carrying the legacy of his father, "Brother" Moncur, who was the Sultans' bassist; Babs Gonzalez, the inventor of BeBop language and modern scat singing (along with Dizzy Gillespie); Wayne Shorter, Miles Davis's wondrous composer, arranger, and innovative tenor saxophone player; Woody Shaw, one of the finest modern trumpet players, who died tragically; Larry (Lawrence of Newark) Young, organist; one of Duke's great bassists, Aaron Bell; Freddie Redd; Ike Quebec; Andy and Salome and now Ronell of the great Bey family; Billy, Gene, Nat, Gene Jr., the musical wizards of the Phipps family; Melba Moore; Prof. Alex Bradford, the internationally famous gospel singer; Eddie Gladden, Dexter Gordon's great drummer; obscure geniuses like pianist LaRue; Charlie Persip, Dizzy Gillespie's drummer with his big band; James Moody and Hank Mobley were raised here, Billy Ford and his Thunderbirds, there are so many great names to be mentioned when talking about Jazz and Newark. We haven't even got started.

Plus for nearly ten years Newark was the single recording center for the most innovative works of Gospel, Blues, Rhythm and Blues, and Jazz, recorded right here by Savoy records, under the wise direction of legendary A&R man Ozzie Cadena. Charlie Parker, Miles Davis, Max Roach, J. J. Johnson, Sonny Rollins, Dizzy Gillespie, Coleman

Hawkins, Sister Rosetta Tharpe, Big Maybelle, Eddie Mr. Cleanhead Vinson all recorded for Savoy, right here in Newark. Look at the labels of the old Savoy records, the historic recordings of all those musics, and you'll see they were made here.

In every era since the First World War, Newark has had famous venues for the music, from the old days of the Coast to the late '70s, when the Key Club and Len & Len's and Sparky J's made their last stand. But anyone whose name you ever heard of connected with Afro-American music has played in Newark. Whether Billie Holiday in the old "Front Room," or Charlie Parker in the "Silver Saddle," or Illinois Jacquet, Len Hope, Bullmoose Jackson at the Masonic Temple, the Graham Auditorium, or Little Esther and Tito Puente at Lloyd's Manor. They've all been here, and they've left a legacy we must reclaim.

Duke Ellington said, "The greatest place to listen to Black music is in Newark." And the last place I saw Duke was on Elizabeth Avenue in the theater the NAACP used to own, which is now a church.

We say all this to say that this is one of the richest legacies this city had. And it is still alive. If we know today that some of the most important Rappers and R&B singers and players still call Newark their home. Gloria Gaynor, Dionne and Dee Dee Warwick, and my sister, Kimako (Sandra Elaine Jones), and Cissy Houston, Whitney's mother, used to sing in a group out of New Hope Baptist Church called the Drinkards. While Grammy Award winner and musical director of the smash TV hit *New York Undercover*, James Mtume, has always been a part of the Newark scene for many years.

Today, young groups like Rappers the Fugees, Naughty by Nature, Queen Latifa, Ice T, and Lords of the Underground are some of the newest Newark-spawned musical groups. Even the young explosive tap dance innovator of *Bring in Da Noise, Bring in Da Funk*, Savion Glover, is a Newark native. The Poetry-Jazz genre (after its innovator, Langston Hughes) is identified with two Newark Kids, Allen Ginsberg and Amiri Baraka.

But this legacy is only valuable if it is known. If it can be raised again and studied and made public. Then the strength and beauty of this legacy can help transform this city. This is what we of the Newark Music Project (now Lincoln Park Coast Cultural District) intend to do. By archiving all the music (and with that the musicians, venues, movements, trends, producers, record companies, memorabilia, information, audiovisual records) and by making oral histories we can project a new image of the city.

By housing such an archive in permanent exhibits, re-recording the classic records and publishing the history of the great works created here and the great creators that worked here, and the legendary venues, not only can we bring that history and legacy back to life, but we can pump old and new life into the city and begin the social transformation.

Because the deepest aspect of education is gained through the arts. This archive will be organized to be studied, to entertain, but also as one avenue of economic and social development. By identifying the city with its own legacy and making that legacy accessible to a new generation of people we will be restoring the city to a stature organic to its history but now hidden by social economic decline. We will be raising a new city, a New Ark, which will make Newark a "destination city," not only for a broader tourist trade, but also to contribute to new employment, new business, safer streets, more revenue circulating within the city's limits, a broader form of popular education, and the root of new ideas for social development.

Ultimately, the Newark Music Project (now Lincoln Park Coast Cultural District) is aiming not only at the long-term and ongoing work of building for permanent exhibition and also a circulating exhibit, but also at rebuilding the old Coast district itself. Now, not just as a Black Entertainment district, but as a multinational arts and entertainment district, so that the Afro-American culture will take its place in a dynamic cultural milieu that brings together Italian, Portuguese, Puerto Rican, Dominican, Haitian, Jamaican, Asian, African, European cultures in that profound mix that can only be found in America. So that all the people can learn from each other, grow closer and better educated by each other, taste each other's food, listen to each other's music, dance each other's dances, and develop the understanding that America is multinational, multicultural-cultural, and a movable feast of peoples and histories, combined into one living society.

The "Lost Jazz Shrines" project will provide the initial impetus to focus attention (internationally) on the greatness and innovative artistic and intellectual achievements of its many great artists and hopefully point the way for a new generation, and at the same time rebuild a section of the city, change this city's image, and make way for the social transformation the majority of the people so deeply desire as we go into the twenty-first century.

6/30/97

CHAPTER 15

Black Music as a Force for Social Change

Imperialist society removes every thing from humans except Appetites. It feeds those appetites' self-destructive confusion about the nature of the world, and if not stopped will eventually destroy, at least, human life on this planet. For instance, imperialism removes arts from humanity, making "art" a mysterious marketable commodity that must reflect the pathology and philosophy of imperialism to be valued. But art is the ideological reflection of life. Art is Creation. Art versus Aren't. Imperialism pushes Aren't. It wants to turn the world into Aren't. Make all of us Wases.

Afro-American art is an ideological reflection of Afro-American life and culture. Both existing in the world. Art can tell us down to minute breath of detail our whole lives on this planet. For the Afro-American, Slavery, the Slave Trade, the very development of the African American nationality, Jubilee, Reconstruction, "Our Spiritual strivings," past present future, all from our Black hearts in touch with the eye of the living, the whole universal spirit of the existent, but particularized, as our specific breathing humanity . . . all this and more absorbed from the path of our lives, as framework and fundamental content of our being as culture. "Culture is how people live."

From the Slave Trade, certainly one fundamental call in Black art has been the cry of *Freedom*. Whether we are quoting Fred Douglass or Thelonius Monk, the concept and will to freedom always animated our conscious and instinctive lives here.

The drums were banned because they could make specific demands and calls for Freedom. "Free Jazz" opposed the chordal jail of Tin Pan Alley pop commerce. The rapper "Jazzy Jeff" is given the Music Awards and not Public Enemy because silliness and cliché are always preferable to truth under the rule of monopoly capitalism and white supremacy.

"It Takes a Nation of Millions to Keep Us Down" is the title of PE's last rap. Like Rap Brown. "What Do You Mean By That?," zombies moan, stiff-legging by us, including Negro Nazis. Some Black people are still slaves, and slavery is how imperialism eats. It is in bad taste to bring it up. Like talking about nasty stuff at the table. It's bad manners and it ain't art. Bourgeois art lets imperialists eat without disturbance.

Black music is an expression of First, the original slaves, a view from underneath the dinner table, like all Afro-American art, the expression of Americans enslaved by Americans, not allowed to be, i.e., with full citizenship rights, in America.

The art describes our lives, whether statically or as a continuum. It still might sound like "social protest," just describing what you see on 125th Street, New York City, or the Central Ward of Newark, in the space of an hour. The music "calls" also, and it does project a future. Forwards history. "The sun's gonna shine in my back door one day," or "Swing Low, Sweet Chariot," both point an end to slavery.

Whether African Song, Work Song, Spiritual, Hollers, Blues, Jazz, Gospel, etc., no matter the genre, the ideas contained in Afro-American art, in the main, oppose slavery and desire freedom. *Ideas do not require lyrics!* Sound carries ideas, that's why you get sad at one song, happy with another.

Black music is "covered" (songs redone, the original artists substituted for by white performers)

1. "To keep the music lovers segregated" and the people generally, to maintain the status quo.

2. To oppose the glorification and valorization of Black life. Since art glorifies and valorizes the life of the artist and the people. If such art is allowed to exist, it will influence people, even white people. Who could enslave Duke Ellington or Art Tatum? Could you seriously believe someone who told you Sun Ra or Coltrane were inferior? You would have to believe Tawana Brawley if you heard Billie Holiday sing "Strange Fruit." And you would know the awful roar of slavery against which we ceaselessly struggle if you heard "Black, Brown and Beige."

3. To keep the economic cycle of distribution that would permit social equity exclusive and segregated, thereby keeping Afro-American people at the bottom of society and superexploited. Afro-American music is internationally celebrated. It employs millions of people worldwide. Certainly it could support its creators!

The music is created by people in struggle. For whom struggle is one constant tone of life's registration. It shapes every aspect of Black life. Whether merely as a reflection of our lives or as a consciously molded medium through which to reshape those lives, art is one form of social intercourse. A potential bridge of understanding and unity.

But since Blacks are not integrated in the U.S. mainstream, the music is also outside, but inside, at the same time. Creators, in a basic and critical way, as workers producing and ubiquitous throughout U.S. culture. Used, abused, lied about, like a dirty secret or a slave.

On one hand, if we used Afro-American Improvised Music (American Classical Music) in the classroom, we would see big changes. Likewise if we began to use all the arts to teach, because there is no depth to education without art. But the constant presence of the music in the classroom hallway, cafeteria, etc., would help toward providing that "true self-consciousness" Du Bois spoke of, as opposed to the double consciousness these schools try to mash on our children now, where they are forced to look at the world through the eyes of people that hate them (even if they are white working-class children). It is the life of the music's creators that speaks. It wants what they want! It is what they are! It is no coincidence that the old spirituals could be used as civil rights marches, that's what those spirituals were about anyway.

Commerce in the U.S. is the transformation of nature into commodity. Commerce wants art as commodity, not feeling and intelligence. Imperialism has turned nature itself into a prostitute. It covers Black Art for the same reason it covers Black people.

We need a Cultural Revolution in the U.S. and internationally, to reorient the world and ultimately transform it where we and everybody else is self-determining. Our music naturally will be a big part of that because that is how we communicate with ourselves, each other, and the world.

In any movement for social transformation (e.g., 19th-century Anti-Slavery, early 20th-century "Harlem Renaissance," the mid-'50s, '60s, '70s Black Arts Movement, there is an arts movement, spawned by the social struggle. Slave Narratives, Harlem Renaissance, Black Arts Movement arise because the most sensitive artists reflect the society (the culture) the people and speak to the same issues, reflect the same interpretation and response to conditions.

Art is shaped by the world, but it also helps, in dialectical fashion, to shape the world. And even though Black people, worldwide, are at the bottom of imperialist-dominated world society, our music already has great influence. The feverish covering of it by imperialism means to blunt its influence, its ideas, its passions being taken up by the world, as it takes up its rhythms.

CHAPTER 16

What You Mean, Du Wop?

One thing about Black People, we always got our music. It come with us. To make a way in the front and the back, like the colors on a map, our music is our path, it shows where we been, where we goin, and where we at.

We were filled and surrounded by our music even before we arrived. Church songs, spirituals and gospel, on this side, are recast from the other side, different but with the same essence, spirit worship. We heard people groaning for the ONE. Moans and screams arising up from the hollows of the world. But mostly no answers came, just other people's cries pleading up through the sky a billion years.

But there was always a ring of answered questions, like life itself do give. That *whatever* you is and will. Real life by what it presents, each moment we can feel as breath. Ain't no coincidence in West Africa we even dressed up in the blues. The pretty blues. The Guinea blues. The under the big sun talking about being alive, and living, as full as that was, blues.

Say it! We always left a trail. A tale, of who we was. That's what we blew. And blowing was knowing. The thought has a self. The music is the self of thought.

But our blues come with us and tell our story. From the church, or through the church, up out and across the ocean and fields. Carrying our single endless multiple billionic lives.

And any basic song could always be sung. It could be a chant, like Du Bois's grandmama made, across from "Afriky." It could roll inside and out the old Sorrow Songs. Or beat with the pitiless fire of the sun on us, as we bent and were bent to harvest other people's profits. And so we had to become our own prophets.

But the real blues bided its time till slavery was spent, at least on paper. And here it come, like walking away from the plantation. Not running, but "hatting" in a steady rumblin' beat. A yeh, "good-bye low crackers / I'ma harvest me a life of my own."

When the deal went down, we had got away from that there and made it as far as this here. It turned from country and went to the city. Still blue, it carried both proof and evidence. As memory and the poem of being.

We was always our own instruments. We could use our hands and turn dead trees to long-distance telephones. Ancient blue rappers that made the forests talk and sing. Could Michael Jackson the air. Look up and see the Moon Walk.

But our blues was always with us. Turn your hat around or not. It was something ya walked with, something carried. The expression of We-Us-I, Black and what-up-Blue.

It could be in a hallway, fire from the cold, the dead slate industrial big city streets. The beat would stir up some heat. Some light. Some of that old-time brightness would come. No matter we be hittin', some-times, some hardass things. Life, when it move you to sing, has made an impression. It didn't just pass by anonymous.

But when the blues come in with "freedom" it was still not free. The gray cavernous concrete and shadow cities. Blood be blood. Blood turn into blood. Your hands so cold, with nuthin in em. You must make a fist just to keep warm.

The old quartet voices was from the Sorrow songs. First made when they banned the old-style rap. Like the devil could actually burn up the map pointing the way out and up. To which we said, "Swing Low Sweet Chariot." Before Duke, there was the Angel Band, and they map was in they rap.

The quartets was like that Angel Band, whose rap was now strictly in they mouths, they moves, the great invisible wings drumming against the air.

Because on these northern streets, where the blues brought us, and that these cold cities taught us, we still must have word from the Angel Band. In those close tight harmonies of the mouth rap, the burning song that carries expression, the blues is wound in tragedy, this carrying on, yet must speak somehow of brightness, if only of being alive, yet, and registering our hearts, perhaps, still racing at the prospects of breath, our spirit, would open up a part of the sky for us, to trace the sun, to see ourselves, if only for that moment of rhythmic brightness.

So Afriky, and middle passage, and work songs in the white ghost fields, and the sorrow songs, moaned tightly woven harmonies, after Tom told the ghost, "Massa don't let 'em beat on that wood. It make 'em open up from inside and get intolerably happy. It move 'em, Massa! It move em!" (and so became winner of the "Genius Award").

But Blues itself come from such a distance of forms and with much baggage. Like the country boy run up the road, stone free, yet the stone falls where it must.

I grew up on old blues and spirituals, church music and gospel. Yet Louie Jordan, Ruth Brown's "Teardrops . . . " and the sweet poetry of such as Larry Darnell, "Why you fool, you poor sad worthless foolish fool. . . . "

The quartets were carried directly through the church. The drumless harmonies of praise and survival. We knew the Dixie Hummingbirds, the Mighty Clouds of Joy, the Southernaires, Sister Rosetta Tharpe, the Five Blind Boys, that gospel had another added life and memory, a harder pulse. And at the same time the quartets start coming out with the names, first it seemed, of birds. As if the Sphinx, half-human half-animal, had become BA, the human-headed soul, Bird.

So out of our hallways, four steps down, stoop-born song, our music just as quickly took flight. As Orioles, Ravens, Larks. It was a city bird. A city soul. A bird come right out the South to light upon our heads. "If you don't love me / Tell me so," Sonny Till touched us with "It's Too Soon to Know." He said, "Am I the fire, or just another flame?"

"That's the story / That's the glory of love!" There was plenty swirling and heavin' up under those skies. The Screamers was also on the scene, like Bull Moose Jackson, Illinois Jacquet, Lynn Hope, Earl Bostic, Hal "Cornbread" Singer, they got even bigger than the birds.

Actually, the a capella street song of our youth was going through changes. They sang as the eternal chorus in big bands. Even with hip Ella Fitzgerald, they'd call back, when she wailed about her lost "yellow basket," that she hoped she'd find it, "so do we, so do we, so do we, so do we, so do weeeeee . . ."

It was an old form, yet a transitional form. There were the Cardinals,

Swallows, Robins, Flamingoes, Meadowlarks, Hawks, Wrens, Falcons, Penguins. And we was from New Ark. The home of Savoy records. And there could be not history without Savoy. No history of the Screamers & Honkers and not the whole story of BeBop either.

Like Little Esther, Mel Walker, Johnny Otis was all in Savoy. The Robins, the Coasters, even Lieber & Stoller, the Rock & Roll million-aires, was first heard on Savoy. Big Maybelle, remember "Candy" and "It's a Sin to Tell a Lie"? Varetta Dillard . . . when's the last time you heard that name, "Easy, Easy, Baby," or what about Nappy Brown and "Pitter Patter"! Savoys all.

All that was with us till the payola investigation put a crying hurt on Rhythm & Blues, to clear the way for Elvis Presley and Rock & Roll (just like the Number Runners got busted to make way for Pick-6). The ghost had come back for us again.

It was not hot again until the '60s, when blues people as usual, like the old Black Bird, the Phoenix (where the Sphinx had gone), rose again, though always with us, as we are wrapped with the circle of the slow beat of wings. The moans & hollers, the booma-loomalooma from way cross the sea. Across the beach rolling ocean, underneath which rest a railroad of human bones.

When we heard the Drifters rising from the street corners again, and the Vocaleers, the Clovers, Harptones, the Crows (a real black bird) crossed over to become the Teenagers with Frankie Lyman, who asked us "Why Do Fools Fall in Love?" Little Anthony and the Imperials, the Chantels. Even so covered by the industry beat for beat by white teenagers set in motion by our songs, but employed finally to *keep the music lovers segregated* and our wails under ground, beneath sound. Yet what could that stop but they own heart? Not ours. It beat, we sang, the rap blew on.

By the late '50s and into the '60s it had turned around again, the beat raised even further up. Combining Gospel, Blues and Rhythm & Blues and Big Band, and some of the arch harmonies of the Boppers. Paul Williams's "Hucklebuck," wildly popular in the early fifties, is really Bird's "Now's the Time." The fundamental dimensions of the music, in overview, are Rhythm & Blues, even Sun Ra.

A rising swell of our own feeling. From those 27 cities in and out-side the "Black Belt" nation, from deep South, extending through its ghetto replications across the country, where we make our home. There were scenes in Philly, Chicago, Newark, New York, "the Big

Apple," everywhere we was, now. But at that point of newly emerging productive forces, where the advanced workers were concentrated and congregated, the big black bird rose again with all the vengeance of his cry, "I Rise in Fire!"

Detroit—the Motor City, Jackie Wilson (under whose crib the Elvis pod was planted), Sam Cooke, "A Change Is Gonna Come"), Otis Redding, who brought country into urban dimension. The Impressions, who signaled a new consciousness in the music with "Keep On Pushin," "People Get Ready," "Amen," "We're a Winner" . . . Gladys Knight & the Pips (surfacing in '61), the Temptations, the Miracles (dig that) with Smoky Robinson, the poet laureate of the everywhere. Certainly, "The Tracks of My Tears" confirmed that. The Four Tops, Martha and the Vandellas ("Dancing in the Street" prophesied the rebellions). The Supremes, when Diana was herself, only one of the witnesses.

So many in the Motown-dominated '60s, because Motown combined the older blues reformation, Rhythm & Blues, with the fresh harmonies and meters of contemporary jazz. Motown paralleled and voiced a wailing sensuousness, like the Hard Bop trend that emerged as response and correction to the "Cool" and "Third Stream" déclassé Commercial dilutions of BeBop. So Motown was re-combustion and motored the genre beyond the by-then dreary faux funk of Rock & Roll.

Yes, and the great Marvin Gaye (Gaye is Wolof, a Senegalese name). "What's Going On" is the most expressive summation of an era. Plus the wonderful sound and brilliance and consciousness of Stevie Wonder! Who was never really Little.

And then there was, is, Aretha, the Bessie Smith of this generation. Warm, rocking, funny, funky, the voice of the time, "Respect," "Dr. Feelgood," "Do Right Woman," "A Natural Woman," "Everybody's got a story . . . about love and the good things. . . . "

Aretha sang with Art Blakey and the Jazz Messengers before she got into her later Motown glory. Marvin Gaye was a Johnny Hartman kind of rhythm crooner before "Stubborn Kind of Fella" and "Baby I Need Your Loving" set the classic expression of the Motown groove. Marvin was so heavy that even after Gladys Knight and the Pips got a big hit with "Grapevine" he could take it in his own direction, so forcefully that the original tune was obscured by his high art.

James Brown was the other large icon of the era, combining the free expression of the oldest "Shouts" with some of the most advanced musical arrangements. Brown's musicians were high tech omni-styled wailers who could drill Coltrane's nuclear sonic colors into James's funk . . . the sound of the other further!

Yeh, and even Michael J, before he "beat it" and left the other Jacksons to separate insanities, was there, and Lionel before he got so Richy. With that same spirit had come Mary Welles, "My Guy," Dionne Warwick, "Walk On By." The Iceman, Jerry Butler. It's really a short few breaths between the Drifters and Aretha Franklin and James Brown. A brief ever flickering Blues spirit that Charles Brown and Little Jimmy Scott could lay on Ray Charles (after he got away from Nat Cole).

Recent Rap is the continuum, certainly, of Rhythm and Blues, and the poetry of the real. Rap, as old as how we spoke across space, beating on the log. That's why the sea men(?) called the records of their voyage a Log. And as connected with history as Rap Brown railing against the prehuman rulers of the world, during those Motown Coltrane years.

Confronted by commercial domination and distortion, which finally covered the earlier more political rappers and groups, Africa Bambatta, Grand Master Flash, Curtis Blow, early Public Enemy and KRS-1, the slick pushing of a so-called East versus West conflict among Rap groups, thereby shortstopping any collective and cooperative alternatives to the Big Pirates, the carefully orchestrated tragic madness of Biggy and Tupac's assassinations and the takeover of Death Row. As Mao said, "Make Trouble, Fail, Make Trouble Again, Fail Again." The Devil has got deep into the Rap. But the strongest and most meaningful examples of the genre will resist and reform its voice and its focus. History explains how the runaway slaves could only stay in one place a short time, then they had to split. The same with the culture, if we stay in one place too long, the carriers of the Skull and Cross Bones will show and cop.

Tupac did not fully understand that just his name, Shakur (viz., a Black Panther reincarnation), would set the slavemaster's dogs loose on him. The same dogs that locked up his mother and sent his aunt to exile in Cuba. So that the easy greasy road provided for him to proclaim "Thuggism" (maxed with media ink) was clearly a setup for his wished-for slaughter.

There is, as well, a historically consistent raising by the industry of the most backward of the trends, groups, and performers to prominence in order to cover the explosive vitality of the truest representations of our world. This is so in all areas of art and letters. Why Paul Whiteman was "the King of Jazz," Benny Goodman "the King of Swing," the Rolling Stones "the greatest Rock and Roll Band in the World." But as a poem of mine puts it, a Low Coup (the Afro-American syncretic form of the Japanese Haiku):

IN THE FUNK WORLD
If Elvis Presley Is
   King
Who is James Brown . . .
   GOD?

CHAPTER 17

Classical American Music

Classics teach a standard of excellence, by which subsequent expressions of the genre can be evaluated and analyzed.

Parker, Gordon, Dorham, Garner evoke an era of musical revelation. Bird transformed formal instrumental style with Black vocal tradition, falsetto, blues, soulfulness armed with aggressive technology, sleek, swift, streamlined.

Dizzy's "BeBop" media-named the genre, but the music was revolutionary, reincarnating Jazz, distancing Tin-Pan Alley. Broadway finessed Blues into the mainstream. Bird reorganized the same materials, using the chordal base of popular song as one resource for improvisation and composition . . . innovative and practical (since only melody is copyrighted).

"Bop," Bird, initially assaulted by the critical establishment, were later, to save face, re-reviewed. Bop countered the blurring and softening of the music made to fit the pockets of commerce, restoring the critical relationship of rhythm to melody, harmony, the centrality of improvisation, blues intonation.

Stunning works . . . Bird's "Koko," "Ornithology"'s narrative wholeness, "Hot House," the contrapuntal "Chasin' the Bird," "Confirmation," "Anthropology." Amazing tempos, thought at higher speeds. Explosive melodic flights. Klook, Max freed from the old 4/4, Equalize the kit.

Diz, co-creator, composing, playing, singing ("Salt Peanuts"), capturing the essence, freshness, wicked humor, confirmation! the music, jagged, surprising, rhythm evidenced melodic line, still sang and danced.

"Tunisia" Diz's Afro-Latin with Candido, Pozo, Bauza, the Indo-Caribbean ("Barbados" a Calypso) African Continuum, American residence.

Dorham, Gordon were front-line creators. Blakey called Dorham "the Uncrowned King," consummate, lyric melodist, ubiquitous on the most creative scenes, not "sidemen," contributing innovators.

Miles's ("Ornithology," "Grooving High") and Dorham's ("Pastel," "Fool . . . ") first love was Diz. Diz left Eldridge to find his voice, Miles and Dorham left Diz, through Navarro and McGhee. Bud's "Pastel," "Fancy," and new ensemble timbre are Dorham exiting Diz's spell. "Conglomeration," cooler, muted, French horn, like Miles's *Birth* sides the same period. "BeBop," "Saucer Eyes" are Dorham's heart, edgy intonation, laid back but salty.

Gordon synthesized Hawkins's weighty reediness, Pres's fluid lyricism, into a singular style that became the ubiquitous sound of contemporary tenor. The rousing entrance on "Dextivity," "Dexter Digs" are coming attractions of Trane.

Errol Garner, like Nat Cole before commerce "stood him up," made early Bop sessions, with a stride-like Blues rhythm piano that caught the popular ear with infectious re-creations of standards. "Waterfront," "Laura" are actually *haunting* and on jukeboxes long before "Misty" made Garner known outside jazz circles.

"The Man," "Moonglow" mark Garner's commercial rise, blues underpinning frequently transformed to syrupy sentiment. "Fiddle," "Dark Eyes" (with Slam Stewart) demonstrate the quicksilver funk animating Garner's hippest jazz recall.

CHAPTER 18

Singers and the Music

A Theater Piece

These are the largest names I know,
To be so included that they spell the entire
Direction of the Flow. The flow of Song
Through them, from way back beyond
And forward, to and through us, lie a
Melody, heated and transported by rhythm
Touch you, carry you, as it do, as harmony

BESSIE SMITH is always connected to LOUIS THE SATCHMO, America's
"Pop." For the combining of Blues and the instrumental diversity and
copiousness of the new jass. The original innovation of instrumental
Blues. So LOUIS + BESSIE is the beginning of the 20th century.

Next ETHEL WATERS is the link, from the two-part chamber of America's Heart, where the slaves were where they were, by chattel condition,
set apart. She had absorbed Bessie and the deepest source, Ma Rainey,
and got with Louis to get down in that blues, herself. But Broadway
was beckoning in its serpentine summons, and the commuters between
downtown and up put the stage into their sound And turned America
around. Made Blues not just unique but a part of the speech, so that the
song was American Jewelry, sparkling Blue and White, Could load it
with Ellington, Fats Waller, or Irving Berlin and George Gershwin and
it would still be all right.

What Ethel did was stroll like Duke, to check everything happening, with the map Fletcher Henderson provided for the hip, created the big jazz band, so the music could expand.

So Duke could perfect it, and Ethel reflect it, she was around when Mamie Smith and her Hounds made the first recorded Blues, and whoever had got down recognized that sound. But America had put out its hand, it had the white, and so the red, but now the blue came in, as long as it brought the green. So Ethel understood, there was a new American popular song, listen to her deal with Porter's Heat Wave, and you wouldn't be surprised that at the next wave's play would be BILLIE HOLIDAY.

Billie Holiday was the child of Bessie and Louis, but so was Bing Crosby. Later, Sinatra sang his Billie song of recognition. But Billie was the whole cloth of classic combination, where the ex-chattel and the ex-immigrants would hook up, the city blues with the social ballad, and from that we got the classic American salad. Those songs we hear in our head and from everywhere every day, *Taking a Chance on Love, A Foggy Day, Night & Day, Lush Life, Mood Indigo, Sophisticated Lady, It Had to Be You, Solitude, Honeysuckle Rose, But Not for Me,* not only Duke, and Fats, and by Gershwin, and Porter, and Berlin, and Rogers & Hart, and the floodgate of the 20th-century American voice, black and blue and white and red, for the blood, of ours and everybody else came to this place or was here when the comers first came.

Billie brought the deep feeling, the intangible memory and up-front pain, straight up into the American ear and mind. She began bright and breezy with those same songs, but as her life in this place went on, so the songs got more like her, inside and out, they got darker and starker and the hidden pain began to sit up front where everybody could see, so the old pain of Blues mixed with the diverse light of America myriad hues. Would register as a resident emotion ancient as our passage cross the ocean.

With Billie comes LESTER, THE PRESIDENT, who named her Lady. She had the soul of Louis and Bessie, and with her was also Bean, Coleman Hawkins, who likewise copped both the weight and the majesty the diction and the tone, and like Billie made his own.

Lester Young was coming from somewhere else, he took what was given and gave it back from where he had been.

By the '30s the American Dream for everybody was exposed down to the marrow as not what it seemed. All the colored people knew that, the native peoples, the ex-slaves, the Mexicans and oppressed peoples, whose land had been took and whose color made them crooks, they already knew that. And from Grapes of Wrath, which came out then, even poor whites got to know the whole score, that there was nothing in the constitution that said you was gonna stop being poor.

That is, an Irony set in, a tongue in-cheek chuckle that was heard during the national anthem, just who was chuckling, well almost everyone here, but for different reasons.

Pres was Ironic from the first blue he blew, this is this, or maybe it ain't, or whatever it is, should it mean what it mean to me what it mean to you. Billie was like that, from the easy rider motion of her early pop hits, there was a diction, from a deep blue jondo canto bottom to the flying verses on the top. And that changed colors, and went further down, and as her life changed her, it also changed her sound.

Like Blue in Africa, before our trip to here, was our favorite, so beautiful we wore on our beautiful selves all the time. But in America Blue is a memory, fired black for face and red for blood, and wet with tears and the grip of the ocean. Blue is what we remember, what we left and what we cannot bear to recall. What we lost, what we sing, you blew you blew, Blow Blow, What did I do to be so Black and Blue. Lady Sings the Blues tells the whole tale. But then You've Changed or the side Lady in Satin will bring you to your knees. Will make you understand the pain of memory and desire in this land.

And the President, who had his own speech, understood this in his isness as the being he lived. And so the horn is first the sound of what is not, and what is gone, and what was blown what is known. Like Billie, there is a sad tenderness, like being born for the billionth time and knowing the drill. Almost happy to be here, and feeling anything, but song is the soul's effort, its confirming presence. So what is recorded there, the registration of our lives, brings even inadvertently the pain of all that with it, and if that feeling is broad enough, deep enough, i.e., human, then it carries all of us in it and with it. It is the irony of Pres, embossed with its deepness and blueness and sadness and tenderness, that is Billie's sound as well.

But the '30s becomes the '40s and ELLA FITZGERALD, who was the next bright being of this sky of music, enters. With the big band, because fundamentally that is what she remains, the big band singer. She is also the transitioning sound of Swing so-called into Bop so-called.

Ella brings the scat with her because she is linked still to Louis, who is speaking his lost, probably, Bantu tongue. When the Boppers reasserted the primacy of rhythm and blues and improvisation, the scat, the lost Africa returned, shoobie doobie, again.

Ella had hope in her delivery, sound, the bouncy optimism of those strong enough to get through America with some kind of grace. Ella always reminded me of a working person's muse. She was open and bright and verging on laughter, it was spread throughout her sound. A Tisket a Tasket, Bei Mir Bist Du Schoen, a breezy clarity of lyric and musical direction. Ella made the Blues, Jazz, Funk directly accessible to the American everybody. Whatever she did she did with the same popular timbre and approach. The Calypso period, the Louie Jordan period, her collaborations with Louis, Basie, Sinatra. Ella brought the music directly up front and center in American popular music. Where Billie had been a trifle too urbane and sophisticated for the cornier parts of the joint, Ella could at least pass by, humming or scatting and they might call it JATP.

SASSY was my early passion. She came with Bop, or Bop came with her. "The Divine One," as Symphony Sid intoned from the old Birdland, not the fat girl pumped up by Hollywood. Sassy was the singer of the new sounds. Just as Bessie came with Louis and Ethel with Louis and Fletcher and Fats and them, and Billie with all them and the line of new inner demarcation with Pres. Just as Ella came with the big band Chick Webb, and Basie. When you image SARAH VAUGHAN, you got to bring in the new music of the '40s BeBop, and Diz and Bird and Miles and Max and "them" all them.

Sassy was the beautiful voice, the breadth the deepness (deeper as she went on) the seamless transformative modal plasticity of it. She could bend it and stretch it and send it in all directions, funky as the breath of a drum. What Sassy did was take Ella's impeccable diction and blithe lyricism into the newly reshaped musical field of BeBop, not just the trendy media fixed version, but via Bop's innovative approach to harmony and restoration of the sharpness and insistence of the music's rhythm origins and its improvisational openness. She made all that the new singer's standard tools. There is no modern jazz singer, of any substance, who can say they have not been influenced by SARAH VAUGHAN and ELLA FITZGERALD. Although Betty Carter took this legacy and transformed it, somewhat, by removing, by the end of her stay, lyrics, as a focus of the song. Whether by a trendy slurring of them or merely reducing them to sound and accent. Still, it should be no surprise to anyone who has listened how deeply Betty Carter was shaped by SARAH VAUGHAN.

The continuing mastery of all this tradition, of what is called Jazz singing, though Duke and Max object to calling the music "Jazz," since given a label, the clowns of animal presumption and largesse (calling themselves "human beings") will name Kenny G, like Paul Whiteman or Benny Goodman or the Rolling Stones or Elvis, the King of . . . you and yours and whatever yall created. As I was saying, the continuing mastery is ABBEY LINCOLN.

ABBEY is the continuum of all this, at its highest level. The oldest Blues and its original instrumental innovation, transferable, from Bessie and Louis through Billie, with the continuing development and "modernization" of Ella and Sassy, so she can be "anywhere" in the spectrum of feeling and history, of form and content.

ABBEY is the story teller, the Djali, the Blues Singer, the lyrical balladeer, the popular Romantic, the Jazz Singer, and the constant reorganizer of the materials of art, so they are alive and touching. Always with the syncopated rush of contemporary funk. ABBEY is the FLAG, the GUIDON, the PREMIER CREATOR, the live paradigm and continuum of the Blue Jazz Song.

Of course, there are others. But, for me, these are the largest.

12/4/98

CHAPTER 19

Newark's Influence
on American Music

The totality of U.S. culture is still mainly shrouded from Americans, who know less about the whole and complex character of American, even North American, Culture than mountains of people all over the world. One reason is obvious, i.e., to the extent that racism, segregation, and discrimination have permeated this society, the ignorance of the whole of the culture is registered in direct proportion.

The grim commercial of America as the Great Democracy has always been a Lie.

The inequality of simple Recognition of the multinational multicultural nature of the U.S. is straightforward enough. If we look at the best-funded and supported and academically forwarded arts culture in the U.S. we would think we were in Europe or a European Colony.

Just a few weeks ago in the *New York Times* arts section, one courageous soi-disant intellectual told us that all U.S. drama is mediocre (he lists O'Neill, Tennessee, Miller, for starters) vis-à-vis Europe.

This is so because White supremacy mandates that Europe must be the paradigm of Greatness in whatever aspect of civilization. This is projected from the illusion that Europe is White! And that civilization itself is an expression of the "pure whiteness" foisted on the world as Europe. The deep ridiculousness of this is the fact that once all of what is now Europe was populated by Africans, from Scandinavia to Russia! Certainly, anyone who thinks this is 1999 should not be taken too seriously about history!

This political propaganda also functions to make the whole of the Western Hemisphere a neocolonial outpost and client for all things European, in the classic mode of Imperialism, as sources of raw materials, markets. One of the main reasons that the racist white guys at Rutgers went to such lengths, requiring Three Elections to the faculty, two of which I won, the final rump gimmick of sending the ballots out was because I had questioned the continuing Colonial cultural aggression of U.S. universities principally teaching European Culture but not the cultures of the Western hemisphere including the U.S.

The tragic irony and oppressive result of this is that the fundamentally democratic and multinational/cultural character of the U.S. is "covered," as the record industry says, squashed, hidden, exploited. That's why there are well-funded Orchestras playing Europeans' concert music across the country. European opera, likewise, enjoys stable and well-heeled venues, and the musicians in both these operations, celebrated ubiquitously as the Greatest Expression of Human Civilization, are very well paid. Another irony, since the market share of this music is about the same as Jazz, but less than Blues. When, with the recent exception of Lincoln Center and Carnegie Hall,* there are no permanent institutional Jazz Orchestras to speak of.

This is national chauvinism, of course, racism, white supremacy. But it is also a repressive limitation on the basic Productive Forces of the nation. Because the repression of the people and music of Afro-America removes revelation, education, and finance from the society as a whole. Given the deep and ubiquitous integration of the Music and Jazz culture into the US at some more than subliminal levels, to the extent that the so-called mainstream has always used it as both resource and commodity . . . from Blackface minstrel shows to Rock and Roll . . . the contradiction between all-around use, usually without credit or remuneration, coupled with the constant abuse, from Slavery to Kenny G, any recognition of the music as one artistic projection of a people or a culture is always sub rosa, at best. Except for the Gee Whiz folk, the hobbyists and children with living toys, who will call the players "Genius," but like Monk said, "Watch out when they call you genius, it mean you ain't gonna get paid."

Since the BeBop '40s the owners have decided to move the music out of the creators' communities (now that the segregation by color is not as strict, but the segregation by money works almost as well). They

*Since this writing the Carnegie Hall orchestra has been terminated.

move the music into the high-rent commercial districts, unlike the old caravans into the Land of the Blacks, Cotton Club like, to dig and to split. Now we must go out of the community to see and hear our most advanced artists. This is a steady brain drain, in an already beleaguered community, as well as a flow of resources. It also reduces the positive role models and sources of positive intervention to reroute our youth toward light.

So about Newark. New Ark, the Brick City. Half country Half City. Half Funk Half Pretty, the South always and yet still ring in our bones. From mouth, trumpets, drums, and saxophones. (A verse sidebar to keep my poet's license.) From early in the 20th century, as more Black people flocked into Newark (Black Russians, they called them, since they had just rushed up here from the South) to hit it in this growing industrial town, some worked on the old Canal, now Raymond Boulevard, in an area where Italians, Jews, Irish also lived . . . imagine Mayor Koch and Willie the Lion Smith both raised on Academy Street. There arose in the early teens of the century now leaving a red light district, Black entertainment district.

THE COAST, where working people used to go after work and have a good time. Roughly, from Branford Place to Lincoln Park from Martin Luther King to a few blocks below Broad. It was called The Coast. Hell's Kitchen in New York City (pre-Harlem, post-Village), the Levee in Chicago, and the Barbary Coast in San Francisco, which was run by an enterprising sister named Mammy Pleasant.

Newark's "Coast" in a few years became the testing grounds, the University of the Box, i.e., the greatest jazz piano players of the day came through here, and if you hadn't been here, you didn't have credentials nor had you paid dues to be known as a Bad Tickler. A Tickler, that's what the great stride pianists were called, Willie the Lion, James P. Johnson, Lucky Roberts, Donald Lambert, Fats Waller, the great Duke Ellington, and many others. They were all here because they had to be tested by the Lion, and all were shaped by the Lion, who was the acknowledged Master of the Ticklers, and Newark's Coast was his lair. Duke Ellington gives an appropriately Dukish narrative about the Lion.

After World War I, the Lion went to New York, when the happenings were still down in Hell's Kitchen, from the '40s to the '60s (streets) on the West Side. Where the boats docked and the new bloods swarmed north from places like Charleston. That's why James P. named his number "The Charleston," cause that's who was in Hell's Kitchen,

Geechie to the bone. But here also the Lion held court until the vibe rolled uptown, meaning the blood had got run out of somewhere else when it started to make money. Just like they ran us out the Village, the first New York City black community, in the 1863 draft riots.

The Lion's mastery dominated Harlem, along with his two sidekicks, students, running buddies, James P. Johnson and Fats Waller. The Lion would always come back cross the river to the Coast even when he was the toast of the Apple. Because Newark's magnetism was that it was half country, half city, half funk, half pretty. There was always raw dirt black blueness to this working-class town that could get slick as the skyscrapers but never let go of the old-time hard-knuckle blues. So the New York connection was also a resource, since in the city, before the great migration north, even the Black music sounded more like Broadway pop than beat down blue. Check Eubie Blake and Jim Europe ca. 1915.

Newark's country insides provide the soulful funk the music must carry with it to be itself. Ask George Gershwin, he sat at the Lion's feet, and Fats' and James P.'s too. Listen to "Rhapsody in Blue," then listen to James P.'s "Yamekraw Rhapsody," then talk to me . . . or his Blues Opera with Langston Hughes, *The Organizer,* or the Lion's piece he dropped on Gershwin and friends the night of the *Rhapsody in Blue* premiere, "Finger Buster." Or if you can find any of "the Lamb's" incredible pianistic miracles, e.g., playing Chopin and the Fire Dance at the same time. Or listen to Duke's "Portrait of the Lion" or the Lion's "Portrait of Duke Ellington." Oh, Yeh! The powerful motifs of rhythm and blues that stride piano encompassed were initially projected from Newark's Coast, when the city was known as a "Ticklers' Town." And this style and its influence became internationally known and will remain historically significant, as long as there's music. Nor did that influence ever cease. . . . If you know Monk's music you hear the stride continuum, or dig Sun Ra, that's how heavy Newark's Lion and his posse of Ticklers were, and are.

This city's closeness to New York was always one of its resources and one of New York's. And at the top of its hipness, which will come again, anything you saw in the city you could dig somewhere in Newark. Not just jazz, but rhythm and blues, old blues, gospel, whatever, any genre of Black music was always pumping here. As Duke Ellington said, the best place to listen to Black music is Newark! Why . . . because there were always so many places to play, musicians came through from everywhere, from the old Coast Ticklers period and forward.

In every period of transition and reorganization of the music, Newark has contributed virtuosi, who bring the double-edged sword of country bottom blue city top, as harsh and sweet as that mixture be in real life. Particularly in New Jersey, the last northern state to free the slaves.

Whether it was Paul Robeson from Princeton, or Bill Basie from Red Bank, or James P. from New Brunswick, Newark was one epicenter of that world. During the Renaissance Twenties, the whole pantheon of stars trooped through, Bessie Smith, Ethel Waters, Mantan Moreland even lived here for a while, "Shuffle Along" had a Newark company with Florence Mills. Sissle and Blake brought Chocolate Dandies to the whites on the main floor Blacks in the balcony Shubert, when the Proctors was like that too. Buck and Bubbles, Bill Bojangles Robinson, they all came through. You could make a gig at the old Black Orpheum (Court and Washington Street) and get back to the Apple in a minute or vice versa.

When the Swing trend came in, this city contributed not only to all the major bands, but there were great bands located here. The Savoy Dictators was one very popular group, led by Al Henderson, with Harold Mitchell, who played with everyone from Benny Carter to Lionel Hampton, one of the finest and most respected trumpets of the period. Dizzy Gillespie called Mitchell one of his favorite trumpet players. Plus, Bobby Plater, who would later become for many years Basie's second in command, and arranger. Mitchell, like many other very skilled and creative voices in this city, never got the fame he deserved. Even in my own generation, great players like drummer Eddie Crawford, tenor magnificence Jimmy Anderson, both went out of here with none of the recognition such artists should receive. All three of these wizards worked day jobs till the end of their lives, though they never stopped blowing.

The Whys of this continuing tragedy are to be found in the lack of self-determination by the indigenous majority. Clubs, theaters, hot spots come and go, usually owned by somebody not even aware of who is who or playing what. The Savoy Sultans was another group emerging in the Swing Era, the Sultans were so original and funky that it is said even Duke Ellington feared them at the famous Savoy Cutting Sessions which put the great bands of the day in crowd-pleasing shoot-outs and cutting sessions. What was so wild about the Sultans, some real Newark stuff, they would actually go into "circus time," some Globetrotter antics, like passing the horns around with slick steps and turns, while blowing holes in every body's soul. Grachan Moncur's father, Grachan "Brother" Moncur, played bass, Al "Razz" Mitchell was the drummer, Al Cooper, reeds, and leader Rudy Williams, saxophone. They were the intermission band at the Savoy, and Basie is quoted, "Them bad Savoy Sultans . . . they ran the hell out of us . . . I don't ever want to see those cats again."

The Newark bands were stylists and they always swung down to the bottom of their shoes because they were rooted in a sensibility that demanded whatever you did, and however you looked, or called your-self, for sure you better make sure you heard what Duke said, "It don't mean a thing . . . et cetera . . . ," so Newark groups generally always came out of a heavy funk blues up top background, no matter where else they wanted to go.

So that jazz musicians were also Bluesicians, they had to be. Lyrical crooners like Little Jimmy Scott is so blues bound, or Andy Bey, as smooth as silk as he be, do still get down, like up under the ground, to retrieve the One, the universal "funkcopation" that characterizes the deep social character of the place. No-nonsense Brick City,

Not only is the blues an internal characteristic of the socialization of the town and its citizens, but it has always been the most ubiquitous entertainment, emotional staple here, outside the church. And quiet as it's kept, you go in many of the churches the Blues be in there still, but Jesus be in it. Newark still is one center of Jazz Organ, I'm told of all the programs in the hopelessly misproduced Newark Jazz Festival, which must be rethought and redone . . . you don't have to bring in a lot of names, give the musicians in this town a break and build an audi-ence that can develop with the music, not only save money and give a much deeper more satisfying program and recreate the city's image as a city of creative artistry to which all so stimulated must come.

Freddie Roach, Larry "Lawrence of Newark" Young, Rhoda Scott, Jimmy McGriff, Big John Patton, Radam Schwartz, I bet there's some folks in here old enough to remember when Milt Pittman played while your ribs got seasoned. An organ town cause the basic funk must be included.

The town was always a place the greatest voices could come and try they thing, like how Broadway shows start out of town to get their number together. Newark was always a testing ground as well as a public "Shed," where you could find out right away whether your

whatnot was tight or not . . . they'd let you know quicker than Amateur
Night at the Apollo.

This has always been a basic Blues and R&B town. Ammons, Bostic,
Bull Moose, Lynn Hope, Big Jay McNealy, Jacquet, Little Esther, Ruth
Brown seemed to be always somewhere in this city. All those quartets,
bird named or not, lived here. The Orioles, the Ravens, the Platters.
And it goes on today, with the Rappers, Naughty by Nature, Queen
Latifah, Ice Tea, Lauryn Hill was in Kimako's basement a long time
before Variety knew the Fugees. You can hear her on my son Ras's
great CD (I'm taking orders) *Shorty for Mayor,* and you can hear him
on a Fugees album and on Public Enemy too, and people in Newark
only think of Ras as a Political Activist.

In the early '40s, when there was a recording ban in New York, the
major BeBop, Gospel, and Rhythm and Blues recordings were made in
Newark by Savoy records, still one of the greatest catalogs in the music.
Bird, Diz, Max, Kenny Dorham, Miles, Dexter Gordon, Errol Garner,
among the many, are all on Savoy. Newark Music Project has already
began investigating whether we can get the new owners of Savoy to
bring the company back and build a museum, warehouse, business
office, to help in the renovation of the old Coast District, a project we
are deeply involved in and hope you will be too. The rebuilding of the
Coast, now called the Lincoln Park Coast Cultural District, would give
new life to the city, and while we hear much talk about Renaissance
Newark and are happy to see the New Jersey Performing Arts Center
built here in our town, unless there is development on the other side of
town then any talk of Renaissance is just Corporate Hype.

When the BeBop revolution transformed the music and scandalized
the Official Knowers because they knew not, and frightened Tin Pan
Alley cause some real what not had come out of the real alleys, Newark
was, as always, right in the center of it. My man Babs Gonzales from
Hillside Place was the actual creator of the BeBop language, and had
a dictionary to prove it. With Dizzy at point, and Bird on nuclear
saxophone, Bop and Bop language spread around the world. Oo Pa
Pa Dow . . . beep beep . . . check *Weird Lullaby,* it's just been reissued
on CD. Babs had the greatest of the new musicians with him, as they
were just emerging, J.J. Johnson, the great composer-arranger, Tadd
Dameron not only played piano on some of Babs's dates but sang the
Bop vocals with Babs. Benny Green, Sonny Clark, Wynton Kelly, Roy
Haynes, Sonny Rollins, Julius Watkins, Art Pepper, Ray Nance, Jimmy
Smith, Don Redman, Paul Chambers, Herbie Stewart, local wailer Art

Phipps all played with Babs. So that BeBop as a vocal and instrumental phenomenon had deep roots in Newark.

Again, close enough to the Apple to dig what it was, far enough away, in spirit, to come up with something totally out. Lo Pow, Oo Papa Dow . . . ooh ooh . . . In fact, one of the acknowledged greatest of the musicians to emerge during the Bop years was the great Sarah Vaughan, whose very artistry spoke of a deep church bottom rising up through a solid Newark blues body up through the U2 jet flight the bopestry took her on, where she could wail like some magic bird screaming out the sky. It was in there. The church, the Blues, the wailing zig zag of Blue bop and the magic of actual flight. Again, it was the components of her socialization here in the Ark, before she reached New York, that made her so special that she could combine all those elements seamlessly in a triumphant Artifact of great artistry. Sassy is yet more evidence of the brew in the place and how it does get around.

The Outest of the Brick City wailers still are much rooted in the Blues. Whether Lawrence of Newark, or the marvelous Woody Shaw. As weird as Wayne Shorter came on, what makes his Buhaina works so lovely is that combining of the out and the definitely in, which sing together in a newly unique harmonic and melodic mix, still funky to the bone. Throughout the years, whoever and whatever have emerged from the place and its environs, it could be the Houstons, or Warwicks or young Savion Glover . . . it could be Allen Ginsberg or myself, from off these gray intensely vibrating streets, there is a bottom of reality to the place we carry. The Blue song carries the blue of the machine, of nab's ugly vine. Of the steel gates of the closed factories or the vamping shadows clogging the empty insides of the ghastly projects or armies of abandoned buildings.

Our innovators have been distinctly "other," highly skilled, but basic as the sidewalks. This is certainly one of Newark's gifts, not only to the Music, but to all the arts we find ourselves redefining. Cause whatever it is, it ain't all told till our particular funkiness get in.

And this is the promise, actually, that we can recreate, for the first time, if that's not too way out, a whole city as we build. Not just a one-sided, corporate-fattening illusion, but something really whole, whole enough to include all the new Little Jimmy Scotts, the next wave of Miss Rhapsodies, the contemporary Savoy Sultans, the next Wayne Shorters or Babs Gonzaleses, some more Sassys and Ginsbergs, and Boobie Heards and Amiri Barakas and even yet another George Clinton, who used to be a Barber on Chancellor Avenue before he got crazy enough to help form the Parliaments, then the Funkadelics, crazy as that might seem, one nation under a groove ain't so bad. It beats Kosovo and Columbine, Colorado.

The task is to build venues for the indigenous artists, an arts district where the citizens and all so moved can groove without the chill of commerce killing them off like colored people.

In order for the whole of society to move, in this era of the single superpower U.S., now rampaging madly around the world, while downsizing workplaces, plundering the national treasury, all the time screaming that the Economy is doing great, well not here it ain't, and in the many Newarks across the land. And it seems if we follow the hideous unfolding of news about the presumably safe and moral communities of the Well Off, we will find a vacuum of purpose and human focus that leads to self-inflicted horrors as ugly as the 41 bullets shot at Amadou Diallo, for essentially the same reasons as the children murdered in Columbine. That fundamental emptiness is the place where art and contemplation of truth and beauty have been removed. Where local culture is almost totally replaced by vapid or pornographic commercial culture. The creation of new indigenous institutions and venues for the emergence of homegrown art and cultural work, created out of the self-determining focus of those communities themselves, is one clear way to sidetrack the monster stalking our cities and our suburbs. One cannot live by television, video games, top ten CDs, and dumb movies alone . . . there must be reserved in the center of all of our socialization and growth, space for the production of local art and culture as simple confirmations that we are alive, independent of Channel whatever, and that what we create reproduces our selves in ways realer than we can buy from any store. We are working to see such a space be created in this city and inside all of us here. To do this would be perhaps the most profound influence Newark could ever have on the culture of this nation.

4/23/99

CHAPTER 20

Ritual and Performance

From the words and their origins as signs: What is the law, or has been written or, before that, done (i.e., what is RIGHT . . . the weakness of the human evolution is that it is one-sided . . . the RIGHT hand, etc., side of the brain, side of the political aisle). At this moment we are moving sharply to the right, politically, to the more conservative, headed toward Fascist society. That is, the naked domination of the most backward reactionary jingoistic sector of finance capital (see Dimitrov, *Against Fascism and War*).

Drama (a smaller portion of life, a dram of it . . . the ma like matter mother earth, more, "mo," etc.) And we are faced with the disposition as antagonistic opposites of the two, Ritual and Performance. What is said (as the law, constitution, laws, e.g., the American dream, the American heritage), what has been "given," which, by now, I hope, all the slowest of us know is a lie, when we measure that rhetorical idealism against the performance, against the actual practice of They Nited Snakes.

For instance we are told, in the ritual rubric of what this all is, that it is the greatest democracy, yet the U.S. has NEVER been a democracy, certainly if you understand that settler colony genocide, chattel slavery, and imperialist annexation (we speak of the native peoples, the African peoples, the Mexicanos) are not democratic and these peoples have had to live under this antagonistic contradiction between American ritual bullshit and the actual performance of U.S. life.

So from the depths and essence of this body politic, body social, body economic, must also be likewise shaped the body cultural. From Brooks Adams, the revered New England Brahmin socio-economic historian from the same family that gave us Anthony Hopkins's grand performance, which now will create a ritual of historical relationship, heretofore obscured because the good guys still would not talk about their dominant badguyness. But now it's OK, "Yeh we were slave masters but some of us were not altogether lawless."

Amistad was nowhere as ugly as *Schindler's List,* which is some solace. Again, the performance of the Nazi state in its annihilation of Jews and now a performance re: the "Dunkle Engel," Schindler, who, NO KIDDING, saved a few, for his own extra religious Profit (Spelled P-R-O-F-I-T). Are we given the heroic struggles of the doomed in opposing the Holocaust and Nazism itself? Of course not, we are given one sanitized Teufel saving his slave workers!

Why, because at the beginning, you remember . . . I know History will soon be banned under the New World Odor as subversive . . . but the Chinese and Russians were the U.S. allies in fighting FASCISM, but now the Germans and Japanese (plenty perfumed Nazis and Japanese Militarists in the crowd) are U.S. allies. Does this mean that World War II was not to destroy fascism but to see who would be in charge of it? (See Cartels, by the Under Secretary of the Interior under FDR, and the agreement to keep profits between Standard Oil, Krupp, Farben, Mitsubishi, Matsushida, no matter who won the war!!!)

So that Ritual is something given as history, manners, religion, social action, even politics and economics, while performance is Practice. They have the same relationship ultimately that Theory and Practice have. Jazz Ritual, for instance, is rooted in collective improvisation, syncopation, rhythm and blues, at least as the known history, from Africa, spread throughout the West.

Performance has been, as it created a classic music, mainly of that ritualistic teaching and doing. But it has also, the performance of this music, been subject to and frequently subjugated by the ritual of COMMERCE and its performance. In each phase of Afro-American music and culture, what develops spontaneously, usually from the continuum of real life, i.e., material life and its reflection, there is also recurrently the intervention of American social life, wherein such initial impulse and process is surrounded. The initial rejection until, like the dunk, the surface of the expression is overstood, from the first dis, and cover, then it is discovered then covered then co-opted, till Eureka,

Paul Whiteman is the King of Jazz, Benny Goodman the King of Swing and Elvis Presley the King of . . . whatever . . . add that to the Rolling Stones as the Best Rock & Roll Band ever . . .. and you have it. But a poem of mine says about Presley, "If Elvis Presley is / King / Who is James Brown? / GOD?"

U.S. society in its antagonistic relationship to African Americans has either stopped, stunned, blunted Black expression, e.g., the banning of the drum, or, when faced with the refusal of the expression to vanish simply because the Slave Master didn't dig it, this expression would be co-opted, taken over, claimed, etc., as commerce or even as social enhancement. White movie stars have historically been BLACK even literally to cover and dismiss Black life and use it to macho U.S. proto- types or simply to make money. Paul Newman as chain gangee. Bogart is the name of the street where Bumpy Johnson was born in Charleston. Name the number of white musicians and boxers and athletes of dubi- ous distinction in films and then compare that to the Blacks or anyone else. Sugar Ray Robinson beat LaMotta and Graziano so many times it was not humorous, yet these opponents have had films, Robinson never.

But to get into the drama itself. Look at the masks of drama and you have the ritual of what it is, but still obscure for most of us. The frown and the smile. These are actually a Geosocial aesthetic description of ye world. The smile at the bottom of the world versus the Frown at the top. The Africans were reviled by the Greeks for smiling too much. The African and world black religions all value "possession," the "frenzy," said the young Du Bois, the "going out" process, gettin happy, the folks in the church say, getting the gospel, the good spell, be on the good foot, etc. That religious passion of ecstasy at possessing the life force as a total consciousness. To become that part of life which lives forever.

College told us that Tragedy was the highest form of Art! Sophocles, Aeschylus, what about a dude who kills his father, sleeps with his mother, puts out his own eyes, and wanders the world looking for Harvard? Nietzsche in *The Birth of Tragedy* tells us that Emotion interferes with Thought. But to me if you are not emotional you cannot think. What cannot feel cannot think sums it up. That's why we ask the philosophers when we see them, "How you feel, Man?"

In the language, "a drag," that's tragedy. These "squares," the ancient Egyptians from their ritual of becoming and understanding, tell us. A square is the angle of failure. The pyramid the angle of success. Hence if we know Oedipus, the clubfoot daddy killer, his most frequent historically surviving characteristic we relate as "That lame motherfucking square!" And for the Black people that ritual of our encounter with the slave masters and their performance goes on correlating exactly.

The term GRIOT, which is supposedly related to Africa, is, in fact, French and means CRY, but the traditional historian-musician-storyteller of Africa was a GLEEMAN (see Glee Club), a DJALI. And the performance was described as DJELI YA. Hence Jelly Roll Morton, or "It must be jelly cause jam don't sound like that," or Mr. B singing "Jelly Jelly Jelly made my father blind drove my mama out of her mind." The laughter at the bottom of the world. The frown at the top.

Theater in the American spelling means "getting down to earth," returning to reality, so to speak, "Getting Down," as the Africans still say. Reflections on material life that give revelation. In the English spelling it means return to inspiration, rejuvenation, touched by divinity, but now these both are mostly commerce as ritual and performance. The Great White Way is White Supremacy at base, its philosophy, the Great Path of gloried Whiteness (read colonialism, imperialism, conquest). But that is openly about money, greed, and vulgarization ahora, at best. In the U.S. commercialism has triumphed in the popular culture and U.S. commercial culture has driven all forms of intelligent, courageous, thoughtful, artistic, powerful, socially precise people's reflections of society into the margins. Off Broadway is exact, off-white, etc., foundations replace corporations, but the result is similar.

The U.S. has no national repertory theater like most of the industrial countries. Why: Because the great drama of the U.S. accuse, as the GF said, "some of the people in the room." Early O'Neill, Hughes, WPA (Works Progress Administration), FTP (Federal Theater Project), Ted Ward, Odets, Tennessee, Arthur Miller, Hellman, Hansberry, Baldwin do not flatter the real history and life of the U.S., which disguises itself in a ritual rhetoric now of broad mediocrity and dollarism. Such theater is also education and a broad popular sense. And the Pows that bees do not need this. Plus the U.S. is now ruled by an imperial class, even its national nonmonopoly bourgeois (See Pee rot's rejection at Pres Debates) is frustrated and driven to frenzy by the usurpation of U.S. national sovereignty by international finance capital. All nations, post the fake cold war and the overthrow of the USSR, must line up to borrow from the IMF, World Bank. Here they call it Budget Cuts, Downsizing, Belt Tightening, while the president of Nike make 96 million dollars last year in salary and 4.5 billion in stock options, a man gets 60 million from Disney for failing!!

What is ritualistic in the majority of us is the will to survive and even to develop and for some the struggle to understand the world. Our art, our theater is a part of this. What we must further understand is that the common rituals of the people themselves, in the Black U.S. for instance the church, contain both the form and content of our efforts but must be transformed by substituting science for metaphysics and collective development for individual epiphany and enrichment. We are not preachers but teachers and not sycophants or "a flock" but artists and intellectuals and activists, cultural workers who must understand ourselves as part of the whole and use that understanding to inspire, educate, and reorganize the whole for all of our collective development and ultimate triumph, i.e., the reorganization and development of society itself.

I say this because our role now, at this last part of the 20th century, must be to fight in the superstructure. That part of society created by the economic base, which includes the institutions, organizations, and philosophies that seek to maintain to continue the present society. We must develop an alternative superstructure. Certainly, in these years where the U.S. resembles nothing so much as the Weimar Republic, the last few years of democracy just before Hitler's fascist domination of Germany. The ubiquitous serial killers, sexual madness, immoral social mores, unprecedented greed, and social horrors are what characterized Weimar. The soporifics of sex and greed and sensation replace any realistic understanding of the world and ourselves in it. We are being desensitized by all forms of madness and urged to run away with the rich and the famous while all the profound issues we fought for in the last social upsurge of the '60s are being eliminated and the social groups at the head of that upsurge, the Revolutionaries, Activists, Blacks, Minorities, Women, anti-imperialists are every day denigrated to justify the Sisyphus syndrome of American social reaction and loss of sovereignty to international finance capital.

Every day we lose more and more democracy and national sovereignty, every day the quality of life of the broad multinational American population is degraded and the U.S. becomes a modern version of nazi Germany, the corporate state. Privatization is justified mindlessly by people who stand to lose most by it and the news pumps at us the good news of how strong the economy is while people lie in the street, die of poisons, executions, police anarchy, and our popular culture becomes an open cesspool of corporately manufactured filth.

What is to be done, said Lenin. We must oppose the present superstructure of imperialism with a superstructure of science, art, and people's democracy. We must rejuvenate and reorganize the popular culture of the U.S. by going to the grassroots of creativity and productivity, the masses of the people, of which we are hopefully one of the most sensitive and thoughtful parts. We must create our own theaters, concert venues, magazines, newspapers, journals, publishing houses, art galleries, schools, and not merely toll away like drugged monks at the bell of vicious moribund capitalism, called imperialism.

We spend too much time, those of us, who have sworn to fight the destruction of human life and culture by imperialism and national oppression, we spend too much time criticizing the BEAST and not enough time creating alternatives. More time should be spent creating an alternative to Hollywood than merely criticizing it. The major publishing houses are being sold away, merged in the final paroxysm of corporate capital into a dead body which will poison all of us if we let it merely fall on us with its dead irrational weight. We mourn the leaving of Simon and Schuster, but what has it done for the people anyway. Where are the thousands of small publishing companies on a collective economic basis that can and must replace these huge Dinosauric enemies?

Kimako's Blues People, which my wife, Amina, and I direct, produces plays, poetry readings, concerts, the last Saturday of each month for the last ten years. We must energize the indigenous popular culture of our communities. Rather an art gallery in your garage, a theater in your basement, a collective publishing house, than to stand around yapping about Knopf or Fox and waiting for them to discover us and turn us into what we now despise.

Where are our national arts and science journals? Our two-thousand-dollar epic films and videos? What is worth 160 million in *Godzilla*, except the lifestyle of the greedy and infamous and proof that we are gophers that will go for anything. Use our resources collectively, our friends and colleagues together, to produce an alternate superstructure. This is the first step in social revolution, to change the minds of the people.

As teachers we must go to the source of strength in U.S. life, its diversity, its post-European openness and earthiness. If we claim to be Americans we must claim the whole of the culture. Anything American is African, European, and Asian (Native), and to be American we must not only be that but claim that and seek to reorganize the whole of the culture to inspire, educate, and social-economically develop the whole people. We seek Majority rule, the control of society by the majority, its workers, and farmers, its oppressed nationalities, its democratic petty bourgeoisie, and even those of the national bourgeoisie (shaky at best) who oppose imperialism. This is our task. Let us get at it.

6/10/98

CHAPTER 21

Bopera Theory

Theater in the U.S. is obstructed in its development by the same forces that obstruct the general positive development of human life and society. Frequently, we are stalled by our very amazement at the rulers of this society shrieking for years of their "superiority," when one has only to witness the world, itself, under their Dictatorship of the Beast, to understand that superior they ain't. Even "lower" animals cause less trouble to the Planet.

But the superstructural control of intellectual development is critical to our penetration of aesthetic theory in the fake democracy real imperialism of U.S. Life. For instance, we must step outside the parameters of this society's version of just about everything. Often I seek to use, as one alternative, practices found in the oldest root of performance, ritual, but not in a frozen atavistic way. We take the wholeness, the freshness, the penetrating emotionalism and spiritual relation and renewal, the direct speech and touch of what the ancients meant.

We want to educate but we want to do that through the transformation of the human consciousness. We want to open it. We want to make the known world as irrational as it actually is and the approaching epoch of human equality a known factor our open embrace brings closer to reality. We want news we wants olds we want the constant beat of life in its material existence as the pump of image perception rationale and use. The feelings we want are feelings that are drawn into intellectual understanding and of even higher relevance to the human condition, use. The use of music must be understood. Music is the feeling as thought as feeling raised or transformed into a less static entity. Music goes into the spirit deeper because it has physical properties that carry intellectual and spiritual correspondences not limited by its physical properties. Music is a living creature, a human intellectual and emotional creation of time and space, with a readily apparent physical spirituality that transcends the visible world of its creators. It goes out of the world as the colors of the world. It is not bound by our physicality. The sounds carry whatever information rests in those frequencies and rhythms and harmonies. Some unknown to us.

We have been given senses, yes, but those are merely the ones the present world is prepared to use. And those not nearly complete. The level of society is the lower register. The reason we are essentially one-handed. The right hand representing the gross physical world. The imperialists are worshippers of idleness. Idol Worshippers. Things. Expensive Feces is their principal achievement. Money is helped by the idle, it is an idol, God. Goodness is a missing Nut.

Add five more senses to the five we know, at least. See and See into forward or back. Hear or Hear back and forth gone and coming. Smell. From a distance & permanent registration, as to essence, as identification, as a register of finer stimuli. Taste. Taste essence. Understand what it is and what it does by the taste. Function Touch. Touching is our projection of it. That is, to register at finer levels of perception and rationale. To touch as a sympathetic presence in tune with, etc. Sound is the registration of feeling (the senses). Our feeling is limited by our ignorance. There are probably five more senses at the level where we exist now, stunted by the RIGHT, the focus on force as social development.

Plus . . . but that's something else. The question is Music as a profound speaking, moving, raising, perception, and teaching. The "Frenzy," DuBois called it. Getting Happy, my grandmother called it. The Gospel. The Good Foot. Dance, that must be in it. But not as the dance we now have presented. But the common dance. The every minute moment-to-moment dance. Which everything actually is. I want the movement of the players to take on the rhythm of the music without "leaving" the dramatic context. The dance must be heightened movement. Emphasis. Further Explanation. Integrated with the Whole.

Actually, every element we know must work together for the revolutionary people democratic workers communist theater we envision.

Lights. Music. Dance. Sets. Speech. The BOPERA to me was poetry and music and heightened movement.

Sun Ra brought back the Pythagorean application of Egyptian understanding that everything is everything, and that music, color, number, emotions, the laws of matter in motion are revealed and are inextricably tied. Ra's introduction of the Space Organ at the Black Arts in the sixties, which the Dangs copped as "Light Shows." The one-ness of the animist view of the world must be restored to reach the deep drama I feel. The words are poetry, as heightened rhythmic speech. But not, by this, outside the current of everyday life. Rather our use of the rhythm and motion, image from which ideas, which grasped by the people, become a social force. Everyday life is not perceived by us in the deepness and grandness of its actuality. What is happening. The feel-ings. The transformations. The reordering. The emotional totality of us or whoever in it. The BOPERA should take our lives and render them understandable as emotional and intellectual experiences, which teach and add to our way of seeing and being. Like the church. The preacher is to get people "happy," trying to get them "possessed" so they start jumping up in the aisles spinning like James Brown. So they become a part of the animating element of existence. We want the experience of entering the whole, not only as emotion, but as heightened rationale, so that the social "use" of the information we are distributing is an experience registered on several levels.

I was on this path with *Slave Ship* and the ritual dramas of the '60s. I still think verse is the language of drama. And the world of the theater is a deeper world (canto jondo) wherein we see this world. Not through a glass darkly, but clear as something funny or sad, which makes us respond and informs and changes us by that. The responsibil-ity to inform is our deepest task, but information is alive and can only be deeply grasped as a living entity passed to the living. The theater should wake us from the "dead" of the blunted sense, the mediocrity that day-to-day evil has wrapped our feelings in, and as we heighten the audience's feelings, it is these feelings which become the enhanced antennae of learning.

Feeling predicts intelligence, I wrote, many years ago. So that it is the feeling, the emotional catalyst that is the dramatic motor. From scene (seen) to act. The Play itself is motion, game, ritual, form, and content. But the point is to the audience, to move them from the confines of the brutal lie world. Truth and Beauty are the content and form of our most advanced works. But these are obstructed (per time, place, and condition) by Lies and Ugliness. These are the shapes of the outline of what we create. We are shaped by what we are not to be what we are. We are always struggling against what we are and what we are not. The theater must present both states as the dialectic of living birth, maturation, transformation. The ancient world was communist primitive communalism. The old African aesthetic still speaks directly of this, whether the polyrhythms of the music, the polychromatic bright multicolors of the visual art, passed even yet to us in the western world. Afro-American music is still fundamentally a collective and improvised communal expression. The call and response and frenzy of the earliest song forms can be heard in Stevie Wonder or John Coltrane.

So the BOPERA is Re Creation, Inner Attainment, gained by tightening our everyday languages into verse and lifting it into the zoom zone of the spiritual, emotional, and intellectual impact with music. Lights and sets are to give an even more specific touching of what we present. The limited creativity of the neorealist set is a continued mediocrity of imagination commercial theater has trapped us in. The set, the props, everything in the scene must relate to what we are saying, not to a world where that can't even be said. The extent to which we are not Broadway, for instance, but imitate them, is the extent to which we are dismissable as revolutionaries or even serious dramatists.

We should relate to the known world but, like the Africans, or the revolutionary German and Russian theater of the '20s and '30s, create from our understanding of what we are trying to present, what we are trying to say, what emotions and ideas and acts we are trying to explain and agitate. The sets must have to do with this, by expressive creative means, not by passive reflection of a world ruled by our enemies.

So the stage must speak, from outside the confines of imperialism and national oppression. It must show these things so we can destroy them, but we must go far beyond them with our presentation, so that even our presence weakens the rulers with the audacity and intellectual and emotional depth of our statement.

Recently at a play of mine where election machines were called for, the presenters wanted to reproduce the election machine. Why? A cardboard flat. A modified ballot. An expressionist image. The election machines are not real in what they are proposed to do in the world we are oppressed in. Why should we give them more reality than they have? Making them is the point!

The rappers show what the musical versification of the word is. But our concept is that words be verse by their insistence and rhythms, not by redundant patterns which dull the perception. The BOPERA is meant to be a musical experience in the sense that the action of the play must be predicated and take its tone and motion from the music as its basic underpinning and only secondarily on the descriptions of character psychology, and commercial theater uses. The "method" of Stanislavski is acknowledged as the principal task of the actors, i.e., to become the character. But the motion, the path, the dramatic "dance" of form, content, and meaning must come from the music. The speech, acting, singing, and movement must be a function of the music. This last idea is difficult for some folks to dig. Directors think you are lessening the particularity of ideas and meaning. But it is exactly the reverse. In the music should be found the deep essence of what is meant, as feeling, mood, tone, psychology. If the actors tune in with the music, then what they say or sing or how they move or pause will be rendered as a whole and in that context, filled with more life.

Life connects us with rhythms. What is rhythmless is not. From Heart to the Day Night pulse of visible nature. To the extent that we tune in with the rhythm and that the ideas that we project have a basis in the emotional and intellectual rhythm of their whole meaning, we move the audience past the purely intellectual guesswork of what it is, so that whatever is is.

CHAPTER 22

"Jazz and the White Critic"

Thirty Years Later

The second article I published about the music, in *Metronome,* was "Jazz and the White Critic." The theme was, broadly, that a fundamental contradiction, sharp, at times antagonistic, existed between American Classical Music, its creators, mainly Black, and the majority of commentators, critics, critical opinion about that music, which historically are not.

The cause of this is obvious, whatever the slaves created was owned by the slave owners. The fundamental social philosophy characterizing American Capitalism (and feudalism before that) has always been shaped by white supremacy, whether it was slavery or the national oppression and chauvinism that still exist today.

The fact that an oppressor nation could judge the creations of the people they oppress is not strange but "natural" in the context of the relationship between ruler and ruled. Just as the slave was part of the "Means of Production" (and, when feudal slavery changed to capitalist slavery, variable capital), so whatever was produced by the slaves was, by definition, part of what the owner of the slave owned.

As "art," the music was useful as entertainment, social control, pedagogy, commerce. "Blind Tom," the amazing 19th-century slave pianist who knew 10,000 pieces of music and became a touring novelty, known throughout the South, even during slavery, is said to have "made" a million dollars for his owners!

In contrast, there were thousands of slave "entertainers" confined to a single plantation. At first despised in a utilitarian way, but ironically, as democracy made its tortured way toward Afro-Americans, their cultural product was more and more co-opted, commercialized, and, nowadays, even claimed.

To read Lincoln Collier or Richard Sudhalter and their bizarre Ubermenschlichkeit is to be annoyed with a tinge of melancholy that our oppressors are, to quote poet Robert Creeley, such "uncertain egotists." Like a poem I wrote, "MTV": "We can have your life, without being poor, etc."

The New Orleans Rhythm Kings, after the first years of the music's emergence, claimed that the Black musicians were white. The context of a white racist superstructure, i.e., institutions, organizations, and the curricula, ideas, and philosophies those are meant to maintain and forward. They are a reflection of the Monopoly Capitalist imperialist economic base, almost completely defining, "evaluating," advancing dubious or ingenuously chauvinist theories, explanations, about Black Music, at this point through writing, other media, reaching incredible proportions. Each year floods of such mainly superficial materials (from books, TV, and radio series, even calendars, T-shirts, postcards) defining and classifying Black Music are produced.

It is this superstructure, with its various critics, scholars, journalists, that has even succeeded in naming Afro-American Music "Rag Time," "Jass" and "Jazz" (in their musical and nonmusical definitions), "Swing," "BeBop," "Rock and Roll," all coined as media-driven generic titles by this collective entity. Since the creators of the music did not have the same access to publishing, writing, etc.

Max Roach tells how Duke Ellington first told him that when we accept and forward this essential commercial nomenclature, foisted on the music by others, same presence can then identify any thing commerce want as that.

So that Paul Whiteman became "the King of Jazz," Benny Goodman "the King of Swing," the Rolling Stones "the Greatest Rock and Roll Band in the World." Then dig the grand larcenous essence of commercial Copperheads inducting Black Musicians into the Rock and Roll Hall of Fame when, Naw, Jimmy, them dudes was playing Rhythm and Blues BEFORE THERE WAS A ROCK OR A ROLL!

There is no general commercial label for the works of Bach, Brahms, Beethoven, etc. That music is called, more precisely, "the Music of Ludwig Beethoven," "the Music of Bela Bartok." Then why not, says Roach, "the Music of Duke Ellington," "the Music of Thelonius Monk," etc. But then that would confer a station and dignity on the Music that the racist superstructure has never wanted to allow.

To this day, there is not a single Afro-American writer heading up the Jazz Section of a major newspaper! (Imagine if there were only Afro-American or other nonwhite writers who entirely monopolized writing about European Concert music!) During the hot sixties there were black writers about the music on the *Village Voice, Philadelphia Inquirer, Washington Post,* but dig this, when the hot times passed, the most fortunate of these were made sports writers! Get to that! (Now what that mean, Jimmy?)

Stanley Crouch was the last surviving name bylining writing about the music. And I told him at a forum at the Village Gate that the *VV* was going to sic him off in another direction, e.g., politics, novels, the former about which he is completely off the wall, the latter . . . well, ax his boys, Bellow or Updike! I told Stanley, Gary Giddins was going to get that main *VV* gig. And while the editorial Iblis is working his number, Stanley has still not put out a single book on the music, though he is more knowledgeable about the straight-up history of American Classical Music than most of the chosen at the *Times, Voice,* etc.

Why? (A good question, bu . . . oy!) Is it, in this case, because Stanley could say some heavy stuff that perhaps dem udder guise wouldn't dig? It seems Die Ubermenschen hate for the darkies to sound knowledgeable about anything, even their own lives. But tell me this glaring ugliness of arbitrary (racial?) exclusion from access to professional position in a subject which must bear some relationship to Afro-America is not dagger-sharp proof of the continuing national oppression of the Afro-American people, right now!

The ownership relationship of Big America to the Music has meant denigration, marginalization, "covers," and dismissal. While European concert music is produced in major U.S. concert halls, theaters, played by permanent resident orchestras in cities across the country, the authentic Classical Music of the U.S. has historically been marginalized, performed in the worst venues available. The conductor of the New York Philharmonic is paid 1.5 million dollars a year. This music is called "Legit," i.e., "Legitimate"; historically Afro-American music, by inference, is "Illegitimate." In the *New York Times* and *New Jersey Star Ledger,* there is a category called "Music," another called "Jazz"!

What is even more disingenuous, as it is dishonest, is that within the last decade or so there has been a distinct movement issuing crablike across the chauvinist U.S. superstructure to systematically distort the history and development of the Music, but also its class origins in the marginalization of this only recently recognized by Congress "American National Treasure." One main distortion made essentially by positing a simultaneous development in the white and black communities. Obviously chauvinist commentators, like Sudhalter, Collier, sickening with their disinformational denigration of Black creativity, seek to construct, at the same time, a completely ersatz metahistory for its actual evolution.

Collier's idiotic and bluntly racist attacks on Duke Ellington, claiming, as the New Orleans Rhythm Kings, that Ellington's music is just an imitation of European concert music, flies in the face of astute European commentators like Ernest Ansermet, Ravel, Stravinsky, Horowitz. Likewise, the testimonials of even American popular artists like Bix Beiderbecke, Frank Sinatra, Bing Crosby, etc.

Obscenities like Collier's racism confirm and pipsqueak some continued legitimization of the general historic American chauvinism toward Black Music, including an earlier travesty such as the American Pulitzer Prize committee's refusal to award Duke Ellington that prize in 1967, even though their own group of judges named Duke to receive the Pulitzer! The bitter absurdity of all this white supremacy is that Afro-American music is in its total possession by the American people, American Classical Music!

People like George Gershwin, who literally learned at the feet and elbows of Willie "the Lion" Smith, James P. Johnson, and Fats Waller, could be named Great Composers and live sumptuously, while his teachers always struggled for recognition, even survival! Gershwin's internationally acclaimed masterpiece *Rhapsody in Blue* is clearly a skillful recombining of essential elements of James P.'s "Yamekraw Rhapsody," orchestrated by William Grant Still, performed at Carnegie Hall in 1927, with Fats Waller as soloist!

Johnson himself was an awesome composer of extended works, at least two symphonies, *Harlem Symphony* (1934) and *Symphony in Brown* (1935). Operas, one of which, *The Organizer* (1940, with libretto by Langston Hughes), was performed, like "Yamekraw," exactly once, at Carnegie Hall! Duke's extended work *Jump for Joy* was performed, to my knowledge, about the same number of times. While Gershwin's estimable "adaptation" of these composers' works is given grand presence as an American Classic! Or consider for a split-second, in contrast to any of the great Afro-American composers, the awesome tribute and major repertory status given to Gershwin's *Porgy and Bess,* a work derived directly from and shaped by Afro-American life and culture.

The arrogant cultural and musical "autonomy" that American critics bestowed upon Gershwin and the work was so aggressively and subjectively chauvinist that it even caused Ellington, usually a consummate diplomat about these things, to express his irritation openly at such haughty white nationalism.

Yet, to be bluntly precise, just as the history of European "Classical" music would not be essentially changed by the exclusion of the many non-European artists who have contributed to it, by the same measure Afro-American music, which is the Soul of what must be regarded as American Classical music, would not be changed if not a single white artist's contributions were included. And, face it, this analysis is not black chauvinism but, like they say, hard fact!

One important development and change in the U.S. since my earlier article is that where I saw, as principal, the contradictory relationship between Black Music, its creators, on one hand and the White Critical establishment on the other, today it should be more and more obvious that that contradiction, still at times antagonistic, is, at base, the contradiction of class and class "stance," distance and alienation, which exist generally in bourgeois society and are no less clearly perceivable in the context of this relationship between "critic" and creator. Even though this contradiction is still most obviously visible as "Black versus White."

That is, there has been, since the late '50s, a very visible and impacting increase in the size and influence of the Black petty bourgeois (middle class). This has been caused directly by the political-social upsurge of the period, of the Civil Rights–Black Liberation Movement or more precisely what substantive changes occurred because of the interlocking force of the twined Afro-American national movements for Democracy and Self-Determination, one aspect loosely labeled "integrationist," the other "separatist." (The essentially anti-imperialist antiwar movement should also be factored into this analysis.)

Ironically, but predictable scientifically, this development has created a much larger "gap" between the burgeoning, but still mustard seed sized, recently emerging Black petty bourgeoisie and the great majority of Afro-Americans with considerably more distance between the black majority and the so-called "neocon" (neoconservative) Negroes, now hoisted into profitable visibility with attendant official "Hoorahs" as a fallacious display of American "democracy."

This has meant that more and more we see "well-placed" Negroes co-signing the most backward ideas of the U.S. rulers. The most bizarre for instances, the "three blind mice," the Colon, the Skeeza, and Tom Ass, at the top of Bush-2's junta. They have been made seemingly ubiquitous by the power of relentless duplicity. At American Express, Newsweek, across the media, as film stars, etc.

In the field of Jazz commentary, we have Stanley Crouch, Albert Murray, who have taken up many of the reactionary, even white-chauvinist, ideas of the racist U.S. superstructure and its critical establishment. A few years ago, at a midwestern seminar headed by Dave Baker, Crouch, in a discussion on intellectual contributions to the Music, and in response to this writer's statement that it should obvious that it has been Black people who have contributed the fundamental and essential intellectual innovations to the music, spontaneously ejaculated, that "Black people have not contributed . . . " Breaking the statement off in mid-ugly, apparently shocking even himself, at the ignorance of his intended comment. Especially, I would imagine, in the face of several scowling "Bloods," most of them prominent musicians, including Muhal Abrams, who commented immediately on the tail of my repeated requests for Stanley to finish his thought!

Crouch also wrote more recently in the *New York Times* that Black musicians didn't like George Gershwin because he was a better composer than all of them (except Duke). It should be clear to most folks with any clarity that both statements are false and reek of the national (racial) foolishness that characterizes white supremacy. And this from a "Negro" (as Crouch, with objective accuracy, prefers to be called)!

What it means is that the creators and artist-guardians of American Classical music must create, as part of a revolutionary democratic movement, an alternative superstructure, i.e., institutions, organizations, venues, critical journals, in order to rescue its history, socioeconomic productiveness and potential, and even artistic strength and free them and themselves from dependence on the socially exploitative and artistically diluting mechanisms of corporate commercialism and its attendant racism.

There is a howling need for more independent journals, performance circuits, educational institutions, whose form and content relate directly to the artists, the history, and the socio-economic and political needs of the masses of Afro-American people and to the whole of the U.S. majority itself.

The title *Ken Burns Jazz* is disheartening up front. Whether there is an apostrophe or not! It's always gratifying to see tapes and cuts of the musicians and hear some of the music. But it is maddening, in the extreme, not to hear them speak for themselves!

For all the petty jealousy that Wynton Marsalis elicits behind his Lincoln Center visibility, even from otherwise knowledgeable people, Wynton was the single saving element to the series. Without him it would have consisted of almost random images and largely superficial injections by Burns's obligatory clutch of "ultimate" critics, "scholars," "Gee Whiz"-ologists and now a smaller group of Negro autodidacts, Crouch the most prominent, but also a Negro "Gee Whiz"-ologist, Gerald Early, who was an embarrassing tourist of very limited relevance to any serious discussion!

At one point, Crouch referred to the musicians in Ellington's great orchestra as "knuckleheads"! You mean Hodges, Gonsalves, Webster, Carney, Tizol, Cootie, Tricky Sam, Blanton, Strayhorn . . . etc.? What kind of thoughtful analysis could come from such contempt? But such is one of the seamier products of the vaunted "social equality" of the fake "post–civil rights era." But in addition to this direct class-deformed commentary, a more subtly obvious ignorance and dismissal character- ized the series as "white critic, black musician apartheid."

From the top, Burns said he knew nothing about the music! Then how did he get to do a series? I wonder if the producers would allow some similarly self-described "Non" to do such a series on European classical music? Please!

But this similar "Gee Whiz!" essentially nonintellectual attitude and method has always been allowed in what passes as serious commentary on the music because of the predominance of Afro-American artists. It is a ruthless paternalism! This is one reason I support Marsalis's work of, to some extent, archiving the music at Lincoln Center. By re-presenting the music's classics in repertory, a consolidating stability and status is accorded to it, not seen before. Just as Lincoln Center does its annual "Mostly Mozart," we should be gratified to see something like a "Mostly Monk" repertory established. Even if Marsalis's orches- tra is sometimes not fully up to the task of, say, reincarnating Duke Ellington, but could Bernstein improvise like Herr Beethoven?

The essence of Burns's piece is the implied ideological dictum that the collective "brain trust" Burns gathered, largely white, mainly "unhip," is the paradigm for the intellectual source for any lasting analysis and measure of this music and that is the deepest content of its vulgar chau- vinist presumptions.

This accounts for the general absence of any impressive philosophical analysis of the music itself and, except for Marsalis, scant discussion of its changing genres as music as art or social expression!

What the music means, at a given period, as aesthetic, social, and philosophical expression. Why it moved from one genre or style to another. Why the abiding classical elements of its constantly reconfigured continuum?

Often specific musicians were characterized by raconteurish gossip or cliched retellings of flaws in their personal lives. Sidney Bechet described as "a thug." The drawn-out docudrama of Bird's drug addiction, likewise Billie Holiday, without a similar depth of musical, aesthetic, and philosophical analysis of their music. Nor was there a historical overview of these constantly developing factors intrinsic to the music.

Just serious interviews with a representative group of the great musicians still around would have offered a much more profound composite and intellectual and social access to this still unplumbed cultural treasure chest of American culture and art. Far from opposing the interviewing of critics, scholars, writers, club owners, the greater and more informed inclusion of the artists themselves (not just contemporarily but from existing archives) would have provided a much more incisive, scholarly, and entertaining document to inform the ages.

Before saying "Later!" I would add that like Fred Douglass, after he whipped on the "white church" in his majestic "Fourth of July" speech and so had to make some slight qualification, if my analysis of "white critics" seems inaccurately sweeping, I should point out that at root it is aimed at "the establishment" of what passes and has passed, for over a century, as "Jazz Criticism."

I say this because of some of the young critics I met when I first came to New York, Dick Hadlock (whom I worked for at the Record Changer), the always penetrating Martin Williams (though we had a running argument about whether Billie Holiday sang the Blues or not). Others, like Larry Gushee, Dan Morgenstern (once he began to dig that the music did not stop after Duke Ellington, if he ever really believed that), my man John Sinclair, the mixed-up Frank Kofsky, I have always had respect for, whether we totally agreed or not.

Still other "white critics" like the great Sidney Finklestein were immense contributors to what storehouse of scientific discourse there is about this music. I could add the redoubtable Stanley Dance, Ellington's shadow, not a deep thinker (but European analysis of the music for a long time was always more objective and scientific), the anthropologist Herskovits. There were even some dudes we will always jump on we learned something from (I won't even mention Nat Hentoff till he returns from the land of liberal social-equilibrium). Suffice it to say, there is That and there is Them. I know the difference.

But just to add some reminder of the kind of stilted hollowness most commentary on the music resembles, recently there was an article in the *New Jersey Star Ledger,* which some of us call the *Star Liar,* by writer George Kanzler (How are you spelling that?). In claiming to list the musicians coming out of and associated with Newark and environs, he left out the following:

SALOME BEY, lead singer with Andy (Bey) and the Bey Sisters; JACKIE BLAND, leader of the legendary teenage BeBop orchestra out of which came Wayne Shorter, Grachan Moncur III, Harold Van Pelt, Hugh Brodey, Walter Davis, "Humphrey" the BeBopper's BeBopper, Blakey's pianist for years; EDDIE GLADDEN, Dexter Gordon's regular drummer; VICTOR JONES, Getz's regular drummer, the last years; HAROLD MITCHELL, who played with Willie the Lion, Basie, Lionel Hampton, Gillespie's Big Band; NAT PHIPPS, leader of the other wonderful '50s teenage orchestra, which featured Nat and Billy Phipps, Moncur III, Ed Station, Wayne (and Alan) Shorter, Ed Lightsey; DANNY QUEBEC, one of the earliest Bop saxists, also with Babs Gonzalez, Tadd Dameron, J.J. Johnson in Babs's classic 3 BIPS & A BOP; Lawrence Killian, longtime hand drum master; SCOTT LAFARO, Ornette Coleman's bassist; LARUE, an unsung master piano teacher to Newark musicians, ask Moncur, Gladden, Morgan, etc.; FREDDIE ROACH, one of Newark's organ funk-masters, along with Larry Young, etc.; CHRIS WHITE, one of Cecil Taylor's early stalwarts. Also absent: the entire Newark Phipps family—Harold, Ernie, drums; Gene, Nat, piano; Billy, Gene Jr., and the rest well-known saxophonists; Robert Banks, piano; Herbie Morgan, tenor and reeds; Jimmy Anderson, tenor; Ed Lightsey, bass; Bradford Hays, tenor; Steve Colson, piano; Ronnell Bey, vocal; Chink Wing, drums; Chops Jones, bass; Rudy Walker, drums; Pancho Diggs, orchestra leader, piano; Rasheema, vocal; Eddie Crawford, drums, piano, orchestra leader; Santi DiBriano, drums; Pat Tandy, vocal; Charyn Moffett, trumpet; Hugh Brodey, saxophone; Eli Yamin, piano; Gloria Coleman, vocal; Bernie James, sax; Ed Station, trumpet; Art Williams, bass, club owner, "The Cellar"; Shad Royful, orchestra leader, piano; Harold Van Pelt, tenor; Geri Allen, piano; Wilber Morris, bass; Connie Pitts Speed, piano, vocal; Gene Goldston, vocal; Everett Laws, vocals; Warren Smith, drums.

Longtime Area Residents: RAY BROWN, DIZZY GILLESPIE, DONALD BYRD.

Recent Residents: David Murray, tenor; Reggie Workman, bass; Oliver Lake, alto, reeds; Andrew Cyrille, drums; Steve Turre, trombone.

So thirty years later . . . you dig?

5/7/01

CHAPTER 23

Random Notes on the Last Decade

Besides *Fo Deuk*, DAVID MURRAY has *For Trane, Gwo-ka, Creole, Pushkin*, a string of important CDs. Murray remains a principal creative force in the music.

CRAIG HARRIS's *Souls within the Veil* is a wonderful emotional sounding of the DuBois classic *The Souls of Black Folk*.

The album *Cause & Effect* by ABRAHAM BURTON AND ERIC MC-PHERSON is, hands down, one of the most dramatic, intelligent, deeply moving CDs I've heard in the last ten years! These two young men (and the others on the album) are two of the most intensely creative artists on the set today!!

D.D. JACKSON is one of the premier "Ticklers" you need to dig today. Check *For Now*, his solo debut, and *Suite for New York*, an extended large-ensemble instrumental and vocal work as somber yet surprising as the city itself. *Anthem* is the kind of flippant small group happy virtuoso piano sound D.D. does. Jackson, Vijay Iyer, and Rodney Kendrick are three of the most important "Ticklers" working today, coming from three very different directions. Iyer, a harmonic explorer of the music in deeply satisfying consciousness altering modes. Vijay brings the sound of his Indian background fully into play, in a wonderful cross-seasoning of funkishly thoughtful reflection.

RODNEY KENDRICK came on like a house afire a few years ago. A journeyman who has played with Abbey Lincoln and James Brown,

Kendrick raises Monk in his own sweet way in *Last Chance for Common Sense*, but we hear an excellent and exciting pianist.

The tragedy of Blue Note sitting on ANDREW HILL'S great works, e.g., *Time Lines, Passing Ships*, for nearly thirty years! Demonstrates one again how reactionary institutions can penalize artists if they think what the artists are doing in their private lives is not in tune with the corporation's ideological vision.

In this case, Hill was music coordinator of the Black Arts Repertory Theater School in Harlem, in 1965, which I directed. Hill's "crime" (and the rest of ours) was that he brought Trane, Ayler, Sun Ra, Moncur, Tolliver, Jackie Mc, etc., etc., to Harlem to play in playgrounds, housing projects, parks, vacant lots, along with four other trucks we sent out Summer of '65, carrying Poetry, Drama, Graphic Arts, Dance into the Harlem Community (before Jazzmobile!).

So a couple years after Blue Note feels the onus of Hill's "violation" of sub rosa institutional racism can be voided, his great CDs are released and he is given acclaim he should have gotten forty years ago, a "minute" before he dies of cancer.

I must mention OLU DARA, the great multiaxed trumpet, guitar, blues-singing hypnologist. His record *In the World*, with Olu singing on every track and playing guitar and trumpet (and on one wonderful track juiced by his celebrated Rapper son, Nas) with a chorus of sisters extending, Amen-ing, and providing some righteous harmonies, is one of the gems of this period.

Hail again STEVIE WONDER on *At the Close of a Century*. The grand lyrical funk master's anthology of Wonder full gifts to the planet.

One of the finest experiences we've had was MCCOY TYNER'S great show at the Iridium with Pharoah Sanders and Ravi Coltrane. It was, like they say, "The Joint!" McCoy and Pharoah, all serious diggers by now should know, are grand artists of the highest magnitude!

Just last weekend a great group led by young pianist MARK CAREY with ABRAHAM BURTON (Sameer Gupta, Wiggins) brought some new configurations of the hardest swing. Sometime in the midst of this fusion-cool guitar-furniture music, cliché-ridden era you can disremember what the hard stuff be. Dudes like this can bring it back!

PART TWO

Great Musicians

CHAPTER 24

Panthalassa

Miles Davis

Miles was among the most mercurial of recent jazz masters. His music, a constantly shifting expression of his whole self, though the "persona," what was projected to his international audiences, might seem less so, in that he was not so easily understood, i.e., what he felt and how he presented it, as a person. The music is somewhat skewed in this sense . . . he could play, would play, whatever he wanted to. Always with that provocative "Me-ness" that allows us to identify his playing instantly.

Not many who have actually listened to Miles through the years would deny his exquisite mastery of his instrumental voice, so distinct and personal, nor should they dispute the fact that for fifty years Miles Davis was one constant source of emotional and intellectual revelation through his music.

Longtime diggers might contradict each other about "which Miles" they preferred . . . what were the masterpieces, the near misses, the placebos. Any discussion about Miles's personal life will be loud with disagreement, but about the music there will be a much more universal acknowledgment, even without including the "Gee Whiz" group of superficial name pushers.

Early Miles, with Bird, still halfway playing Diz, in that altar-boy musical relationship to the "Holy Family" of BeBop, where he learned and began to find his own voice. Inventive and psychologically wired to the whole mad spectrum of Americana, from the outside looking in, or

as a self-proclaimed outsider, inside *being* "out"—Miles wanted always
to be what he thought, what he perceived as "what it was."

The motion away from Bird was not just the result of Bird's "yard-
ness," which could sometimes be extreme. Peeing in the phone booth of
some swank North Chicago nightery, using the band's bread to feed the
Gorilla which accompanied him, rather than pay his musicians. Many
of us know the real or the mythological Ornithology.

But there was also another musical, i.e., aesthetic, expression Miles
carried puffing itself larger inside him. He told me once, "Bird was playing too fast. It was all over too quick. I needed some kind of bottom."
Miles wanted a "place" to stand and be Miles, himself, as he registered
that totally. Not just be a hip companion in the ultra zoom of Charlie
Parker.

Next stop, *The Birth of the Cool,* with its expanded orchestration
and "cool" ensemble textures, showed Miles in another "place." He
spoke of trying to create a "soft . . . unpenetrating" sound. As well, he
brought the feel of contemporary dissonance and contrapuntal motion
to this music (as Duke had earlier), with some of the freshest young
composers and arrangers on the scene. Bud Powell, John Lewis, Denzil
Best, George Wallington among the more established, and some of the
newest white musicians, composers, and arrangers, Gil Evans, Gerry
Mulligan, John Carisi. This album was also the first shot in what the
young West Coast, mostly white, musicians carried on as "the Cool
School."

Miles, the son of an East St. Louis dentist and gentleman farmer, who
had come to New York to go to Julliard, but actually "Looking for Bird"!
We know BeBop wasted Julliard—at least in that initial confrontation.
But by *Cool,* you can hear the resonance of Julliard or the "non-jazz"
presence in his conception. (That record *Conception* with Lee Konitz,
for instance.) The personnel and music of "Venus DeMilo," "Budo,"
"Godchild," "Boplicity," "Darn That Dream," "Israel," "Move," are
striking and fresh.

It is so weird that from time to time infidels have pictured Miles as
"antiwhite," probably because of his killer stance on racism, but quite
the contrary, almost from the beginning, Miles blew in "mixed company." First, because in the early Bop context, the jams and blowing
sessions and many of the groups playing the "new music" were socially,
aesthetically, and psychologically "open," particularly in contrast to
the earlier, more segregated, U.S. social conditions in which the music
had to be made. Plus, the young Getzes, Mulligans, Konitzes, Sims,

etc., were *actually hip*, not the recently manufactured icons of commercial fakery.

Miles was reaching for that deeply "American" resonance, perhaps the placement of his sensibility according to the parameters of an essentially "middle-class" rationale of his sensual perception of "what it was," from the funk to the blues to his own lyrical recycling of them. The music Miles made with Gil Evans seems a rather deeper and more thoughtful "American" music, in the fullest sense of that. *Porgy and Bess, Sketches of Spain,* etc. The Bill Evans chordal austerity (Miles actually using a scale, in a modal sense) on *Kind of Blue* is a miraculous mix of blues and the *contemplation* of it.

The classic jazz of the Philly Joe, Red Garland, Paul Chambers, . . . Trane, Cannonball groups are expressions of the "Blackest" Miles, that marvelous use of the "hard bop" motif to give his own lyrical persona a dynamically percussive context in which to fly. To me, these are the funkiest, the bluest Miles. Yet even in these sides the projection of the music called Fusion is shot out of Cannonball, a simplified blues line consistent with Miles's penchant for pop ballads, e.g., "Someday My Prince Will Come," "If I Were a Bell," "It Never Entered My Mind," etc.

Miles is the great alchemist of popular American music, transforming it by his own organic relationship to that part of America which ain't never really got in it! His personal antics reflect this self-conscious desire to be "outside" even while, in some ways, being an insider (except he *was* Black). Something like the rebellion of the American middle class.

Miles now moves into a modified, perhaps more formally oriented version of this classic music, with the Herbie Hancock, Wayne Shorter, Ron Carter, Tony Williams groups. He also begins to move into a more pop-based modal otherness, with clear aspects of the later sharper departures into the world of "backbeat" and electronic atmospherics. While capable of really stirring music as a group and individually, all these musicians following Miles's lead move like Cannonball to the "Dis Heah" and "Dat Dere," "Jive Samba," where, with another Miles alumnus, Joe Zawinul, they created the chart-topping Fusion and, for Zawinul and Shorter, got to the commercially astute vehicle that *Weather Report* became. The paradigm for what Miles had created, an R&B funky bottom with a Cool pop top.

Fusion can be seen as a logical motion of Miles's American pop-connected aesthetic, as his solo voice, atop, within, beneath, any rhythm clearly shows, as well as his choice of materials. Though two of the tunes on this album, "He Loved Him Madly" and "Get Up with It," are dedicated to Duke Ellington, I can think of very few of Duke's tunes that Miles did. But like Billie Holiday or Ella Fitzgerald, Miles could transform otherwise banal pop music into American classical music.

In the '70s, Miles's titles did reflect the will to social transformation, Black and African Consciousness that emerged during the '60s, "Mr. Freedom X," "Red China Blues," and, when Mtume was playing hand drums in the band, "Calypso Frelimo," "Maiysha," "Zimbabwe," but with the same "dualism" that always characterized his music.

Alongside the perception of political and social upsurge, Miles also carried the impact of the Flower Children, Hippie, Fillmore tip, like the coexistent presence it was during the period, the less strident "peace" ethic of the bohemian, beat, hippie cute reformism of the loyal opposition. Miles's near-reverence for Jimi Hendrix, like his later extolling of the "Ex-Prince," and his concomitant social and musical decision bear this out.

Miles always had the deep ultra-appreciation for the "good life," as a normal psychological persistence of his class. The dope, street, pimp, near-gangster persona served to muffle this, but it was always quite evident. The night Miles called one of his oldest dearest friends to say, "Hey, Jimi Hendrix gets $30,000 a gig," was more like a farewell to one stage of himself than just awed information. After this, Miles told his agents he didn't want to be listed with the Jazz players. He felt he could do what he wanted musically, and it would still be hip. AND he could get paid!

From *Bitches Brew*, which was the biggest commercial success Miles had, his movement away from classic BeBop was obvious. We should be clear about this—that Miles, as a solo voice, remained near himself until the end. And despite the electric or R&B context which "purists" and traditionalists dismiss, Miles was still making a very Milesian music, in the "elsewhere" of his solos.

This record is very representative of Miles, from "Bitches Brew," a brew indeed, mixing pop musings, wildly contrasting rhythmic bottoms, electronic serial sound (a la Varese, Cage, etc.), and the fragmented sound placement of Webern . . . What? From there, Miles stepped off into "the other world." The first part of this record is outtakes of "In a Silent Way," Miles's sensuous subdued lyric voice maneuvering adeptly among the "ambient sound." The repeated vamp a repeated emphasis that some critics called "non-Western."

All the music is connected in segue, as if we are drifting with the whimsical darting of Miles's musical consciousness. The various textures of electronic instrument and sound, with the synthesizer stitching broad fields of romantic color/mood. "In a Silent Way," Miles said, "about time." As if 1969 characterized Miles's self-conscious movement in himself away from the Bop, Hard Bop paradigm he himself helped create. But it was all there, where he picked them up, all the elements of his later music, it is the interpretation that makes it specifically Miles.

Agartha uses a frenetic Indian tabla presence at bottom, referencing a few years back when Ravi Shankar got large in the West. Part of the impact of the period when the East was "transported" (again) to the West, in various ways. From Trane's worshipful mediations and Sun Ra's visionary excursions, as well as Miles's and his musical cadre's use in their versions of the newly emerging fusion that Miles is the creator of, come full out, for instance, with something like the Mahavishnu Orchestra.

Miles uses the tabla rhythmically and harmonically, as propulsion for a zoom tempo and battery, a fusion-rock base, at times it is almost a melodic line in its rushes and breaks and centering of the music. You can see that in all this music Miles felt that he could combine the outest of outness with the solid funk of R&B/Rock and achieve a synthesis that would allow him to stretch yet be easily accessible to the popular sensibility. "On the Block" makes reference to this focus on Afro-American popular music, R&B, conditioned with the miracles of electronics, the abstractness of the "serious electronic" musicians (not only Europeans but Jimi Hendrix, etc.) to cast a new spell. What was not fully commercial when Miles initially produced it in the mid-'60s and '70s, before he went into a semi-retirement, was by time he came out almost de rigeur for the rock-fusion that he spun into being. Miles was not totally succumbing to commercialism, he thought he had created a place he had customized to be himself, and "what it was."

All of him is carried with him to this new place, though sometimes we are distracted by what we want to hear from Miles, and so cannot fully hear what he is actually doing. *Black Satin, On the Corner, Agartha,* in long segue, tabla, the "otherworldly" ambient sound. Themes rising and leaving. Miles himself with the horn sounds like the "sci fi" sounds like guilty bystanders wrapping themselves around him.

As he moves, Sonny Fortune, for one, appears to let us know of another depth that can move through the Davis concept like the sun from behind a cloud. Clear, emotional, hopeful. And then from underneath, the wah wahs and sound lasers, which Miles uses as both rhythm and harmonic trope, even a melodic dimension as it slides in and out securing the otherness of his trumpet voice. Though he *becomes* a wah wah, as the rhythm reaches into the very shape of the melodic repetition.

The electric guitar and fender bass mark this music. Whether in heavy rhythmic emphasis or legato asides. The repeated theme out of which comes another theme, or it seems another until we realize it is the same theme stated another way. Often the R&B rhythm under the still sustained synthesizer. The synthesizer became Miles's main "color," suspense, suspension, exaggeration, strangeness. Again like sci fi music, but suddenly the straight-out R&B, the tabla back under like a rocket ship. He is "on the one," like the musicians say, wrapped up in the back beat, but it is a much more complicated "one" than many would give him credit for.

Miles could also lay something like "Rated X" or "Billy Preston." Like a laid-back, cool march or exaggerated step, a plastic step. With a drifting dreamy bottom via the sustained synthesizer following the theme underwater. He comes with mute, or wah wahed, in echo, himself the synthesizer, like an oddly bizarre ballroom with the room itself shifting and drifting, headed away like a dream.

Miles also used the organ, e.g., "Billy Preston," to give the neighborhood organ trio (referencing Duke's tribute and use of Wild Bill Davidson on *Deep South Suite*) to transform that ubiquitous ghetto bar feature into a Dali helicopter with a pipe organ propeller. Plus, dig, when we used to "grind" in my teenage 1950s to Jimmy Forrest's "Night Train," none of us knew it was from Duke's *Deep South Suite*. Duke's profound *funk* (likewise on *Afro Asian Ellipse* and *Far East Suite*), those examples of a funk deeper than the backbeat. Miles is after this combining as well.

For all the talk about Miles going commercial, no one can tell me there is not some worthwhile music on this disk, and there should be no mistaking pieces like "Tutu," "D Train," "Human Feeling," among others—it is Miles, like it or not, still trying to get a freshness or newness, despite the wires. I cannot say that all the electronic Miles is immortal, but it is still a body of work that cannot be dismissed. Like you didn't dig Beethoven's 8th? Remember the 7th? (You better get ready for the 9th!) Just as it would be foolish and philistine to dismiss Herr Ludwig on the basis of a small section of his work, likewise with Herr Dewey. (Though I repeat one phrase from the eulogy I read at Miles's funeral, "Let us all always be able to hear 'Straight No Chaser' anytime we want to.")

All that to say, this record is a piece of Miles that is old, new, borrowed and blue, in his wedding with "the one," the straight-out funk. Though often, it seems a funk invoking (certainly, inspiring) Rock as much as R&B. But you can't dismiss this music. The synthesizers. The Rock. The aural gimmickry. A lot of it still as slickly perverse and thoughtful as Miles himself, as is much of his music.

Actually, I still believe (see *Black Music*, "The Changing Same") that that which is still evolving will be a music that absorbs the entire spectrum of Afro-American, American, Pan-American, Pan-African, and International music and still simplifies this complexity into the *Djeli ya* itself. Not the mostly commercial, so-called "world music," but something that grabs you and bounces you around in ear-blinding revelation. Miles heard something, and some of it we can hear.

6/97

CHAPTER 25

When Miles Split!

Someone called me and said you died, Miles. Yeh, that cold. Here in North America, with all the other bullshit we put up with. You know. I know you know. Knew. And still know, where ever you is.

I'm one of yr children, actually, for all the smoke and ignorant mimmy jimmies . . . you know / I can say that. I was one of yr children / you got a buncha children man, more than you probably dug on the serious side. Not innocent ass fans. But the school of the world you created from inside the world's head. You gotta buncha children brother. I still am. Will be. In some important ways. For instance, I will never take no shit. Yr legacy. I will never believe anybody can tell me shit. Unless they are something I can feel. Like Aretha said. Something I can feel. You were that. I cd feel you, I cd be you when I was a little boy, up the street with the trumpet bag. I wanted to be in that music. I wanted to be that hip, that out, that whatever it was I felt you were. I wanted to be that. All my life.

What it was was the place and the time. But it was you describing it with your feeling. For me that place was Newark, where we grew, and then here you come so hip. I cd dig that I needed to be that, but more I knew, I was that. I was with you in that fingering, that slick turn and hang of the whole self and horn. And the sound. I had never been in that place, there wasn't no such place in Newark, before.

I mean I never thought of the shit you made me think with *Godchild*. I never thought of nothing before like *Venus De Milo*. There was nothing in my life like that before you brother. And then the persona, what it all spelled. Yeh, I wanted to look like that. That green shirt and rolled up sleeves on Milestones. That cap and seersucker on *Dig* I always wanted to look like that. And be able to play *Green Dolphin Street* or *Autumn Leaves* or *Walkin* or *Blue Haze* or *Round bout Midnight*, or yeh yeh yeh yeh hey, even the mammy jammin *Surrey with the Fringe on Top*, as whatever he wanted, as tiny lyric, or cooler than thou, hot pointillist funk-mares, cubist, expressionist, impressionist, inhabiting yr being into a plane of omniscient downness (dig that!)

It was the self of us all the way without anything but our saying, our breath, night times, or walking where we was. We could be whole and separate from any dumb shit. We could be the masters, the artist, the diggenist knowers, the suave, the new, the masters.

This is what art doos. Your voice, that out sharp growl. That was how art should dig itself to be talking. *So What* is probably a prayer in the future.

I held my horn like that, and rolled my body like an ark of music, just looking at things. The cool placement of emotion. The information. I carried that consciously. No one could put me down, I was Miles child. His man. somehow. anyway.

And then each change, stage, was a path I wd walk. When I heard you as a little boy. Then went to see you. You was me alright. You was one of the few I could let be me.

Now some motherfucker wannta tell me you outta here. No. No. Miles. Why? You left? So right away I figure none of the shit still here is cool. But dig, Dizzy and Max is still here. So that's the pain. And I know I dig you. I know I carry *Dr. Jackle* in my speech. And *Godchild* and *Miles Ahead* and *Kinda Blue* and even Porgy and Bess, somethin Gershwin can't do.

Cause no one was that tender, that touching the where touch cd ultimately is.

They taking all the Giants. You. Trane. Duke. Monk. Billie. Your whole band is dead, man. Paul. Philly Joe. Cannonball. John. Red. Your whole band. and what does that do to us, but leave us on the shore watching the waves, and trying to write music from that regular funk.

But what it says is that our youth is gone. That we are the adult. What that? That you have it in yr hand now, to do. That if it will go, this life, this memory and history, this desire for freedom and a world family. That's it's on you.

Like I dug, when Philly Joe hatted up. On us. If we are the ones. If it is to be, something other than the savages and bush mens. Then we got to. The giants. Our fathers and mothers. Sassy split last year. Monk. Count. LTD. If it is to go then we are the goers. The comers. In that whole sound and thought. That life that makes the blues. That makes the dark hip, the roll and rumble. Yeh. Then if, all that long two hundred centuries of slick, is to be on bein. Then we are the only carriers.

I cd dig the way you walked and held that horn. That gorgeous chilling sweet sound. That's the music you wanted playing when you was coming in a joint or just lookin up at the sky w/yr baby by yo side. That mixture of America and Remerica and them Changes, them blue Africa magic chants. So I am a carrier. I got the stick. I aint stopping. If you, whoever else you tapped, then them too.

Headline the Giants are murdered. Then we got it. All of those who finally must dig, dont say it brother, truth and beauty. But who am I talkin to if you split, Miles, Man, and what the fuck is there to listen to.

Except you did leave jabillion ultra hip notes, 70 billion swift blue cool phrases. And how many millions of unheard dig'its, them nasty silences right in the middle of the shit. Bee-bee beep beeppp, ba dee da dee da . . .

So what about it, like they say in the tradition, what about it, is Miles and them, John, Duke, Monk, Sassy all, the giants, does it mean our shit is over with? I know about the records and shit. I'm not talking about that. Does it mean, with the crazies vampin and now even some things look like regular niggers can break out with bushy tongues. Where before with your cool Boplicity in our heads it was somehow not only soft yet gentle but like a weapon against such square shit as most of the rest of America is. That all of you giant figures that we emulate and listen to and hear and visualize night after night inside our heads, from the nightclubs, the concert halls, the bars, the records, the t.v. . . . is this, your death, like some hideous omen of our own demise, and I mean everybody here, not just niggers, cause if we go, this whole playhouse go up in smoke.

No I mean either this death is the beginning of death in cut time, or it means that one earth has turned and another begun. One age, one era, one being. Listening to you now, and knowing that whole of change you went through, from life to life, from music to music, from revelation to revelation, even evolution can be dissolution or devolution.

But you was Bop when you got here, flying w/ the human headed soul Ba, Bird, the doped up revolutionary. Next, you was Cool. It was like your own creation yet, of course, very Presidential. Then you got with Philly and them for the harder Bop and then got Ball, the Dis Heah and Dat Dere of we funky story. Then you sic'ed the straight out vision monster on us Trane, in that perfect wonderful all time classical hydrogen bomb and switch blade band. Let us all always be able to hear *Straight, No Chaser* anytime we want to.

I know the last few years I heard you and saw you dressed up all purple and shit, it did scare me. All that loud ass rock and roll I wasnt into most of it, but look brother I heard *Tutu* and *Human Nature* and *D Train*. I heard you one night behind the Apollo for Q, and you was bashin like the you we knew, when you used to stand coiled like a blue note and play everything the world meant, and be in charge of the shit too. I'll always remember you like that Miles. And yr million children will too. With that messed up poppa stoppa voice, I know you looken up right now and say (growl) So What?

The next evening, 9/29/91

CHAPTER 26

David Murray, *Ming's Samba*

Portrait/CBS, 1988, Portrait 44432.
David Murray (tenor sax, bass clarinet), John Hicks (piano),
Ray Drummond (bass), Ed Blackwell (drums)

Some years ago I wrote, "Albert Ayler is the dynamite sound of our
time." Now, I think, that can be said about David Murray. Not because
he comes out of "Albert's Bag," whatsom ever that is, but that David
is the high fire of this time's sense expansion. To be further than "the
given" as far as this horn, this music, this line of feeling, yee must be
into David, oh yes!

This album is simply further confirmation (in the key of "Smoke!").
It is his sound, which begins *beneath* us, as an understanding of what
will bring the feeling. His skills, to make the point, that it is partially
about that, what rationale you can make of your perception, and how
that can be translated for Use! His spray of knife points of note, how
the technical can aid the emotional. Some of the things that Trane
did on "Nature Boy" and "Crescent" and some others, which I never
thought to hear again. The whirl of feeling erupting in multidirected
threads of tumbling fire. Yeh, David's into that—Dig "Samba" and
"Spoonin.'"

The statement of feeling as the whole *message* where self is telling,
choosing sides, as it were, arting, *art* means create, be, etc.

His intelligence, which is everywhere all the time, on display. His
selection, taste, the movement of the music he plays. His composition. Even his choice of Butch's, compositions and this tight smoking
quartet. John Hicks, a young master; Blackwell, an older master; and
Ray Drummond, who is a distinct and much sought-after voice always

found in the company of masters. All spell a heaviness that makes the feeling in the music keep moving in us, raising and lifting us, and answering questions we have even forgotten we asked!

What makes David combine so much and give so much, if we are here-ing, is, like Pres said, the story he tells. The content of this story is how the form, the articulation got that way. Form is part of content, an extension of it, Dualists. So that when we are jumped on by the heat of the blue rhythm and the blatant ambition of the hippest ducality, intellectual declaration and stance, when that all comes together as it does in Trane, Albert, Duke, Monk, Billie, it's all going and coming, the lines like lava jism. The seeds (stored visions—ideas) are genius babies of funk we make—call it jass. David Murray is always jassing. The music is ejaculation, which was Holy before we were mashed in the bottom of the boat headed West to be eaten by Ghost. Because it is about Creation, Art, the only God goodness acknowledges wholly. Bringing into being what was not!

I begin to understand that "modernism is an attitude," a way of thinking not tricks or opportunism or commerce—certainly not ignorance. The most sensitive always want to be in the way of everything life knows, and emotion, deep feeling, are the fundamental description of being as opposed to nothing.

David's modernism, his innovation and "newness" are because he knows in his actual feelings some precision of description about "what's happening." It's new, because the more sensitive, the deep feelers, now before others, in other words, they knew, and for you to know, you must embrace (K)new. Remember, Noah?

The music on the album is superb—funky, tender, aggressive, inspiring, blues smoked. David is alive and on fire with dynamic pulsing rhythms. This is the real number, hip and broad enough to reconnect jazz and blues and funky as an escaped nigger!

The music on this album is "evidence" to get Monkish. The title piece, after David's wife, is dance & image. Brazil, but a vehicle for dynamic improvisation. John's piano insists it's Sambo's Samba, from Brazil's early blue church. Blackwell mentions Africa so you don't forget. David's horn is narrator and the narrated.

Fats, the happy genius. A great pianist and musician, folklorist and dynamite sit-down comedian. Reflected here, in "Rememberin' Fats," as pushing pianistic steppin' boogie. David's "newness" on one hand is a restating of "the tradition" for these times.

The ballad "Nowhere" . . . is another of Butch Morris's gems. Nowhere is a real place, the composition and the creativity. The tenderness as memory peaceful traveling. Forever the everywhere of everything softly communicating! Tender, tender piano and sax ride. Breathless, breathy.

"Spoonin'" is very, very hip. The high-note blue New Orleans strut. We walks like this even without a plan! Usually in love with whatever part of life animates us so. The second line is all the time and Spookish. But the players are us too. Hicks embroidering the step with information. He is reporting. In the funk language. With a concerto depth, e.g., strutters, or are they marching? And there is a tango to it, the Latin tinge.

What will we see when we get where? What will we be? David asks and Asks. Predicts. But Sings Drama, i.e., Plays way higher than everyday prisoners or security gods can dig. The idea of this music breaking out suddenly at a Bush-Dukakis debate would be better than a lie detector test.

"Walter's Waltz" a song for his father. It is storyful, telling and listening. Learning and remembering. The bass clarinet of our waltz through before young till after old. 1-2-3 the three sides of the pyramid. Mama Blue. Papa Knew. Heat rhythm till funky is jazz. Art is the baby's name. And Baby is what we call our souls.

CHAPTER 27

David Murray, *Fo Deuk Revue*

Justin Time Records, Montreal, Canada, 1997, H4P, 1P7.
David Murray, tenor, bass clarinet; Doudou N'Diaye Rose, sabar, vocals; Positive Black Soul, vocals, rap; Didier Awali, rap; Oumar Mboup-Djembe, percussion; Hamet Maal, vocals; Tidiane Gaye, vocals; El Hadji Gniancou Semben (Dieuf Dieuf), keyboard; Abdou Karin Mane (Dieuf Dieuf), bass; Ousseynou Diop (Dieuf Dieuf), drums; Assane Diop (Dieuf Dieuf), guitar, xalam, percussion, backup vocals; Jamaaladeen Tacuma, bass; Hugh Ragin, trumpet; Robert Irving III, piano; Darryl Burger, drums; Craig Harris, trombone; Junior Soul, vocals; Amiri Baraka, poetry reading; Amiri Baraka Jr., rap vocal.

I admit I am on this record, along with one of my sons, Amiri Jr. Still, even without our contributions, or even if they had been done by others, the conception David Murray has projected to put this record together is impressive and the results powerful and innovative.

I wrote an essay in a book of mine a few years ago called "The Changing Same" in which I proposed that soon the most daring players would begin to use the whole of the music as basis for composition and improvisation. I meant that Black Music, internationally, is a treasure chest, from ancient traditional Africa, spread across the planet in its myriad diasporic expressions. I was not talking about the commercial superficially similar concept of "world music," which usually results in a pastiche of fusionlike profundity, i.e., "cheap furniture." I meant that the deepest and most lasting elements of the great music of the world created and planted worldwide by the Pan-African presence can be plumbed for ever new and fresh musical entities. What the fusion hucksters do is take the surfaces, the resemblances of both jazz and rhythm and blues, and slap together a commercial mood music that pulses like it is truly rhythmic. But rhythm is not just pulse, it is direction and connection. It is not just a hitting but a *wiring. It carries the current.*

David Murray begins his conception with the rhythm, and his playing has always been an excellent example of how rhythm is used as melodic and harmonic organization and direction. So this whole record depends on the deepness the broadness, the richness of its rhythmic insistence.

The combination of the Senegalese African traditional drummers, including the great Doudou N'Diaye Rose (composer of the Senegalese national anthem and revered throughout Africa), is a fundamental statement of where Murray is coming from and where he is taking us. In fact, *Fo Deuk* means "Where do you come from" in the Wolof language of Senegal.

The rich African bottom of the music is the fundamental sensuousness of the music, a rhythm that describes what is added to it, by carrying it as a whole presence. The djembe, dun dun, and the Sabar and other traditional percussion are joined by the Afro American "kit," a western industrial product, and they provide a bottom for each other, so that both percussion presences are on top and at the bottom, distributing emphasis as the music changes.

This is a truly innovative feature, to use the African and Afro-American bottoms as interchangeable song rhythms and funk vehicles. Likewise, Murray uses both African and Afro-American rappers. The Senegalese "Positive Black Soul," famous throughout Africa, rap in Wolof, and the sound of this alone is an intriguing timbral addition to the whole sensuous feeling of the music.

The Afro-American horns on the top are melodic and harmonic but also rhythmic cursors, sound events, coloring, and statement. Hugh Ragin and Craig Harris are just the kind of daring and technically advanced voices needed for this enterprise, swooping in and out sometimes, as well as air-sculpting the infectious heads of the tunes. David has created a music, advanced, yet melodic and breathlessly rhythm oriented.

The music on this album would be extremely popular in the U.S. if it were given the ink and air the commercial buccaneers give mountains of trash hourly. Blue Muse, Chant African, One World Family, Village Urbana (by Robert Irving) are works whose melodic grace alone would capture a broad audience. Yet David's concerns are perhaps troubling to the Bigs. Certainly, "Evidence," which springs out of the Goree Island experience, that both David and I (with my son, Ras) have confronted, which carries the still bleeding memory of the Slave Trade, is a theme some would eschew. Yet such denial merely prolongs the ignorant confusion that prevents the coming of the One World Family, on the real side.

The mixture of Wolof rap and Afro American rap is one aspect of the rich fabric of sound this music brings. David mixes the classic West African tenor of Titiane Gaye with the black American song form, so there is a broad palette of musical and emotional registrations ignited. The songs "One World Family" and "Too Many Hungry People" (a Robert Irving rap, recited by Amiri Jr., on loan from his group, "One Step Beyond") are topical and inspirational, but grooves with international relevance.

David has been touring with the Fo Deuk Revue, recently, New York City Central Park, D.C., Oakland, Seattle, San Diego, Chicago, and I fully expect the grapevine to make the side catch fire on the charts. The stirring funk provided by Jamaaladeen Tacuma is the constant flow of the one throughout everything. Tacuma is one of the freest of the fender funkers, but one of the steadiest in laying down the line. Even in his outest improvs, he never turns the line around or lets it lag or speed up.

David's playing remains one of the marvels of the music. He is, in the same solo, capable of rage, tenderness, thoughtfulness, and grace. Always inventive, always rhythmically oriented, hence swinging. This *Fo Deuk Revue* is a grand expression of his personal aesthetic, experimental but earthy and melodic. This side will be around, like something too good to be lost or covered for too long. It is one of the finest records to come out of anyone from anywhere, certainly in the last decade or so.

CHAPTER 28

David Murray,
Addenda to a Concert

What makes David, his music, his approach, so important to all of us is that he has stepped back as it were to gather all of the truest tradition of soul music to him, in him, and used that as a forward thrusting recoil like a jet to propel him into the newest regions of feeling. That is the key, to keep to the hot wire of deep funk trad, the rocking, the shocking, niggers with purple stockings, yet at the same time, and because of this to a degree, to be doing the truly fresh the truly new. Because the blackest tradition could never be wholly digested in the American mainstream because truth would kill this thing outright like a funky dog. So much truth. So much of the real. Like the milk would be cocoa or coffee or darkest night with only the smiles of slaves to light it if there was gonna be any light, if you couldn't see in the dark. Like the darkies.

The music is like that, makes you see in the dark, cause the dark be you first. Understand. Can you see in your self? See the mission and the magic. The way and the cross. The hope and the double cross. The music is like that. That's why they keep black culture and art out of the schools, our children would be too strong to handle. They are terrified of them now, black boys especially terrify them, turn them into murderers. Black girls challenge them, they have just recently found out a way to cool out some of their parents, they never discover a way to cool out the youth! Why? Because listen to David and you will hear the whole erupted landscape of our historical lives. All our ecstasy and the heap of dead pain, the weight of it like a growl, like a sudden greasy honk, like a blue moaning star leaning on an emptiness unable to pay your rent with its lonesome beauty. Because our art valorizes makes glorious and beautiful our lives. The lives of the slaves. How can you oppress Duke Ellington or Art Tatum—can you be believed if you want to say that Coltrane or Sun Ra are inferior? You must believe Tawana Brawley if you listen to Billie sing "Strange Fruit." You would know the weight of oppression you had to move and overcome when you hear "Black, Brown and Beige." You could not think of Larry Byrd as intelligent and Dr. J as only instinctive when you hear the World Saxophone Quartet. Louis Armstrong make an idiot savant get funky.

The art of the African (and we here are Africans, African Americans, that is our nationality, African heritage and American history) is very ancient. In that art is our whole . . . being. This is why it is called soul music. Soul like Sol the sun, the core of all life. Our jazz is our birth replication of this life, our ideological/psychological replication of our lives on this planet. Our lives as they are described, our needs laid out like notes on a page. These needs cannot become everyone's needs or they will be answered, the society altered the world changed thieves and murderers punished. Ignorance after a while would become obscure maladies of prehumans.

That's why we need the Davids, the Johns, the Eddies, the music in our schools, to reinforce the highest aspirations of our lives for our children every day. They would be intensely interested. They would not have to be dragged to school if they did not get drugged once they got to school or got sold drugs on the way to school. If they were hearing their own lives, reading of their own history, their own escapes and triumphs, if it was their own experience reinforced, they would emerge too powerful for white supremacy to handle. This is the fear. Education spoils you for slavery, Douglass's reading teacher was admonished. Don't teach em to read. The music teaches you to read even deeper into things. To discover your own face and signature at the very heart of things. Self -Consciousness, a necessary aspect of Self-Respect and an absolute requirement for Self-Determination. That is the tradition you hear so clearly in David. Self-Consciousness and Self-Determination. What does that music mean, the squares would ask, assaulted by our pyramidal ideas? Self-Determination. "Freedom," Monk said. "More than that is complicated."

Newark, 4/22/89

CHAPTER 29

On Reissuing Trane

I listen to Trane every chance I get. Still. And it's always a new thing, something valuable and deep, for me. Even when I hear Trane on WBGO (our 24-hour Newark jazz station) I still am genuinely transported. Not in any nostalgic way, but re-ignited emotionally by the continuing power of the music.

What is that "continuing power," drawn out of the insides of where he and it and we too been. What we felt and remembered of our lives. That part of the world we are and can feel and be conscious of. What can be described or evoked somehow. That remains with us.

This is what a human classic is, what scribes, that cutting edge that registers the most. That carries as its description the essence of the material, emotional, and intellectual context of the world he was in and the world that continues.

The changes in human society, yeh, the changes, like we say, in the music, in our selves, can be charted fundamentally. The most valuable aspects of human life can be expressed and endlessly reproduced.

So Trane, reflecting the highest consciousness of what existed, is a historic truth. What I speak of in "Legacy" [see page 191]. Because so much *has* changed in the world since he split, so much attempted destruction of human development, denigration of human spirit (what about that? they wants to de nigra the world, that's why the music biz got "covers." To hide the nigras that cannot be killed. This is called de nigra shun). These are put out by coverments.

So much has changed in the meanest of times. Yet it is all a Sisyphus syndrome, especially with "Bloods," that we must continually roll the boulder up to the top of the mountain (like King said, "I've been to the mountaintop"), and see mammy jammers try to roll it back down on our heads.

For instance, check the corruption of the music with con and fusion, since Trane, where things have gone. The social, political, and spiritual fabric of the world. How totally sick that "Long Island" is being spread across the world. Like the freaky tricky weak dumb lie music of corporate domination of art and culture.

So when we have a reprise of the music, our entire world of history and ideas is re-expressed. There is also the history that the music and its creator evoke.

Listen to the amazing "Venus" on the CD and check where it takes you. That feeling that the world is knowable and ultimately explosively endlessly beautiful. (From a live recording.)

It is very negative that this collection could not include the Miles sides on Columbia (now SONY). I guess you know that Rockefeller sold Columbia to himself disguised as a Japanese multinational corporation. Yeh that's Rocky in the kimono. Along with Rockefeller Center, so they can escape U.S. taxes. So now Columbia Records and Columbia Films belong to SONY (Standard Oil of New York!) But anyway, my man, those sides, along with Billie, Miles, Benny Goodman, Duke, or Sidney Poitier, Rita Hayworth, Orson Welles, even the Capra potboiler *It's a Wonderful Life,* belong to SONY & they wouldn't give up the rights.

How droll. (What goes a round, Comes a round, even, apparently, for the square. Conscious folks can tell you what happens when somebody else controls access to your own culture! Oh Oh!)

The historical track of the music, even as chronology, can reveal both the changes in Trane and the changes in the world. You hear the music going through changes, from Trane making the transitional swing to BeBop changes. Even the earliest Gay Crosse and Earl Bostic sides, that sound, what it was, and since we also know where it is going, and hear the focus of that arrival even in the early travelin, it is stirring.

With Diz and Bags on the early Diz sides, here "Hot House," "Good Groove," and the wild "We Love to Boogie" ("ReBop & BeBop Too" . . . which shows how the music was one thing, with different expressions, before the corporate labelers got to work, to keep the music lovers separated).

Listen to the distinct "Trane/ness" that leaps at us, no matter from how far back. It's there, it's coming. What we hear later, through the years, is Trane coming to meet himself, the stunning, yet certain, development.

The Gay Crosse piece here included, "Sideways," when Trane was just out of the great Earl Bostic band (in fact I hear Earl Bostic on this tape), was once reported as "unknown details, not established if this has ever been issued." (See "John Coltrane Discography" by Brian Davis.) Trane loved and learned a great deal from Earl Bostic and his "electric" toned alto that was so popular in the late '40s and early '50s in black communities.

The poem printed here [see page 185], "AM/TRAK," was an earlier attempt to chronicle something of Trane's life as the narration of his music's development. The learning in North Carolina, the migration to bad funky Philly (so like the Newark-NYC funk matrix). His "walking the bar tops of Philly" with Big Maybelle. 3 Bips & A Bop. Even his sojourn in the navy, you got to believe all that got into the music.

What was important to me was that Trane in becoming Trane carried all that gradual but enormous buildup of experience, musical and sidewalk. That accretion of living language which can be expressed and even gathered as "anything."

So the poem calls the names of the Rabbits, Cleanheads, Dizzes, Big Maybelles, on Trane's winding route to be himself. But particularly the two "stops" of Miles Davis's "funny time" School of Hip and the great University of Thelonius where Trane received his Ph mf'n D in Theloniuspheric studies.

"Miles stood back and negative checked." Well not exactly negative. I dug them at the old Cafe Bohemia, downtown, just coming in from the Error Farce. Miles's thing, however it seemed to whoever, was always presented as part of Miles's persona. Beautiful, funky, like "So What," which might one day be the standard question for artists and scientists and intellectuals. Miles had mastered his own expression, to whatever degree of self-consciousness.

But like the great unsung Chicago poet Amus Mor laid out in "The Coming of John," when Trane joined Miles it was like "Miles come in an be doin / alla right things. Ya understand! Takes the hord'overs from the / lazy susan with so much finesse, en be so correct when he be talk- / in to them big fine socialite hos. Understand. They be sayin 'Oh Miles' ya understand. En mah man leave the door open. Nah / here come Trane. He wrong from the get go. Ya understand. / Reach his hand down in the tray, say 'gemme one of them little / samaches.' . . . What he try- / ing ta tell yall with his horn is that yall cant expect to / get nowhere being what the gray call intelligent. If yall expect / to get somewhere in america, you gotta start bustin down dos an / shit, pitchin a fit, and poppin these lames upside the head."

So that the next stop for Trane was the pyramid school of T. Sphere ("Trinkle, Trinkle"). I saw Trane that first night with Monk at the 5 Spot, and most nights of that next 13 magic weeks. How he struggled to get that music. It was funny the way a new baby looks, all awkward, but with time becomes truly beautiful.

Monk had laid the music out on the piano and Trane would be reading those wild heads. Monk pounding out the chords (Miles said he couldn't use) and Trane struggled, Jim, struggled.

It wasn't anything about Trane's fluency with Herr Sax's thing, the earlier and contemporary Prestige, Savoys, Blue Notes (Trane was blowing with some of everybody, all the "cats") was proving that. Trane would come by Monk's house and Monk would get up and start playing the tunes. He wouldn't say nothin. And finally Trane would fall in. "Can you play this shit . . . Life asks."

And "in a minute" Trane could play Monk's music, as we saw in our nightly diggings at the 5 Spot. We saw Trane confronted with the new and a new aspect of his own developing self. And it was smoking.

We were sure of that cause once Trane "got aholt" of them heads, and started to stretch out, Monk would come off the piano bench and go into his low down dance, which, if you could dig it, was really the way Monk conducted. And we was all conducted, Jim. Conducted like a mammy jammer. In fact Monk invented "break dancing" right then. (With Wilbur Ware on bass and Shadow Wilson, drums. See poem.)

Unfortunately all those Riverside/Milestones dates with the Monk group are not included here, but you can hear "The Coming of John." The fact that all this music cannot be reissued singly is the ugliness of the corporate muscling of the world. But this collection offers the products of some of Trane's wonderful journeys towards his whole glorious self. But even in the earliest of cuts that musical glory has already begun to assert itself.

The great body of the music heard here, "Giant Steps," "Cousin Mary," "Naima," "Mr. P. C.," "Equinox," "Body and Soul," "Favorite Things," "Greensleeves," "Lush Life," "Central Park West," are what you should call John Coltrane Classics. Classics of vision and execution.

In Trane's many incarnations, reinventions of himself, from the hard
boppish Dexter Gordonish sounding blues tenor full of hippest of funk,
he began to hear in 16th notes instead of Bird's 8th note Bop. Just as
Lester was the bridge that brought the music from Louis through Bean
with the directly stated quarter note rhythm/melody to the 8th note as
speech. Now Trane heard "something else." He wanted to "make sense
at faster and faster speeds."

This implied a harmonic freedom as well since he was already somewhere else. It suggested more harmonic alternatives, substitute chords,
etc. The critics (the same ones who had to re-review the old Bird and Diz
and Monk records because they had originally given them "no stars")
began to talk about "sheets of sound" or "barbaric yawps" depending
on the shape of their souls and the cultural accuracy of their ears. The
fullest expression of this would come still later.

But as he went into Trane speed, he began to jettison the old ties to
the Tin Pan Alley plantation. The album *Giant Steps* contains all Trane
originals and marks the entrance of the Giant himself. Trane and Miles
speak of Miles's help with harmonics, and from Monk I think Trane
learned that the entire world was his, that he was in every bit of it, as
human and therefore musical reference. Every stop, every sound, every
silence, every motion. Like he now could enter entirely into the music
so that it became a truer and fuller expression of himself.

Trane said of Monk, "I always had to be alert with Monk, because
if you didn't keep aware all the time of what was going on, you'd suddenly feel as if you'd stepped into an an empty elevator shaft."

On the *Giant Steps* sides you hear the transition from the cats and
Miles time, expanded through Monkish inside investigation. Tommy
Flanagan, Paul Chambers, Art Taylor were all old Miles alumni. Miles
said about Trane then, "I don't understand this talk of Coltrane being
difficult to understand. What he does, for example, is to play five notes
of a chord and then keep changing it around, trying to see how many
different ways it can sound. It's like explaining something five different
ways. And that sound of his is connected with what he's doing with the
chords at any given time."

Around this time at the clubs Trane began to stretch out even further.
Sometimes "explaining" twenty-five and fifty different ways. Some
solos would last one and two hours. One tune would become the whole
set, as Trane searched and searched and stretched on further out.

The incredible "Equinox," "Body and Soul," "Central Park West"
are from this transition period as well ("Coltrane's Sound"). Though

now McCoy Tyner and Elvin Jones have come into the picture. Who with Jimmy Garrison would be the personnel for the later classic Trane quartet that will forever be recalled and replayed as part of the music's greatest accomplishment.

"Lush Life," "Russian Lullaby," "While My Lady Sleeps" are from the "cats"/Miles period, Trane lush and bluesy, expanding the form and content of funk saxophone into something much heavier. With musicians like Sahib Shihab, Mal Waldron, Red Garland, Al Tootie Heath, Johnnie Splawn, Earl May, Art Taylor, Donald Byrd, Louis Hayes, hip journeymen of the music, many stars with their own light.

But Trane would keep gettin up. Ironic, that for the Afro-American people a train was always so impressive because it was a way you could get up, and get away from there (the South) as fast as possible. Also it spelled the coming of modern times past old slavery times, and the possibility of going somewhere and seeing some new things. Check out the hundreds of Train Blues and Trane Whistle Blues from the old blues people.

So that the word *train,* become Trane, had been lodged in the blue black psyche for a while. And when it returned, as I said in a poem, "the only trane faster than rocket ships."

And Trane did keep gettin up. Harmonic innovation (listen to Coltrane Jazz), dispensing with chordal music eventually and going into modal forms, embracing Africa and the East, musically and philosophically (*A Love Supreme*) and beyond.

The poem "I Love Music" was written to recall how, when I was locked up in solitary confinement, after the Newark rebellions in 1967, I sat one afternoon and whistled all the Trane I remembered. And then later that afternoon they told me he had died. But I knew, even then, that that was impossible.

I LOVE MUSIC

"I want to be a force for real good.
In other words, I know that there are bad forces,
forces that bring suffering to others and misery to the world,
but I want to be the opposite
force. I want to be the force which is truly
for good."

Trane

Trane

Trane sd,

A force for real good, Trane. in other words. Feb. '67
By july he was dead.
By july. He said in other words
he wanted to be the opposite
but by July he was dead, but he is, offering
expression a love supreme, afroblue in me singing
it all because of him
can be
screaming beauty
can be
afroblue can be
you leave me breathless
can be
      alabama
            I want to talk about you
                           my favorite things
                                      like sonny
can be
life itself, fire can be, heart explosion, soul explosion, brain explosion.
can be. can be. can be. aggeeewheeeuheageeeee. aeeegeheooouaaaa
deep deep deep
expression deep, can be
capitalism dying, can be
all, see, aggggeeeeoooo. aggrggrrgeeeoouuuu. full full full can be
empty too.
nightfall by water
round moon over slums
shit in a dropper
soft face under fingertips trembling
can be
can be
can be, trane, can be, trane, because of trane, because
world world world world
can be
sean ocasey in ireland
can be, lu hsun in china

can be,
        brecht wailing
                    gorky   riffing
                        langston hughes steaming
                                                   can be
                                            trane
                                      bird's main man
                            can be

            big maybelle can be
        workout workout workout
                            expression
                            ogunde
                            afroblue can be
all of it meaning, essence revelation, everything together, wailing in
unison
                    a terrible
wholeness

AM / TRAK

1

Trane.
Trane.
History Love Scream Oh
Trane, Oh
Trane, Oh
Scream History Love
Trane

2

Begin on by a Philly night club
or the basement of a cullut chuhch
walk the bars my man for pay
honk the night lust of money
oh
blow—
scream history love

Rabbit, Cleanhead, Diz
Big Maybelle. Trees in the shining night forest

Oh
blow
love, history

Alcohol we submit to thee
3x's consume our lives
our livers quiver under yr poison hits
eyes roll back in stupidness
The navy, the lord, niggers,
the streets
all converge a shitty symphony of screams
   to come
    dazzled invective
Honk Honk Honk, "I am here
to love
it." Let me be fire-mystery
air feeder beauty."

Honk
Oh
scream—Miles
comes.

3

Hip band alright
sum up life in the slick
street part of the
world, oh,
blow,
if you cd
nigger
man

Miles wd stand back and negative check
oh, he dug him—Trane
But Trane clawed at the limits of cool

slandered sanity
with his tryin to be born
raging
shit
    Oh
    blow,
yeh go do it
honk, scream
uhuh yeh—history
        love
        blue clipped moments
        of intense feeling.
"Trane you blows too long."
Screaming niggers drop out yr solos
Bohemian nights, the "heavyweight champ"
smacked him
in the face
his eyes sagged like a spent
dick, hot vowels escaped the metal clone of his soul fucking
  saxophone
tell us shit tell us tell us!

4

There was nothing left to do but
be where monk cd find him
that crazy
mother fucker
      duh duh-duh duh-duh duh
      duh duh
      duh duh-duh duh-duh duh
      duh duh
      duh duh-duh duh-duh duh
      duh duh
      duh Duuuuuuuuuhhhhhh
Can you play this shit? (Life asks
Come by and listen

& at the 5 Spot Bach, Mulatto ass Beethoven
& even Duke, who has given America its hip tongue

checked
checked
Trane stood and dug
Crazy monk's shit
Street gospel intellectual mystical survival codes
Intellectual street gospel funk modes
Tink a ling put downs of dumb shit
pink pink a cool bam groove note air breath
a why I'm here
a why I ain't
  &who is you-ha-you-ha-you-ha
Monk's shit
Blue Cooper 5 Spot
was the world busting
on piano bass drums & tenor

This was Coltrane's College. A Ph motherfuckin d
sitting at his feet, elbows
& funny grin
Of Master T Sphere
too cool to be a genius
he was instead
Thelonious
with Comrades Shadow
on tubs, lyric Wilbur
who hipped us to electric futures
& the monster with the horn.

5

From the endless sessions
money lord hovers over us
capitalism beats our ass
dope & juice wont change it
Trane, blow, oh scream
yeh, anyway.

There then came down in the ugly streets of us
inside the head & tongue
of us

a man
black blower of the now
The vectors from all sources—slavery, renaissance
bop charlie parker,
nigger absolute super-sane screams against reality
course through him
AS SOUND!
"Yes, it says
this is now in you screaming
recognize the truth
recognize reality
& even check me (Trane)
who blows it
Yes it says
Yes &
Yes again   Convulsive multi orgasmic
                 Art
                 Protest

& finally, brother, you took you were
(are we gathered to dig this?
electric wind find us finally
on red records of the history of ourselves)

The cadre came together
the inimitable 4 who blew the pulse of then, exact
The flame the confusion the love of
whatever the fuck there was
    to love
Yes it says
blow, oh honk-scream (bahhhhhhh—wheeeeeeee)

(If Don Lee thinks I am imitating him in this poem,
this is only payback for his imitating me—we
are brothers, even if he is a backward cultural nationalist
motherfucker—Hey man only socialism brought by revolution
can win)
             Trane was the spirit of the 60s
             He was Malcolm X in New Super Bop Fire
             Baaahhhhh

          Wheeeeeee . . . Black Art!!!
Love
History
   On The Bar Tops of Philly
in the Monkish College of *Express*
in the cool Grottoes of Miles Davis Funnytimery
Be
Be
Be reality
Be reality alive in motion in flame to change (You Knew It!)
                                        to change!!
          (All you reactionaries listening
          Fuck you, Kill you
          get outta here!!!)
Jimmy Garrison, bass, McCoy Tyner, piano, Captain Marvel
   Elvin
on drums, the number itself—the precise saying
all of it in it afire aflame talking saying being doing meaning

Meditations
Espressions
A Love Supreme
(I lay in solitary confinement, July 67
               Tanks rolling thru Newark
               & whistled all I knew of Trane
               my knowledge heartbeat
               & he was *dead*
               they
               said.

          And yet last night I played *Meditations*
          & it told me what to do
          Live you crazy mother
          fucker!
          Live!
               & organize
               yr shit
               as rightly
               burning!

LEGACY

(For Blues People)

In the south, sleeping against
the drugstore, growling under
the trucks and stoves, stumbling
through and over the cluttered eyes
of early mysterious night. Frowning
drunk waving moving a hand or lash.
Dancing kneeling reaching out, letting
a hand rest in shadows. Squatting
to drink or pee. Stretching to climb
pulling themselves onto horses near
where there was sea (the old songs
lead you to believe). Riding out
from this town, to another, where
it is also black. Down a road
where people are asleep. Towards
the moon or the shadows of houses.
Towards the songs' pretended sea.

CHAPTER 30

John Coltrane

Why His Legacy Continues

"Why does his legacy continue to influence our lives, our music, and the arts?"

Trane emerged as the process of historical clarification itself, of a particular social/aesthetic development. When we see him standing next to Bird and Diz, an excited young *inlooker* inside the torrent of the rising Bop statement, right next to the chief creators of that fervent expression of new black life, we are seeing actually point and line, note and phrase of the continuum. As if we could also see Louis and Bechet hovering over them, with Pres hovering just to the side awaiting his entrance, and then beyond in a deeper yet to be revealed hover, Pharoah and Albert and David and Wynton or Olu in the mist, there about to be, when called by the notes of what had struck yet before all mentioned.

Trane carried the deepness in us thru Bird and Diz, and them, back to us. He reclaimed the Bop fire, the Africa, Polyrhythmic, Improvisational, Blue, Spirituality of us. The starter of one thing yet the anchor of something before. In the relay of our constant rise and rerise, phoenix describing its birth as birth as a description of yet another (though there is no other) process.

Trane, carrying Bird-Diz bop revolution, and its opposing force to the death force of slavery and corporate co-optation, went through his various changes, in life, in music. He carried the southern black church music, and blues and rhythm and blues, as way stations of his personal development, not just theory or abstract history. He played in all these musics, and was all these persons. His apprenticeship was extensive, and deep, the changes a revealed continuity.

The point of demarcation was Miles's classic quintet with Cannonball the other upfront stylistic vector. Style and philosophy confirm each other. As I have said before, Cannonball was Miles's confection of blues that would be called later Fusion. Simple and charming in that context, but very soon commercial on the way to not. Trane, on the other side, was the way of Expressionism. Nuclear and carrying the rush of birth and death and rebirth and redeath and new life and yet again forever, what is, as the Africans said, Is Is. Ja Is (Jazz) the Come Music.

Trane emerged as the confirmation, the parallel reference to the being identified faultily as Time. The Times. He carried the power and sway, the explosions of that period (the end of a sentence). But the conversation, the exposition, of the Book of Life uses periods only as rhythmic emphasis. Like beats. The music is continuous and all of what was is will. It is rhythm finally, changing motion, that Trane describes.

The '60s when he appeared full up was a period, a rhythm of intensity, the Giant Steps of revolution. This is why we turbulence. Trane's annihilation of the popular song, so-called, was its restatement as a broader more universal popular. His "Favorite Things" could not be Hollywood's, since Hollywood is to make animalism and exploitation glamorous and Trane was trying to speak of what will exist beyond animals, what had created them, and what will carry them away as waste. What is disposed.

Trane's constant assaults on the given, the status quo, the tin pan alley of the soul, was what Malcolm attempted in our social life. And both African Americans, they carried that reference, Black Life, as their starting point and historical confirmation. The word *Truth* sounds bland only if we don't understand what it is said in opposition to. Since it is transcendent, invincible, existent even past whatever else we claim exists. Even the lie must use real life as a reference to trick us, it claims to be truth. But Trane made no claims, either in his life or his work, what he did he got from life and we either recognize it with our selves or risk being wasted. Like Malcolm, what he was was reality, not to grasp it defines the quality of our consciousness, our closeness to what cannot finally be denied.

Even in this backward period, this post-revolutionary retrograde era, when the social gains of the black revolution and world upsurge of liberation struggles have been thrown back for a time and we must face the open betrayal of many of those heretofore posing as revolutionaries in the Soviet Union, China, and the rest of the world, including the U.S., as we watch the steady deadly march to War. Today, we even have a trend of Negroes who tell us the American Dream is now and those of us who have not gained access to it are self-destructive sluggards, womb-bred muggers, a priori dope addicts, or prehistoric welfare cases.

The Fusion garbage dump heaped around us as "contemporary" music we know to be commercial reinforcement of social betrayal and prehuman addiction to animal limitation. Many of the ills of society we thought we had bypassed, transcended, eliminated, have returned in all their ugliness, whether supreme court recidivism, white supremacy, corporate domination, violent racist attacks on the streets, at our jobs, through the media. Trane like Malcolm represented our will to destroy these animal outrages. To break out of the clichéd chord changes of primitive social life. Free Jazz! was parallel to Free Angela! Free Huey! The Ballot or the Bullet! Free Black People!

Since Trane's moving on we have been Paralyzed by the Imperialist Ray Gun, now 1/2 doped up by its Bush, but Trane still sounds inside us as the freedom we seek, the total expression of our lives as the expression of the Human headed Soul, the teaching that the flaming paradise of his music is in us to create as the world we live in.

CHAPTER 31

Some Memories of Alan Shorter

Interview with Wayne Shorter

"He had some ideas about breaking through the hold of the (commercial) mass-aimed forms. The way that he did what he did on those records . . . speaks to that . . . in that short time . . . limited . . . no bands behind him . . . on arrangements . . . not really equipped with the science of music. . . . It was like he was saying to those people (the companies), 'Sell THAT!' He wanted everything . . . to bend to his will. . . . He was, like, a Voice!

"I found a play of Alan's in the garage called *The Innkeeper*. It's out there too. He's got like the Dramatis Personae. . . . There's a woman in it named Chance. There's a Sentinel. It takes place in a labyrinth, a subterranean labyrinth. And the characters are going up a stairway toward an inn. The inn's called 'More Wine.' And they're going up these stairs, having a conversation. It's full of cuss words. . . . I guess he was ahead of his time.

"Maya Angelou read it. It's his thoughts on life. What he thought about life. He'd written novels too. One chapter of a novel he wrote is called "On France." When he was leaving Paris an immigration officer said, 'Will you return to Paris?' My brother wrote one word . . . 'Pourquoi?'

"Roscoe Lee Brown and Maya read it. My mother took it around to publishers. But I think it was too far ahead of its time. Maya said it was brilliant.

"Alan was in and out of the army in six months. He was at Valley

Forge. He wrote a letter to his commander saying, 'You know why I ain't got no business in the army. . . . You know the history. . . .'

"And he got a reply . . . 'I understand.' They let him out because they said he 'was unable to adjust,' that was on his discharge.

"Alan always played tenor when he was younger. . . . Why'd he change to trumpet was a question. 'He loaned the horn to a guy who said he'd bring it right back. But he disappeared.'"

But why trumpet? "Flugelhorn. Well, one time he walked past Miles at the Bohemia. Miles and Alan had on the same style suit and some jodhpurs. They both Geminis . . . one's May 26 the other May 29. Miles said, 'You trying to look like me!'

"Wayne said, 'NO, you trying to look like me.' That cracked Miles up. He came over to me and start laughing. 'Your brother's something else, man. . . .'

"Alan created his own world. He had papers all over where he stayed. He kept writing music without knowing how. He would hum it and sing it and put it down like that. He was influenced by Dracula movies and Frankenstein . . . you know . . . Deh, Deh, Deh, Deh. . . .

"'Orgasm' was a shock thing. He thought, 'Ain't nobody doing this. The bottom line.'" (For people like the interviewer who thought Alan was influenced by Ornette, 'Orgasm' is pre-Ornette). "When we were young in Jackie Bland and Nat Phipps's bands. Before that we had a group, me and Alan, called the Group. Jackie Bland couldn't read music either. But Alan got him to get out front and conduct. IT was me and my brother, Eddie Lightsey on bass, some other guys I can't remember. We had a contest once with Nat Phipps's band. They had music stands. Alan went up in the balcony with two chairs and a newspaper, like he was playing it. He had on gloves and galoshes and reading the newspaper. He had his horn in a shopping bag.

"We played 'One Bass Hit.' We were a BeBop band. As best we could. We played 'Manteca' with no trumpets, so we took the mouthpieces off the saxes. We would play at the Court Street Y and the Jones Street Y. Me and Jackie Bland said, Let's get something together. We rehearsed after school, with Mr. Lawson who ran the Y, at least he had all the keys. He got us 'Things to Come,' which we used to play at a very slow pace, trying to get it together. We played 'GodChild.' Nat and them were playing more standard dance numbers, but we wanted to play BeBop.

"Lawson used to tell us we had to be 'Clean and Correct.' I was learning how to read. I was playing in the concert band at Arts High.

Alan went to East Side High. That's where we lived, so you had to go where it was zoned. But one teacher caught me drawing . . . and got me to take the Arts High test.

"In army I played dances, had to read real quick in that Army concert band. One guy in there with me, a composer, got to be the head of Julliard. Alan went to Howard. After I got out the army I went to NYU. We used to talk about how difficult it was going to be in the U.S. to get the music going. Alan lived in Europe about five years.

"When we talked, we talked about the same things . . . that not much headway was being made . . . with the world. He'd go off . . . he was nomadic. The strongest and most lasting thing you can say about Alan is that he was original, as original as you can get. He was for that kind of thing. He didn't want any academic guidelines to equip him to reinvent the wheel. If he saw something like that, he'd go the other way.

"A lot of other things in life like that. He was always in confrontation or there were confrontations on the horizon. Nine times out of ten, he would be in some kind of action, some kind of confrontation . . . with record executives, rehearsal places, front offices, professors in school. Teachers would mark his papers and he would ask why on the top of the teacher's mark. He went to CCNY, NYU. And that was strenuous for him, put him under great stress . . . to sit through that.

"I did Alan's 'Mephistopheles' on *All Seeing Eye*. . . . I'm gonna look through his other things . . . see what's happening . . . and do some others.

"I'm doing a concert of my things at Lincoln Center, April 23–25, with a twenty-five piece band. They're calling it 'Speak No Evil.' I woulda called it 'Duty Free—Duty Bound.'"

Asked about his proclaimed record of seeing *The Red Shoes* more than anyone else: "I've seen it about seventy or eighty times. I've got two thousand laser disk films now and a big screen. Trying to write and listen to the music and make some music that will let me find out where my wife is now so I can eventually be with her again."

CHAPTER 32

High Art

Art Tatum

Art Tatum is a giant who is still not completely understood, though apparently wildly "appreciated." Tatum's pianistic "100 Fingered" virtuosity is most widely referenced, his unusual harmonic imagination, even his unbelievably expressed rhythmic drive is mentioned.

Very often Art's melodic embellishment is cited either with the highest positive comment or, to the contrary, some critics charge that it is Tatum's seeming "ornateness," his decorative melodic complexity, that makes him less than omnipotent.

And even some of those critics who must drop in every other paragraph the "extraordinarily gifted" or "incredible virtuosity," discussing the breathtaking arpeggios, arabesques. They speak of Tatum's "greater technical means" and claim he had a "better imagination than any other pianist," and yet in the end there is the sneaking subtext that, as Andre Hodeir said in Martin Williams's *The Art of Jazz,* "Tatum is no genius." In fact there is a school of critics who subtly detract and undermine Tatum's obvious claim to "Master of the Music," who use the naked virtuosity of the giant as their reference. Suggesting, in some expression of bizarre irony, that anyone who can play at such awesome often supersonic levels of pianistic articulation cannot possibly be a genius. They imply that such virtuosity suggests superficiality and musical vulgarity. Sometimes such commentators sound like the voices of jealous meat hooks exasperated at the dexterity of flying hands and racing super-articulate fingers. Alas, what frustration, what pain this must occasion.

But in my measure, Tatum is the paradigm of American popular music, which at the same time is its so-called actual "High Art." A measure constructed through performance, and the expression of musical concepts that are still obviously influential in the music that came after him, from Bud Powell, Oscar Peterson, Errol Garner, to Cecil Taylor and through Charlie Parker to John Coltrane and beyond. Like the Masters, Louis, Duke, Billie, Bud, Sassy, Trane and Tatum's influence was hardly limited to pianists. Bird, for instance, is Art Tatum on Alto, but expanded into a new post-swing rhythm and harmonic expression. Like Louis's impact on Hawkins, or Lady Day and Pres's influence on each other. What these sub rosa subtractors don't understand, as for instance Hodeir saying that Tatum had "easily discernible flaws" while Horowitz (who, by the honest way, said Tatum was his favorite pianist) was "perfection," is that Tatum was not only a premier jazz player, who was most times not *memorizing* text but *improvising!* An incredible piano virtuoso who was, as well, one of the highest expressions of a way of making art in the West. Perhaps a denouement, the whole ripening of a particular approach to the creation of works of art.

Tatum, a concert artist, created his technique designed to raise the instrument he played to the self-contained musicality of the music of that era, replicating the wholeness of the full orchestra. The piano begins with this proposed incarnation with its construction. The entire orchestra, the potential of the whole music, is contained in its basic physical form.

Not only would the a capella blues singer add guitar and whatever, but could become a Hot 5 or 7, a grand Dukish *Transbluesency,* could also, in the most developed skits, become the entire expansive history contained in the exquisite musical consciousness of a single player. The work songs, "Hollers," spirituals, blues could become at some point the expansive complexity that distinguishes their progeny, the music called "Jazz." (That is objective history.) But Tatum demonstrates that the whole history and consciousness of the music is simply the depth of that form's defining content to touch and communicate. Tatum is not any single type of jazz performer; he is the "place" the music was, at one point, carrying past and future to shape itself *as contemporary.*

America is the Western world, the Pan-American wholeness. Europe is not the West. *Not to understand* this is the result of Canon Shock, which promotes such erroneous geography and racial chauvinism as cultural heritage. "You leave England headed West," I wrote in a poem, "you end up in New Jersey."

So factually, Western Civilization is actually the Americas, the New World. This actual Western Culture is the whole culture of the Americas. And this culture is a composite, a polynational multicultural expression that is African, Indian, Latino, European. It is a polylinguistic spectrum as well. In English, Portuguese, French, Spanish, native American languages, African tongues, Dutch, Scandinavian, Asian, and the various so-called Creoles. It is a combination of national cultures, a hemispheric culture. It is also a dialectic of the duality of social organization in that these are characterized aspects of each culture relating to the whole, one oppressor, one oppressed.

In the Americas, the most historically impacting processes that have shaped this culture have been slavery and colonialism, white supremacy, racism, imperialism, national oppression. The paradox is that these social barbarisms have sought to segregate and freeze in separation the whole cultures' diverse elements with motives that are economic, social, political, and subsequently psychological and emotional. But often, they have forced these elements together.

Americans hoodwinked by the official imperialist theory and practice of culture still do not even understand they are Americans. And that Americans are not merely, as a culture, solely white or black or yellow or red or brown, but by definition are all as one or one as all.

For instance, to isolate American speech to its European derivations linguistically is to render every sentence in our language meaningless. Neither standard English nor "Ebonics" is a reflection of American reality. Even the term *jazz* is an African phrase, *jasm* for "jism," so the music is ejaculatory, an orgasmic expression, "come-music." Olaudah Equiano in his famous narrative says of the West African antecedents of many Afro-Americans, "We are almost a nation of drummers, dancers, singers, and poets. . . . Our favorite color" is blue. Black Guinea Blue. So the blues, from confirmation of an existence as free spirits, changes with the middle passage confirmation of survival as slaves.

Jazz. Ja Is! Yes Is Is Is Everything Is Everythings.

As history, American culture has always been held in a jealous lie of power to mean Europe, but by doing this the imperialists deny a culture to America itself. Our curriculum in all schools today still points backward to Europe, as maintenance of a slavery/colonial status quo. Our children when "educated" are made Eurocentric. Even the militant blacks who discover and grasp Africa too often, if lacking clarity, dismiss their American experience, covering & hiding slavery thereby.

So that the entire cultural consciousness of Americans, that they are the inheritors of the whole world, all the continents and nations live here and the richness of our history is the dazzling polyexpressiveness and depth of the total Pan-American culture.

American music is "pop," European concert music "classical." Slavery, colonialism, white supremacy make colonials of all of us. Not only do the Afro-Americans suffer from the "Double Consciousness," as DuBois said, "Seeing ourselves through the eyes of people that hate us in a mixture of humor and contempt." But the Americans' standard, even for white Americans, is the Double Consciousness of being "white," thereby denying real national histories. And by subjecting themselves to the Eurocentric legitimatized chauvinism Americans attribute all great beauty, classicism, and intellectual profundity to a racist ideal in which they exist only as hayseeds and crude Uncle Sam, having no culture or art except as secondary mimics of static European models.

At base, this is political, the politics of imperialism "the most concentrated expression of economics," says Lenin. A cultural aggression intended to maintain slave and colonial relationships.

We say this to point out that many of the most powerful official commentators on American culture consider it, whether in brown, red, black, or white, a priori inferior and limited. Apparently the Tories won the cultural revolution after the American Revolutionary War. Compare the power of English Departments versus American Studies! (Not to mention Black, Latino, or Women's Studies!)

The history of Afro-American music as a vector from Africa spread throughout the hemisphere, through its multicultural multilinguistic development carries with it very specific parallels to the historic motion of the people who carry it.

American popular music and popular culture, in general, has been in any free development, since the African arrived, heavily African influenced. The African rhythmic legacy is one defining component of Pan-American popular music. An quiet as it's kept, it is also a conspicuous factor in the composition of any indigenous so-called American art music.

The Europeans (see Brahms, Debussy, Ravel, Stravinsky) have actually expanded their own musical resources with Afro-American music and the African antecedents when "official" U.S. slavery/imperialist cultural commentators denied its existence constantly.

Stravinsky, for instance, spoke of the immense stature of Duke Ellington. Horowitz said his favorite pianist was Tatum!

Tatum is a profound study because he suggests in his musical aesthetic and practice the historical development of Afro-American culture and thus of America the real West. Even Europe.

Afro-American music takes its form and content from the historical lives of the Afro-American people. The very name of the nationality explains the character of that culture.

The culture, as music, begins African, is transformed by the Western experience of chattel slavery. Its development is an expression in one aspect of the level of productive forces of the Afro-American people. Their social development, education, the sophistication of the tools used in production, etc.

The single slave shouting in a field, or work song of cotton pickers, the single guitar or harmonica characterize one period of Afro-American music as reflections of the people's level of social development. It was difficult for chattel slaves to develop twenty-piece orchestras, fully equipped, a trunk full of charts, a succession of wonderful venues, and the time to experiment and perfect their creations.

New Orleans brings the classic singers and the early jazz bands. The small combos. But this is post-slavery. Access to a sophisticated urban environment, modern instruments, more freedom of movement and life choices and expression creates jazz, and eventually brings Fletcher Henderson and Duke Ellington.

Ellington is the eye of the pyramid of Afro-American orchestral expression. The transformation from the single country singer to "Black and Tan Fantasy" is an expression of social development, the expanded sophistication, additional personal freedom allows, and the artificating of the richest (broadest) culture in the world, the Pan-American, from the bottom up. As an expression of personal and national history and specific human experience. Black appropriation of the soi-disant high culture of the ruling classes. The co-optation of Napoleonic marching bands, Euro-projected clarinets, bass fiddles, saxophones, etc., and utilizing these to present the entire spectrum of our emotional lives. From the bottom up. This is more profound than we think. It is new, yet it is a continuum.

As the Africans become Afro-Americans, as the separatism of slavery, the intense segregation of the neoslavery that came after the destruction of Reconstruction was diminished through struggle, black people had increased access to a more complete presentation of the society's resources.

American classical music is at base Afro-American Classical music. And what's called American popular music, e.g., Cole Porter's, George Gershwin's, Irving Berlin's, etc., when touched by the whole emotional consciousness of the Jazz Idiom, is raised to the level of classics as well.

These composers, like most American musicians, have created even initially a music derived in significant part from Afro-American musical culture. The Cole Porters, Berlins, Gershwins, Kerns, like minstrel shows, Dixieland, Swing, Cool, Fusion, Rock and Roll, or white Rap, have used American culture, African rhythmic and linguistic (vocal) base, blues scale, the tragic patina of black life as a canto jondo of touching emotional lyricism.

Tatum was so important because he expressed the motion of Afro-American and American social and aesthetic history. Just as Louis was the classic soloist and improvisor of that freedom his music means, so Duke carried that as a collective orchestral total. Each instrument is part of a whole blues soul. The orchestra is black history and American context.

Duke charges his orchestra with translating black life human feeling and memory into an expression absolutely accessible to the whole world, as profound and exquisite art, the most elaborate and emotionally transforming human statement.

Art Tatum absorbed the technical, formal, aesthetic stance of European concert music along with his earliest training. The black piano tradition is, like the main vector of Afro-American music, vocal and percussive. Just as the whole history and tradition of African American music derives from the oral, the vocal, the spoken word, the ground of the voices, but also with that the turning day/night funk of the heartbeat. The drums. The beat. The Be at, right here. Be At! Right now. Be at!

Tatum was heir to the great tradition of Black piano players. The Blues percussive piano tradition, but also Tatum is the inheritor of the Scott Joplin, Jelly Roll Morton school of pianistic technique.

Both approaches are consolidated in the great ticklers like Willie the Lion Smith, Lucky Roberts, James P. Johnson, Fats Waller. There is the percussive rhythmic drive, sometimes like Tatum even as catalyst carried in the most dazzling runs and super arpeggios. Duke Ellington, the pianist, is also in the group of piano masters, but Duke's harmonic voicing and impressionist colorings are what made him unique in this group. The orchestra is his big piano. For Tatum the piano was an orchestra. Not a single instrument but a collection of musical potentiality that could be expressed the way Duke's orchestra would express.

What Hodeir and others do not understand is that Tatum's embellishment is not ornate but orchestral. "Begin the Beguine," a masterpiece in simple journalistic terms, is something seen as the height of Rococo melodic impasto. But Tatum's statement of melody is not presented with the limitations of a "tune," it is a catalyst of musical reorganization. Tatum is not embellishing "Begin the Beguine," he is orchestrating the materials for piano. The melody is not a figure for one important aspect of the music. "BeBop" begins to improvise from the harmonic and chordal base of melodies, dispensing with the original melody since it is a limiting entity. The melody is reorganized as improvised dissociation.

Tatum was also a master improvisor. His great improvisational sweep, which is the equal of any composition, is so awesome because it is seemingly so "formal" or heard as organic extensions of not only melody but harmony and rhythm.

Tatum's dazzling runs unleash harmonic and rhythmic dynamism that can be exchanged as melodic values. All these elements are part of the whole story, Tatum gives them narrative quality in that they are equal contributions to the language and grammar of the music's tale.

One of the longest-lived nonmusical jobs Bird had was as dishwasher at New York's Chicken Shack while Tatum was playing. Just to check the master. And for both Bird and Tatum, any composition they played was approached as a formal collection of musical elements to be reorganized into their personal music. No one so suggests Tatum's improvisational blue virtuoso dynamism as clearly as Charlie Parker.

Tatum used the piano as part of his organic consciousness and clearly the piano was Art, he was not just playing it. He was speaking and in telling his rousing complex tales perhaps his physical blindness helped, ironically, to banish the separation between musician and instrument. For Tatum, who sometimes played for eight or twelve hours a day with a few breaks and naps, was speaking, singing, laughing, shouting, crying.

Tatum seems in essence a solo performer. He takes up the formal history of the piano as an instrument of "classic" "Western" culture. Even the solo form is very western. Art made many small group records and wonderful collaborations with Eldridge or Webster but in the main we perceive him as soloist. Like the classic ticklers but also, it seems to me, as confirmation of one fundamental philosophical principle and certainly of mythological America of so-called "Rugged Individualism." Which is why all of the industrial states in the world have social democratic health and education programs except the U.S., whose leaders can even make the word *Freedom* a hype covering exploitative personal and class gain.

Tatum often seems so self-absorbed in his improvisational sweeps that accompanying musicians seem to retreat, with preeminent exceptions, into various kind of tails. Tatum's performances are concert presentations. His approach to simple thematic materials is often concerto-like, stating quite formally, at whatever near light speed, introduction, elaboration, variation, denouement for unassuming pieces of music that are no longer simple or unambitious. It is the stance Art took basically to his performance, and to the music itself.

The "gap" between the Afro-American possessors of the backward culture of chattel slaves and the "highly cultured" artistic creations of the artists and intellectuals of the oppressor nation was rendered obviously nonexistent by Art Tatum.

Listen to the great collection *Art Tatum, 20th Century Piano Genius*. Not only to "Beguine," but to the marvelous "Someone to Watch Over Me," or "Body and Soul" or "Love for Sale" or "Too Marvelous for Words." American popular music enhanced through the completeness and consciousness of a Pan-American and Afro-American specific expression, transformed to "High Art."

Usually I am distressed by that phrase "High Art," since it implies the elitist fakery of racial chauvinism. Dig the Encyclopedia Britannica's collection *The Great Works of Literature. High Art*. Not one black name, only one white woman.

But I am using this phrase to suggest that Art (and Art) has taken materials, estimable certainly, when he found them, but profound when he leaves them.

Art Tatum, like Art itself, transforms the works by making them more expressive of much broader and deeper human experience. As Billie does with "Yesterdays," so too Tatum makes the piece speak of more people and to more people. It is not simply lyrical and nostalgic, but a living memory, personal history, but everybody's.

Sometimes when forced to deal with the shallow superficialities of poseurs who cover their banalities with the fig leaf called "Art" I respond, "It might be art, but it ain't Art Tatum!"

Tatum, for all his orchestral pianistic concept and amazing technique, was still a blues player. And the blues always provides an irony to what it reports. "Life like this is transitory," blues says. "Tragedy" ain't just a life style, like victory, it says something about where we been, where we are, where we want to go.

"These compositions are what I create to explain how unlimited music is, how endless is possibility, how natural is variations and contradiction. Plus no matter how deep, how grand, how difficult, or how elementary these materials, they are effortlessly combined into the conscious whole of my own experience. I am inside the 'Beguine,' my spirit is 'Humoresque.' Whatever this piano has been, now it is my stream of feeling and consciousness."

Some commentators object to Tatum's all-inclusiveness (as they did to Louis, Duke, Miles, Trane, Sassy, Billie). They say, "But those materials, those pop songs are so slight, so limited." But whatever is not whole is incomplete. Tatum wanted completeness. The sweep of the whole emotional spectrum of this place. From its silly ditties to its soi-disant masterpieces.

Duke's *Such Sweet Thunder*, his various suites, do the same, collect the various fragments, the diverse aspects, like "Black, Brown and Beige," from work song to symphonic largesse, and makes them seamless parts of a new more expressive whole.

Any historically and socially honest portrait of the real Western El Nuevo Mundo must combine and raise its diverse polycultural register nations, Afro-American, Indian, Latin, European components as equals, as parts, dimensions, of the whole experience and vision.

The classic Afro-American artists, like the great artists of the world, dig deep and climb high to collect and reorganize the politically alienated portions of their culture into really authentic portraits.

The strength of Afro-American African music comes from its exclusion from American commercialism (until after the fact) (despite the staggering "covers" co-optations and outright thefts) but at the same time, dialectically, its aesthetic and political power is the result of its ability to combine the socially ostracized with the mainstream, the basic with the profound.

Tatum's eyes were replaced with his musical vision. His virtuosity was his signature. His omnivorous attack sings of his feeling that there were no limitations, no boundaries, nothing unrealizable in the music, and that the music finally was everything and everybody, late night, after hours, endlessly funky.

Tatum was an example of the Afro-American artist whose style and approach seek to include everything, as opposed to another school, e.g., Pres, Monk, Miles, which creates its penetrating masterpieces by excluding what it deems dross.

Tatum is "High Art" because in his broad inclusiveness there is also a blessing, a rite of passage and transformation, a realization that finally the whole world is in its truthful essence profound.

CHAPTER 33

Max Roach at the Iridium

4/16/96 Opening: Max Roach Quartet with Odean Pope, tenor saxophone; Cecil Bridgewater, trumpet; Tyrone Brown, bass.

The group, now, together for years, is at a still rising level of aesthetic growth, organic expression and wonderful power.

Max is still the Master of the trap, the industrial western percussion ensemble, the kit, the set, the Afro-American drum combination.

From the one-man band of post-slave necessity and invention. Without orchestras, we would have to be the whole thing ourselves! (to paraphrase Max). Like a film I saw of Tony Williams on the West African coast playing his set into the forest. And when the Africans responded to his "call" they thought he was a bunch of us!

Max Roach is a bunch of us, and his present sums up a lot of hims, as well. The quartet moves around and extends its reach from the essence, the inside, of Max. He is the Center. The music, whether Piano or Forte, is drum music.

The passion implicit and direct, of the beat. The Be and where it's At. We grasp the living instant becoming, in time and space, what life is, expressed through the music, from them, around and through us.

Max's beat is passion. The insistence of the Messenger, the Djali, the Griot, the Town Hip-Switch.

Africans put a city under the high sun called ON. Where from they could dig the R, the B, the light, the heat, time, motion, the seasons, the endless.

The swirl of the heat
R AY AY
Nut

The music is cheer of electric Rah Rah. Laughter. Making love to revelation.

Odean Pope is a moving presence, crying wailing howling with feeling. He turns the straight-ahead rush into emotional information. Search. Up and down modal harmonies, chromatic sweeping in all directions for the next question. Philadelphia tenor as answers.

Max flings the group out of his drum feeling. From Odean, the exploding point, to Cecil Bridgewater of the impeccable material entity of after Miles stopped being Dizzy and just before he got to be Miles, a space there, a memory sound encircled with his own telling.

Tyrone Brown, a virtuoso of drive and harmonic colors. His pizzicato is a percussive "re-being" of Max, as jet-propelled strings, melodic events discussing the meaning and direction, a zooming cradle of perception.

The quartet is, has become, a mighty organism of deeply touching music. Highly organized sound, but deeper, a living narrative of awesome feeling. The Music of Max Roach. Advanced (but very traditional) Afro-American Creative Music, i.e., American Classical Music, called Blues, Rag, New Orleans, Boogie, Swing, Jazz, Bop, Hard Bop, New, etc., etc., etc. What is so great about this quartet is that it is one of the actual Masters, at work. Still able to perform at the cutting spearhead of his creative power.

If you were civilized by the music of Bird, Monk, Billie, Klook, Bud, Diz, Miles, Ella, J.J., "and them," in the hot '40s & '50s, through the cultural revolution of the Music (Max hates the word *BeBop*, a commercial tag used to claim it and contain it, by the minstrel thieves of commerce, to paraphrase), then dig this fiery living deeply articulate expression of *The Souls of Black Folks,* and your digging will be to the Max!

4/96

CHAPTER 34

Paris Max

I'd been to Paris a few times over the years, but never with much registration. A couple of readings, one I'd been traveling with one of my main
mens, Linton Kwesi Johnson, the great Jamaican ("Black British") poet,
going through there on the way out somewhere in off-the-beat France
for a reading. Another time, another reading, Ted Joans, another of my
poetry comrades, he'd taken me down to Shakespeare & Co. (to meet
Aimé Césaire). Some other times. But this last time it really registered,
to whatever extent I could dig what the Paris thing was.

I went over to do a gig with Max Roach, the master drummer, at the
La Villette Jazz Festival. Because of the Atlanta, Black Arts Festival,
Max and I couldn't go together. I came later. But the circumstances of
this going were still deeper than you'd believe off the top.

When I got to Kennedy, I thought I'd miss my flight, which would
have been a large drag. But it had been storming and whatnot up and
down the East Coast, so that the flights were delayed. Yeh, just enough
for me to get there in CPT (Colored People's Time . . . which is . . . late)
and the plane hadn't even gotten nearly ready to split. A luck you need
in this world. Like Lightn'n Hopkins said, "If it wasn't for bad luck, I
wouldn't have no luck at all!"

But running to the counter, the voice over the loudspeaker was
calling people up to the counter for standbys. I had my ticket, first
class, Max insisted. And the voice was saying, "So and So, So and So,
Coltrane." That registered. "Coltrane!" And lo and behold here comes

Coltrane, not John, but Ravi, his amazing look-alike son. Who is also a tenor saxophonist, and not a repeat at all, but old Trane plus something entirely this Trane. You'll hear him, if you into the music, without a doubt, make sure you do. . . .

But young Trane comes rushing up. And we embrace and whatnot, but by then the plane was boarding. Dig this. It was TWA Flight 800, regularly leaving each night from Kennedy at 7:30, for Paris. Yes! The same flight that a couple weeks later got blasted out the sky . . . (by what? Probably by politics, somebody's . . . even if it was simple post-Reagan deregulated non-maintenance!)

Young Trane and I had to go our separate paths onto the plane, he was a standby in coach and I was upstairs in airplane luxury. But then when I got up there, a young white dude I was ostensibly to sit next to declares, "Oh, I don't want to sit here!" So right away, being Black and made paranoid by reality, I figure he's got a color code in his what knot that makes me a bad companion.

But it was paranoia this time, he wants to go downstairs with his friend. He asks me if I have a friend downstairs who would like to come up and exchange seats. Oh, yes, I say . . . his name is Coltrane! This guy looks at me as if I was maybe high, because the dude knew the name. But he rushes downstairs, arranges the switch, and, Voila, here is the newest supersonic Trane sitting next to me.

This cross-the-sea airborne dialogue is the subject of an entire article. But suffice it to say, I talked the poor boy almost into invisibility. I felt that Trane was hovering over me saying, "Talk to him, tell him everything you know, man, about the music, Afro-American history, the world, philosophy, and on. A young course in the RAZOR, i.e., Revolutionary Art for Cultural Revolution!" He nodded off a couple of times, but hung tough for the entire cross-the-water lecture. Yeh, Trane, I did it! I thought I owed it to you . . . and to him!

At the Paris airport, they'd lost my bag. Was it really lost? Whattayou mean? Oh, the big P again? Big P, my ass. But the next day the bag showed, plus TWA even got off some money to assuage my sweatily wrinkled pissed-off persona.

Max had us staying at one of those down by the Arc de Triomphe heavy places you hear about. So old looking and formal it's a sharp but pleasurable contrast to regular U.S. out the box characterlessness. That in itself was a groove. All kinds of doors and panels. Elaborate, rococoish, elegant wood, all kinds of services, a huge room, a view of the sweet boulevards of wealthy Paris. A tucked-in feeling, as if you were being cared for by everything you could see. (So that's how rich folks feel all the time?)

And this joint had the food, the service, the quiet response to your endless needs, now that you needed less than most, since it seemed to be all around. Old friends of mine came by too. Ted Joans and his young-ish companion of years. . . . They sign their name in concert "Paula Ted." A breath of antimacho idealism. We trooped around in the damp gray brightness of the glowing downtown. Ted always the consummate travel guide. He even took me to the Dapper Museum, created by an African named, that's right, Dapper! With some of the most exquisitely crafted masks I've ever seen. Just up the street, and through a little oasis of African imported flora, where we stayed for hours, inhaling the grand hipness of the ancients, to confirm our continuing connec-tion with the magic.

Plus all kinds of Americans live or are always in Paris. It is still, in that sense, a city of lights. That light being the sparking remains of the Paris Commune, the model Marx used for laying out the Dictatorship of the Proletariat. And the still evocative throwback to the older Bour-geois revolution and the Jacobin ascension past feudalism. All this, even in the street names, still murmurs the high vision of human lib-erty, equality, and fraternity, though we know since the Commune was overthrown to demonstrate that old capital had been transcended and the era of Imperialism was upon us. Just about the same time Black Reconstruction in the USA (as Du Bois named it) had been crushed by the "Bourbon Reaction" of resurgent U.S. slavery and the reconstruc-tion smashed dead as a doornail. And Paris, now in its Chirac reflec-tion of the momentary triumph of post-USSR neofascism that spreads around the world, with the new nazism of the skinheads, Klan clucks, and the New World Odor of U.S.-led big-teeth-vicious greed, must also carry that same smell seeping into our nostrils from all directions. Oklahoma City, Lebanon slaughters, Burundi massacres, and the proof finally that Stephen Kemble of *The Fugitive* did not lie when he said that it was a one-armed man that really killed his wife. Who now is running for U.S. president and Kemble, poor guy, long dead.

But the greatest part of the trip was, of course, being with Max Roach. Max, the consummate classical artist of Afro-American music, and world intelligence and international revelation. I'm fortunate enough to be working with Max on his autobiography, which I have wanted to do since I was a sophomore in high school when I first dug the old Guilds, Manors, Dials, and Savoy records with Max, Bird, Diz,

Miles, Monk, Bud, and the rest of the great pantheon of marvelous creators of the music labeled by the stone-age minds of pipsqueak racial negation as BE BOP!

The La Villette Jazz Festival was a wonderful experience for me. Every day we were there there were top names performing, e.g. Roy Haynes. But Max opened with one of his patented solo performances which should be mandatory digging for those proposing to be intelligent in this world. Max plays the drums as articulate speech, the rhythms carrying the most sensitive recall of the world, in so sensitive reflection of himself and ourselves, we learn through our ears what our hearts can be if we were allowed really to understand the world through revelation.

We did, together, two afternoons of discussion about Duke Ellington, the first, and Thelonius Monk, the next. And those things were gems of experience and even as a lecturer, absorbing a teaching that will remain at the base of my knowing. But then the last night, Max and I did a word-music performance. My reading to his playing, improvising together, myself raised in expanded understanding creating at the top of anything I've ever done, raised by the "oom boom ba boom" of the all the way back to the beginning of what we still presume to be humanity.

What the religions obscure is that when it was said, "In the Beginning was the word" . . . what is meant. That is what separated those who call themselves humans from the four-legged predators, the growl had become the word. The paw had become the hand. (From Monk's leap up into the tree to get away from old hairy tooth and the bloodsuckers, where he broke his big toe and turned it into a thumb. At that same time, the growls became A E I O U, you dig, the black keys and the ultraviolet became indigo, and the Blues was on the way, swinging from limb to limb, talking about, Hey, them squares can't get us up here, checking out the sky in another harmony with the everything. Like the Signifying began. Hey ANIMALS, kiss my whatnot and what not.

CHAPTER 35

The Great Max Roach

Almost the only unanimous co-signing of Greatness of still living Musicians is that accorded to Max Roach. For anyone remotely aware of the history and development of American music in the twentieth century, this is obvious. Max Roach is a name at the core and nucleus of the main innovations in percussion and the advanced creativity of the whole of the music for the last fifty years. From the time he first sat in with Duke Ellington at the Paramount for Sonny Greer, at eighteen years old, and with that acquired an instant peer prestige and historic persona, until today, Max Roach is always synonymous with the new, the adventurous, the delightfully innovative.

Max Roach is the defining nuclear fuel of the classic Charlie Parker new music insurgency of the forties; in fact, Max, to his constantly stated annoyance and chagrin, is immortally linked to the dread media albatross "BeBop," which as Max readily points out, is just a commercial boxing that allows the pirates to steal your creativity by like-naming their not so solid waste.

That new music of the forties, from Bird, Dizzy, Bud, Mingus, Dameron, Monk, is, first, a collective entity, but in any thoughtful analysis of the music, Max will always stand out as one figure of continuity, from beginnings through the many variations and masterpieces, not just as individual instrumentalist, but as the Voice, the classic paradigm for his instrument, and for an unceasing commitment to uncompromising artistry, for the last five decades.

Even beyond the mythic halcyon days of Bird and company, blowing

Tin Pan Alley and the music *business* apart with unbridled creativity and daring, with open defiance of the willful dilution and denigration that commerce had worked on the music that proceeded them, this new music, the music of the great musicians who were co-creators, individually and collectively, recreated the deepest excitement of the genre's origins and essential aesthetic.

The new music released the drummers, Klook and Max, to freely sweep across the set, with counter-rhythms of the fundamental poly-rhythmic tradition, with, as well, melodic inference and intervalic col-oring that set the drums apart as another voice. The new music restored the polyphonic, polyrhythmic, percussion-derived dynamic of what was demeaned as Jazz, it also restored the blues roots and primacy of improvisation.

Max was also part of the Milesian stylistic trope called "Cool," which brought in the chamber concertizing of contemporary European harmonic explorations, with Mingus, Russell, Tristano, Evans, . . . voicings and compositional influences.

It was Max Roach again who was the catalytic source for the cre-ation of one of the greatest small ensembles in the music, i.e., the Max Roach–Clifford Brown groups that were the cutting edge of post-bop elaboration of what the new music had taught. Only the Miles Davis classic groups of the same period exist at the same intensity of artistic power and influence.

Max stepped out again, in the middle of the political turbulence and militancy of the revolutionary democratic struggles of the late fifties and sixties that marked the Civil Rights movement. Max utilized his powerful musicality and consummate compositional skills as significant weapons in the struggle. WE INSIST! Cried Max. FREEDOM NOW! Together, now, with a beautiful young singer, who became his wife and principal collaborator during the period, the great Abbey Lincoln. As much as Max Roach–Clifford Brown instantly identified not just those players during the post-bop funk restoration but an approach to making music, now MAX ROACH–ABBEY LINCOLN became indel-ibly linked in the international Jazz Culture and in the annals of the democratic movement as great Artists who volunteered to help end the open apartheid and racist national oppression black people endured across the world. TEARS FOR JOHANNESBURG, DRIVA MAN, wailed Max and Abbey, and the progressive world was inspired.

We should note as well, that to the extent progressive people were energized and empowered by Max Roach, the musician as freedom

fighter, and by the powerful Max Roach–Abbey Lincoln collaborations, the Tarzan-gods of the money jungle reacted in just the opposite
fashion. They made it hard for MAX & ABBEY, as they do for any
freedom fighter artists, to find work. If they could they would have
made Max and Abbey the New York Two like they trumped up charges
against the Hollywood Ten and sent them off to the tin pan alley jail.
But this is just another reason that Max Roach (and Abbey too) will
always be celebrated across the world, and held with awe and respect in
the hearts of all those who know or understand the continuing worldwide struggle to end the exploitation of the many by the few.

Throughout the years, Max Roach has continued to be not only a
consistent voice of innovation and high creativity as an artist but a relentless voice for social transformation. Witness the myriad groups Max has
authored, each one with its own unique statement and voice. The great
percussion Ensemble MBOOM should stand, if not for the moles of commercial maledict that shroud the incredible creativity and innovation of
the whole of the music, as one of the most celebrated of relatively new
and conceptually unique improvising repertory ensembles in the music.

And Max has been aware, longer than most of us, of the contradictions and opposing forces armed against the clear and honest portrayal
of the music, from both the commercial and ideological fiends who
profit from our captivity and victimization. He has spoken out again
and again against these enemies of Human development, many times
to his own detriment. But it has seldom deterred him.

He has continued to be at the forefront of explosive experimentation
and excellence, as witness his collaborations with Archie Shepp, Cecil
Taylor, Anthony Braxton, venturing into the dance world with Bill T.
Jones, Donald Byrd, into drama with George Ferencz and me with our
(still to be done) *The Life and Life of Bumpy Johnson,* his work at the
Public Theater, Spoken word with Toni Morrison, Video Explorations
with Kit Michael, the new symphonic works or the "So What Brass
Ensemble." Always, as Mao said, creating works that are Artistically
Powerful and Politically Progressive.

But then. Let me fill you in on what you might've forgot, dig this.
Like Roach is actually the Scarab, the ancient Egyptian Beetle. The
symbol for immortality. Now add *Max* to that, uh huh, and then
remember too, he come from Dismal Swamp. A drummer. A native
American–looking blood, who has always been and always will be with
us, and you got the picture. MAX ROACH!! Nuff Said!

4/99

DIGGING MAX

Max is the highest
The outest, the
Largest, the greatest,
The fastest, the hippest,
The all the way past which
There cannot be

When we say MAX, that's what
We mean, hip always
Clean. That's our word
For Artist, Djali, Nzuri, Ngoma,
Señor Congero, Leader, Mwalimu,
Scientist of Sound, Sonic Designer,
Trappist Definer, Composer, Revolutionary
Democrat, Bird's Black Injun Engine, Brownie's Other Half,
    Abbey's Djeli-ya-Graph

Who bakes the Western industrial singing machine
Into temperatures of syncopated beyondness
Out Sharp Mean

Papa Jo's Successor
Philly Joe's Confessor
AT's mentor, Roy Haynes' Inventor
Steve McCall's Trainer

Ask Buhaina, Jimmy Cobb, Elvin or Klook
Or even Sunny Murray, when he ain't in a hurry,
Milford is down and Roy Brooks
Is one of his cooks. Tony Williams, Jack DeJohnette,
Andrew Cyrille can tell you or youngish Pheeroan,
Beaver and Blackwell and my man, Dennis Charles.
They'll run it down, ask them the next time they in town.

Ask any or all of the rhythm'n. Shadow cd tell you, so cd
Shelley Manne, Chico Hamilton, Rashied knows, Joe Chambers,
    Billy Hart, Eddie Crawford
From Newark has split, but he and Eddie Gladden could speak on it.
Mtume, if he will. Big Black can speak. Let Tito Puente run it down,
He and Max been tight since they were babies in this town.

Frankie Dunlop cd tell you and he speak a long time.
Pretty Purdy is hip. Max hit with Duke at Eighteen.
He played with Benny Carter when he first made the scene.
Dig the heavy learning what went with that. Newk knows,
And McCoy, CT could agree. Hey, ask me or Archie or Michael
    Carvin
Percy Heath, Jackie Mc are all hip to the Max Attack.

Barry Harris can tell you. You in touch with Monk or Bird?
Ask Bud if you see him, You know he know, even after the cops
Beat him Un Poco Loco. I mean you can ask Pharoah or David
Or Dizzy, when he come out of hiding, it's a trick Diz just outta sight.
I hear *Con Alma* and *Diz and Max in Paris,* just the other night.

But ask anybody conscious, who Max Roach be. Miles certainly knew
And Coltrane too. All the cats who know the science of Drum, know
    where our
Last dispensation come from. That's why we call him MAX, the
    ultimate,
The Furthest Star. The eternal Internal, the visible invisible, the message
From afar.

All Hail, MAX, from *On* to *Digitaria* to *Serious* and even beyond!
He is the mighty SCARAB, Immortal as our music, world without end.
Great artist Universal Teacher, and for any Digger
One of our deepest friends! Hey, MAX! MAX! MAX!

CHAPTER 36

Billie Holiday

Read "Dark Lady of the Sonnets." That was written in 1962, for a record called *Lady Day in Berlin*. It's out of print now. But recently, and I think I have to give some praise to my wife, Amina, who began using Billie's works to extend and bring to further life her own poetry, and I feel that has helped reintroduce or first introduce Billie's works today.

Billie Holiday said there were two great figures in her life, musically, that she learned from, Bessie Smith, the Empress of the Blues, and Louis Armstrong, the first great soloist in jazz. Louis also remains one of the most important vocalists in the music.

Billie came on the scene and took the blues matrix, the basic blues feeling, which rises from African American life and speech, and extended that blues feeling into its modern jazz vocal form. There are some slow academics, formalists who tell us Billie Holiday wasn't a blues singer because she didn't sing AAB, twelve bars, the classic blues form. But blues is first feeling and a feeling. It is the African American cultural memory, the experience of our long lives, reproducing the context of our western lives, it's all in there, in that music, the middle passage, slavery, national oppression, and the fundamental dynamism and struggle of our lives. It is language, history, economics, culture, politics in every syllable.

The fact that Billie could take so-called American popular songs and transform them into blues and jazz artifacts of inestimable beauty is part of the African American tradition. Our whole lives have had to be transformed to be bearable in this slave empire. A slavery which is still going on, and which our artists and leaders constantly make reference to.

Billie also was deeply moved by saxophonist Lester Pres Young. They moved each other. He naming her Lady Day and she naming him Pres, the President of the tenor saxophone.

First there is the story, Billie's attention to the lyrics is amazing, she is telling a story, it is a musical story, it is dramatic as life, as hard and as sweet, as terrifying and as emotionally transcendental.

She is also never tied to "the given," either the form or the intended content. Billie handles them, changes them, she comes from behind the beat sometimes, sometimes rolling on top of it, sometimes running ahead, her voice stretching or shortening the vowels, the sounds, like a singer, but also with the attention to the specific emotional charge in each syllable like a poet. Indeed Billie Holiday is the poet of jazz singing.

Billie said she got her inspiration of Louis and Bessie in a House of Prostitution, she said that's the only place they had the music playing, if it had been in a church she would have gone there.

Today, we face the same problems. We have to make certain that the arts are in our schools. Billie Holiday's "Strange Fruit" could teach more about black history than several white supremacy style social studies courses. Pres, or Trane, or Bessie could teach more about our lives, our children's lives and future than most of the curriculum now. "God Bless the Child Who's Got Her Own" should be the anthem the schools start with each day. Our history, our lives, our struggle, our ecstasy are all inside our arts, and our artists are still griots, historians, and poets, carrying word from bird, from the oldest ancestry, to prepare us for the future.

Is Billie Holiday taught in our schools in black Newark, of course not. She of the deep pain and unwavering love feeling looking for completion. Billie was also victim of the racist nature of U.S. society, many times she could not work because they took her cabaret card away. The fact that Billie Holiday had a problem with drugs should also be part of our understanding. Just like our children have problems. Just like our friends and family. To me the decriminalization of these substances is the only future we have.

Our losses of Trane, Bird, Billie, and countless others in the drug mania ought to teach us something, the slave masters make it available then arrest us for using it.

But Billie must be learned from. There is a whole world of understanding of this society in her songs. There is a whole path of further strength and wisdom in her songs. You need to go out and check them deeper further. Find out about Billie Holiday, don't just drop her name, get down with the real life and feelings she talks about. It's about freedom, like Monk said. It's about freedom.

CHAPTER 37

The High Priest of BeBop

MONK'S WORLD

'Round Midnight

That street where midnight
is round, the moon flat
& blue, where fire engines solo
& cats stand around & look
is Monk's world

When I last saw him, turning around
high from 78 RPM, growling
a landscape of spaced funk

When I last spoke to him, coming out
the Vanguard, he hipped me to
my own secrets, like Nat
he dug the numbers & letters
blowing through the grass
initials & invocations of the past

All the questions I asked Monk He
answered first
in a beret. Why was
a high priest staring
Why were the black keys

signifying. And who was
wrapped in common magic
like a street empty of everything
except weird birds

The last time Monk smiled I read
the piano's diary. His fingers
where he collected yr feelings
The Bar he circled to underscore
the anonymous laughter of smoke
& posters.

Monk carried equations he danced at you.
"What's happening?" we said, as he dipped &
spun. "What's happening?"

"Everything. All the time.
Every googoplex
of a second."

Like a door, he opened, not disappearing
but remaining a distant profile
of intimate revelation.

Oh, man! Monk was digging Trane now
w/o a chaser he drank himself in. & Trane reported from
the 6th or 7th planet deep in
the Theloniuscape.

Where fire engines screamed the blues
& night had a shiny mouth
& scatted flying things.

A story that is factual, but seems to all who have heard it apocryphal,
was played out one night near the old "new" Five Spot, on St. Marks
Place.

   A group of us, the hip, some hipsters, and no doubt a couple of hippies, were standing around running the world back and forth between
our mouths when Thelonius moves by, between sets, on his way to
the where ever, which was not far, but far enough out he wasn't takin'
nobody else.

"What's Happenin' Monk?" I called, as a greeting not an investigation. But let it be.

Monk called across one shoulder, never breaking his stride, "Everything. All the time. Every googoplex of a second!"

And there we were, knowing Monk was in the beyondusphere hip in the first place, now given further living, walking down the street proof. Monk, indeed, was hip. And to me, one of the hippest persons I've ever encountered.

Actually every time I've heard or run into Monk, over the years, which is a bunch of times, Monk has indeed been out there with himself, radioing back—was it radio?—in a blue wavelength. That's what we need to understand. Why Monk was so hip!

When I first spied him it was in *Downbeat,* one of those veiled photographs. Like it was dark, and Monk had on a beret and dark horn-rimmed glasses. And he was staring through the dark veil, his eyes with the glint of other in them.

I had just got hip a few minutes ago, when my Cousin laid all these fantastic BeBop records on me. Bird, Diz, Max, Buhaina, Bud, Getz, Miles, and I was just getting down a little bit, having let the music soak through me for a few months.

And then there was an article in *Esquire,* Dizzy Gillespie, with beret ("tams," we called them back in Newark), horn rims. The caption said, "To Be or Not to Bop." And that was the public recognition. And whatever the article said, all it said to me was that Diz was the leader and I knew that. I'd heard "Ooo Bop Sh' Bam" and "A Night in Tunisia." I wanted to be like Diz the way these kids today want to be like earlier Public Enemy, or KRS-1.

But then Monk was something else. Not only the steep mountains of hype the media laid down. (They always do that when they getting ready to steal.) That the boppers were crazy. (Yeh, that's what we said. "Crazy!") But what was wrong with crazy, if sane in the late '40s and early '50s meant Harry Truman and Dwight D. Eisenhower?

Crazy, wild, frantic, were our normal passwords to where we wanted to go. And that was one overarching sense of what BeBop was to me. That it took me somewhere I hadn't been before, made me think of things I hadn't thought of before. Just the names of the players took me out . . . Dizzy Gillespie, and then Thelonius Monk. Wow!

And the only thing I thought was that was how BeBoppers were known, that they were "weird." Yes, of course, that was another aspect of my attraction. I was fascinated by the weirdness of it all. Not only the names, Bird, Klook, Max, Bud, Miles. Damn! and Monk's middle name was, what? Sphere! But the music, from that first wailing 78, maybe it was Max Roach and his BeBop Boys. I was all the way in it.

But Monk seemed to take me all the way where I wanted to go. Diz was weird, funny, and finally could swing the world into a really new order, for me at fifteen-sixteen years old. But Monk was weird past just funny. Monk was "deep," "heavy." And in my unwinding literary mind, that was the quality I seemed to seek. What was past "the given," the ordinary, what spoke to me of a world way past the gray concrete streets of 1950s working-class Newark.

Sitting in my room with that music jamming new images into my mind, or uncovering old perceptions now being transformed into new rationales. So, of course, I became a Bopper. Like, trying to be hip . . . as that came in more clearly. Always hip, not square. Never square!

There was in all of the Bop that grabbed me that quality of high intelligence being transmitted. Brought home with the flailing emotion of the music. No matter what various fools and nitwits said, "Squares" (I got to know them right away, and lo and behold, I had known them before, just didn't know they had their own phylum and could be identified).

Not only did the music get down and through me at an intense emotional level, even an intense physical level, but it carried ideas. Heavy ideas. It had a distancing quality at the same time an interior focus and life to it.

I could not have run it all down then, but the Boppers were actually rescuing the music. They were spiriting it out from under the dictatorship of the mediocre swing bands, the imitators of Ellington and Basie, who with the blessing of the giants of commerce invented "Swing" as a noun, trying to get rid of the verb, and assassinating improvisation and the blues on the way to the bank, and reinvoking the ban on the drums.

So that even unbeknownst to me, off the top, BeBop was a movement and a spontaneous cultural crusade. To restore the music to its deepest and profoundest originality, the essence of what gave it important cultural meaning.

Diz, Monk, Bird, and the others were restoring improvisation as the critical factor of jazz creativity. They were restoring the blues, as its sensuous history and self-consciousness. They were reinserting the polyrhythms of Africa and freeing post-1940s jazz from the Tin Pan Alley prison.

The fact that the Boppers dismissed some of the most brackish melodies of commercial music, its principal "popular" hegemony, and made a new music, improvising and even writing it off the old song's chords. To take it away from "the given"!

It provided the voice of "the Other," a deeper description of American culture than the "official," the standard, the academic, as well as its sanctioned, i.e., commercial, popularization.

So not only did the sharp and abrupt zigzagging polyrhythms bring Shango with the lightning and thunder to blow a hole in the Alley so the swiftest could escape. But the harmonies, from the attention to chord structure, reclaimed American music, at its most expressive, as an advanced Afro-American music.

Clearly class struggle, e.g., Afro-American big band jazz bowdlerized by commerce into American mediocrity. Against which the Boppers reassert the Afro-American origins of the whole music by appropriating the so-called "refined" commercial product (the standard goal of imperialism's control of "raw materials").

The irony was that now the "refined" product was used as a "raw material" for the Boppers' reclamation of the music. Dig Monk's "Evidence" as a totally new creation based on the stale remains of "Just You, Just Me."

(But at the same time, the Boppers, particularly Monk, could take some of those same old horses and transform them into gold. Check T.S. on "April in Paris," "Ghost of a Chance," "I'm Getting Sentimental over You" (Tommy Dorsey? Yipes!). What about "There's Danger in Your Eyes, Cherie"? Or "Just a Gigolo"? "Lulu's Back in Town"?

Yet Monk's formidable handling of these bits of commercial fluff is not just humorous, he digs down deep into the song's innards and makes it speak of what it would become if Monked with. And even though he has made a reputation Monking with such songs, he has an even greater reputation, again like Duke, for playing his own music.)

The blues, the national consciousness of the Afro-American people, by the '40s had also been jailed on "Race Records" or co-opted by commerce, e.g., "Blues in the Night," etc., or cast into disregard.

But Rhythm and Blues, which combined a modern "shout" with the big band, recreated the "outside" quality of contemporary blues. Literally, the sound of the field, not the house.

The screaming saxophones of R&B (Jacquet, McNeely, Lynn Hope, etc., were the harbingers of the big Hard Bop and even avant sound of

Shepp, Ayler, etc.) took it all the way distant again from commercial imitations (until Rock & Roll).

So that those young people who flocked after hours to Minton's and Monroe's in Harlem, and wherever else, were experimental artists and scientists. Reconstructing the new from the wasted!

Monk carried all this, then, with him. All the great Boppers, image, word, and music, did. Bird's instrumental majesty, the burning lyricism, so ultimately sweet (like Johnny Hodges) but at nuclear speed, reorganizing American music so it sung in Afro-'merican contemporary.

Diz's stratospheric improvisations. His rhythmic signature *was* "Be-Bop." The flatted fifth of we original pentatonic language. Then the new scat, like here recome Satchmo, and pre-Satchmo New Orleans. Even before we spoke the language, hip. The scat is the cultural memory of African languages, so essential in its fundamental powering of the music (Black Speech!) that it demonstrates it exists without and before American lyrics.

BeBop speech, songs, jargon I took up with the heat of the whole hip music. What I first dug as "otherness," as Grachan Moncur III would say, "some other stuff," I took to because the narrow definition of the world, regular America, and petty Bourgeois Afro-America, I felt unchallenged by.

But "Ooo Bop Sh' Bam" opened a door. Bird's "Repetition," why was it called that? "A Night in Tunisia." "Salt Peanuts." "In the Land of Oo Bla Dee." "Kush."

Monk was, even in that context, something else. Not only the difference, the alternative, the "escape" (from where?) from the obvious gray corniness, but I sensed in Monk a more advanced consciousness, why I thought, of them all, he was the "furtherest out."

Monk's music, even without the visual persona and personality, is, to me, one of the highest expressions of African American music (with Duke, Trane, Louis, Billie, Sassy).

What Monk "says" in his music is why it is said like it is. First, it is the Sound. Part of the Bop genre, but not altogether located completely there.

Monk brings the older traditions to you in such an organically recycled way. He is a Rag player, like Duke; a Boogie Woogie stylist, also like Duke, to whom he is most indebted to stylistically. No matter what *Downbeat* thought when they first reviewed his and Bird's and Diz's records and gave them no stars!

Monk is a dyed-in-the-wool (under his many weird hats) tradition-
alist. He has taken black piano music and made it account for all its
historic transformations and continuing characteristics.

I think Monk's famous debt to Bud Powell (you can hear Bud's debt
to Monk more clearly) was in his digging the fluency of the piano line.
The melodic possibilities of new harmonic improvisation, although it
seems to me Monk was already way high into that when I first heard
him. But Bud did bring a new emphasis to the use of the left hand as
accent, rhythm, and harmonic catalyst.

Monk's chords are part of the whole song, not just an anonymous
vehicle to carry the melody. They are rhythmic insistence, harmonic
recombinations of melody to surprise the common melodic line, to signify its "narrowness" as a complete statement, that it is not the whole
"story."

Miles "could not stand" Monk's comping, his irregular zigzagged,
still weirder harmonic emphasis: Monk implying that even the ultra-
modern zoom of the BeBop line (Bird and Diz's) could be too fixed and
predictable.

Miles told me he "needed a base," a consistent pulse and frame under
his post-Bird, after Dizzy, melodic lyricism. *The Birth of the Cool* begins
to spell this out. Gil Evans's arrangements bring it out even further. The
negative aspects of this narrow harmonic rhythmic base are what led
Miles to fusion and then to warmed-over Rock & Roll.

Miles made the popular song hip. Monk dismembered it, and ate its
heart. So all that remains is a mysterious irony edged with droll, acidic
blue laughter.

Diz, like Louis, was up-front funny. He had an open joking humor.
To describe America must be funny, a joke, a square illusion of the real
world of human feeling and vision.

Monk, on the other hand, seemed altogether withdrawn from the
square world. Unlike Dizzy, Monk said nothing. But like they said
about that tomato sauce, "It's all in there." Both the humor and the
seriousness. Monk is always, like Pres, "telling a story."

"Round about Midnight" is one of the most articulate narratives in
modern music. A place, a mood, a lyric of black drama, an introspective voice, a story extolling self-consciousness.

The "otherworldly" aura of "Midnight" is the classic narrative of
feeling as the basic component of reflection. Where the emotional scope
and depth of the music, the perception created by the manifest spirit of

the life force, how the soul comes, mind jism, brings new life, history fertilized by forever's electric memory.

For Monk, the seed was the blues, not just as genre or form, but as the emotional essence of its origins, as feeling, as the self-conscious interior of objective experience.

Monk, like Bird, Diz, restored the blues as a contemporary experience. Producing a classic new music, as a continuum of a classic old music.

"Misterioso," "Blue Monk," "Monk's Mood" leap out at you as glowing for instances. Blues as the deepest reservoir of black emotion, expressed as the feeling of thought, the idea of feeling, backed into itself so it speaks, sings, drenches us in it, like hip blue rain.

These are classic pieces. That is, they are constantly renewed by life itself. No matter when we hear them. The fact that these pieces are not symphonies or cantatas or suites, etc., is like the whole question of Afro-American life, the problem of the lack of self-determination.

Grachan Moncur says that "Light Blue" is "a symphony in four bars," that is, the sweep of statement, the depth of its intended explication of what it all is, that is us and animates us as well as surrounds us, Monk runs down in four bars. Not having the 100-piece orchestra (by virtue of our enforced travel to ghost land, etc.), just the profound self-consciousness to speak as the entire spectrum of the whole, from the realized life consciousness of the one.

This is why Monk can write a blues ballad, a lyric that is edged with the pain of we self, yet with tenderness and deep desire, like what it is and what it ain't, each circumscribing the other.

It is Monk's openness to the world, no matter he might seem distant and oblique. The hipster's wisdom, to be love armed with information. To be calling ultimately for understanding. To understand that evil is another name for death and to attack it with the rhythms of your own life, spirit, breath, to reorganize the heartbeat so it expresses what will always exist: we call it truth.

Monk said one time, "There's two kind of mistakes. The regular kind and those that sound bad." So that the whole universe could speak for him. What he began with and whatever happened. Like people today speak of "found objects." Monk knew accidents and incidents, as well as our "intentions" (in a world we still don't understand), like Jung said, are all part of it. How could something be outside life? Like he used arms & elbows as well as his fingers, *to Work*. His feet constantly kicking the underside of the piano so it could feel the funk as well.

And did you ever see Monk dance? I've always said that Monk created Break Dancing. When Trane finally got beyond the complex simplicity of Monk's "heads," his fantastic rhythm melodies (during the historic Five Spot engagement that ran 13 weeks, and I was there every night) and began to stretch out. Monk no longer just beat those chords out to give Trane a route. Then he would get up from the piano as Trane soloed, and dance, jim. Each part of him would neon the rhythm: arms, knees, head, ducking, and spinning. Each beat would be highlighted by some part of him registering it.

The Break Dancers got that characteristic of Monk's aesthetic together. Where the dance was an exact expression of rhythm, some-where on or in the dancer. And this was another aspect of Monk's hip. And I dug the dancing as much as the music, it was part of the music.

Monk's melodies were always part of the rhythm. Which is why so many people claiming to play "jazz" can't get to it. The tunes are rhythm expressions, which is what I always dig about the best of the music. The melody reaches out of the rhythm. It is not some less strik-ing alloy. The melody is rhythm given another medium in which to expand the rhythm's tale.

Monk was part of his music. It did not just come out of him, it was him. The persona was the song. The surprise, the weirdness of the tunes. The daring dissonance and sudden changes of direction were all Monk.

One night Monk finished a piece, and without stopping his motion, his hands still held up in front of him as he had ended, he shuffled (like the tune "Shuffle Boil") from the piano all the way around one wall of the club, and up to the bar, and called out, "Gimme a double bourbon?" So all eyes could dig, "Straight No Chaser." The tune he had been playing? I just told you.

FUNK LORE

Blue Monk

We are the blues
   ourselves
   our favorite
    color
Where we been, half here
         half gone

We are the blues
   our selves
   the actual
    Guineas
   the original
   Jews
   the 1st
    Caucasians

That's why we are the blues
   ourselves
   that's why we
    are the
    actual
     song

   So dark & tragic
   So old &
     Magic

     that's why we are
       the Blues
       our Selves

   In tribes of 12
    bars
   like the stripes
    of slavery
     on
    our flag
    of skin

We are the blues
   the past the gone
   the energy the
   cold the saw teeth
   hotness
   the smell above
   draining the wind
   through trees
   the blue
   leaves us

black
the earth
the sun
the slowly disappearing
the fire pushing to become
our hearts

& now black again we are the
whole of night
with sparkling eyes staring
down
like jets
    to push
    evenings
    ascension
    that's why we are the blues
    the train whistle
    the rumble across
    the invisible coming
    drumming and screaming
    that's why we are the
    blues
    & work & sing & leave
    tales & is with spirit
    that's why we are
        the blues
        black & alive
        & so we show our motion
                our breathing
                we moon
                reflected soul

    that's why our spirit
     make us

       the blues

    we is ourselves

       the blues

What I felt in Monk was a consciousness of the real world retold to us through his music. That it was, at least in its present concatenation of duress, jive, corny, frustrating, yet full of unseen beauty. "Ugly Beauty" is a tune which speaks directly of this. He was like the philosopher who said he did not carry a lantern so he could see the road, but so that other people wouldn't bump into him. He knew where he was going.

So that persona, that daunting "distance" we beheld each time we dug him, was a shield of a sort, an anti-square device. The music is like that, it sounds so "out" and certifiably deep, yet the humor, the irony, the straight-out get-down cooking, is constant. In the pieces and their titles.

Monk's deep traditionalism allowed him to go as far out as he wanted to, yet shape what he did with something familiar as our collective memory. Something like "Four in One" or "Friday the Thirteenth" goes off into the Monkesphere alright alright, but at the same time sounds like Jelly Roll or James P. Johnson. Like we say, "in the Tradition," demonstrating continuously that time and space were an illusion squares hemmed you in with. That labels were to sell stuff.

I thought Monk knew not only the baseness of this world, but the heights of revelation within it as well. Many of his titles and shot out the side of the mouth epigrams carried a sense of the dialectical nature of reality. He was always saying, "Two is One!" and likewise "One is Two"! That things are always changing, like he said, "Every googoplex of a second." That everything was in motion, never the same. And this was so like his music, his rhythms and melodic lines. Stops and starts, constantly changing directions.

Monk also knew that even the art, music, whatever, your thoughts, happen in the middle of something else, while someone else is doing something else, or that all communication and relationship is partial and mysterious. "Well You Needn't," "I Mean You," "In Walked Bud," "Evidence," "Ask Me Now," "Criss Cross" say so much, just as titles, about Monk's mind. How he understood that most people never understand much of anything, even about themselves. And what you think might be going on is certainly not all of it.

Monk used his well-known "craziness" as a shield, but he also wanted to press the limits of the what it is to get to the next where. If you can dig that. They say when Monk was younger, he used to stand on the corner up on San Juan Hill in the Apple, where he was raised

(Hell's Kitchen), and dig the fire engines as they roared by because he thought they sounded so hip, with that crazy keening wail!

In the movie they made about Monk, you see him in some airport turning around and around in circles. "Monk's crazy," you might say. "Humph" (a Monk title), Monk getting high. Literally, the uses of dizziness. I used that title, by the way in the first poem, "Wise 1," in a long work, a book, called *Wise/Why's/Y's*. It is a poem of Afro-American history and the beginnings of slavery. It ends:

humph!

probably take you several hundred years
to get
out!

The point too is that Monk never let anybody ban his oom boom ba boom. His very "craziness," like Bird's, and Diz's, it seems to me was a basic defiance of the thoroughly hypocritical non-crazy world (actually so insane as to torture people with national oppression or drop A-bombs, put em in gas chambers, etc.).

His titles are tongue in cheek, speaking in his sardonic drollery about the world from inside just as the music itself, looking out from inside his wild head at a "Nutty" world and or being outside in that world strolling up the street in a funny hat talking about "Humph." Rolling his eyes and chuckling at the absurdity of everything, including himself. His inside music was "out" and his outside music was "in." A "simple" scalar melody, actually a hidden blues, is "Misterioso." Gorgeous and funky.

Monk wrote some of the most beautiful ballads in the music, like "Midnight" or "Ruby My Dear," "Crepuscule with Nellie," "Reflections" (also known as "Portrait of an Eremite"), "Monk's Mood." His playing of Duke Ellington's works alone are great classic performances of nuance and contemporary reinterpretation, absolutely true to the spirit of the work. And the trio Monk uses is one of the classic groups (Oscar Pettiford and Kenny Clarke) still not quite appreciated for the clear mastery of that music.

Likewise on another incredible standards album, *The Unique...* (Pettiford and Blakey). Dig, for instance, Fats Waller's "Honeysuckle Rose" or something like "Tea for Two."

Monk also wrote his swinging Bop numbers, "Epistrophy," "Straight

No Chaser," "Little Rootie Tootie," "Off Minor," "Brilliant Corners," "Monk's Dream." Some of them with that strange anthemic brassiness "Jackie-ing." "Rhythming."

The traditionalist-sounding rag and boogie pieces like "Four in One" or "Trinkle Trinkle," which sounded old and all the way out new at the same time. "Blue Monk" is one of the most funky and gripping blues I've heard. It's the piece that made me write "We are the blues / ourselves."

Yes, it was the weirdness, the outside "distance" of Monk and his music that drew me to him, that bound us together, as comrades of the hip soul forever. And I guess I've emulated him in many ways I wasn't even hip to. My wife, Amina, is always telling me how people used to do imitations of me imitating Monk. And that got so in, all people had to do was a gesture or two and they knew who it was.

The last time I saw Monk, it was outside the Vanguard. I hadn't seen him in a while, and we had never been really that talking close, mostly it was my deep admiration from the audience or with a group of musicians after the set. I had started writing about Monk when I was a young man, writing for the old *Metronome* magazine and *Downbeat* when my name was still LeRoi Jones, and I always signed, as was the custom, with my initials. Anonymous enough. Yet that last time I spoke to Monk, he answered, "What's happening, L.J.?" I tell you, it meant the world to me.

93/94
Newark

Eric Dolphy

A Note

What always seems missing in any discussion of Eric Dolphy's work is the influence that the great Jackie McLean had on him. Commentators always seem to pick up the Ornette inspiration on Eric, but listen to that distinctive Dolphy intonation, always sounding just a little sharp, like he's wailing so hard the sound is bending the metal out of shape. Then check any of Jackie Mc's classic blowings and you should get my meaning.

The sound of the horn, in both cases, is itself a phenomenon of harmonic shading. Once you heard Eric you can never forget that sound, and to me that's Jackie Mc's bag.

But Eric was also a sensational technician as well as a wondrous feelnician—like Jackie Mc. He could stretch all the way out into the waygonesphere and still be bulletproof funky.

I remember when Eric used to live down on Water Street down by the East River, where he sublet this incredible loft. On the outside it was just another run-down lower manhattan factory building. But inside the place was outfitted like some wealthy aesthete's digs in the "Yellow '90s." Complete with rugs and a piano.

But no matter what time you walked by the building you'd hear Eric up in there practicing, projecting fresh life past his fin-de-siecle environs. You'd hear him scaling and wailing, playing on and on, tirelessly, in the morning, lunchtime, and late evening too if he had no gig.

So it was cold irony when some ersatz critic reacting to the way outness of Eric's sound focus would idly challenge his "technical" pedigree. But ears of paper never hear what's happening "enty" (as Al Hibbler might say) way!

CHAPTER 39

Jackie Mc

By the time I had got fluent in the understanding of BeBop and its revolution, and had begun to recognize the historical development of the music, I heard Jackie McLean. And from the first times I talked to my partners about him it was always Jackie Mac to the hip. He was one of the young geniuses Charlie Parker's life brought to revelation. Not only the musical innovation that will historicize Bird's life but the personality of himself as artist, and the social philosophy, the cultural explosion and introspection these elements together worked upon America. Birdland is an actual place, even to the capitalists.

Jackie came up the charismatic New York hipster, but he could play. Not only was he carrying the feeling of a generation but the sensitivity of the artist, the illogical truth of reason. What was so hip about the young Bird freaked musicians, artists, intellectuals, people was that Bird played Beauty & Truth. Even his life was truth, how tragic. But even that was simply Confirmation of the death rule of squares. The corniness of authority, the banality of a slow walking insensitive society in which art could be ignored, artists driven to suicide, and the people beat down all kinds of ways.

Like Bird, Jackie came up as young and as wild as he had to be. As penetrating in his grasp of this world as he had to be. The music was supreme judge and purity. Life should be as hip as the music.

Jackie spoke as he grew in respectful artful admiration of the new learning, its accents and he drove his sound on alto up high like Bird's, but something more personal also developed, it was a harder, more gut shouty sound in that metallic bop alto. It was as articulate as the

Parker paradigm, and in Bird there is always the homage to Johnny Hodges as well as Lester Young, but it wanted its blues street wailing and screaming.

Jackie was from his appearance part of the whole development of that music, BeBop, both in his association with Charlie Parker and Miles Davis. The Miles connection made us understand how another younger generation was emerging. Miles & Jackie on "Dig," or "Morpheus," "Down," their look and the hard blues they pushed were carrying us into the next period of the music. Hard Bop.

When Horace Silver, Sonny Rollins, Art Blakey & the Messengers, Clifford Brown–Max Roach, Bobby Timmons brought the church directly into it. Those post-cool Blue Note sides. Especially I still always listen to Jackie Mc's "Dr. Jackyll." With Miles developing the ensemble style that would later lead to the Trane-Cannonball–Red Garland–Philly Joe Jones–Paul Chambers classic period.

When the Freedom Militant Funky '60s emerged, Jackie had not only developed into an alto maestro but an important composer. "Little Melonae" is another of his gems. The bands and music of *Let Freedom Ring, One Step Beyond,* his work with Grachan Moncur III, Tony Williams, Bobby Hutcherson, Freddie Hubbard, and many others is outstanding, innovative, yet as drivingly funky as anything in the music.

One story that indicates for me how art is related to society as intrinsically as human thought and feeling is one day during this period I wandered into a Village record shop and asked for Jackie's *Let Freedom Ring.* The squat joweled bespectacled clerk resembling a Nazi sympathizer in a '40s movie began squealing, "If you people want to be concerned with such things why do you have to put it in music?"

He was actually angry, agitated, and puffing. I made some nasty remark, amazed at the hidden maniac posing as thought in the American mind, and thought for a minute about murder and explosions.

Jackie created a music that continued the Parker Bop tradition and the hard bop development and restoration of blues and polyrhythms, but parallel to John Coltrane, Sonny Rollins, and the coming of Ornette Coleman and Eric Dolphy and Pharoah Sanders and Albert Ayler and Archie Shepp, Jackie McLean contributed a highly distinctive voice which told a very broad story.

Jackie starred in the Living Theater's controversial production *The Connection,* where Archie Shepp later blossomed. He played the downtown New York spots in profusion. Even made a kind of headquarters of Slug's on the Lower East Side. But there is a kind of slow death amidst lights and noise that spends the artist's energy that Jackie opposed. That he saw hurting so many of his friends. Till, finally, he says, when Trane died, it signaled his departure.

Now in Hartford, Connecticut, at the Hart Music School as director of Afro-American music, Jackie Mc has re-emerged as a continuing master player and innovator in the music. He sounds as swift and hot and funky as ever, his soul is certainly right where it supposed to be. Listen!

5/89

CHAPTER 40

It Ain't about You

The night Albert and Black Norman, the Wizard, and I went up to Lincoln Center, my wife, Amina, whom I had yet to meet, was sitting out among the huge audience, with a Newark contingent. But not many people knew Albert Ayler then, and even those of us who knew him never knew exactly what Albert would do. But he had said something on the way up about seeing if the musicians featured up there at a concert this night, John Coltrane, Eric Dolphy, Cecil Taylor, Pharaoh Sanders, Elvin Jones, McCoy Tyner, Jimmy Garrison, "and them," thought the music was "about them." That was Albert's consistent conversational polemic. "Oh, you think it's about you?"

So at one point in the concert, in which all mentioned were up on it, rising like the Black Bird, BA, the human-headed soul, Albert strolled, stepped to (like the kids say today) the players on the stage (from the wing where we three stood digging), his deadly ax tilted, with his head all the way back, playing something nobody anywhere had ever heard, except invisible Albert and the Black Wizard.

It was a terrifying alarum of *Entrance*. The rest of us then were the Romans digging the big H come wailing across the Alps, Ax blowing Blue nuclear Flame!

"Wow!" (An old Blood battle cry.) "Wow!"

And "Boo!" (Not its later derisive meaning given by the vanquished, but another old Blood battle cry, ask the early Brits!) "Boo! Boo! Wow! Wow!" Everybody on the stage was transfixed by and transfigured in this roar of cataclysmic Soul. Like Henry Dumas said, this Blood could set the whole world afire!

It was amazing, stunning, past Bravos to "Holy Jesus, what is that?!" Albert roared and roared, in that inimitable, still to this day, inimitable blast of romantic fury. It was amazing, mystical, dangerous. Alive!

No one has ever sounded like that! Believe me!! The records are not records, but rumors. At the end of it, all the musicians came off the stage, still in concert, with the amazed awe-full screamings of the crowd. Who in the whatever was that, or more like, what in the whatever was that?!

And I remember, Trane, our father who art much hipper than Heaven, step to Albert and say, "Hey man, what kind of reed you using?" You know what I'm saying?

9/18/96
New York

CHAPTER 41

You Ever Hear Albert Ayler?

We are all products of Time, Place, & Condition. What we bring, we are "given." By heredity, those prearranged characteristics, mostly physical, a range of proclivities, skewed possibilities, &, most profound, the shifting contours of *Environment*. Including, to me and the most influential whatever *interventions,* entrances, shapings, that help construct & reconstruct us as we go.

Albert, from whatever complex network of all these, arrived in my life in the middle '60s. I never knew or found out very much about his origins and early life. Only that he'd come from Cleveland, apparently with, at least, striking distance from the well-heeled Shaker Heights section. At least close enough to have been a frequent caddie at those shiny golf courses that go with wealth.

I found this out from Albert, who was given to describing his mastery of the sport, still unusual (for Afro-Americans) in the '60s.

Albert must have arrived at my door late in '63, early '64. By then the world was flipping & shuddering from the assaults of the oppressed, as well as the historically maintained wrenching of the oppressors, the conflict bore. This fundamental contradiction, *Labor versus Capital,* had reached such awesome international political, economic proportions by this period that they I had given rise to another principal contradiction, *Imperialism versus the People.*

So Mao said of the period, from '47, India's independence; '49, "The Chinese Stood Up!"; '54, *Brown v. Board of Education* (supposedly desegregating U.S. Public Education); '57, Dr. King leads the newly formed SCLC in organized resistance to segregation on public buses, created by Rosa Parks's historic refusal to move to the rear of a Montgomery, Alabama, bus; '59, Fidel Castro leads the Victorious Cuban Revolution; '60, Malcolm X appears nationally, Greensboro sit-ins, and the formation of the Student Non-Violent Coordinating Committee with Foreman, Carmichael, Rap Brown, and the breakout of a nationwide student movement; '62, Patrice Lumumba, first premier of Congo, assassinated; '63, JFK assassinated; '64, Vietnam; '65, Watts Rebellion, Malcolm X assassinated, etc. In that "Then" world, the world's environment was resistance, revolt, revolution.

In the arts, the world pointed the way as well and much of the most significant art created likewise (however the objective definition of it) was full of this ideational surge of revolution, even in the expression of that as merely the "New"! "Innovative," "Highly Creative," even "Shocking" were frequent descriptions.

In those days, just after Kennedy got shot and just before Malcolm X, when Lumumba had just been lynched by Rockefeller and the Belgians, and Africa raged with Liberation organizations, MPLA, PAC, ANC, ZANU, FRELIMO, PAIGC, and leaders like Toure, Nyerere, Cabral were soon to be widely known. When Fanon was an opening name, Fidel & Che up in Harlem, Nkrumah alive, & Jimmy Baldwin had come home. Du Bois would just have died in Ghana. The day before Dr. King led the March on Washington!

At the same time Robert Williams, the central figure of a book called *Negroes with Guns,* had stuck up the Klan and pulled off their hoods in North Carolina, and some preachers in Boogaloosa, Louisiana, called "Deacons for Self-Defense," had done likewise, and so tuned in with an obvious international consciousness which carried real knowledge for use (Remember the dance "the Boogaloo") which still could be made into a casual social code!

Concomitantly, the reformist aspect of the journalistically hyped "Beat Generation" did prove the bridge of necessary attention to the emergence of another generation of Americans. So the Beat, of the music, Jazz, Rhythm & Blues into Rock & Roll, like Paul Newman on a chain gang, was an appropriation of "Blackness" by the class that will "rule," as a *class!*

Every generation of white people must take on a "Blackening," not only intellectually but connected by *blood*. As Jimmy Baldwin used to point out, but as *one people*, regardless of the segregation, discrimination, racism that mark Black National Oppression. The connection between Black & White Americans (as well as all the Americans social- ized as parts of one American Culture) by politics, the economy, histor- ical precedent, etc., creates an aspect of that culture that must register the influences of Black Americans as an essential aspect of that culture. Speech, social mores, arts, psychologically, positively or negatively. E.g., contemporarily, even to the emergence of an altered dress code, which has the wealthiest Americans wearing "casual" or bohemian uniform that simulates poverty, e.g., stained, ripped, or merely formally infor- mal, a trend so strong even corporate culture begins to reflect it. Or the jailhouse, droopy trouser, stringless, open sneakers look, to which is added the turned around baseball cap of the "Hood."

So whether it is the 19th-century white Abolitionist or the "Black Face" minstrelsy of the of the same period, or later "Dixieland," Paul Whiteman, "King of Jazz," Benny Goodman, "King of Swing," or the myriad white "swing" bands (with a couple of exceptions, the noun, not the verb) that all sounded the same. The "Cool" school of "Jazz," which functioned as a "white" style, or contemptuously contemporary, what they call "Fusion" (discreetly leaving off the prefix "Con"), both spawned by Black Miles Davis! (In addition, names like "Rag," "Jazz," "Bop" are all the creations of white media!)

The ubiquitousness and profundity of a certain "Blackness" to American culture should be obvious. Even before we speak of Rock & Roll, which is Rhythm & Blues played by, with its content reshaped by, white players . . . internationally. Essentially a *class altering*, but in the U.S. what's called Race is a Class Distinction!

Particularly Greenwich Village, the Lower East Side, later the East Village (& a few other twilight zones of "egalitarianism"), the assump- tion, co-optation, very consciously, though many times still superfi- cially, of an aspect of Black American culture was obvious.

The so called "Beat Generation" context of the period re-ratified, not only the existence and value (see Karl Marx) of Black American Arts culture and those near-stereotypical mores that could be refer- enced "off the top," but this actually traditional cultural absorption honored itself by claiming to have positively taken some of those pre- sumed qualities as part of a "new" and "radical" American life style.

By the early '60s, more Black people, as residents or as a broadening presence, had come to "the Village." In addition, the most innovative Black Music now made its principal home there. The Charlie Parker generation had brought the music effectively not only out of Harlem, but eventually out of the 52d Street (Birdland, Royal Roost, Bop City) entertainment quarter, which then, became again, an oasis for the "Swing" and redux, mostly white, "Dixieland" style (Eddie Condon's, Central Plaza, Metropole), downtown to the Village by the '50s.

New clubs, Village Vanguard, Open Door, Village Gate, Café Bohemia, later the Five Spot (1), a Bowery hangout painters started to go to, and with them the new Cecil Taylor, with Denis *(sic)* Charles, Buell Neidlinger, pre-Ornette Coleman. Then Five Spot 2, the Jazz Gallery. New venues for the new music, which itself had loudly pronounced its radical disaffection with the Tin Pan Alley American popular commercialism, musically by refusing to play those melodies, actually from Bird on, with the use of the harmonic structure, the chords from which to build new melodies and improvisation.

By the early '60s, John Coltrane and Sonny Rollins were the leading voices of innovation, from the forwarding presence of the two Key groups Max Roach–Clifford Brown, Miles Davis, with Cannonball & Trane, and of course Art Blakey's graduate school of Funk, the Jazz Messengers, out of which Horace Silver, Bobby Timmons, Kenny Dorham, Hank Mobley (the last class included Wynton Marsalis).

These groups broke the '50s post-Bop dialectic of "Cool" by reasserting Rhythm, & Blues, even Gospel, as a corrective to the flattened dimensions of the emerging "Man in the Gray Flannel Suit" new conservatism of rhythm-alienated formalism.

Roach had even raised the focus of the music's lyric content to an openly Black Liberation, Anti-Apartheid, Civil Rights stance with "We Insist" and the sides he made with the great Abbey Lincoln.

So the period's premier players came out of the three premier groups into the Hard Bop reform of the cool, and then, with the fundamentals restored, went on "past that."

Monk's deep creativity came into a wider window of public attention. The oldest rhythm and harmonic elements of the music, reconstructing the stride piano classicism of Willie the Lion, Fats, James P., Duke, as well restoring BeBop exploration and innovation in the "style," and caused a kind of reappreciation of the music's origins as original, "new."

Rollins and Trane went through the pantheon of origin, commercial dilution, restoration, and with the philosophical "zeitgeist" of the period Mao Tse Tung described as *"The World's in Great Disorder—a Good Thing for the People!"*

Why? He added, *"Revolution Is the Main Trend in the World Today!*

Countries Want Independence, Nations Want Liberation, the People Want Revolution!"

Rollins was particularly innovative in the creative reorganization of melodic and thematic elements, e.g., in his improvisation on "Freedom Suite" is an awesome (& check the title's focus), combining of Form, Content, and Political Direction. His sound was the "Bean" the pre-BeBop thick timbre. The elegant statement, re-statement, and melodic transformation, shaped in the sensuous depth of the sound.

Trane came later, from North Carolina, son and student of a preacher-musician. To the big city Philly Rhythm & Blues. Living the neo-romantic urban night club organ trio gig experience. Walking the Bars, Honking and Wailing. From the Illinois Jacquet, Big Jay McNeeley, Joe Bostic, Lynn Hope, Gene Ammons sound, sometimes "flat on the floor, kicking they legs in the air!"

Then to Diz & Bird, check that flick at Birdland, Trane with his mouth hung open, digging and learning. Into Diz's Big Band, leaving alto for tenor, becoming a journeyman of the Neo-Bop, Funk, Hard Bop rebirth. The Prestige, Blue Note, records. To Miles and that nuancing into the NY scene as a peer.

The modal funk & opening search for a newer more complexly informed "hot" . . . to *Smoke, Work, Cook, Wail*, as the collectively expressed.

Monk was "Weird," Trane was "Bad" ("a Genius"), Miles was "Hip," Rollins was "Out," Max was "Sayin' It!" Buhaina (Blakey) was "Funky."

Past Miles, through Monk, Trane went out to meet his self in another place. Ornette arrived and aggressively suggested a "BeBopier BeBop," as an innovative voice. The decentralized "Harmelodic" improvisation. "Free" became the rubric, the oath of commitment to the "New."

Mile was "Free Wheeling," Max said "Freedom Now: We Insist!" Duke "Diminuendoed & Crescendoed" at New Port re-materializing through Paul Gonsalves, 24 choruses, as the continuum of what it all was! That solo a preview of the profound historic constancy that Trane would make "new." The Pres's bar-dissolving inference of his swinging! Using the rhythm as a quantitatively accumulated expression, refusing to be enslaved by *the one*, but always reflecting its rhythmic insistence.

Sun Ra was another fresh entrance into that Village-centered scene. With his complete address to innovation, creativity, a fundamental commitment to the new, the unknown. The intellectualism that focuses on Art, the Spiritual, Metaphysics, the *Raising of Consciousness*. The Song's "story" as Myth, Symbolism.

As bizarre as Ra might seem or sometimes Be, past the costumes, camp, theatrical devices (some, like "the space Organ," was paradigm for "the Light Show" of Rock & Roll), still Ra remained, and is yet, a little-known composer, orchestra-creator, innovator of grand proportions!

There were players in Ra's various Arkestras who were most the most expressive and innovative players of the "New Music." John Gilmore, Marshall Allen were among the most important influences on their peers. Trane is reported to have approached Gilmore, praised him, and told him he was going to "cop" certain of his techniques. He did!

There are very few alto saxophonists yet at the same level as Allen. Ornette, perhaps, Jackie McLean, himself a great neo-Bird stylist, was likewise later inspired by Ornette. Eric Dolphy was a Jackie McLean–influenced voice, as later reflection of Bird. With Monk, and the reappearance in Miles, Trane emerged as the newest point of the Blues-based improvisational instrumental style.

And armed with the whole history of the Music, John Coltrane, inspired by the spirit of the times and the material context that shaped his thinking, took up the challenge of the New! Of experimentation & courageous innovation. *Giant Steps* announced this, 1959, as Fidel Castro marched into Havana.

Trane's motion gathered around him attitudes, stylistic, young Radical, revolutionary, & contrarily, conservatism of some of "the Cats" which began to question him, and of course, the reactionary poison captions of the critics who cryptically serve as Bouncers for the trite, the formal, the commercially sanctioned repetitiousness which are generalized distortions of "tradition."

The New Frontier had been murdered away, the new beginnings of a Confederate coup that has, with the national elections in 2000, raised that confederate insurgence to state power! Trane & Rollins claimed the inner and outer planes of the "OUT." Rollins played on Brooklyn Bridge. Trane played the post-Miles, post-Monk Bridge to "Oh Oh!"

Both JFK and Lumumba had been slain when *My Name Is Albert Ayler* (1964) appeared. As a confirmation, it seemed, of the sharp transitions that were taking place in the world. By now, Trane had become "A Master . . . the slightest sound from his instrument is valuable" (to quote myself ca. 1963–64), the Guidon of the hip, but nervously reconsidered by the flatfoot hippies (old meaning) who co-signed things rather than actually Dig. Trane was getting outer and outer. While Ornette, these same people thought, was on the awesome ledge of overt foolishness, with his yellow plastic alto, "no huddle" offense, offending some even with the little waiter-like Eisenhower jackets his band wore.

Ornette & Cecil did scramble the old hip. Put the hippies, the co-signers, on armed alert that something further out had arrived to redefine what was happening and they weren't sure, yet, if they could co-sign it. Ornette was on a ledge. Yeh, we said, some threw their hands up. And after all, what the freak was this Cecil Taylor *really* doing?

Ra was so far past the easy groove of what the hip can be imagined to become, if not freshly watered with the absurdity of willful desire and the courage to turn corners, open doors, answer inverted questions! Ra was some kind of carnival orgy got loose. Cosmos, Solar, Intergalactic, NASA was doing it, but Ra desired more than just walking on the Moon. Sun Ra.

But in the circumference of that boiling, for a moment it seemed that Trane & Sonny were in a relationship of perfect balance. As if working from a specific place in the Sunshine, where they each did and developed, showed, and moved. Two paradigms of the ever changing Hip. With the others, confirming we had moved deeper into the rising turbulence of the decade.

Sonny now became "weird," shaving his head, except for the so-called "Mohawk" strip down the center. Why was that? We never asked. He was just getting "weird." Monk had *been* weird. Monk was still weird. Sun Ra was talking about "Outer Space."

Trane had got "Deep." Down into the evil *Dooji,* which was not weird, but by now an infamously mainstream of Bop and a demonically incarnated environmental default in Afro-America! Rollins had begun to leave the stage and walk around the club blowing. First, in one corner, then, never pausing, as he crossed the room, another. Sometimes poking the horn at this or that patron, his manner impressively stoic.

My Name is Albert Ayler reflected "the Great Disorder" that Mao spoke of. The style of the record was itself mixed. His explosion of the "Next," less apparent under the gauze wrappings of a standard Europeans rhythm section. Still he had a deepness, a kind of "gone behind himself," that summoned the close listener that there was something else yet to come.

That same *achiote*, sharpness, characterized his person, so that whatever he said, just above the lightning flash horror flick metaphor of the dramatic white "fright" gash of white at the edge of his modest beard, added to the "challenge" coming out of his mouth, as if he was his horn!

Albert eased into my crib in that space in time between JFK's killing and Malcolm's. By now, the gauze of old BeBop chords and concept had been lost and a space had been "newed" apart, so when Albert appeared, his eyes stretching like something come out from behind the clouds, the look we exchanged and the words must have lit up something, because first thing Albert did was laugh.

In those days Albert traveled with a dude named "Black Norman." From him resonated Weldon Johnson's metaphor, "a hundred midnights down in the cypress swamp."

Norman's eyes, as they flashed, were an event, against that jet Black skin. Given to a cracking silent smile, another row of lights. He was Albert's confirming icon. To second Albert's "Outness" with weirdness!

Cecil and later Ornette had rushed through the door Trane & Rollins (& Miles & Max-Brownie, Blakey) had opened. With Denis Charles, Buell Neidlinger, Jimmy Lyons, Henry Grimes, Sunny Murray, Blackwell, Charlie Haden, Scott La Faro. And the continuum of the new began to be a visible and audible presence. Pharaoh Sanders, Eric Dolphy, Archie Shepp, Marion Brown, Grachan Moncur III had been on the scene with "the Cats" for a longer minute, emerging from another direction. Then Milford Graves, Don Pullen, . . . Oliver Nelson, in the name of "Avant Garde," "Free Jazz," "the New Thing" as a rush of definition and personalities, reshaping the brooch face of the music.

Half Note, Slugs, were new venues, on the Far West and Far East Sides. But the rush overflowed the already given, and so the "Loft Coffee Shop" scenes began to open. (See *Apple Cores*.) The Lower East Side had become "the East Village." And aside from the impromptu, one- or two-time hit places, there were more stable places like the White Whale, the Dome, the Ladies Fort (tended by Joe Lee Wilson and Sam Rivers), Galleries and Theaters, Coffee Shops, at one point Café Avital, Metro, the Ninth Circle, the Cinderella Club, Harout's, the Speakeasy, also opened, Nonagon, the Living Theater, St. Mark's Theater, Maidman Theater, and so many others, plus the personal home lofts of people like painter and musician Marzette Watts. In this explosive swell of transition and change fundamentally in the axis of the material world, Albert swept into and out of the center of all.

Albert came to see me, I guess, because my name had been associ-

ated with the new music, as publicist, critic, as poet expressing the new
consciousness. "You think it's about you?" His favorite question. A
challenge, more than inquiry. In other words, is it about the music or
about possession, ego trip, getting over, and employment, something
superficial?

It was also a challenge to my definitions, analysis, evaluation of,
hierarchy of artists. "You think it's about you?"

Or at times, talking about other musicians, usually his peers, Albert
would come out with, "He thinks it's about HIM!" The emphasis on
the word was exclamation pointed with sudden stretched eyes and a
growl of half-erupted laughter. Black Norman would snort knowledge
and ultimate approval, his own eyes twirling in deep appreciation.

Those conversations were about "the Music"—of course, in whatever direction, though always laced with his re-occurring Socratic
interrogatory oaths. The loudest exhortation was always if some name
was used as the direct object. "X thinks it's about Him!' And we all,
myself as well, would crack up!

What emerged in these meetings? Well, several things. That "the
Music," in its *selfless* performance and the widespread acknowledgment of its "glory" and revelational purpose, was absolutely primary!
This was the reason that the vulgar "use" of it, as self-promotion for
commerce, etc., was a violation of it and a stain on the morality of its
perpetrator!

The music was *Holy* (see the titles of Ayler's compositions). "Holy
Holy!" The Truth Is Marching In," "Spirits Awake," "Spiritual Unity"
form the metaphysical embrace of his focused theme. This was the Sunlit
Idealistic presence filled with the bright beautiful arrogance of the creator aggressive from digging his own strength and power, his understanding that he, in fact, was a vehicle of Truth & Beauty. On the other
hand, there were demons surrounding that glorious vision, Witches &
Devils, Ghosts. So the music is dimensioned by both seeings.

Another aspect of Albert's metaphilosophy was in the technique and
method and approach to creating the music. That "Other" kind of wail
promised underneath the standard BeBop context of *My Name* had
sounded, the mouth of a different stranger wail. And when we met that
clearer presence had emerged. The next record on Debut was exactly
that, as the real monster leaped out!

That sound, the horn's timbre, unbuckled, broadened, deepened,
assumed a Wolfsome metallic echoing bottom. And at each succeeding
record, that signature thundering klaxonic aerodynamic keening crack-

edged blast *"Blahhwaonnkaad,"* a sonic-born electricity, blown into ringing continuum as music.

It was a drum, but blared. The hammer of Human Feeling against the Anvil of the Air! There are no *records* of Albert (no precise replications), only *Rumors*, but more faithful, more moving.

It was this wonderful sound that really marked Albert Unique! And, live, or, as they say, "In Person," that sound was literally devastating. It Wailed and Wawed, Not a scream but something nature only sowed the seeds of, like the singing from a Black Hole, something very Loud and very Hard. It confronted, attacked, took hold, it was nevertheless touching, but its touch was "past" aesthetic/psychological, but physical, not just being heard, but being *felt*. It was not just the ears that dug Albert, the whole body became a field of sonic ideational penetration!

That overwhelming sound was, I felt, the principal focus of Albert's *musical intentions*. That that brass "Waw" carried a new understanding, A *canto jondo* religious vision. And as such, it provided both the overarching form and content to what he played. Every other feature of Albert's approach seemed to be shaped or the result of that Sound! As astounding as they are, the recordings only get the *tops* or edges of the sound, but not the unnerving deepness, the "Dish" (as in the video dishes) of the sound's force! The actual human, physically aggressive wail of it!

And Albert would elaborate on this leading shape of force and power that came to characterize his playing. "It's not about Notes!" he'd proclaim imperiously. Sometimes about some subject musician(s), with that defining scoff of laughter, usually chorused by Norman's stretching eyes of affirmation. "He thinks it's about Notes!!"

Albert meant it was the Sound & that force & ultimately that Spiritual Power that were the real purpose of the music. To bring & raise & spread the Force of Spirit. That fundamentally, the music was, if comprehended and sincerely projected, a Holy Spirit, a Soul/ar Force, an instrument of Revelation, even Salvation.

The spirit of the times colored Albert's defining of the spiritual, the metaphysical bent of his thinking was wound into the actual material existence that marked the Civil Rights Movement, that described Nkrumah (and dialectically what overthrew him). The force of that as reality, of Montgomery, or Fidel, or King or Lumumba or Greensboro or Malcolm. The combustible continuum of Real Life, e.g., Political confrontation worldwide.

Because those "things," "events" are actually deeper processes filled with emotional, philosophical, and psychological animation, communicating lives. The feeling, etc., provoking the acts signifying what indeed meant "Revolution Is the Main Trend in the World Today!" All connected Albert's definition of "Spiritual Awakening," "Spiritual Unity," "The Truth Is Marchin In." So that the metaphysical often referred as well to the non-metaphysical, so there are Real "Witches & Devils"! An extension describing the enemies of "HOLY HOLY," etc., foes to the essence and spirit of the new Freedom!

"It ain't about notes!" we heard as the sound of the horn. Blasted most times into clear direct simple "melodic" lines. Melodic as a vehicle carrying the timbral sonisophical force. Both rhythm and harmony redefined in the Freedom of Ayler's intention into aspects of the Powerful sound.

The compositions were marked by a sharply aggressive explosion of the line, or by a marching cadence, frequently employing a terrifying vibrato or harmonic "phrase" of tones, notes, yelps, shards of dissonant washings, many times in a kind of marching cadence. Later this wash of vibrato waverings distilled into a simpler gospel-like (sanctified) phrasing. The gospel record was surprising in its more simplified statement of the fundamental melodies. But by this later recording something else had crept into Ayler's approach. It was getting absolutely "simpler" in its broadest Presence.

When I began an *Apple Cores* column (in 1966) with "Albert Ayler is the dynamite sound of the time!" the context, just earlier, was what Shepp, for instance, had taken from the Rollins-Hawkins-Webster! sound making it a blues heavy shimmy of extravagant funk. Trane, by now, was the "heaviest spirit" as the conductor of the newly unfettered "Out" and Pharaoh his amanuensis, Pharaoh was Trane inspired but lifted that presence into a hyper-sonic imaging of Trane as paradigm of a new freedom! Ornette was a contemporaneous reprise of a BeBop field far from the deadening counter-creative effects of the Tin Pan Alley penitentiary of commercial and conceptually repetitive stasis.

Albert used the big Bean-Rollins bottom, Trane had dug it but burned it sinewy as air by a kind of Pres-Gonsalves (Bird-taught) facile dynamism of the coming & going of his overall melodic harmonic rhythmic line. Albert put it all in the explosion of his sound.

Trane's improvisational aero-sonic dynamic inspired and unleashed, i.e., forced Albert's overblowing (to be NEW), so that where Trane's beauty had a deep sensuousness to it, Albert replaced that lyricism with an attacking force that only valorized Power!

It can be understood that that approach was aesthetic and political, as I have tried to explain, as a reflection of the social forces at work as context and influence. The question of Power is at the base of all revolutionary struggle. The question of Revolution is "the seizure of power!"

As well, if you can dig it, there was a "geography" to the New, as location of its sensibility. Sonny had got down to the absolutely domestic (Way Out West) to show that everything was indeed everything, then drew on the Caribbean Island Connection (St. Thomas, etc.), a subjective stimulation for fresh improvisation.

Trane, armed with (what Miles told me came from his instruction) the chordal reductionism of The Mode, souped by the impacting presence of the emotional entrance of "the East" (Africa, Asia, Latin America) whose struggles (India, China, Bandung, African Liberation struggles) demonstrated his perception of all this by likewise echoing a new awareness of the East.

Diz had decades before expressed a new bonding of the music to the Latin and Caribbean world in his import of an Afro-Cuban genre. (With Bauza, Machito, Chano Pozo, Mongo, Manteca, "Night in Tunisia," "Cubano Be Cubano Bop," etc., the Cubans had declared themselves an Afro-Cuban nation at the beginning of the 20th century!)

The Afro-Cuban African presence grew heavy in the music, though there had always been that element, from Jelly Roll's "Latin Tinge" to Duke's multiformed uses, e.g., "Caravan," to Bird's "Barbados" & Bud's "Un Poco Loco."

So Trane pressed Eastward, *Kulu Se Mama, A Love Supreme, Exotica* (his contemplation of Eastern religion and musics deepened this, *Africa, Africa/Brass, Afro-Blue* (Mongo's tune). Not only as far as some formal structure, but in the use of hemi semi demi tones, sounds, harmonics that flushed notes out of a running line, seeming to thrust in all directions (See "John Coltrane, a Jazz Great," as well as review and analysis of most of the musicians of the period in *Black Music*, by this author).

But Albert absorbed all that, making apotheosis of the "non-western" timbres and scalar insinuating harmonics. "It's not about notes!" And with those albums and appearances between 1963 and 1967 the music he produced verified that what he was doing had little to do with the formalism of note to note expression. The music gathered a blistering anomaly of omni-tonal sonigraphic phenomena, like narratives of his persona. The music was about his feeling, whatever it sounded like.

But, of course, the same people who first gave Bird, Diz, Monk "No

Stars" in their magazines, & years later had to re-review the same records with overwhelming acclaim, still dirtied minds, calling Trane's playing "Barbaric Yawps" and "Sheets of Sound." Like the A-Hs who told us Monk had "no technique."

So what could they do with Albert, who very consciously was trying to make his horn a Summoner of Livingness, i.e., live images of the soul's awfulness. Ghosts? Witches & Devils? Even John Litweiler, a "sympathetic" critic, says repeatedly that Albert's tempos are "bizarre," "maniacal," and speaks of the "craziness" of Ayler's vibrato. but that vibrato was meant to be "crazy," "out." Albert felt the sound was the soul's munition.

One night Albert, Black Norman, and I, at Albert's insistence, journeyed up to Lincoln Center. It was a Trane concert, armed to the teeth with some of the most impressive of the new musicians, who were now magnetized to the master. Eric Dolphy, Pharoah Sanders, Cecil Taylor, Rashid Ali, and Elvin Jones. We arrived backstage, Norman's eyes shifting the shadows of the darkened staircase from which we checked and dug the fantastic out bad doom a doom whooah of the heavy jam.

The whole of the mise en scene entered the playing, as the playing danced and hugged everybody (alive's) tender screamings or head casted to the rest of the audience like a transfusion, the blistering molten blood swishing through our hearing. Oh Yeh! (My future wife, unknown to me then, Amina, then Sylvia Robinson, was in that audience. See what I mean . . . what a connection.)

At the top of that nuclear "My God!" What emotional convergence turned Albert into the horn he suddenly had in his hands? He began to stride out onto the stage. The horn raised high above his head, as if he wanted to take Pres manque all the way out. The bell pointing as much as possible at the embroidered ceiling of the place. And then, Lord, with that pose as his heart's signature, he began to open a hole in the roof so his angels could descend, summoned by his exploding plaints.

I mean (lovers of a graphic prose) that sound Albert created then was of an actual frightening nature. It had no older reference, it was like a thing born then, that we all witnessed, flying out of the womb of his horn, screaming, it seemed, in its suddenness, with a thousand times more force than all the assembled around him! It was like a thing that you could hear and feel and be made "other," because it swallowed you! (Is this exaggerated? No. I ain't come to that part yet!)

The musicians on the stage, among the greatest in the world, stared in some kind of amazed awe as Albert folded the world in his meaning, as sound! When he finished, there was a beat of . . . "What the F . . . was that?" Then the explosion of recognition. Later, after the program ended, the first one back to the stairway was Trane. (Albert had left the stage, after his nuclear display, for the hallway, where Norman and I waited.) Trane came right up to Albert, his only words, "What kind of reed you using?"

Albert's presence, "the dynamite sound of our time," blew large through that world of ears (as large and as small as it is) after that night as he became the most talked-about insurgent of the new music. Between the murders of JFK and Malcolm X, Albert Ayler is historian and prophet of the Apocalypse!

And for many of us the assassination of Malcolm X was the end of what we called "Downtown" as a center of "new learning." Its meaning was altered and diminished. In the wake of this assault on the Afro-American people and the concomitant rising of the Black Liberation movement there was an even sharper emergence of Black Nationalism.

Many young intellectuals, myself for instance, fled the Village, frantically seeking more direct involvement with the Afro-American struggle. It was almost immediately after the murder that a group of us young Black patriots split from the Village, outraged, guilty, impossibly incongruous with the actuality of material practicality. Yet we had been burned into a bloody sensibility shaped by the deep daring of our self-consciousness, the aggressive caring of what we wanted to think we wanted!

That summer of 1965 was a spectacular thing. With our exodus from "downtown" up to Harlem, opening the Black Arts Repertory Theater School on West 130th Street & Lenox Avenue (now Malcolm X Boulevard). Brought some of the advanced Black artists from the area, as well as from anywhere word of our efforts reached, into Harlem. The Artists marched down West 125th Street when we opened the BARTS, led by Sun Ra's Myth Science Arkestra, myself at the front with a flag designed by painter William White!

Every day that summer, we sent four or five trucks out with improvised stages that painter Joe Overstreet thought up, four banquet tables held together with clamps. Music, Drama, Poetry, Dance, with one truck with easels for the daily exhibition of graphic arts, all over Harlem. We performed in parks, vacant lots, playgrounds, Project Spaces, on the sidewalks, in the streets, alleyways, Sun Ra, Pharoah, Cecil, Milford Graves, Don Pullen, Sunny Murray, Charles Spaulding, Eddie Blackwell, Denis Charles, Olatunji, Jackie McLean, Grachan

Moncur III, Charles Tyler, Archie Shepp, Marion Brown, Albert Ayler, Don Cherry. Andrew Hill was our music coordinator.

Larry Neal, Roland Snellings, Clarence Reed, Ojijiko, Steve Young, Charles Patterson, Sam Anderson, Sonia Sanchez, Barbara Ann Teer, Yusef Iman, my sister, Kimako. It was a total assault of Black Arts into the currents of Black political struggle, a precursor to our understanding of what Mao called for, Cultural Revolution. Though the BARTS itself lasted as an organization in Harlem less than a year, its influence was international. Black Arts Theaters opened in the South (Black Arts South, Val Ferdinand, the Midwest (Woodie King, Ron Milner), the West (Black Arts West & the Black House, Ed Bullins, Marvin X).

The line was Black Art should 1) be identifiably a product of Black Culture and History, as identifiably Black as Monk or Trane or Billie; 2) be a mass art, and go where the people are! 3) be revolutionary.

Sun Ra was among the musicians who came and played regularly to the Arts. Ra came a few days a week to sit and rap with young Steve Young & myself. His Myth Science Arkestra was there performing once a week, and as far as I know Ra pioneered the "light shows" later copped by the Rock shows (Bill Graham of Fillmore West was first) with his Pythagorean-inspired "Space Organ." High sound bright color, low sound dark color.

Albert came less frequently, a few times with Black Norman, who once put one of the Arts's troublemakers into "check" by welcoming, with his eyes and teeth electrically enhanced, a physical conflict that said t-m backed away from. Then Norman took the Bass he often carried . . . (I didn't tell you that?) and wailed extraterrestrial combustion on it, grinning, for an hour!

Albert was in the flow of the Black Arts, but mostly he was still downtown, as were most of the rest of the musicians then, before a bunch more got away, plotting, I speculate now, to become the dominant force in the music he knew he should be.

When the Arts collapsed, from the internal contradictions of its spontaneous mix of ideologies, using black, an impossibly diverse catch-all as a definition for political direction, so that it could not find stability, I returned home to Newark. Perhaps, not so weirdly, Albert had already been coming to Newark, drawn to a Newark Arts space that was also a venue for the new music. Marion Brown, Sun Ra, Charles Moore, Pharoah Sanders, Burton Greene, John Sinclair had made that scene. So when I got back in 1966, the Cellar, as it was called, operated by a local bass player, Art Williams, was doing it to the top of its capacity, and drawing folks from New York as well.

More ironic is that the Cellar was a split off from another similar venue called the Loft, on the top floor of the same building, one member of which was my soon-to-be wife, Sylvia Robinson, now Amina Baraka, one of the principal movers and shakers of the place.

Later, I opened the Spirit House, which was to produce, drama, poetry readings. The Spirit House Movers were the group that emerged from this, made up of people originally drawn to the Black Arts idea. Yusef Iman, Rosita Broadous from California, Amina Baraka, Larry Miller from Newark were key movers.

We began later to produce LPs on our Jihad label. *Black & Beautiful* was the first, with me reading poetry backed by Yusef, his wife Doris, and a DuWop group. *A Black Mass*, a play of mine on the mad scientist Jacoub's creation of white people, as told by Elijah Muhammad with Sun Ra's Myth Science Arkestra. *Sonny's Time Now*, with a group led by drummer Sunny Murray, with Albert and Donald Ayler, Charles Tyler. . . . (All these will be eventually re-released, *Mass* is out already.)

I saw Albert a few times in Newark. But he was still based mostly in NYC. The movement was rising to full blast, with the variously defined impact of Malcolm's assassination. The rebellions would begin in earnest in 1965 Watts, 1967 Detroit and Newark. In Newark, Amina and I stabilized the Spirit House and brought together several organizations as the Committee for a Unified Newark. Even though we still gave programs and traveled with the Spirit House Movers, and read poetry, and Amina organized the African Free School, our main attention was becoming political action.

We had scheduled another LP with Albert and managed to record a concert of Albert and Pharoah Sanders together in Harlem at a Rally. Larry Neal, A.B. Spellman, and I put together a magazine focused mostly on the Music called *The Cricket,* from which the piece "Mr. Jones Asked Me," by Albert, which should be instructive on where he was coming from in 1968.

But I lost direct close touch with Albert, and by the time *New Grass* appeared I could not really say what Albert was up to or doing. Except that record surprised and shocked me with its centerless fluff. From *Lighting and Thunder,* it seemed Albert now wanted to do something he thought "commercial." I wondered and still wonder what happened.

And then I heard that he had been found floating in a River, cause of death unknown.

THE DARK IS FULL OF TEARS

When Albert returned from
the grave, he had no horn. He
asked us to look for it &
we agreed.

He sd he wd return when
we found it. He was somewhere
in space, drugged about Religion
& The Mob.

I asked him had he been
murdered.

"Of course," Albert wd answer
most things like this though,

"Murdered by God! That's why
it was stupid to believe
in him!"

That was in 1970, the same year we finally elected a Black man as Mayor of Newark and organized the Congress of African People. But in a few years, that surge of Revolution had been co-opted by the same Black elected officials we bled to get elected.

The world keeps changing for the Afro-American people, Du Bois said our historical path resembles the story of Sisyphus, so that our "Sisyphus Syndrome" sees us roll the huge boulder of national oppression, racism, up the mountain of desired democracy, only to have cruel "Gods" roll it back down on our heads. Certainly we are at the near bottom of that Syndrome today. But that old tape we have of Albert and Pharaoh, blowing fire at a Political Rally in Harlem ca. '67 blows me back, for a minute, to that time and that place, and the feeling leaping off the tape is "Revolution Is the Main Trend in the World Today." Just like these sides here, make you think "Truth Is Marching In" still. It will, though, that's why these sides are so valuable.

CHAPTER 42

Albert's Will

Albert spoke singing from the deep mixed up clarity inside us, everybody human, everybody who feels or cries, or laughs, or knows something. Albert erupted from out of the shadowy interior of everybody's soul, where the sky burns its crazy omen of allness. That blast of ON-ing fire. Hmmmmmmmmmmm&c.

"You mean?"

. . . Yes,

"You're saying . . . ?"

. . . That's right,

"That Albert was in touch with something More Than ourselves?"

No, Pilgrim, Albert was in touch with the whole of us with no shucking or one-eyed whispers. Africa, the Middle Passage, Ghost Furnace America, Slavery straight out, the runaway angels sailing back overhead, the cold-blooded deep down hope to die, fly if you wanna, heavy, absolutely colored, blue dirty chained Black Ass God of the Slave Nigger Church . . . and all them tears and all them screams and all that cussing and swearin and believin and forgetting and crucifying and drunken stumbling grace. Plus underneath or overneath all that some almost contra-tonal divinity of sweetness. That's why he spake in them kinda tongues. That's why he cd say what he saw. That's why, I guess, he had to pay for it.

And like a heartprint of his soul's intelligence and understanding of what all this is or was, or will be, or whatever the taste of morning makes us see, he left this. . . . Yeh, A Box!* Dig That!

"And . . . ?"

Huh, it's on you now!

10/3/04
Newark

---

*Albert Ayler's complete works, *Holy Ghost*

CHAPTER 43

Sassy Was Definitely Not
the Avon Lady

But she was the divinity from Avon Avenue between Belmont and the Circle, Right around the corner from the old Silver Saddle, where we first dug Bird. Her '50s landmark crib, for little Bop anointed hipsters, going back home, up the, to the, Hill, digging, not pausing . . . Hey, that's where Sarah Vaughan lives . . . a crazy million times on the way to the Four Corners where we lived. Near Babs and Little Jimmy and Brody and Grachan, the Holy Temple of Belmont Avenue where we got saved every Sunday night by Nat Phipps, Jackie Bland, Bull Moose Jackson, Lynn Hope, Illinois, Ammons, Bostic.

The Hill, old 3rd ward, wherein, also, Booby Heard's *Howard Street* is the raw tip, the under-over wailing rhythms where rid oh Blues leaped out the souls there, turning the streets and the people's faces Afro-Hillian blue. Where, like tasted memory, reached back, the place, as a face of faces, beyond our conscious knowing, until we stumbled into ourselves.

Yes, she was Divine, the true origins of that word. To see the future. Which is what Sassy was singing. For the diggers Sassy's voice was an instrument expressing the exact sensuousness of our hearts. How fantastic that was, how she swooped and bent the beauty of it, ascending like our hopeful vision, the emotional touching of our would-be rationalized reflections . . . what we had picked up trying to dig the world.

Ella was the umbrella of vision, the common dimension of our AT,

the house, the windows, our parents. Dinah Washington, the ubiquitous encirclement of sound in which we stanced across those streets,
Ruth Brown too, "Teardrops from My Eyes" had held us in those tee-
nybopper Belmont Avenue and Spruce Street Masonic years.

Then we heard Sassy, maybe one night, on (Sid growl) "The alll
night all frantic one . . . ," Symphony Sid, our main man, pulling apart
night shadows to show the burning blue and fire inside. "From the Jazz
corner of The World. The Divine One, Ms. Sarah Vaughan."

. . . oh, and altogether at once right then, the radio glowed, rose
and became sacred . . . made your ears incredible treasure, make you
stand up inside yourself reaching beyond where you could see, all the
way out to where you could dig another world. Unfolding with the
glide and turn and whipping moon-flecked speed of the ancient Black
Bird. Or get down with the Charlie Bird, Lullaby of that world, of the
human-headed soul, of Bird Land. And even if somebody blew, well, . . .
"You're Not the Kind of Boy for a Gir-ir-ir-irl . . . like me. . . ." Sudden,
surprising, possessing your wanting with her desire. Like it was . . .
"Just One of Those Things," you dig.

Or at sun speed, she re-blued the tale of "Perdido" or, in deep indigo,
"Lonely Woman" or the acidly anthemic "Sassy's Blues," and let you
know, with sound and word and utter gorgeousness, what hip is, to
hold in our knowing for ever. You want to know where she would take
us she spun a thread of living wheres, like "How High the Moon."

If you told me, some where any body could go, past that sailing
soulfulness . . . I would say you was probably still saying "Hep" and
wearing pegs. Sarah's voice was dazzling broad, instantly re-imaging
re-hearing re-sounding. The voice alone was unbelievable the way it
lit excitement through you. Clear strong blues-shaped church-muscled
and intense, with the wide open conquest of where it touched.

Sassy was the Scatters' scatter, the BeBop horn mouth of our song.
Ella before her, the paradigmatic mistress of high scat, Sassy picked
whole, on her way to her self's wonderfulness.

But Sassy was hippest, the most daring, and innovative, the clearest
voice of the new music. She was not accompanied, she was organically
part of the One, the fluid Outness of the whole. She was the beautiful
song trumpet banner of the emerging Gone. The voice that told the
whole story of what the new music was being, its ultra-gonic tempos,
rhythm-born "jooking" melodic lines, harmonic innovation, the re-
incarnated "newness," freshness of its sound.

Underneath all that glorious wailing was the church, and this is not much understood, Mt. Zion Choir, like many of the "hincty" middle-class Black churches, was pushing the Fisk Jubilee Singers' "concertization" of the Sorrow Songs, moving them from the field to the house, but slavery limited class distancing, so that the essence of the songs' beauty remained intact. In fact, Sassy's mother and my grandmother helped form the William P. Sims Gospel Singers just to make sure the upwardly mobile Negroes at Mt. Zion and Bethany Baptist (which also sang Handel on Easters) still stayed in touch with the traditional gospel funk of the Black working-class church.

So Sassy carried the swooping keening ascending and descending vocalism identified with opera (unless we know the traditional West African vocal style), drawn from her peepas' transatlantic appreciation of that style, before she hit Julliard. It is the combining of these "techniques" Sassy opened our ears and heads with. That even when she was all the way hot funky wailing, grooving, "straight ahead," in a beat, she would be gone, up up and away, circling, diving, turning, gliding, like the glowing Black Bird she was, aloft, but still "getting down." She was the Charlie Parker of the Voice, and remained so even when she went all the way out, past Serious, as is all our destination, back to the Sun.

What could you be
When you heard Divine all around you
Floating I Am misty elegance across the streets of The Hill
Where could you be but where your self Divined you would
    have to be to be digging what had helped shape you
    before you even knew there
Was a you to do that

Plus, we thought, absolutely, that Sassy was one of the most beautiful women we'd ever seen. Like that, the entire umbrella of sky, magnetized to her breathing, transformed then into sonic images of light. Ahhh, and then we thought, anyway, all that world-altering revelation, the flood and flash of what the Imperial Ghost word-packaged as "BeBop." All of what that did to us, in our open youngness, was transforming, and convinced us we had been sanctified with knowing. A knowing from incredible feeling, made us think we could know whatever there was of value in the world.

So We were Sassy's "Funny Valentines," in a world of "Polka Dots & Moonbeams," all us, including "Cherokee," "Old Folks," any groovin being who could "Shulie Bop." Or understood "Don't Blame Me" or

"September Song," even in July, or could feel with "Poor Butterfly" in our "Misty" Disposition, that "It Shouldn't Happen to a Dream," why we say, Sassy, Sassy, Oh, Divine One, "Lover, Come Back to" . . . We. . . .

And as she booked there was . . . a climbing rush of whispered Blue ness, introed the silence her leaving left, Spirit splitting across the sky, trailing lyrics, sad ironic, made us cry. . . . "Send in the Clowns," that wonderful haunting deep with tears, "Send in the Clowns. . . . "

And then, lastly, from the stunning Outness, of Sassy's flying where, That last sound, to those on the ground, "Don't bother . . . they're here. . . . "

CHAPTER 44

Fred

On Feb 1999, at the Aaron Davis Hall of City College of New York, David Murray, Craig Harris, and some others led the way in organizing one of the most artistically sensitive and musically expressive memorials I've attended. Fred Hopkins was commemorated by a spectrum of his peers, who showed not only why Fred was so central a figure in the last decade or so of new music, but that those who cared most for him are among the most innovative and moving players out here.

Read the program, and lament your absence:

Chief Bey to give the libation and invoke the transatlantic savaging, and the music's origins.

Muhal Abrams's grand effusively effervescent yet tightly wrapped big band, how the large sound carries the newest orchestral approach and remains contemporarily the great voice of the music, something we need to hear, to dig our selves, all the time.

A bass unit to give homage to Fred, "Bass Guard," with Wilber Morris, William Parker, Mark Helias, Andy McKee, Michael Logan, F. Vattel Cherry—who played and returned—playing an extended version of one of Fred's works.

Craig Harris's "Slide Ride" trombone unit (Ray Anderson, Frank Lacy, Gray Valente) is as hip as expected, unique simply because we can't see enough of them for all the squalling imitation the media hoists to defeat our quest for beauty.

The World Saxophone Quartet, now with James Spaulding and the

exciting younger voice James Carter on soprano, in Cab Calloway's
"vine," along with David and Hammiet, was at the top of whole art
form. Add Micki Davis, a dancer who provoked and evoked and
spread the instrumental force and archness, its lovely harmonic bond,
into steps and gestures and living rhythm images hooked to what we
know of each other's lives. This was the highlight of an evening of
highlights.

D.D. Jackson, the emerging piano point, supersonic muscularity
and thoughtful sensitivity, with the unique musicality of drummer
Andrew Cyrille and John Stubblefield, whose reed mastery is yet to be
sufficiently dug, along with guitarist Kelvyn Bell, presented a tasty yet
out traveling quartet which also should be gigging regularly, in all the
places where mediocrity now reigns supreme.

Lester Bowie's Brass Fantasy performed the exquisitely tasteful
dirge, complete with L.B. walking it off. Again, a musical treat we
cannot hear enough of. The entire Memorial should have brought back
to all in earshot how much great music is forcefully kept obscure and
seldom heard by the resistance to authenticity and originality that
characterizes the Money Jungle of clubs and recording companies, the
society itself.

3/5/99

Modesty almost caused me to drop my own participation in the program, with Pheeroan Aklaff, drums, and Frank Lowe, tenor.

CHAPTER 45

Fred Hopkins's Memorial

Tragedy is defined, ultimately, as a Drag. Comedy, the collective orgasm electricity. I first checked Fred as part of AIR, which now, except for its Navigator, hopefully safe in India, the other 2/3rds of 3/5ths of the metaphor for Artist in Residence, Breath Song, or Yes, in the peasant tongue, have gone on, turned completely Spiritual on us.

What tragedy combines in its dialectic is that both Fred and Steve McCall, the other wing, were new when we first dug them, stayed new when well known, i.e., by the cognoscenti, and were still new when they went on.

Fred was articulation. A sharp throbbing pulse which made a Jake Lawrence visioning to his note to note, to chord, to phrase, coloring. The motion glowed, as a beautiful "Thing" voiced from a thing by a Thing thinking. Perception to rationale to heavy use.

We miss Fred so deeply because he was the voice and impressive parade of the music that evolved to carry Pettiford, Mingus, Wilbur Ware, Chambers, the unsung Henry Grimes, Garrison, Workman, all the badnesses through Trane, Albert, Ra, and them, representing an advanced technology as the means of expressing contemporary feeling and understanding.

Fred was feeling playing (as) himself, the matter whose motion was thought. Matter that has grown a brain, which thinks and makes tools, which expresses itself and its place and vision in the world. An innovative creator of the continuum of the music itself, which exists as re-creation re-birth. Like the crocodile from Upper to Lower Nile, half hid, half seen, a legend underneath, covered here, in the Money Jungle, Duke said, by the Sea of Money.

Any slave trader, whose specialty it is to make Bucks green from Bucks Black, would have paid glittering chump change to ride Fred's Black. If he just wasn't carrying all that Blue Deep, Story, Rhythm as the infinity of meaning, speech, song. The visible thought, the poets' mood. The Cow Cow Boogie. The Black Ox Moan.

Art lights up the world so the world can identify and understand itself. Earth, which has grown a brain, from organic sticks and stones, from feelings. Production teaches, dimensions spirit, the breath of life.

Rhythm is the first speech/song, as always, imagining every as a question, a divining visionary of origin.

Destiny is the spine of our where, we, anything, is, going, been. The future is always a head, time is motion, space. And why Fred is now gone. Do we dare define the coldest most outlandish margin of our is? Dare we admit our brother and most of the other "Blowers of the Now," Where they were are, were, are cut down by the horrible but familiar Beast master world of our continuing Chattelphilia.

Or say this, a nation's most advanced thinkers are secure, no matter how brilliant they are, only in direct proportion to how secure that nation is. And then, given the risk to which highly developed, discursive, and applied rationalization, experimentation, and specific practical use put the individual, the particular being reflective of that Whole being and history, time, place, condition, then if we got three out of five of our children in jail, two out of five of us in deep poverty, and live in a place so hostile to genuinely creative thought and even mental and physical health, then to the extent that we cannot protect each other, our people, most people, workers, including our intellectuals and artists, our cultural workers, then we got real problems, terrifying deathly problems so ugly that barely a century after we create an internationally acknowledged artistic genre of transforming beauty, somebody else can say, with absolute impunity, that No, it wasn't we, it certainly wasn't Fred, it was Elvis or Kenny G. If we in that kind of situation then we got a fiend problem, and must deal with it not only for us to survive, but even our memory and history.

And I know I have said this before, at each tragic passing, too early, of our most advanced creators. That we must use all of our energies and resources to transform such a place where even our vision is in danger of being vision-napped, or benignly appropriated and co-opted or assassinated. That we must even create an art whose force and beauty and profundity help make ourselves and the people of the world secure and more self-consciously sensitive. And for our artists and intellectuals, as righteous cultural workers whose souls are part of and extensions of our own, we must struggle to transform this torture chamber and create a world where such valuable beings will be secure and honored, even paid and fed.

So the Freds, like the Steves, the Hemphills, the Blackwells, Pullens, and Dennis Charleses, the Aylers and Tranes, and "Fat Girls" and Brownies and Birds, and Sassys and Betty Carters, and so many others, are doomed each day like Gray's flower "to blush unseen," or like Henry Dumas or Fred Hopkins, slaughtered or suicided by America, the Beast, who "rose smoking from the Western Sea." What is to be done, we will have to do, they are our lives, our thought, our feeling, our expression, and no amount of submission and begging will save us, only Self-Consciousness, Self-Reliance, Self-Development, Self-Defense, Unity and Struggle. Think of Fred and all the others, and understand and act like we got some sense. Because We Really Do!

2/19/99

CHAPTER 46

Duke Ellington

The Music's "Great Spirit"

Duke's collective work sings and "speaks" as a reflection of the social and political economic character of the historic African American culture. Its aesthetic character is itself artistic expression as the most evocative summation of that people, contexted by their mean experience of the "Whole" world encyclopedic African presence as development, journey, summation.

Africa, the actual, as it disappears into the Been is entrance into recorded history. The music comes from before that, its blue pentatonic polyphonic polyrhythmic human voice. We are carried with and transformed by him in that becoming, voice to instrument, become itself, from what it come from. Not abstract but the historical materialism of Wheres—as Continuum, as Consciousness, Testimony, social presence, art, aesthetic projection, style, and confirmation . . . as the Djeli ya of the "Gleemen," by the consummate Djali (*Griot* is a French word) of American Classical Music, the greatest keeper of its Afro-American soul. Soul is its great force, its Sun, from whence all the colors come.

Duke's music is the evocative human experience of its Being, Origins, Destiny. In its multiple forms, vectors, rays, halos, crowns, its function as generator and what has been generated.

Ellington's Blues is his breathing life inside the works. The Blues is always a presence, form, content, spiritual essence and reach. Blues as the Being wherefrom the Being re-being as Music (Thought seen— Sonic Light).

But Blues for Ellington is a life and life force—from the "favorite color" it was in West Africa (see Equiano) stretched twisted tortured. Soaked with a deadly abstraction of invisibility soaked in Blood. Therefore across the whole spectrum of color, sounds, speed, direction, Ultra Violet (invisible as it emerges from Blackness, Indigo as it appears as the twilight diameter of touching worlds, history now memory now Mood. The Doom of the Slave trade and Middle Passage is thrown dialectically to its origins as Mood (Doom!).

So Blue (Beauty) post–Middle Passage is Loss, Sadness, Memory as Recherché, Redux, yet afire as it remains. Laughter, Joy is often the ironic contemplation of sadness. Happy Blues. Crazy Blues. Billie's Blues, Blue Monk, Potato Head Blues.

You Blue

You Blew!!

Yeh, Blow!!! (Express)

He really Blew (Like Trane)

The dialectic combines as a link like the "Railroad of Human Bones" (Jacques Roumain) . . . at the bottom of the Atlantic Ocean. My God! A railroad of human bones!

Ellington is the Classical American composer, with a world-encircling understanding of the singularly expressive, pointedly *sensuous* possibilities of Music. His use of voice, vocalism, chorus, the incredibly beautiful harmonies . . . almost never fully reproduced by those who seek to . . . are literally stunning.

Duke's Harmonic conception is Western Blue, the depth, Blue Black Deep, inferring a natural "unison" use of the whole fabric of sound, placed precisely to caress the broadest chromatic spectrum of itself as color and drama, mood and emotion. Ellington's music is fundamentally *lyric drama* . . . Dramatic as sensuous ideation, containing narrative, call & response. Tales of passion or revelation, pain and uproarious joy.

Some recent highly touted interpretations of Ellington seem superficial, the orchestra playing the written notes but unable to create the deep colors, powerful moods, and transcendent imagery of the works, particularly the extended, more complex pieces, like the great Suites.

Duke always tells a Tale or continues it, in *ideosonic* images, as rhythm-melodic verse, chromatic color mood sound emotion as living musical drama. This is the heavy historical presence the music brings, narrative images. The formal rationalization of Duke's music are the complex and inventive compositions. But the maestro always explained to the orchestra *what* the pieces were about. Their narrative Tale. The Mood's Meaning. E.g., "Characters," Settings, Dramatic Contexts and Scenes, as musical creations, musical relationships whose aesthetic whole is itself Narrative, i.e., how it is put together . . . Musically! Ellington explained in his rehearsals what those relationships, of note, to phrase, to theme to emphasis, style, tempo, create & evoke the particularity of the image he sought. Its *story*, description, structure, musical functions, which propose a relationship direct or as a result of, as indirect, that exist as an infinite number of paradigms and examples. Metaphor is a function of anything, according to its context.

Max Roach, describing the sessions that produced the great *Money Jungle,* relates that at the first rehearsal with himself and Charlie Mingus, before any music was played, Duke explained the "Mise en Scene," i.e., the dramatic world he wanted to create with that music.

But whether the initial material and inspiration originate as Stride, Rag, old or new blues, they are expanded in their *use* and meaning in the music that follows. Ellington combines, through the classic historical summation and convergence of cultural elements, All the Music We Know!

The ancient pentatonic scale is African . . . the Old World and the Blues. Duke, the pianist, is insinuatingly black-key (one form of the pentatonic scale) based. But he uses the white keys as part of the whole, all related more organically. The sharps and flats are part of one integrated scale (as the Twelve-Tone composers demonstrated to some extent). So that "minors" and "majors" express each other as dialectical relationships existing as a living whole.

One wonders did Duke ever discuss with Paul Robeson the profound research Robeson did, internationally, on the relationship of the worldwide existence of the ancient pentatonic and the later diatonic "tempered" scale Europe created with its ascendance (ca. 15th century) and the resulting segregated piano. The very existence of the White/Black key segregation, exclusion from the diatonic as "flat" or "sharp," of what? These sharps and flats actually speak of the historic existence and ancientness of the Pentatonic Scale (Blues) as found throughout ancient world cultures, from Africa to Russia to Mexico, etc.

The European Diatonic scale is a psychosocial privileging of some notes over others, as a fixed "tempered" scale. Actually, the black notes are the ancient vowels of speech, of languages, the five senses (5 + 5), the hands, the feet, the organs on the face of the senses.

The music speaks, sings, as a totality of its own historic actuality, the confirmation of all the aspects of which it is composed. In other words, it is what it tells about.

The refusal, in 1967, by the Pulitzer Prize committee to give the Pulitzer to Duke, after its own music judges had selected him, is just another bizarre proof that the U.S. has never been a democracy. Just as the same embarrassing national chauvinism enabled "great musical minds" like Irving Mills and John Hammond to pass judgment that Duke had betrayed "Jazz" when he began to produce the extended masterworks and suites. Or *Downbeat* and *Metronome* writing in the '40s that the emergence of Bird, Diz, Monk, etc., signaled the "death" of the music, giving their records "No Stars" initially, and then years later, to save the unface they had left, re-reviewing the records!

Still it goes on, with frequent *New York Times* writers like Richard Sudhalter contributing such gems of national chauvinism as saying that the music did not originate in the Afro-American community, as a vector of that culture, but was actually co-created by white musicians. Certainly, Mr. Sudhalter is entitled to his opinion, but in the context of the historic racism and national oppression under which Black people have suffered in the U.S., and the fact that there are yet no major newspapers in the country in which a black writer is featured writing about Jazz, such tedious subjectivism as Sudhalter's seems only another shell from the scatter gun of white nationalism, Black national oppression, and racism! (Let us imagine there was no major newspaper with a featured Euro-American writer writing on European concert music!)

As for the Pulitzer salute to the Klan, when Duke heard this incredible confession of lynch mentality by the Pulitzerwaffe, his rejoinder was, "I guess the Lord didn't want me to get famous too young!"

Ellington's 2,000 registered compositions, his leadership of the Ellington orchestra for over 40! Years, without a break, continuing even when the Basie band broke up, by hook and with a crook (Mills), is another testament to Ellington's real (as distinct from legendary) Ducality.

The national character of Duke Ellington's work, African American and American, the very nature of what Duke combines to produce his great body of composition, makes it seem as if Duke was, himself, the most gloriously aestheticized paradigm of Du Bois's (his spiritual father) description of the "twoness" of the Afro-American people. The "double consciousness," which we have been taken aback considering, but have yet not quite understood, is the actual configuration of Afro-American social, psychological, and cultural sensibility.

Are we Black or Americans? the distressed Afro-American prototype consciousness tortures itself asking. The fact is we are both, but
that "twoness" is the basis of schizophrenia only if we cannot realize
both aspects of our Western experience. This is the same "twoness" we
must arm ourselves with politically, that is, to fight for democracy and
equal citizenship rights, but at the same time to assert our right to self-
determination, because it is only to the extent that we do self-organize
and project our own historically confirmed summation of the tasks and
methods facing us in forwarding the overall struggle that we will be
able to advance the "other side" of this twinned struggle successfully.

We need not be almost "torn in two," as Du Bois lamented, by the
contradictions of being Black in the national chauvinist fiction called
"White America." We are both, Black and American, and I hope I scan-
dalize Black cultural nationalists into near-sanity by repeating, Yes,
Black people are Black and Americans, and this is our double-edged
sword.

This is the dichotomy, the dialectic, of our fully conscious Black
selves, not a schizo-paranoia, but the fuller recognition of our own
history and experience. This is the powerful perception, given philosophical and aesthetic dimension (rationale) through an understanding of the historic parameters and existent continuum and paradigm
Ellington drew upon to inspire his USE of the concept that Black People
are African and American and we can authentically draw upon the
entire range of psycho-cultural aesthetic choices with which to express
ourselves. For to be an American we must be shaped (even if we are
not aware of this) by three cultures: the African, the Native Peoples',
and the European, at their deepest incursion reorganized as American
culture.

So Duke, the most American of composers, the Afro-American Soul
of American Classical music, is at the same time the most cosmopolitan and most expressive avatar of a grand art registered as profound
across the world, including the metropoles of Europe. Ellington is at
once African and non-Western, as Western, international and local,
Pan-American, Pan-African, American, Occidental, Oriental, etc., his
amazing gifts to us, at times universally lyrical, at others jam hot or
some other times an innovative Symphonicopation still unreplicated by
the soi-disant replicators.

How? By absorbing *all*, from where to when, like even the backbeat,
rhythm and blues signature Duke used for a long time. (Check "Night
Train," i.e., the second movement of the *Deep South Suite,* or the funky

denouement of "Happy Go Lucky Local," or for that matter extended works like *Afro-Asian Eclipse* or *Far East Suite*.) That's why Miles, when he got into exclusive backbeatdom, wrote the piece dedicated to Duke "Love You Madly," for Ellington had provided myriad examples and, one imagines, "permission" for Miles to appropriate what he must have considered a similarly advanced use of backbeat.

Duke was "far out" and "way in" depending on what aspect of our experience he was musicking. It's why, say, Stravinsky, when he came to the U.S., always made it a point to dig what Ellington was doing (like if you asked Horowitz who was "the greatest pianist in the world" he'd tell you Art Tatum!).

For Duke was both artist and historian-composer and raconteur, the West African cross-the-water, Afro-American *Djali* (Griot) of the Deep and the Very Deep.

6/8/99

CHAPTER 47

Duke Was a Very Great Pianist!

I know I was guilty of saying this numbness, in print, somewhere, which I understand recently has been attributed to Billy Strayhorn, that "Duke's real instrument is the orchestra." And probably, if he said it, he meant that in the way of emphasizing Ellington's unparalleled creative expressiveness through the artistry of his composition and orchestration, and conducting. But make no missed snake, Duke Ellington was one of the finest pianists in the music.

Because the piano, like all the other instruments in the magnificent orchestra, is organically linked embedded embossed in the whole cloth of blue lovely wailographic sonifunkestry as a whole a completeness of expression, we might sleep the specific grandness of each of its parts. But if you miss the masterful chords Ellington lays down behind any thing, from *Money Jungle*, or with Louis, e.g., on "Do Nothing," or "Duke's Place," "C-Jam Blues," "Fleur Africane," "Subtle Lament," or myriad others, pick up his solo works, "The Pianist," "The Shepherd," "Solo Piano."

Duke was one of the "Stride" masters, from his earliest days, one of Willie "the Lion" Smith's grand charges, like James P. and Fats, and his piano playing gives the basis, the fundamental sound corridors his ear glides out of, to put together the immense profundity of his orchestral works and approach to writing and arranging. Moreover, Ellington, even without the orchestra (unthinkable, and an abstraction, since Duke's piano was, dialectically, a cameo of the orchestra), would be a Giant, just from the grand aesthetic scope of his musical conception, expressed however.

CHAPTER 48

Blind Tom

The Continuity of Americana

John Davis Plays Blind Tom: The Eighth Wonder, Newport Classic, 2000, NPD 85660.

Tom Wiggins, born in 1849, a slave, in Columbus, Georgia, later called Blind Tom Bethune (after the slave master), was apparently an "autistic" slave (what they called an "Idiot Savant"), though, with the ugly jumble of white supremacist mumbo-jumbo which passed, certainly in the 19th century, and still passes for science, we cannot really be sure of this. That is, Wiggins could have been just a sightless brother with an amazing skill at playing, almost immediately, any music or sound that he heard. From accounts I've read, any piece of music played in his hearing he could duplicate almost spontaneously and, as well, recall a piece instantly he'd heard years ago. At any rate, whatever Wiggins's physical handicap, his worst handicap was slavery itself.

This can be confirmed by just reading the title of one of the brochures which advertised his appearances in the 19th-century U.S.,[A] "Blind Pigs & FireProof Women" . . . , "Unique, Eccentric and Amazing entertainers . . . e.g., Stone Eaters, Mind Readers, Poison Resisters, Daredevils, Singing Mice," with the picture of a pig with a number in his snout over Wiggins's name. (Likewise, the characterization of women reminds us of women's oppression, a triple oppression for working women of color, even today!) Ah, Yes, fellow citizens . . . "the good old days!"

Wiggins was able to play, literally, anything, European concert music, and a monumental conglomerate of the popular songs of the time. By 1878, James Trotter, in his book *Music and Some Highly Musical People* (purported to be the first book written by an African American on Black Music), wrote that Wiggins "remembers and plays full seven thousand pieces . . . every piece he has ever heard." "Blind

Tom" began playing at four years old, and the amazed slave owners had him concertizing throughout the South before he was ten! The general amazement at Wiggins's skill was so peculiar because, until the end of the Civil War, he never played outside the South!

Blind Tom was characterized as "near animal," able only to mutter unintelligible grunts and odd sounds, though he could, according to these same observers, play Beethoven's difficult 3rd Piano Concerto, with his back to the piano, so that his right hand played the left-hand part and vice versa! Most of the amazement and awe was inspired by Wiggins's ability to whip through the panoply of European "Classics," but this was bluntly tied to the kind of appreciation such people give to, as they advertised, stone eaters, fire eaters, carnival geeks, etc. He was called "a curiosity," "The Eighth Wonder of the World." By characterizing Wiggins as a "Mimic" (Houdini said it had to do with "Psychic Powers"), the fact that the man also composed hundreds of his own compositions could be generally trivialized. It reminds you of how Black athletes today are "instinctive," whites "intelligent."

The importance of John Davis's resurrection of "Blind Tom" by playing Wiggins's own compositions, and the historical materials he has made available, in a series of concerts and with this recording, the first one ever done, should redraw Wiggins's image so that he can be seen not just as some "black freak" but as a creative personality, performer, composer, no matter his physical limitations.

As Du Bois put it, "Many suffered as badly as black people . . . but none of them was real estate." Even after the Emancipation Proclamation, Wiggins's former owners still owned him. And while he made an equivalent of a million dollars as a result of his tours, even playing once for President Buchanan, he died in poverty and was buried in an unmarked grave. How cruel was slavery, one might say, but as late as 1967 the Pulitzer Prize committee refused to give Duke Ellington the prize, and the number of Afro-American musicians who have been dealt with by official U.S. culture keepers and lived and died the way Thomas Wiggins did, even at this very hour, should let us know that "Blind Tom" is perhaps a metaphor not only for Afro-American Artists but for the creative forces of any oppressed people, whose state, if they are truly a reflection of their culture, must exist as a more remarked-upon replication of that whole people.

On the tape I have, though there is other music to be released on the CD, Davis plays "Wellenklange" ("Voice of the Waves"). Wiggins, it is reported, could "mimic" "German, French, Greek and Latin but could not understand it" . . . still one category past most Americans, who can neither speak it nor understand it. Frequently Wiggins's compositions were modeled on the phenomena of Nature. Additional "proof" that he and Debussy? (e.g., "La Mer") were mere mimics. "The Sewing Song," musical onomatopoeia for a sewing machine, "The Rainstorm," another . . . what is that word . . . example of Wiggins's sound-centered . . . *Impressionism* (Ah . . . yes) and "Reve Charmant" (literally "Charming Dream"), translated here as "Nocturne."

Listening to Wiggins's compositions dispels immediately the canard that he is merely imitating. Though the pieces played reflect the Romantic European concert "classics" of the period, the careful balance of the form, the delicacy and lyric grace of even the most impressionistic passages, the skillful use of arpeggio, crescendo, the movement of the work from the lightest Piano to roaring Staccato mark Wiggins's compositions as the thoughtful musings and deliberate organization of sound that can only reflect a humanity and creativity ironically much more developed than the Yahoos who unquestioningly accepted his characterization as "less than human." But this distorted rationale of the man does reveal the incredible ignorance and/or generally depraved psychology of the characterizers and should confirm the all but absolute disconnection of such a society, based on exploitation, from any form of civilization based on a collective self-consciousness of human commonality as well as from very simple forms of feeling which must mark developed humanity.

The music, played with much emotional empathy by John Davis, puts one in mind of Fred Douglass's famous soliloquy on some bluff overlooking the Chesapeake just before he made his dash to freedom. Identifying with the free sailing ships which whip his mind with the contrast of his own bondage, he whispers, ""You are loosed from your moorings, and are free; I am fast in my chains, and am a slave! . . . You are freedom's swift-winged angels, that fly round the world; I am confined in bands of iron! O that I were free! O, that I were on one of your gallant decks. . . . Go on, go on. . . ."

The music expresses a similar emotional metaphor, if one can but imagine the tragic irony of two humans (among many) with such sensitive and creative consciousness enslaved by beings who claimed humanity yet enforced an inhuman social obscenity in which actual bearers of a more truly human civilization are ruled only three-fifths of Dracula, and imprisoned as "Real Estate"! Makes you wanna holler . . . etc.

7/99
Newark

CHAPTER 49

Don Pullen Leaves Us

Don, you too, already? So many of us away away. We were here &
sang and spoke and danced and played and even made war. Acted.
We did—

And from that time I first met you and Milford, your man. That
homemade self-made intro side. I donno, people kept saying this and
that, you was more or less than this or that one. It didn't and don't
matter. You was hip as Don Pullen and very few can claim that.

So, sad, brother, very few of the citizens even know your name. Very
few even got to know you—your music. Very few . . .

Don, so beautiful, yet still in my mind a young man. Don, Don, so
beautiful. Yet like my whole gang of great genius motherfuckers, so
quickly gone. Don, so beautiful, Still, I see you, still so young. With so
much fire and incredible vision, loveliness blue gleaming funk pouring
out of your fingers. Don, Don, so beautiful. I see you, still a very young
man, and yet so quickly, like so many of our gang, already gone. No
glibness. It just ain't hip enough here. It is the ugliness and terror surrounding this little light of ours.

We wanted in and wanted out! We needed, like that song, and you
did appear and grow and gave the gift the Dr. spoke of. The gift of
song and story, and yes, the gift of labor and the gift of spirit. These
are the gifts of Black Folks, the visible daylight fire that alone keeps us
alive prevents our death by frostbitten heartlessness the maniac hea-

280

then who own this space bloodily maintain and claim, no shit, that it's civilization.

Yet with these gifts of ours, the gifts of Black Folks, just this week, you, Julius Hemphill, and Gil Moses, all here less than six decades, have gone, been swept away—By what? And that's the question plagues me, that what that why and lack of wise.

Swept away by Dis. And Covered. Even while living. From lost Columbus given the word by Isabella (a lie) that the Moors was whipped. El Sid had triumphed (and was getting a radio gig at Birdland) and that it was cool to hotfoot to "India" to pick up some taste for the grit. But they meant a dimension, a thing, for their newstyle "Christianity" of pretense.

So the D at the end of Go. De fense against Go. Against life. The D. The Thing of Heathen fusion of lie with death. The Idol. For life is eating and drinking and farting and belching and rape (the f word) and rope their last name.

And then to give it Greatness. Here, Everywhere. They could not lead, but give it the same timbre as Dead. Without life. If we were Shines, they could get Shiny the God—Better the Thing the Stopping of Life. GOLD.

Space becomes Speech becomes money. The Sun's very rays are said to be in competition with each other. As they race across the not see, these blind heathens saw Races, of everyone. In order to belch and fart more. The most deadly animal can pretend.

And here we come, the Afro'mericans. The source of the riches. Af—Before, but seized by Romans. Roaming ourselves, dragged here to the money lovers' (Americans') stolen palace.

Our chants at night under the decks. Our screams to whatever it was we'd forgotten. Because we seized ourselves and gave ourselves to Rome, we were so high. And that's how we got down.

When I met you, like me. We knew we could win the world. We knew it didn't belong to no Heathens, that's why you wailed so hard uptown with us. We Black Arts them nights. Cooking us black Harlem magic.

We owned Black Art! We cried We Black. We coming Out, All in the Street. We cried we was revolutionaries. That our hearts beat tempos. Our language itself was syncopation. And Blue we painted on us from the inside. So our spirits were dark like our mother night.

So Don was Out! All of us was Out. Trying to get out. Already Out! Going Out further. Trane was our underground railroad. Albert Ayler was the high whistle you heard that broke the nights into dances the stars sparkling notes the sky played.

You see, we thought Art was Tatum, Blakey, at least Farmer, that it was the prayer the dark folks whispered, "And Thou Art with me." Our Art was our comrade in struggle. It was the creation the creating that wished us here. Ain't's enemy. We played the Blues from our memory. When we were Home. And so came again to Harlem to try to get back.

We knew what then we had to do to make us so Black & Blue. The out was to be counted (along with Count & Duke, & Billy & Bud & Monk & Bird & Pres). The Out was to escape—this jail of colorless evil. We were our own spices.

Besides we knew Columbus was a torturer and a criminal and he brought spies to seize our goods and make everything else bad (in english) and call himself God. Removing the second circle of infinity the Art would turn upside down like a smile becomes a frown (womens got sad) and vision would become a broke carrier an unmoving cart to carry something that does not exist. Tragedy's taxi. (You know, God riding a machine!)

If G is the Sun Gone from Nut the speech of the balls track through space like the earthy clitoris touching itself and becoming the Ark, the SDG, the coming, the Sea man, in waves, ultra purple invisible to the circle of lo! To the second circle of go! To the 3rd circle of soul created and gone. Then what created is good. What Is created. And it is alive. Not a statue or a statute (a paper statue). A low opposite. It is the truth. The they is it going. The ing in we connected to coming. The jism is the jasm. It says I AM. JAZZ. Signed with Shango's initials. I AM. We say through eternity. Speaking from the sky. SHA-N-GO! ZZ JA (Yes! Eye! I! Aye!) AM. We could feel that we were invoking that goodness and truth and beauty was swinging. That like come it was hot. We were the Out of Ja who could C. We were Ja's colation. A little food from thought, the arc was Blue. Our memory too. And we were like every thing forever, Black. But when we studied and worked and fought we had read the book of life, and our outness exploded Red. We knew we were new. So we blew what we knew. What we blew, that made us blue. And we read every body.

We wanted to Change Everything. The Changes we went through we saved like Black mama becoming the first Say lore, our needs were Know I see. The So—the Sown. The Changes were sewn in us. And we spread them like the seeds of our thoughtfulness.

Like the nigger of eternity we loved freedom. We could see it when we got in to the Visionary thought, the question that beats Are I Them! The answer the down of the turning waves, possessed by their going and coming, the rise and falls, and the curves of the five senses, the black notes of Human Number, the symbol of Self—connected to the circle of going, Knowing, a speed measured in knots, the body of our rise the swift swoop and funk of our fall. Getting down is the motion and Time and Art. Like Sisyphus rumbling to the bottom of the mountain, again.

We knew we had to go on out to get past the dead and the executioner's symbol they bid us wear to show we loved the prophet's murder. They said they would give us candy, to show how the dead could rise again a few days later. And the prophets' betrayal would be our namesake, the graves to trick us with Sweet History Month, they covered with chocolate. That world, the moon, matter, the motion, became Peter-Paul's Mounds.

We would play the new world. Not be hung by our balls like the old father who denied us or the self-hating convert who covered us on the Road to Rome, who never was an apostle. Peter and Paul were the creators of Rock and Roll.

We were new souls, children WHO.M.B. The WE of US & I. Albert, Eric, Sun Ra, We all was on the same Trane. With Henry Dumas and Larry Neal, out's children. An army of RAZORS. An army of Bloods. (Check *Richard's Tune* and *Big Alice*.)

We seemed Strange because we were the change. Don was telling us Jesus never been in Europe! He was telling us Everybody talking Bout Heaven Aint Going There. Listen to Malcolm and Betty. He was telling us The Ballot or the Bullet.

Don would play the black notes as vowels. Five of them. And the 21 consonants, a sea of trouble. Don was explaining why Ali Baba on reaching Europe ate fish on Friday. To eat up the old religion. He knew why the imposters called Christ's day of execution "Good Friday." And that Friday was a day of freedom for the Heathens, since they had killed the Son and taken Summer north and named him Remus.

He knew how the Sun Man's lost child was kidnapped to the out lands. And at the opposite side of the whirl was called Romulus. How the brothers Romulus and Remus were Sumer and Sulumoor. And how Bird swept up through the nut of his black mama, black rising against blue bursting into flames at the top. Celebrating himself and everything that Are.

He was our Eye. That Black Fetish Djeli Ya Bird. Inside his mother watching the wolf, where the flood waters swept, suckle them and whisper about Johannesburg.

Don knew Gold was a Dead Thing. That money was a blind liar chanting that Heaven was a plantation full of slaves. Don spoke in a swirl of pictures. Like the voice of our mother the sky, when she is wet and on fire. Only truth is royal. Only reality.

His self was a thought of laughter. The smile from the bottom of the world. He was the Who that ends as Be. Though at the footstep of down rush spirit, invisible breathing.

Don could get high from smiling. He rode the blue ark of flight. He was U and U the I & I of Birth and Vision. He could sweep across the keys like educated space speaking in colors.

He used sound as the spectrum of particularity. Like the notes were things with lives and business. He was warm and alive yet he would scream and hammer like Shango's boy telling everybody where he was.

He was the romance. The living ocean of human life. Don was communicating what civilization is. He was a spirit reliver. He'd leave you with a spirit embracing you. He turned you Blue. He forced you to act like you read the world every day. He made you fly and see from up there how small, how awe full, yet like the numberless flowers, funky pretty smelling and beautiful waving to the birth nap, the horns and bass.

Don loved Love. He wanted, like, all of us living humans, to be love, to make everything love and the truth. Don wanted everything to swing like it should. To whisper and scream and kiss and embrace themselves as other everybodies cool as the chorus of comets.

Don, I can't love you enough for you to be here now playing. Yet we will someday save ourselves by forgetting this animal world. Letting them go to Mars in a Hot Rush. While we float on the blue water the see of the whole self, the mother of the father, the son of the all's daughter. The vision the fission the colored say lores the tale oars of the wordship, the go past, this world, must change, even while we sit here or blow the devil, backward life, away.

I want to hear Don inside me like that beyond the space of time the lies of how wise got to be spelled w-h-i-t-e.

We are the Razor, Don would play, We are the Blood. He was new, like we all were. He came from Out to bring those hundred flowers of his fingers, to return those hundred schools of spiritual fish back home. Don was a point guard of the new, the yet, the will, the beauty of humanity still emerging. Don was post-Heathenic loveliness. Post-imperialist musart. Eye him later Who first was the me you can't see.

We were there, the answer electricity gives to the be seer. Beau Peep! Hot eye the blue spook, afraid of a thing who says it lives and is dead, the backward dog. The lead foot of the lame who left home a murderer who went north to be a mf and get blind and eat people. Later he started calling it religion, the prize for bribing judges, the cost of becoming Holy and the Vampire. Yet still We color the world. Co-author it with the birth of each you reliving.

Don was not known widely because he was a tour few take. So he rode the ark in the asking cycle. And hammered like old speech the keys to open tomorrow.

We got high possessed and rose blue like flying, to escape these animals before. Up this tree of life and made hands of our feet and thumbs of our toes. The apples the naked liars copped (the adman and the imaginary woman he created and their pet serpent) were actually solid waste. And for the predators this was money. Yet they were insulted by our high ness. They did not understand we were possessed by what rises into where, not a sum, but an every, each return, on the ladder, like up in the tree you could hear them crying, limping there hairy with a club. And couldn't clam up no how.

My eyes were rolling like the universe. Don speaking. There is no place but what I make travels and loves and is the family looking up at the Sun.

Don was my brother. He could sing to me like from a very old place, and I would feel and hear and understand. And then we would be flying. Black up rising against the guinea blue. In my memory. Don is the future waiting to say hello again. And we know life does not end. Don, if you dig it, is where ever Blue is, still goin out, playing himself, in that moving arc of light, he circles just above our heads, invisible and nuclear, telling quiet stories in the voice of the mother tongue, so we are never alone.

5/95

CHAPTER 50

Black History Month Rediscovers "the Music" in New York City

My wife, Amina, said something like that when I wondered aloud why, this weekend of February 17, 18, 19 (2005), there seemed, very suddenly, given the month's long near-vacuum of quality music, that a bunch should magically appear. Usually the scene for the last years has been spotty to zip.

A year or so ago we saw a great gathering at the Iridium, a McCoy Tyner group with Pharoah Sanders, Ravi Coltrane, Charnett Moffett on bass and drums. And that was exciting and exquisite!

A couple weeks later, Jackie Mc, his son Rene, with Grachan Moncur III, trombone, again at the Iridium, on quite a few of Moncur's classic charts. But such encounters have grown rare. The most advanced music has been replaced by commerce, e.g., fusion, neo-elevator, anonymous "white chicks" (of any nationality), equally anonymous Europeans and white supremacy redux. For a longish spell the Monks, Mileses, Tranes have been disappeared in favor of gnomes named Kenny G, Dr. John, Diana Krall. But this weekend Amina and I were delighted to check the sudden Plenty of Horn the newspapers and WBGO projected.

A Bad start was the weather, Bush like, cold and ugly, blowin' snow like lies. We got to the Iridium early, or at least just before 9:00, and had made reservations, but Cecil Taylor was still hammering through the earlier set, some said because he had arrived about a 1/2 hour late.

So a bunch of us grew into slabs of jabbering ice until we improvised a way into the hallway, and it was time to slide inside and greet the musicians and poets who always grace any of the vaunted musical venues. Soon, we made our way straight back to talk to Cecil. The great bassist Reggie Workman and my own longtime tenor player Rahman Herbie Morgan also made that backstage scene.

For me, since Cecil and I have known each other since the late '50s, about the time he first began to wake up a slouchy crowd of painters (many about to become famous) at a greasy little Bowery club called the Five Spot. In fact, Cecil might have been the first Jazz acolyte of that quality to be in the joint. The rest should be history.

This night, however, what drew us back to him was the alert that he would be leading a big band, and that sounded interesting, very interesting, to me. Cecil's dazzling irreverent tirades on the box are tres familiar to me, having dug and trumpeted them for almost fifty years. The last time I'd ventured to hear him was on the Columbia University campus a few summers ago with Max (Cecil insists on calling him "Maximilian") Roach. And that was a memorably iconoclastic rumble, with said Max furiously pushing Cecil across and back, the connection resulting in something hot, red as fire and smoking.

Since then, or since any time, it's hard to walk up on Cecil because, like many of our artists, he has to spend an inordinate amount of time in Europe. This night, Cecil was indeed himself. Almost as I had known him since my first hearing. Except there has been at times an ambience that somewhat decomposed the strict straight-ahead percussionism of CT licks, the angular saxophonic denting of Jimmy Lyons, at one time Sonny Murray's psychedelic grunts and chings, later Andrew Cyrille spinning mini-ripostes. And the brief conjunction with Trane on that terrible coming attraction (we thought) that never really came again. "Into the Hot," where Cecil projected and was projected into a sizzling after funkistry that we heard as the unifying construct, romance, "classicism" & the next stage of everything!

But the American dream remains just that, and one aspect of it, for that reason, is dipped in fluorescent concrete, but it still hardens. We become what our received desires demand of us, even if that ain't actually super-hip.

To say Cecil became & remains "the monster at the Keyboard," endlessly reminding us that European "classicism" can be "appropriated" as one trope of Afro-American (American) music, must be obvious. Whether it "swings" or not is a question for the poseurs of absolutism (of which I have not been inducted). "Moving" though, doesn't that count?

This night at the Iridium, what had drawn us there was not the chance to hear & see Cecil again, but that he was appearing, the Newspapers taunted, with a Big Band. Hey, we thought, that was something. The mind always creates its own world, only to be "advised" of the contrast of that world with reality.

The idea that Cecil's jet-propelled monologues would be translated into orchestral quotients remains intriguing. Unfortunately that never happened! What we heard was Cecil being his Cecilistic self, surrounded by near-ambient (however placed) sounds.

Cecil would poke, then puddle, then stomp, then batter the box as he does & the various instruments would provide a kind of consonant Bling Bling. There was never any hint of significant composition. It was merely Cecil & some other stuff. Fascinating in itself, but for those who might want to hear Cecil Taylor moving toward some, perhaps, Dukish compositional aesthetic presence, Alas.

And so those fettered with such banalities of now traditional grandeur must continue to treasure what they can.

2/22/05

CHAPTER 51

Black History Month Rediscovers "the Music," Part 2

The Charles Tolliver Big Band at the Jazz Standard

One thing we can treasure and if we cannot it means the "Yet" of this ain't borned where we can dig it. Amina & I, the next night (after C. T. at the Iridium), had plotted to go first to the Jazz Standard (East 27th Street, NYC) to check the Charles Tolliver Big Band, then to a new Japanese spot, the Kitano, a seemingly haughty glistening nouveau on Park Avenue, to see John Hicks.

We thought by leaving the house (Newark) at 6:00 we'd be at Jazz Standard in plenty of time to see the Tolliver set. But we found we were actually "late," people were crowded in the place already, so we had to sit in a sideways corner, though close, digging the musicians from the side and rear.

No matter, Jimmy, this is some of the best music we've heard in a long minute! Tolliver and I go back to *The New Wave in Jazz,* an LP I produced as a benefit for the Black Arts Repertory Theater School, which myself and some other self-determining minded Black artists opened in Harlem, on West 130th Street a month after Malcolm X was murdered.

Tolliver was then a hottening but streaky "Hard Bop/erator" from Brooklyn, one of the knowledgeable graduate students of Professor Blakey's Funkiversity. Tolliver came through Max Roach, Sonny Rollins, with groups that featured John Hicks, Stanley Cowell, and did a year or so with Gerald Wilson's California Big Band.

I'd just about forgotten, in the torrent of the Unhip and the submissive that clouds the scene these days at the bottom of the Sisyphus Syndrome where the rock has been rolled so far back down the mountain of human progress it has almost disappeared into the Bushes . . . that Charles Tolliver and Cowell, in those heavy days ('71) when the idea of Black Self- Determination was a mass expression, founded their own record company, Strata-East!

Part of what was so refreshing this night was that you could hear in the music, the compositions and solos, of this Tolliver-led band the fire of the Blakey/Jazz Messenger CHARGE! type heat, but with an obvious finesse and consummate orchestration of the parts and the smooth yet ever forceful sonic dynamism of the whole, you hear what the leader learned not only from the Blakey hard bop Classicism, but also the orchestral teachings of Wilson, and check it out, what Diz exploded into being with his big bands shot straight out of Gillespie's marvelously wild yet impeccably well-ordered compositions, likewise his overall still much undervalued orchestral conceptualization! Usually Diz the sonic stylist and even his hip comedic antics overshadow the genuine grandeur of John Birks Gillespie, the truly great innovative artist! But none of this is lost on Charles Tolliver, himself one of Diz's freshest and most skilled progeny in all aspects, compositionally, orchestration, conducting, he even wanna crack some jokes.

After not seeing Tolliver in quite a few years, what we witnessed was a source of deep excitement and gratification. Tolliver stood the music up on tiptoe, Dizzy Gillespie Brass-First style, and it was deep down thrilling! Not just the unpreventable nostalgia such magic carries with it, but to hear again such music, such an approach, such charts, such solos, such ideas, played so well, was utterly transforming!

The band, I suspected it, checking the notice, was most likely a squad of skilled veterans, old enough to be funky and conscious, shaped psychologically and socially by "the tradition" to be awesome musical raconteurs of its wonders. And so it was, James Spaulding and Bill Saxton, tenors; Jimmy Owens, trumpet; Howard Johnson (the great tuba player), baritone; Cecil McBee, bass; Ralph Peterson, drums, just to name some of the biggest names, though believe me, there was some young'ns and some veterans who will come to me who carried much heavy in the set. But just from the names I mentioned, experienced, highly skilled, hope to die funky operatives, who have actually heard the masters of our late Golden Age, the Birds, Dizzys, Dukes, Fats, Tranes, Miles, J.J.'s, Carters, Sassys, Billies, Prez's, who have actually heard the wonderful Dizzy Gillespie and Billy Eckstine big bands, who carry Ellington & Basie in the amulets of their hearts!

So the incredible precision, the unchallengeable *swing,* Yeh, that, at undecipherable speeds, spraying visions of grand classicism, yet possessing us, themselves and the place, with the newness of the right now.

A wonderful evening, fully Gillespie-like, but with its own excellence and excitement. The loud thrashing riffs (Check "Things to Come," "Emanon," etc.), the sudden lightning of solos or key changes, all calling on whatever was in charge of the joint to challenge the heat of this truth, this beauty (whew!).

Just before the set, as musicians came trooping over to our table, a couple in front said, "Whooh, you're too popular," and moved so they would not have to be stepped over.

It was a re-unioning of sorts, the musicians to some acolytes, us both and all to the grand BeBoppers of our finest sessions. So dig, next time you see Charles Tolliver Big Band somewhere (he's got a refinery, I'm told, at the New School), don't blow, pick up and go! You'll love me for telling you.

CHAPTER 52

Wonderful Stevie

Stevie Wonder, *At the Close of a Century,* 4 CDs, box set, Motown, 1999, 0121539922.

Learn one more time, the heaviest people come from where they mostly is. For instance, let us dig, one more again, the Great Stevie Wonder. The Stevie Wonder boxed set *At the Close of a Century* is high mastery. So full of the absolutely deepest down of the Black and the Blue. At the same time, packed throughout with an all-embracing musical and lyric social sophistication which is joy, shock, revelation, amazing grace, and Blood hot sweet, burning, beautiful is the word, wonderful grooves to lay in your mind as long as you hooked up here in space and time.

I've always been a Wonder digger, from back in Little Stevie days. That first intro is on this side too. Four CDs take us from the frenetic sub-teeny bopper belting out the just about standard Shouting R&B. You remember this little dude in the dark glasses rocking back and forth side to side, up and down, blasting at us. And one very fine quality of this set is that we hear the brother moving, his voice becoming more maturely his own, with every cut. (Hey, where is "They Had Me on the Front Line . . . but the back of the line when it comes to gettin ahead." Apparently some thinker didn't think this was at the top of the Wonder's wonders. Too bad.)

You hear Stevie's voice getting deeper and smoother, his driving beat coming from a personal concept, not just co-signing the tradition. The voice becomes a thing of physical grandness, but the passion, the feeling begins there, but runs into your own feelings he means the words, is touched by his music so.

To sample some of the obvious beauties, check "If You Really Love Me," a mocking plea, a conversation, a rap . . . or the transformation he does on "Blowing in the Wind" from Bob Dylan or the Beatles' "We Can Work It Out." I said a long time ago that coming out of Stevie's emotional depth, these songs are literally transformed by the context of Stevie's and Black People's real lives. They are deep urgencies, not only serious ballads.

The stunning "Living for the City" is a piece of music to come out in the glorious Motown Sixties that can groove at the ambitious level of Marvin Gaye's "What's Going On." But dig the, like they say, denouement, going out. Stevie adds real home hard drama with the country boy makes bad very quick, plus dig the spiraling aria-like moral as this urban cautionary tale rises back into the ether, as pointedly poignant like Verdi questioning destiny as Aida splits.

What about the jaundiced wail of "Superstition," Oh preacher con man politician ridden folk that we bees. "You Haven't Done Nothin," with the classic vocal vamp, Doo De Wa Doo De Waa. We used to play that for Newark politicians every Monday on a radio show we had . . . "If you really want to hear our views, you haven't done nothin," like a more advanced companion piece to "Superstition."

From every which direction and style and approach, tempo, mood, lyric statement, we must embrace the grandness of Stevie's musical bounty. A recent film has two "superhip" white boys put down a white customer for wanting to buy "I Just Called to Say I Love You," saying, "It's too sentimental." Egad! that's the final Dis, to remove Stevie from the Mainstream of national attention because of the progressive nature of his lyrics and the all the way out-of-sight conceptualization and innovation of his art. Remember Paul Simon, one year at the Grammys, thanking Stevie for not making an album that year so he could get a Grammy. Dig that!

So now the corporations have set their Lilliputians to work at totally Dissing this great musician, after first covering him with hundreds of ersatz replicas. So they can take the public taste to Heavy Metal Devil Worship, Neo-Nazi mania, or the highjacked Afro-American Music they fix our criminal class image with by calling it "Gangsta" (easier to shoot a Gangster) or Hip Hop. But remember these are the same critical minds that refused to award Duke Ellington the Pulitzer Prize in 1967, even though their own jury selected him!!

Instead of Wonderful music we get Marilyn Manson, Madonna, and a bunch of disguised Negroes lying about how they gonna smoke a cop!

The deeper tragedy of all this is that Black Americans are among the most historically productive and innovative artists and cultural workers in this nation, as Du Bois said, The Gifts of Black Folk . . . Labor, Song & Story, Spirit. We are the Air Jordans, Whitney Houstons, Tiger Woods, Michael Jacksons, Muhammad Alis right Now, so why we so cashless. (That ain't really true, the GNP of Afro-America is 470 Billion dollars a Year!!) You know why, because we still have not developed a national circulating commonwealth that will touch the 470,000,000,000 at least once before going back to the Owner. The organization of Afro-American Art & Culture is one of the most critical necessities we face in the struggle for Self-Determination and Democracy.

The great Motown era was also the era of sharp social struggle, shoulder to shoulder with some of the most innovative Jazz since Bird's BeBop '40s. The element of struggle, commitment, innovation, self-determination, all flying head high and full of a vaunting human joy. All this is the spirit of the Civil Rights Black Liberation Movement Sixties. Notice how once the movement was stalled, the arts grew static, the thrust for/Self-determination diminished for the opportunism of economist types who take the money and sit.

Just from this Wonder, "Send One Your Love," "Always," "Pastime Paradise"!! (dig the orchestration, the use of synthesizer and voices, and especially what he be saying, "We spend our lives living in a pastime paradise," or, equally wasteful and frustrating, "a future paradise." "I Am Singing," "All I Do," "Isn't She Lovely," "Golden Lady," the activist missile "Happy Birthday," a clear demonstration of Self-Determination, Dig the Wonderful vamp on "That Girl," or "Ribbon in the Sky," and check "Do I Do," with Dizzy Gillespie and again that marvelous use of big chorus, "Overjoyed," and Yeh . . . dudes, "I Just Called To Say I Love You."

A HIGHLIGHT FROM "BACK IN THE DAY"

In 1970, when we mounted Newark's "Community's Choice" electoral campaign and elected the 1st Black Mayor, Kenneth Gibson, of a major northeaster city, Stevie came in in a bright yellow suit and wailed for us all day, all over town, from the back of a truck.

CHAPTER 53

Abbey Lincoln

I want to believe that for a broadening circle of longtime listeners to "the Music" Abbey Lincoln is synonymous with "the State of the Art" as far as the instrumentally "re-defined" blues song. After Al Jolson or with Kenny G, it's difficult to say "Jazz" and attach it to something profound without a grim shrug in acknowledgment of the disingenuous commercialism heaped on the term almost since its inception.

But if we are meaning blue song, transformed by instrumental adaptation of rhythm and the harmelodic expansiveness of improvisation as acknowledged reorganization of the line the beat the melody the harmonic relationships, then we are talking about Ethel Waters, Billie Holiday, Ella Fitzgerald, Sarah Vaughan, and Abbey Lincoln. This is not meant to be exclusive, in the sense that nobody else could do this. Betty Carter, Carmen McRae, among others, talking about female artists in the music. But from the particular perspective I'm coming from, the combining of the most traditional Blues feeling, sound, timbre, content, transformational form, with the constantly reconfigured newest renewal which creates the continuum of the music, from its various innovators, then these singers are the music's vocal pantheon.

Abbey Lincoln, like the most expressive re-definers of tradition, has absorbed, it seems, all of the past, recent as it is, and, with the chemical equation of her own life and experience, threaded through the rational process of general and musical intelligence honed to light with the endless practice that produces high skill, carries and offers freely a vocal artistry, right now on this planet, that is the main paradigm for revelation in this time and the next.

As voice, instrument, narrator, dramatist, actress, creator of the mise en scene, auteur, improviser, melodist, poet, Abbey Lincoln moves without peer. Knowing her music is to know a lot about Abbey Lincoln, as it is with the deepest artists. Because so much of their whole feeling thoughtful combined selves is used to create their art.

So the sensitive lyricism, the blade-sharp insight very often touched with a droll but wistful humor, the emotional revelation that is one constant dimension of her singing are very evident in the woman herself.

She lives in "upper Manhattan," like they say, where the more expansive cultural motif of high urban sophistication begins to turn, like the enjambment of a poetic line, imperceptibly toward the contrasting otherness of where the Blues People stay. So Abbey is like that, what she does, who she is, the artist and artistry connected as the persona of a sharply defined and articulated, yet delicate humanism, linking the given with the need to be, the deep with the deeper.

Like the apartment, spacious, clearly an introduction to herself, comfortable, self-proclaiming, engraved with not so much decor as confirmation of her own aesthetic particularity and presence. Evocative painting, including one of her mother and another, just parallel, of her father, each holding some of Abbey's brothers and sisters, Abbey herself in both.

Classic photographs, which themselves are archival gems narrating some aspect of the world she has moved through, the many giants and epiphanies she has experienced. Like one incredibly riveting photo of young Mr. B with Bird, and Diz and Lucky Thompson. Stunning drawings and posters and photos of Abbey, herself, making the walls also a visual biography. Still, at 70 (and she wanted to know why "they" want to make so much of this number"), a striking beauty.

"I came to California when I was around twenty. My brother Alex brought me out there with him. I had been practicing, singing, but it didn't sound like much. When I got there I was Anna Marie Wooldridge. But the manager wanted me to have a French name and I already had one. But when I began singing at the Moulin Rouge, they changed it to Gaby. And I got some publicity, I was in some of the magazines. *Ebony* used to like me a lot, before I went social." She says this with that wink in her laugh, cool and signifying.

"I was meeting people like Jose Ferrer and his wife, then, Rosemary Clooney. And Mitch Miller, they introduced me to Bob Russell, really a brilliant lyricist. He wrote lyrics for 'Do Nothing Till You Hear from Me,' 'Don't Get Around Much Anymore.' The classic Ellington songs. It was Russell named me Abbey Lincoln. He thought I should be linked up to my own history. He was very up front about his own. He used to tell me, 'Jews made the world,' and talk about Marx, Freud, and Jesus Christ."

Russell also functioned as Abbey's first manager along with Steve Roland. "They sent me on the road. I went to Honolulu and worked with a group called the Rampart Streeters. They played the music, a drummer named 'Blinky' Allen. He used to blink his eyes when he played. They were playing the music, but there was too much vice and stuff going on, the place was wide open. People thought they could do anything they wanted to. It seems like it always gets like that just before they take your country over. A lot of people got busted finally. That's when they used to call me, 'that square broad that works at the Brown Derby.'"

Speaking of the "Theys," she says of her neophyte days, "They wanted to make me a glamour type, when I first got to Hollywood. I got in this movie, *The Girl Can't Help It* (with Jayne Mansfield . . . Little Richard sang the title song). I sang something called "Spread the Word." No, nothing happened with that. They weren't interested in what I was singing. They were just interested in me wearing that Marilyn Monroe dress. The one she wore in *Gentleman Prefer Blondes*. Roach saved me from all that." One aspect of Abbey's narrative is a consistent and genuine gratitude for the role Max Roach played in her musical development as a singer and as a conscious artist.

"But before that I'd wear this dress, it was orange chiffon and my breasts would be bouncing around. It actually had cotton in the bra. That's all they were interested in, me wearing Marilyn Monroe's dress. They were creating some rep for me as some breasty sexy woman. But I wasn't never really that. I can't stand some man looking at me and just thinking about sex.

"I was never driven by ideas of 'Success and Stardom.' I thought I was that to start with. My family gave me that. I was given this." She is laughing openly now. "I think my ancestors liked me a lot."

"I really didn't know much about the music then. But I began to meet people." Talking about how and what she learned and from whom. "I met Duke coming from Hawaii. He used to stay in a suite in one of the two Black hotels in L.A., the Watkins. That's when it was all segregated. So when Duke was in town, he always stayed at the Watkins.

"So I decided I wanted to sing with Duke. He hadn't asked for a singer. But I just went up to see him, and hit on him, telling him I wanted to sing with the band. Duke didn't say much, he just began to undress and walk toward the bedroom. Then he rolled the bed down, and I walked out of there." Abbey is having much fun running this down. "I never told that to any writers before. . . . I guess he was letting me know . . . up front. . . . so I got right out of there."

"I met a lot of people in L.A. and Honolulu. I met Billie Holiday, Cozy Cole, Louis Armstrong. I never got close to Billie. Actually, I was afraid of her. I mean, I respected her so much. I wasn't going to walk up to her like some of these singers do to me and start talking about myself, give me their latest record." So it is that Abbey describes her relationship with Billie as "kind of standoffish."

"Louis was a wonderful man. He didn't look at a woman's behind, he looked right into your eyes, and he was a great friend. Dinah Washington and Sassy liked me. Actually, they treated me as a mascot. Cause I was still learning the music. I already had a career, as a glamour queen. I didn't have to be there" (she means, not only Honolulu or the L.A. music scene), "but I had to be there. I had to be in the music.

"I remember one time I was in Honolulu with this saxophone player I used to hang around and Johnny Griffin was blowing. I had never heard somebody playing like that. I told my friend, 'You better go practice!' Boy, Johnny Griffin was bad! I was still practicing."

Anna Marie Wooldridge, one of twelve children, born in Chicago, parents coming up from St. Louis. Abbey's conversation is punctuated with frequent references to her parents and the values they gave her and her brothers and sisters. "My father built our house. He built two houses, one in Chicago and the other in Calvin's Center, near Kalamazoo, Michigan, when we moved there. Calvin's Corner was one of the stops on the Underground Railroad. A lot of those folks there were light skinned with straight hair. The runaway slaves married the whites and Indians there. So they didn't socialize with us much.

"My father actually midwifed my last six brothers and sisters. He knew how to do things with his hands. He was a handyman." When I asked what was the most enduring value her family gave her, without hesitation, except for the laughter which accompanied her answer, "Learn how to do something!" And with that droll hilarity, "To go and do something . . . before we got underprivileged or ghettoized!"

"I grew up on a farm. My folks never told me about no storks. Never gave us no names to worship. If my mother had put a white man's picture on the wall. . . ." She is remembering how even after her parents separated, her mother provided a continuity to the secular clarity of the values in the house, mainly, self-respect and self-reliance.

"We had an upright piano in that house. When I was four going on five I would sit in the front room, we called it. If I could sing a tune I could finally play it. No one ever told me to 'stop playing,' it was getting on their nerves or anything. No one told me to 'play' either. Neither my parents nor any of my brothers and sisters."

It is this openness and directness shaped with the direction of self-knowledge that still animates Abbey's telling of her youth and family. "We slept, all twelve of us, on the floor, on pallets. Yet they produced children who became something. My brother, Robert, is a judge. My brother, Alexander, was the first black tool and die maker in California. A movie star. . . ." She is smiling, impishly. "My youngest brother is a VIP at Motorola. There's about 150 of us now, children, grandchildren.

"The first album I did was with Benny Carter, Bob Russell, Marty Paitch, Jack Montrose, *The Story of a Girl in Love* in 1956. I had met Max in 1954, when I got back from Honolulu. Friends had told him about me, that I was a singer he needed to hear. He was working with Clifford Brown at Hermosa Beach. I remember how beautiful his hands were. He encouraged me. I met Clifford that one time.

"After Clifford was killed I came back to New York. I had fired everybody, all my managers and agents. Because by now I had a manager who owned 50 percent of me. I overheard Bob Russell telling some people, 'You don't understand, I own this woman.' I fired everybody, agents, manager. I've not had a manager since. I've got business associates. But I manage myself!

"Influences? Billie Holiday, Duke Ellington, I had a lot of influences. But Max Roach was the main influence. I was still wearing that Marilyn Monroe dress, and one time in Canada, Max says, 'Abbey, I don't like that dress.' I thought about it, then put it in the incinerator so I wouldn't wear it again.

"Max and the great musicians he introduced me to knew everything about theory. He introduced me to the cycle of fifths in B$^\flat$. What I love about this music is the promise of individuality. Variations on a theme. If you can get past the idea of 'Jazz.'" Abbey hisses the word into a chuckle. The dismissal of the term as a loose straitjacket of commerce and cultural patronization she shares with Roach, who told me he got it from Duke Ellington.

("Once they start calling the music Jazz," Max said to me a few years ago, "then they can use the term to prop up some things and some people that have nothing to do with this music. All they meant in the beginning was 'nigger music'. We need to speak of the music of Duke Ellington or the music of Thelonius Monk.")

About the music, Abbey turns directly philosophical. "It's the *human spirit*," she calls. That's why those athletes can run like that. That's the only thing. Everyone has it. But in the music, the Africans practiced it. On this level. That's why they came and got us. You think somebody's gonna cross two oceans to get somebody that can't do nothing?

"But when I met Max I understood what I was involved in. He asked me, 'Abbey, why do you sing everything legato? This is a rhythm music. On the beat!' He'd say that even on the stage.

"How would I have gotten a chance to meet these great musicians, Rollins, Dorham? Max asked me, 'Abbey, would you like to make a jazz album?' I told him I wasn't a jazz singer. He said, 'You're black, aren't you?' The Riverside dates came out of that [Abbey's first sides as leader: *That's Him*, 1957, Riv 250, with Dorham, Rollins, Wynton Kelly, Paul Chambers, Max Roach; *Abbey Is Blue*, 1959, Riv 1153, with Tommy Turrentine, Julian Priester, Stanley Turrentine, Les Spann, Wynton Kelly, Cedar Walton, Philip Wright, Bobby Boswell, Sam Jones, Philly Joe Jones, Max Roach].

With another smiling irony, Abbey remembers, "That's when the jealousy started." And to my incredulousness, she adds, "Uh huh, people who were jealous. I wasn't supposed to be taken seriously." Her tone stiffening. "I would get this from singers. They'd be talking to Max, 'Why don't you let Abbey go make some money, she's not a singer!'

"I wasn't supposed to be a singer, just 'pretty.' After *Freedom Now*, someone of them said, 'Now I'm gonna hear Abbey scream!' But first of all there wasn't anybody as beautiful as Billie Holiday on stage, ever!

"But Max and the other great musicians he introduced me to carried me through all that. When I was getting ready to record 'Blue Monk' with my lyrics, Max called Monk and asked him to come and check the rehearsal. When I finished, Monk came over and whispered in my ear, 'Don't be so perfect'. I didn't know what he was talking about. When I asked Max, he said, 'Make a mistake!'"

The inference being that all the strained concentration on "not making a mistake" is misplaced in this American Classical Music, because such focus would be better used to free the musician's improvisational creativity. Or as T. Sphere himself once said: "There's two kind of mistakes. The regular ones and those that sound bad!"

"Monk started me to seeing myself as a composer. He told these people once, 'Abbey Lincoln is not only a great singer and a great actress, but a great composer.' And I hadn't composed anything then. But I would. The first song I composed and wrote the lyrics was "The People in Me" (*The People in Me,* ITM 0039 CD).

She certainly would, her compositions and lyrics are one aspect of the unique musical artist that Abbey Lincoln is. Since her complete embrace of the most advanced musical forms, the poetic impact of the lyrics, hers and others', is an indelible power that keeps the whole song, voice, words, arrangement, composition spinning in one's head. Always from the stance of singer as musician, instrument, poet, actress, philosopher.

For those who can actually hear the sweet and swinging composite of skillfully wrought emotional and intellectual artifact, we are always stunned and in awe at her accomplishment. Yet like anyone who takes life more seriously than what is "given" to us by those who think life is merely a continuum of paydays, meals, and the passing of expensive feces, Abbey has had to take her share of knocks. For her highly personal creativity and her highly public aesthetic, cultural and social-political self-portraits.

A big for instance is the sizzling records she made with Max Roach, whom she married in 1962. The daunting aesthetic departure of the great *We Insist: Freedom Now Suite* (Candid 9902, 1960) and *It's Time* (Impulse 62, 1962) was clearly inspired by the whole context of the real world in which everyone lives, even though it pays to claim it doesn't even exist. The "screaming" that the one anonymous ignoramus laid at Abbey's feet is, in fact, if said sad person was babbling about "Tears for Johannesburg," where indeed the vocal narrative reaches like the unstoppable juggernaut of rising collective human passion. As if the struggle to end apartheid in South Africa were purely a figment of some black woman singer's overactive imagination. You can go to Soweto today and still be moved to wail with such incendiary beauty as Abbey's to further change the place even years after apartheid has been formally dismantled. Its remains are still visible and still stink.

Likewise "Driva Man" and "Freedom Day," drawn from the historic emotional log of grievous black American memory, and you could be talking about a memory you gonna get after you go outside tomorrow. Abbey sings of a real world, which she paints with her own soul's experience. Max Roach, she repeats, was the agent of her recognition of that soul in music as a function of raising a young artist's "true self-consciousness" already unfolding.

It is a common topic of conversation among the various diggers how Abbey and Max had to pay for their commitment to "the Movement." The very same crocodiles who might skin and grin in their presence would advance almost a boycott of these two internationally acclaimed artists, as payback for them daring to use their art in the service of democracy and the people. But self-determination is anathema to the corpses, even if packaged only as an aesthetic and located exclusively in the world of art.

"Miriam Makeba took me with her to Africa (1975). I was sort of her Lady-in-Waiting. We went to Guinea, where the president (Sekou Toure) was her patron. He gave me the name Aminata. In Zaire, they added the name Moseka. She is a wonderful person and a fantastic singer. She can do so many things with a song, with her voice, with the words. She sings in so many languages."

I was trying to vouchsafe to this grand artist of blue song that I wasn't there to press her for any don't-need-to-be-told stuff about the whatevers of her life. Instead, she volunteered a somewhat stunning raison d'être, coming out of the expressive discussion on what things have shaped her, and I guess booted by the mention of the Motherland. "I'm an African woman. Really. I'm not a monogamist," she offered, seeking to clear up whatever questions she thought she could acknowledge vibing in my knot, that she felt, perhaps, would not be asked but needed to be laid out.

"People don't understand. Max was not a womanizer. He wasn't running around. But I don't want to have to answer where I was last night! I don't want him to divorce his first wife if he can't have me. I don't want my sister to be without. I would never do that again." A high spangled laugh, "But at my age, I'm not gonna do any of that any more . . . any way.

"But the whole thing. . . . I never had any rights. What rights have you? Unless you can kill him. The African women could do that!" She is still light with it, a philosophy of post-was summary. She pauses to reflect, however deeply, "What was wrong with Roach and me was *the approach to marriage*." And with that one must withdraw before the water is over your head.

"The only way I survive is to keep running my mouth. That's how I keep from being wiped out, to keep expressing myself!" The talk goes to the wonders of her last albums, the signifying *Devil Got Your Tongue!* and *Wholly Earth, You Gotta Pay the Band*, where not only are we moved by Abbey's poetic mastery, of form and content whether her own lyrics or the unique creativity through which she delivers someone else's words.

One remembers the awesome aura of simple WOW that she evokes from us on Stevie's "Golden Lady," even the old horses "What Are You Doing The Rest of Your Life?" or "You're My Thrill." What about her amazing "Throw It Away," or innovative new worlds provided by "Caged Bird" or "Africa" or the liberation motifs of "Tears," "Driva Man," "Freedom Day."

Of those classic pieces, Abbey has a penchant for digging up forgotten or neglected masterworks, e.g., "Brother Can You Spare a Dime," the sound of which provides old folks with a newsreel of the Depression, WPA, or maybe Fonda in *Grapes of Wrath.* Another such evocative time machine is the World War II romance "When the Lights Go On All Over the World," which conjures "Casablanca" and "To Have & Have Not."

On her way to Los Angeles to perform at the Masonic Hall and the Jazz Bakery, we are discussing the various trends and camps she is checking, bouncing them around for verification. "Best thing I ever did for myself is practice the arts." She is confirming with delight the wisdom of her own choices: "I was a singer, a painter, actress, a playwright, a composer. I wrote a thesis on Africa and Egypt. I don't want to do an autobiography because of the ugly spirit in this place. They take your stuff and twist it.

"And I'm tired of them talking about 'Women in the Music', like it's new. Women always been in this music. But the men have been at the front of it. The men have a hard time keeping a standard that individual. If the work is to be seen it has to be original. Otherwise you can kick his booty butt off the stage. But John Coltrane, Bird . . . that's the people who are out front. . . .

"Really. I feel attacked when people bring up all the feminist idea in jazz. . . . " It gets funny to her, about the modes of creativity identified with gender. "[A woman] can make a baby. . . . She comes looking for a man . . . takes him home like a sandwich . . .

"I haven't changed, I'm just better at expressing myself. When I listen to the early things. I write songs about my life. It's not an unhappy life. Because I run my mouth" (lyrics to "Straight Ahead").

CHAPTER 54

Four Tough Good-Byes

Jackie McLean, John Hicks, Hilton Ruiz,
Halim Suliman

Though "beginning" travels backward into the wherever, this one was Jackie Mc's. I've already written about it for some weird Spanish magazine (*Matador,* ca. January 2007). That's the way it goes in the craziness where we live, harnessed to the dead. Those who still walk around with the harshing memory of those who don't (not visibly). Right now "Little Melonae" is playing accidentally (not) on the box. I played it, maybe, the day I got the news. Jackie's great album *Let Freedom Ring* (which really marked the high-water mark of that generation's thrust to innovation). The story about how I had to curse out Clerk Eichman at the record store, even to buy the record, is in the Spanish piece. And just before I began (physically not philosophically) to type Whatever this is . . . , this piece, I picked up the old LP sitting on top of the middle-aged box & put it on, not really realizing that I was going to work on this piece.

But the crown of it all is the sense of whooom, woooosh, wheeee, gone, that layers it all. Jackie Mc was one of my touchstones, as far as the developing music of BeBop. That sound and presumed whizzing hip panache were valuable to me, I guess, and in me. Jackie was also, for a minute, one of my road buddies, him and his soon-to-be, lovely, wife, Dolly. This just before we all made our move out of the Lower East Side, of which Slug's Dopery had got to be the white house.

To mean, I could not think of him gone. Did not want to think of him that way, because his leaving carried some of my life with him too.

One cannot remember one's life as fully as one has lived it. For one reason was that Jackie was fully alive when I knew him best, and still full of all that the last time I saw him. The funeral, weirdly, confirmed that for all the other I's, entering our lives through all the eyes we looked into at Abyssinia. And ain't it funny that as unchurchly as all of us was and is most likely to be right now, how the church do seep into our STOPPED lives? (Yet I pledge not to be buried in the church, if I have anything to say about it!)

But this is not just about Jackie, the great paradigm post Bird BeBopper, whose sharp cutting edge, and in and out of the dope world, at full hoisted banner still wailing for the next deepness, I/WE hoped was Our own! This is about the *month of death,* or so it seemed. And it really was for the bare extent of my focus. Though death for my generation has been mounting like Katrina's bath. Each week some other close friend or known personality cuts out. Of the latter, in essence it didn't matter whether they were positive or negative, with news of their booking it meant still more of our world was moving away. Perhaps that is why old folks sometime seem so grumpy because, minimally, they have fewer and fewer to verify the epiphanies or even the rotten little misfortunes of their lives.

So that a few days later I thought I saw something on the net, naw, forget it, it couldn't be that. Not . . . no . . . what??? But a few hours later . . . & I had just seen John at the Iridium, with Grachan Moncur's group. The piano seemed further away from the whole group, off to the side. It's probably always there. (It is, but this week, checking out Charles Tolliver's wondrous big band, it was over there on the side, but during the last intermission they changed it so the pianist's back was to the audience! What dat mean?)

After the set John and I sat at the back of the club, while he ate ice cream and I was telling him about a series we planned in Newark of solo piano concerts which would feature John, Adegoke Colson, Hilton Ruiz, D.D. Jackson, Vijay Iyer, some of the badder young "Ticklers" (piano players viz. early 20th-century hip). Talking with our usual subtle undergarment of humor. John was one of the subtlest and sharpest of the walking-around musical minds, his casual understated persona quite the opposite of the rushing syncopation of his OH AW FUNK FUNK YEH THAT'S RIGHT! approach to the box. John's playing, ask anyone who dug him, put him in line to cop the jazz pianist's equivalent of James Brown's "the Hardest Working Man in Show Business."

We'd known each other for many years. He and his wife, Elise, with me and my wife, Amina, sat together at many sets, in many joints, in many people's houses and ran the world back and forth between us. One of the last was at a party given by another partner of mine, the painter Emilio Cruz, who also split without notice.

I remember John was sitting at the piano and I crept up on him and challenged him to play Billy Strayhorn's "Blood Count." Yeh, he played it straight out, with the kind of lovely lilt that Duke would give it. Or like his own marvelous "After the Morning." Then, just to take me all the way out, he invited another fine piano player, Larry Willis, to sit down, and they played it again four hands. It was an altogether spontaneous stretch of loveliness to add to that party's overall hipness.

I'd also gotten John to come over to Newark to play quite a few times. As featured pianist for our multi-arts presentations at Kimako's Blues People, which went on for 15 years, or for private parties Amina and I had. Once for Amina's birthday. The last time John played here at our house, he wailed far into the night, not only the smoking tunes we know him for, but for the last hour or so he came out of the covers and instead of the constant reference to the church, he went deep into it and the whole place turned into a revival.

It was the suddenness, the it-couldn't-be quality of John's get outta here that was so devastating, disheartening. Jackie Mc's was a deep blow, like Brando hearing his oldest son getting wiped, it is a body punch that threatens to shatter even the pavement you stand on.

And then the music itself trembles, from these disappearances but also from the general dumbed-down condition of the whole culture. The *New York Times Book Review* reads like the possible reject list 40 years ago, with dim-witted professors, right-wing hatchet persons, and straight-out hacks emboldened with dirty lucre.

Looking at New York City schedules for the Music, in the clubs and wherever, is likewise chilling. Occasionally (of which I'll speak in a minute) some brightness and actual reflection of real minds reporting, but in the main the headless whorespeepas run amuck. I've repeated myself saying that so-called fusion is really social & intellectual betrayal.

But we could hear some of the greats playing among us from time to too long a time later, e.g., recently Andrew Hill, McCoy Tyner, David Murray, Abbey is not feeling well, we're told, and that in itself is painful. But for two greats, both warm friends, Jackie Mc and John Hicks, it's like some cruel thing going upside your head with two devastating overhand rights.

We went to Jackie Mc's funeral at the eloquent Rev. Butt's, Abyssinia, where Gil Noble, the dauntless face of Afro-America's television blog, *Like It Is*, and Jackie's roadie since their Harlem childhood, was a eulogist of living and instructive memory. Randy Weston evoked a similar lyrical nostalgic New York vibe to seal the blue package.

A scant few days later Amina and I went to John's wake and funeral, at St. Mark's Methodist Church in Harlem, successive days, plus to the tribute at St. Peter's (May). Amina once had to change the title of her poem to John from "John the Baptist," once he told her, to "John the Methodist." Son of a Methodist preacher! (Still sounded like a Baptist to us.)

The tribute, though it expressed our collective loss, was also an expression of great love and warmth, the large audience and broad list of celebrants, which included Larry Willis, Mulgrew Miller, Joe Lovano, Mickey Bass, Lincoln Center's Todd Barkan, Amina, and me accompanied by Amina Claudine Meyers, the World Saxophone Quartet, Buster Williams, Elise Hicks, and our man Cecil Taylor, so there was all that lyrical and funky love, for us to wander out of the place, still stiff with grief but at least given something of value to go with our loss.

But a few days later, was it on the net, the newspaper later, that again a big NO! flashed and fished through us at this further grimness. Again, one of the young classicists of the Music, and another close friend. How could this be? With the same incredulous terror that stalked us with news of John, unlike the funeral sadness that came with word of Jackie's going, the news of Hilton's death was punctuated with an actual terror! The word was that he had "fallen," but a cynical wonder surged across the jazz community, how could a person receive the kind of injury it was reported that Hilton had suffered—the bones in his face fractured, so badly he went into a coma, from which he never fully returned. From a fall? So that the word "Murder!" was wrapped completely around this news. And no matter what other word came out, for those of us close to him, that lurking horror remains.

A few days before Hilton had gone to New Orleans to publicize a record he made as a benefit for the survivors of the Katrina Bushwhacking, my wife and I had dug him up at Cecil's Place in West Orange, N.J., a place where it's always possible to see some of the best of the Music.

We arrived mid-set and Hilton was at full smoke. A Carnegie Hall performing prodigy at 8, who studied with the great Mary Lou Williams & made his first recording at 14, Hilton's playing was always characterized by constant melodic blues shapes driven by an engine of ever changing rhythms. Hilton would leap back and forth from deep funk blues to Afro-Latino boomaloom effortlessly, cracking himself up at the transformative hip.

That night, as he finished, he went into a rap that combined peddling his most recent CD (*A New York Story,* issued by the Hilton Ruiz Music Company), to serving as a jazz quiz show mc, rewarding correct answers with copies of the CD. To a question answered by some quick dude and my wife almost simultaneously, "What was Clifford Brown's nickname?" Hilton laughed, not knowing I was there, "You sound like Amiri Baraka!" At which I called out and raised my hand from the back. That cracked him and the rest of us all the way up.

Between sets we talked about his recent gigs, his sharp sense of politics, in and out of the music, and how proud he was of himself that he no longer smoked, drank, or "messed around." He also had me touch his stomach to show that now he had become a karate "black belt." Not only that, we exchanged phone calls and e-mails the next couple of weeks, as I was trying to get his schedule clear so that we might invite him again to Newark. Like John Hicks, Hilton had been to our house in Newark to play several times, in the Kimako's Blues People series and for our private sets upstairs. The last time he played here was at a reading, at the Aljira Art Gallery downtown, featuring Amina and myself, with poets Sekou Sundiata and Halim Suliman & grand trombonist Craig Harris on the set as well. We still have some boss flicks about that wonderful night.

After the first word came, mainly from the New Orleans police, that Hilton had accidentally fallen in front of a spot in New Orleans, which Hilton's ex-wife and daughter initially seemed to co-sign (despite a swarm of queries and suspicions to the contrary), in recent days daughter Aida is now suing several folk in New Orleans, citing Hilton's being beaten by some person or persons. Horrible, whatever the case, especially since this great pianist was only in New Orleans to give survivors financial and spiritual aid.

We went to the New York Tribute to Hilton at LQ's on Lexington Ave. A buncha musicians played, Zon del Barrio, Willie Martinez y La Familia, Craig Harris, David Murray, Frankie Vasquez, and more, poet Papoleto Melendez fetched us from one side of the room to dig a celebrant slouched in a corner seat. It was Bill Cosby, mournfully quiet, making us remember that Hilton had provided the music from time to time for Cosby's family show and his *Detective* series.

But as Spike Lee showed in his powerful *When the Levees Broke,* the madness and horror in that ex-Black city is another real terror to be attributed to the Bush'it coming from the Caucasian Crib in Washington, D.C.

I mention a generation seeming to fly out at top speed. The last of the *Good-byes* here is the death of a close friend of ours, the poet Halim Suliman. The personal relationship I had with all these people makes this a roll call of regret. Particularly Halim, who was for several years one of the poets on Amina's and my poetry-music ensemble, *Blue Ark: The Word Ship*. From the earliest days of our Kimako's Blues People multi-arts series, Halim was on the set, reading and even videotaping a few of the programs.

With Blue Ark, Halim traveled with us to the Berlin Jazz Festival, where we made a record, *Real Song*, plus to universities and venues across the country. He also acted in my one-act play *Song* and as part of the company of actor-singers in the Adegoke Steve Colson production of *A Cultural Reminiscence*, playing several parts & in a group singing the freedom songs of the Civil Rights Movement, in one act of the work, my *Dr. King and the Mountain*. The entire work features Colson's music and another act by Richard Wesley. We did that at the New Jersey Performing Arts Center in Newark and also in Paris.

Halim was a poet lit up by the fire of Newark's faces and places like a rocket straight out of the Black Arts Movement. That is, he was still trying to make Cultural Revolution. He also taught at Newark's (should be) world-famous Arts High School, where folks like Sarah Vaughan, Savion Glover, Woodie Shaw, Wayne Shorter, Amina Baraka went. He was the mentor for the string of State Champion Newark High School Debating victories.

Halim was ubiquitous wherever there was a heavy reading in this city. In the Poet-On! Series I put together, at the Newark Public Library and Public Schools, to continue "popularizing poetry" to carry out my work as New Jersey Poet Laureate in 2002, despite the attack by lying pests, Halim, as usual, was one of the stalwarts. How many folks in this city quoted one of Halim's poems to make their comments on Newark politics, viz., "James / Ain't never been Sharp!"

So the loss is up close and personal but also a continuing diminution of the forces of an advanced American art. So these sad good-byes.

8/29/06

TOP: Steve McCall, Amiri Baraka, David Murray; New Music–New Poetry Ensemble; 1982. Photo by Ming Murray.

BOTTOM: Halim Suliman, Wilber Morris, Scoby Stroman, Amiri Baraka; Berlin Jazz Festival, November 1994. Photographer unknown.

Amiri Baraka and Sun Ra (*top of stairs, left*), in front of Black Arts Repertory Theater School, 1965. Photographer unknown.

Kimako's Mardi Gras leaflet featuring Sun Ra Cosmic Arkestra, 1994. Courtesy Risasi Dais.

TOP: Sun Ra and Cosmic Arkestra in downtown Newark, 1995. Marshall Allen, alto sax, *center*; John Gilmore, tenor sax, *second from left*. Courtesy Risasi Dais.

BOTTOM: Sun Ra, Newark, 1995. Courtesy Risasi Dais.

TOP: Hilton Ruiz, Victor Davson, Amiri Baraka, Craig Harris, Sekou Sundiata; Kimako's set at Aljira Gallery Newark, 2005. Courtesy Risasi Dais.

BOTTOM: Amiri Baraka and Ornette Coleman, New School book party for *Blues People,* 1963. Photographer unknown.

TOP: Grachan Moncur III, Cuz Henry, Jimmy Anderson, and Amiri Baraka at Amiri and Amina Baraka's house, Newark. Upstairs over Kimako's, 1986. Photographer unknown.

BOTTOM: John Hicks, Eddie Blackwell, David Murray, Kunle Mwanga, Amiri Baraka, and Ray Drummond, New Jersey Performing Arts Center, Newark, 1990. Courtesy Risasi Dais.

TOP: John Hicks, with Woodie King, theatrical producer, and Pharoah Sanders digging at Amiri and Amina Baraka's house, 2006. Photographer unknown.

BOTTOM: Abbey Lincoln with Amina and Amiri Baraka, PSE&G Plaza, Newark, 2001. Courtesy Risasi Dais.

Nina Simone helped off stage by Roberto Vargas after singing in support of the Sandinistas, July 1985. Photographer unknown.

TOP: Max Roach and Amiri and Amina Baraka with Blue Ark and others. *Left to right:* Herbie Morgan, tenor sax; Tyshawn Sorey, trombone; unknown guitarist; Robert Banks, piano; Wilber Morris, bass; Max Roach, drums; Amiri Baraka; Amina Baraka; James Orange; Halim Suliman; Ronell Bey; PSE&G Plaza, Newark, 1990s. Courtesy Risasi Dais.

BOTTOM: Blue Ark lineup, 1980s–1990s, at Kimako's. *Left to right:* Halim Suliman, Rachim Sahu, James Orange, Robert Banks, Rudy Walker, Amiri Baraka; *first row:* Herbie Morgan, Amina Baraka. Courtesy Risasi Dais.

TOP: Roswell Rudd, trombone; Reggie Workman, bass; Amiri Baraka; 2006.
Photo by Adger Cowans.

BOTTOM: At Kimako's: Herbie Morgan, Rudy Walker, Wilber Morris, Gene
Phipps, Sr., Amiri Baraka, 1980s. Courtesy Risasi Dais.

TOP: Max Roach and Amiri Baraka in Paris at La Villette Jazz Festival, 1997. Photographer unknown.

BOTTOM: Max Roach with poet Ted Joans and Amiri Baraka at La Villette Jazz Festival, 1997. Photographer unknown.

TOP: Archie Shepp, Bradford Hayes, and Amiri Baraka, 2006. Photo by Adger Cowans.

BOTTOM: Nina Simone and South African poet Duma Ndlovu at the Hunter College Anti-Apartheid Program, 1985. Photographer unknown.

TOP: Cecil Taylor and Amiri Baraka, Boulder, Colorado, 1994. Photographer unknown.

BOTTOM: Blue Ark on Cape Verde: Vijay Iyer, Dwight West, Rudy Walker, Amiri Baraka, 2001. Photographer unknown.

Woodcut of Miles Davis by Guy Berard, originally published in a pamphlet edition of Amiri Baraka's *When Miles Split!* (Candia, NH: LeBow, 1995; a slightly different edition was published by Caliban Press, NY). Used with permission of John LeBow.

PART THREE

Notes, Reviews, and Observations

CHAPTER 55

Impulse Sampler, *Act on Impulse*

Promo sampler CD, MCA, 1995.

When they told me about this sampler and the move to reissue the old Impulse catalogue, along with some of the newer things, it gave me a little of that rush of elation that that actual music gives. You mean we're talking about raising the real, the deep, the genuinely moving American classical music of that period from the ghostly prison of commercially engineered obscurity? Dig that!

Because during the storied '60s, the now much-lied-about, disingenuously distorted, purposely covered '60s of revolutionary political, social, and cultural upsurge, there was also, as there always is in any period of aggressively human struggle, an art, an accompanying aesthetic trend, among the most advanced of us, that reflects and speaks from and to that time, that in itself recreates the lives of us wherever we were in it. So that those who perhaps have forgotten or are too young or have since been purchased by the agents of violent ignorance can feel the truth again, or for the first time, and hopefully be raised or ReRaised. Like the old folks when they be whooping and hollerin and entering and re-entering the spirit world, funky Sundays of revelation.

The fact that this sampler is being reissued during Black History Month is important. Because the music, like they say, is one of the heaviest parts of our (American and Afro-American) history. All of us, know it, or like it, or not! You see art is the ultimate RAZOR, the best educator and illuminator of our lives here. And for the music called JAZZ (a word which some of us, mistakenly, don't like . . . mistakenly, because it means, from the African, "I AM" i.e., JA (like Bob Marley and them spake) IS! JA, the divine (seer) energy Spirit of what is. And them double Z's is the first Max, Shango, his sign (scion) Thunder and Lightning, getting a Nut (the sky). So JAZZ is the ejaculation of the infinite! I AM!*

We know when Homer Cupcake first dug it in them Laughing Parlors (Ho Houses, i.e., HO, HO, HO) he confused IS NESS with mere sex, and mostly did not dig that syncopation was not a belly dance but Love as the matter and motion of what lives forever.

(Very Heavy! Ok, please, brother, go on with the what not, like intro.) You see just contemplating it got me rising like the Black Bird we is, rising again, in Fire! Cause if you can hear, for instance, that flying Trane (from underground), that keening, screaming agonizingly revelational "Call," you respond, with hereness. You be's in it, flying with Trane out past the relentlessly irrational.

Because Impulse, during those years, let Bob Thiele loose somehow, and he got it down. The outbursting spiritual fire of John Coltrane and his classic group (McCoy Tyner, Jimmy Garrison, Elvin Jones) and many of the others. The sharp funk of a speeding Freddie, who, with Lee Morgan, were the post-Clifford clarions of re-emerging hip! And dig that group, a "Hard Bop" paradigm, with Curtis Fuller, Tommy Flanagan, Art Davis, Louis Hayes. With John Gilmore (who, sadly, just left us) on loan from the great Sun Ra.

Sampler even brought back Oliver Nelson. He of the rhapsodic consciousness and gorgeous alto poetryphone. Both *Resolution* and *Stolen Moments* have already taken on the stature of classics. Not because Prof Deadpaper decided but because what is in that music remains right on the true and the beautiful. Oliver's group on this piece and the entire album *Blues and the Abstract Truth* is a formidable cross-reference of proven and avant wizards, with Eric Dolphy, Bill Evans, Paul Chambers. A roster of great artists.

There is bad Sonny Rollins, who, along with Trane, rescued the music from the gray flannel fifties and revived the erudite funk of the Neo-Bop called "Hard." To get the Blues back, to get improvisation back, and the talking drums of the Old folks back. Rollins was going into his Calypso mode then, digging the Mighty Sparrow and them and bringing the Caribbean right up in there.

The Music is always a reflection of where the people are, I wrote

*Written before Max Roach explained why he didn't care for the word and neither did Duke Ellington.

thirty years ago in Blues People. Listen to mad Mingus's "II B.S." with his big aggressive orchestration. Giving praise to the Master, Duke, but with the rawer harmonic values of that sizzling period.

And this sampler, they threaten, is just the first taste of that stream of great music from great musicians that dug into the very essence of you, 'merica!

I used to use Pharoah's (I started calling him that back then, when he was known as "Little Rock," a young man from Arkansas with very tender foots and a sound like the Prophets) "The Creator Has a Master Plan" as my theme song on a penetratingly political radio program in Newark during the '60s called *Black Newark*. Some times I'd hear that thrilling spiritual history in my car, speeding toward the station. And they'd keep playing it till I got there! Ah, the rush of those images and memory now reseen and refelt!

And on this first reissue, there is the fly Chico Hamilton, the West Coast boulevardier. A new McCoy Tyner, who was a young wizard in Trane's "all time, classical, switch blade and hydrogen bomb band." Now into the funk mode of the '80s along with Q's "Sermonette" dragging the popular song form into seriousness. Evoking the movement into the postmodernism of funk and fusion. Stanley Turrentine was one of the bluer officers of that trend, the Godfather of which was the Prince of Darkness, Miles Davis, with the other gunman in his greatest band, Cannonball Adderley.

And there's even a bit from two of the greatest masters, Duke Ellington, unarguably the greatest American composer and orchestra leader ever (and the band's here too, he seldom left home without them), with the creator of the modern tenor saxophone, Bean, Coleman Hawkins.

But, you know, there's a whole lot of albums left to get back out here, yall. More Tranes, Trane and Duke, Trane and Johnny Hartman, Archie Shepp, Mingus, Max, more Pharoahs, and on and on. And we waiting.

This was a grand period in the world for the human family struggling to free itself from the big ugly, just as the most innovative musicians were trying to flee from the Tin Pan Alley plantation. There's a bunch of good things here, old, new, and middle Hip. The sampler itself is like a funk-reel of a very socially and musically adventurous time. Something we all need right now, in these willfully backward times. For the "fresh" generation or those who merely want to be refreshed.

10/26/95

CHAPTER 56

Ralph Peterson

Ralph Peterson, drums; Geri Allen, piano; Essiet Okon Essiet, bass;
Phil Bowler, bass

A "new" drummer on the scene is like a new heartbeat. And as the character Heart (played by drummer Steve McCall) says in a play of mine, *Primitive World,* "If the world survive a drummer must be in it!"

Hearing Ralph live at Kimako's Blues People, the artspace my wife, Amina, and I operate in Newark, was not introduction but understanding. With Craig Harris, Ralph was hot as fire, creating a rhythm zone in which everything rocked.

On this album, the emphasis is on the swing, although the heat mus' is for the swing to be so. But it is musical relationships and smooth conception that strike us, though that does hotly insist on very hip grooves. Smooth or no, we are always aware of Ralph, not as some banging acrobat, but it is clearly his motion that animates this tight evocative matter-of-factly creative trio.

Geri Allen is a new star pianist, and here she is the lead voice, daring, self-possessed, but earfully collective. The trio is understatement in some sense but shaped as surprise and freshness. Ralph shows his tasteful sophistication in these bright fascinating excursions, yet he is cooking serious.

These are classic trio performances. Intimate, as well as rollicking. Romantic and yet discursive, penetrating, intent on describing, recalling, making their *newness* "conversational" and clear.

Danny Richmond told me, "In reality the drummer is always the band leader." Jass is the drum's largest body. Blues, its living soul. And each new personality is restatement as well as evolution.

What is encouraging here is that we can feel what is valuable, and its telling is more than advertisement. These musicians are telling us where the music is, where it was, and where it is going. Their performances are already polished and relaxed—seriously innovative as well as straight ahead and at work!

Ralph is young but focused and in motion as well. Denzil Best is such a hip drummer and composer, for instance. Too often overlooked in both his areas of excellence. Miles's classic version of Best's "Move" obsessed and bedazzled my then young trumpet playing. It was part of the seven Capital works called *Birth of the Cool.*

Ralph's take on Best implies both the cool hipness and elegant narrative of the "Klook" side of Bop drumming. Which is where we find Ralph and Co. on this date. Geri Allen is Bud like, in this context, already entered into Cecil!

The early Monk and Bud trios is what this date puts you in mind of. "Egos" in the service of the "Id." Particularly dig the opening of "Bemsha Swing," a Denzil Best–Thelonius Monk classic.

Peterson has four of his own pieces on this album, to stake his own claim as drummer-composer. One tune co-authored by Geri Allen and bassist Essiet Okon Essiet. And there is a freshness to this, as our kids say, to restore its original meaning past the cliché. This whole hook-up is *fresh* and alive! And everyone contributes imaginative solo, ensemble tightness, and the throbbing drive of life anew. Bassist Essiet is a discovery, and Phil Bowler, he of the big dramatic sound, needs to be recorded more frequently. Geri Allen's reputation is spreading like sunrise. And Ralph Peterson is here in living funk. His first album (*Something Else,* 5502) announced his arrival as leader and significant voice (check the solo on "Princess"). His clean "get-up motion" is what Peterson's playing carries. It is explosive, crackling, and in a hurry to get to *then* from now. Hey, he's what then will be!

The opening of "Just You, Just Me," and the off-rhythm accompaniment of Allen to Essiet to Peterson, before the work at tempo, is sweet indeed. Or that drum solo intro to the same number . . . explosive yet tasteful as your heartbeat. The clean brushwork later . . . hmmmmm. This was another of the Monk trio classics.

That's the album which "busts" Monk for his Dukishness. Just as this album "busts" Ralph in the sweetest way for his "Bestness" and Geri Allen for her Monkish finery. But these are all "busts" like in stature or statue you digggg? Like they bust on to the scene right *in the tradition* and new as the next moment. Welcome Ralph, especially, it's your time. Stretch out, brother!

CHAPTER 57

Andrew Cyrille, *Good to Go*

Soul Note Records, 1997, SOUL N 1292.
Andrew Cyrille Trio with James Newton (flute) and Lisle Atkinson
(bass).

Andrew Cyrille first hit with C. T.'s (Cecil Taylor's) fabled energy-mobile
in 1958 and began to play with him regularly in 1964. He was the main
C. T. drummer until 1975. C. T., always the logician, asked Andrew
(according to Valerie Wilmer) what he thought rhythm was! "Dance,"
was Cyrille's answer. I think this is more to the deep of Cyrille's playing
than the usual saw that "he does not keep time" but accents the various
instruments.

Klook and Max (and Bu, with his terrible "shuffle") brought that
in 50 years before. Andrew, like the wave of younger drummers out
of the '60s nouveau, came in with Max/Klook/Bu & Philly Joe/Elvin,
already stashed safely in their funkionaries. Sonny Murray, Milford
Graves, Eddie Blackwell, Dennis Charles, Billy Higgins, Rashid Ali,
Tony Williams, etc., all had that from jump, that was the legacy, the
heaviest teaching. That is why they could leap so far, cause they had
heard the heavies and *understood*.

Their specific variations are from their lives, of course. But the
general "movement," to whatever extent the newer *Ngomas* could be
collectively placed, was to use the accent as the *logic* of the flow, not
just as color. To be specifically personal, in a sense. To speak to and
from the rhythm, at the same time. And this music, at its very essence,
is about rhythm.

The first cut on this new CD should demonstrate convincingly, even
to the all but suffocated by cliché, that Cyrille does, indeed, have that

"riddim." "It don't mean a thing," said the Duke of Afro-America, "if it ain't got that swing." Swing? (the verb, not the commercially flabbergasted noun, which don't. See A. B.'s *Outsidehighoriginia*. "Swing, that perceived manifestation of the dialectical motion between opposite poles, e.g., from Be to At." Swing something hard enough, it increases in temperature. You dig?)

"Bu," Andrew's tribute to the great Art Blakey (Abdullah Buhaina, our man, now on assignment heating up inner space), he begins as African call and then, in a heartbeat, is into a recycling of Bu's "Message from Kenya." It's impeccable Bu, all right, but there is also some Andrew in there, he's "Cyrilled" with the tempo a little bit, yet it remains a wonderful tribute.

The makeup of this group is quite different from the nonstop bashing ensembles we usually connect Andrew with. After the notable residency with C. T., Andrew has been featured with another all-out smoking outfit, tenor saxophone giant David Murray's various jubilant combines.

With James Newton on flute and Lisle Atkinson on bass, one does get the expected subtlety, measured color, and intimacy that that orchestration would predict. Certainly, Newton's introspective "Oblong" speaks from this context very movingly. A deep lingering touching piece. But that is not nearly the whole story. Lisle Atkinson's emphatic bass voice makes certain of this. Atkinson, a highly respected, widely sought-after, and constantly gigging yeoman at the other rhythm post, not only powerfully and dynamically paddles this furthership, but allows Cyrille to circle back and forth inside the main flow without the least loss of drive.

"Inch Worm," the standard that John Coltrane resurrected into groove land, is likewise given a happy re-revival. Newton's beautiful depth boosted into the faster lane by the insistent Atkinson, and Cyrille, who is always pushing and turning and pulling and commenting, as he yet remains the fundamental battery of the vessel.

"Nicodemus," ah, it is always refreshing to see or hear some part of Westory. Plus the African motor Andrew gives this URR is to the point, pointing at the before U got here. You see, there is an inexhaustible deepness to that still breathing monstrosity of Black people's enforced redebut here in the West, that is full of stories and songs and tales and a still emerging politics that artists are ignorant to ignore. Like the good Dr. (Du Bois) said, they are the gifts of Black folk to the joint . . . Labor, Story, Song, and Spirit.

Newton's "Olmecas" reaches down into the southern self of us

Americans. All us here in the western hemisphere, the real "Western World," are combinations of African, European, and Asian (Native), from that combined ourstory & culture. You an American, you that combination!

So from that ancient people, the Olmecs (visit Acapulco, you'll see a giant statue of "Louis Armstrong," who was here before the U.S.), Newton gives this beautiful swirling imagistic present. It utilizes harmonic variety as melodic "track." Then Andrew eases in to speak alone and from under, about "Los Viejos," in a piece that begins as sensuous mystery and emerges an understated near-wildness. I wondered where J. N. been! Wherever, he's still the new measure of what can be done with that ax, on the real side.

"Good to Go" is, A. C. says, "a composition written with the intention to continue to essay and explore original musical works with inspired solos of free group improvisation based not on prescribed chord changes and/or meter(s), but with the intention of relating to and making musical connections to the spontaneous music heard around one in the moment."

Which is to say, if you listen, as these musicians here listen to each other, you can dig, like we say, get down with the already down and go out with the already gone. So we can watch the soul rising. Like the ancient Africans who built the city of ON directly under the sun so they could keep track of the Sol, as it turned, so they were also, by under standing, made creatively as "high," in ON.

"Fate" is a drum concerto in miniature, with the bass accompaniment and vice versa, like we do. Dig J. N.'s howls and harmonic feelographs. What makes the record formidable is these three seemingly limited by number (which is only name) produce a whole art.

Andrew Cyrille is one of the finest drummers on the scene today. This album, with its modest construct yet powerful presence, is a gem! It will be a real find for the humble stumbler, but actually a confirmation of just how musically important and gratifying Andrew Cyrille is and has been, for a while now!

And his friends, James Newton and Lisle Atkinson, don't leave them out. They contribute with equal persona to this wonderful effort. This is the kind of album you like to pull your friends' coats to, so they'll know you know. Now if only somebody would pull the *New York Times*, etc.'s coats. But then, the Emperor don't wear no clothes, do he?

6/24/96

CHAPTER 58

Odean Pope Saxophone Choir, *Epitome*

Soul Note, 1994, SOUL N 121279-2.
Julian Pressley, first alto; Sam Reed, second alto; Robert Landham, third alto; Bob Howell, first tenor; Glenn Guidone, second tenor; Middy Middleton, third tenor; Bootsie Barnes, fourth tenor; Joe Sudler, baritone sax; Eddie Green, piano; Dave Burrell, piano; Tyrone Brown, upright bass; Craig McIver, drums; Odean Pope, solo tenor and leader.

A wonderful, refreshing, and very surprising CD. Pope is a longtime Max Roach stalwart, a daring, resourceful, skilled, and passionate player, but alas, too solid and fundamentally "inside" to get much ink from the "Gee whiz, it don't even sound like jazz . . . ain't that great!?" school of music insulters, who got regular jobs as buffoons of music commentary.

But Odean Pope does sound like, swing like, move you, exactly like Jazz can. The record is surprising because it is mashed flat under the detritus of so many World Saxophone Quartet imitators and poseurs. Odean Pope is none of them. He created the Saxophone Choir sixteen years before.

This is a record the logic of which is obvious, from the first time we heard Duke's angelic reed sections. The saxophone is a marvelous thing because it can come from so many places, reflect with penetrating sensuousness, the multi-myriad diversity of human presence.

Odean gives us, certainly, the arranged palette and brilliance of the horn, horns, harmonized not for flashy bombardment, but to make a very satisfying and poly-dimensional music. Not only the arrangements are sharp, tasty, funky, thoughtful, but he has selected players (most, it seems from Philly . . . like the underground wizards Bootsie Barnes, Middy Middleton, Dave Burrell) who can carry the load. Both section and solo, to where Odean, as paper and instrumental leader, directs them.

Some six of the ten tunes on the album are Odean's, the rest he spread among Green, Tyrone Brown (whose brilliant work on "Trilogy," his and Odean's work, is one of the finest rhythmelodic bass vamps (with a lushness extending into his sensitive solo) I've run on recently. Brown is another Roach sideman. Dave Burrell, the unsung innovator on the piano, contributes "Zanzibar Blue." Plus there is Trane's "Coltrane Time," from the old side he did with Cecil Taylor eons ago, and the Afro-American National Anthem, "Lift Every Voice," the monumental work created by James Weldon and J. Rosamond Johnson, which a great many folks have taken up recently to present with a dazzling array of approaches. More power to all of them. Here, Odean gives us the broad frame of the concert songfulness of the piece, punctuated by an insistent drum break, perhaps to signify what must be endured and encountered. Then another kind of Easternness, as interlude, to the swing that comes off the top, as where we came from and what we brought with us.

But this CD is the kind of item you press on people who don't know it to show how hip you are, digging out the deep ones, the unknown ones. Like dig Odean laying on top of Brown's vamp in "Trilogy." Or the frantic opening of "Coltrane Time," where Odean has taken the piece and took it into a further orbit. Pope's solo speaks to his understanding of where the Trane was going, but it's Odean's own engine. But the very "outness" of the playing is passion, not anarchistic commerce. Odean Pope is the paradigm of a contemporary artist at the top of his consciousness and ability, who has heard most of what's out there, and still got his own voice to sing with.

Yeh, tasty and hip, this whole enterprise.

CHAPTER 59

Ravi Coltrane, *Moving Pictures*

RCA, 1998, 743215588726.
Ravi Coltrane (sax), Michael Cain, piano; Lonnie Plaxico, bass; Jeff
"Tain" Watts drums; Ralph Alessi, trumpet; Steve Coleman, alto.

Ravi Coltrane's debut as leader is a major IS. A birth, a continuum,
a re-being but a New Being. Music! (Like we say, Word!) The music,
from top, is his, Ravi's. If we hear the classic "Engine" *that* Trane,
where can we not? If we are looking for Trane traces, yea, they are in
the every. Ravi, like any of the younger Knowers (at work on their own
Arks) of necessity, Must dig Trane, otherwise they could not Know!
For he is most of them's father, including this one.

What is striking though, is that although those now classic "tracks"
and "stations" are clearly obvious with this young creator, if we listen
past the given, and not even very deeply, we hear that Ravi has not been
distracted by John's incredible nucleotechnics, as most have seemed to
be. That is, they want to explode in that passionate fire ray of sound,
emotion, notes, harmonics, double triple tonguing bombardment and
flight. Which did take the here to somewhere other. But so often the
virtuosity, without the deep soulful vision, empties into a technique
without a cause, a quickly diminishing formalism.

Ravi, like a few others, has actually *felt* Trane, as well as heard him.
He has been touched by the essential *deepness* of Coltrane, his spirit,
which is breath, Ravi has inhaled into his own feelings. So that his
playing is not one of the many attempted replications of Trane's outer
persona, Ravi presents that bottomless Blue Blackness, that ultra-violet
sway, that funky happiness Trane gave us. So that we are touched not

only by the initial roar of fire and brimstone but by the actual tender creation of living understanding.

Ravi moves us like Trane does, not that he is all the way out there in the waygonesphere of meaning, not yet. But whether at the up-tempo cook mode or singing in that sweet lilting way the underground railroad does when he is not racing at incredible emotional rates, there is in Ravi Coltrane's music, from first sound, a lovely sensuousness that fixes and holds us. Frog, Ben Webster, said that the test of the soloist is how they render ballads, which sometimes many of the Johnny One Note Speed Demons cannot. But Ravi, still mastering his whole mind and feeling, even now moves across tempos easily and without pressing to be hip or funky. There is that confidence that what he is playing is that without methodical declaration.

This is an impressive album for several reasons. From the opening piece, "Interlude—Thursday," which seems to lay out a casual space, a playful reflective mood, but very quickly, with excellent percussion of Ancient Vibration, they have all soared across to the Motherland, at a rush, picking up an emergency on the way. Then, abruptly, at the peak of this flight, they are gone.

The band—Michael Cain, piano; Lonnie Plaxico, bass; Jeff "Tain" Watts, drums; Ralph Alessi, trumpet; Steve Coleman, alto (and producer)—are tight and clean as "Dick's Hat Band." This is a well-rehearsed group, and the interplay, call and recall and response, contrapuntal brightness of their collective voice is always exhilarating, many times straight-out *thrilling*.

"Narcine" is thoughtful wandering, the Trane tracks are clear, but the feeling seems spontaneous, natural. Cain's piano, like most of the album, an understated groove sharp enough to season the mix with a kind of brisk intelligence that makes the piece subtly funky. "Tones" is that searching mode, the Why's man working on getting Wise. Underneath the percussion popping, so we know everybody is dancing while they think. And the young man darting up and across, through and beneath, on the horn, ahh yeh, we said, ahhh yeh . . . .

The combining sound of the group is very "cool," complex, but direct and melodic, the unison passages precise and meticulous. But the "coolness" is what the old folks meant, restrained fire. Most of the music is Ravi's and there is a delicious modality the pieces ride on, particularly Cain's chordal sub-plateau of motion.

Ravi, himself is illuminating on this "motion." He says, "The title of the record is 'Moving Pictures.' . . . The Whole snapshot idea about some music representing one place and time. . . . .some music has deeper roots that can go back through a person's life. Some music is only a reflection of what goes on when the red light's on. For me the record I made really reflects my life at the time it was recorded."

There are, as well, not only Ravi's own seemingly simple melodic polydimensional pieces, there are also wonderfully arranged compositions by Horace Silver, McCoy Tyner, Wayne Shorter, and Joe Henderson. All, at whatever tempos, characterized by a quietness, a pulsing "restraint," while at the same time carrying with, under, around, somewhere connected to it, and us, a forceful "swing," free blueness, that is touching, moving, transporting, evoking those moving pictures, like funky metaphors of feeling.

I could go on, but perhaps you got the point, this album is something on the real side, an unveiling, a releasing, an introduction, a promise of some things even more wonderful to come. Like we say, check it out . . . and be in Ancient ON, peeping Dig, able to see Serious, and flying with the Out past there to Gone! Suddenly you might remember what Hip really means, and the magnetism of the Music when we came in.

2/1/98
Newark

CHAPTER 60

Donal Fox and David Murray, *Ugly Beauty*

Evidence, 1995, EVI 22131.
Donal Fox (piano); David Murray (tenor saxophone, bass clarinet).

As I begin to listen . . . with no names . . . what turns out to be the title piece comes on evanescent, thoughtful, delicate, David flowing above, the piano not subdued but as the lifting element that permits Murray's flight.

Next ("Vamping") Murray uses the Bass Clarinet as a percussive thrusting of the melody. This piece a chromatic climbing and stroll, till they both begin almost to scamper. It is not a march. It is a striding with the percussive clarinet pops like claves, and the piano whipping Bartok. The piano grows aggressive, beating a cadence that forces us forward.

"Midnight," with its long intro, is beautiful David. The passion swelling and lyrical. Where "Hope Scope" is transformative from prac-tice-room scales to boundless expressions of rolling rising combustibil-ity. The stark early C. T. playing here is a boost, a partner in the quest, the surge of changing emotions, the search, the crashing movement, pressing up and down the scale and Fox rolling under him following and enhancing the direction.

At every turn and new development of Afro-American music, there are several general trends, ignited within U.S. culture as a whole. First whatever that new trend is, it is roundly denounced, just like the one before it, and the one to follow. New Orleans (become Dixieland), Big Band, "Swing" which didn't, BeBop, Cool, etc.).

Second, there is a spontaneous attempt to ignore then cover, that is, simulate the trend into commercial tender. Next, the attempt to co-opt and claim the music. Whether literally (Elvis, Goodman, etc.) or by surrounding it with the "other," again commerce/store or commerce/academy.

One of the most insidious of the latter I called the "Tail Europe" school, where the music is made a muffled titter inside the belly of European "avant." Certainly, if one has listened to 20th-century European music—Stravinsky, Bartok, Prokofiev, Debussy—one has perceived the influence of Afro-American music.

American music, of any kind, is likewise impressed. Copeland, Ives, Bernstein, Cage, Gershwin. And neither Tin, nor Pan nor Alley is possible without the blues and its children. But American music is part African, just like American culture. American culture is African, European, and Indian. That's what an American is! (Like it or not.) That composite of material social life, history, and psychological development.

So that Americans, from definition, have the whole of that triangle (as posited clearly by the triangular trade) to encompass into themselves. But I mean as consciousness. The true self-consciousness that Du Bois spoke of. That True Self-Consciousness makes us aware of all that we actually are, which is unpresumed, even imprisoned, if we are not fully conscious.

This coupling, meaning Fox/Murray, has some very good moments because each plays the grasp of the interchange, the crossing, that characterizes them. Murray, the young giant of the tenor. (To be sure, Sonny, Archie, Pharoah, Gilmore take up the space called "premier" as well, that's the way we is . . . not to mention altos, baritones, etc.)

But David is the "point" since he is "on the scene" wailing in medias res, wailing "heaven" into our now. So many have died, yet we have still a mighty phalanx of giants on the set. But David has taken the last generation of volcanic sonic prophets, Trane, Sonny, Albert, etc., and carried that claim on revelation into the present. The flaming funky artness of these sound prophets is David's torque as well.

Donal Fox, on the other hand, is young and from the American hipness that persists even inside the conservatories. Like C. T., 30 years ago, of whom I wrote, "He ran through the conservatories screaming 'Bud Powell is what's happening!'"

And like C. T., who likewise had been instructed on the European concert tour, Donal has sought to make his training responsive to the reality of his Afro-American (and American) psychological development.

Fox comes out of the Boston practice rooms (again like C. T.) but he has to cross town to get back home, Roxbury! Clearly, then, an expression of Du Bois's "Double Consciousness"? Only if the two aspects of this consciousness are pulling against each other for domination. But what if they are complementary and understood as the equal hemispheres of one psychic world? Du Bois meant the Afro-American (slave and on) yet exposed & misshaped by the historic "high" kultur (as in drug abuse?) of Europe.

Fox insists that he has absorbed all of it as his own. That if he insists on the second leg of the triangular trade, from the U.S. to Europe and the third leg, Europe to Africa, then that is his prerogative.

We hear the serial verticality of European concert music, but emotionally reorganized as harmonic, melodic, and even rhythmic counterpoint to David's blue red blackness. The pianistic context he creates complements with sharp contrast blue David. It is sympathetic as any true dialogue, significant as the sense it exchanges.

In "Ugly Beauty" (Monk), Fox is lyrical and chordal. Likewise in the great (as classic and in this performance) "Midnight," Fox flows with great effect under and over and parallel to David's always warm to flame blue voicings.

"Ugly Beauty" is so much a Monk expression. Like he said one time, "There's two kinds of mistakes. The regular ones and those that sound bad." It is the existence of these contradictions and the constant surprise of their reoccurrence which Monk absorbed as himself which his music gives the highest eloquence.

If America is ugly, any beauty completes the oxymoron. Perhaps America is, itself, an Oxymoron. Or in the context of the chauvinist canonical formation of the rulers, the "intellectual" superstructure built by conquest and slavery, any truth or beauty is measured a lie, hence "ugly." As the xenophobic measure of the conqueror calls all people other than themselves "ugly" as a formal color, caste (class) scale.

In "Hope Scope" there is an expanding and closing relationship between the two lines. It is musical and cultural, i.e., aesthetic and social. We can hear Europe (actually Euro-America) and Afro-America relating, touching, and sharply distancing themselves to emphasize the extreme limits of their collective expression.

When David and I (along with the late and very great Steve McCall) worked together a few years ago the piece was called "Murray Steps." Part exercise, part chromatic interchordal exchange, part rhythmic song form. The piece draws attention to the closeness of the communion, yet by doing so exposes the ocean of history and condition of their contradiction.

The collective expression of a future Afro-American music will grow to absorb all places and faces it is and has been (as it always does). I was critical of the TE people because I felt they belittled JAZZ by insisting it look backward at Europe as a substitute for the real advance of the music which will collect everything as it always has, seamlessly and with the black funk, the hot explosion of feeling (jism = jasm = jazz = I AM) and revelation.

But the value of this work is that David Murray's depth and broadness and powerful voice is never smothered or undermined by Donal Fox's C.T.-like Afro-Euro anthemic formalism, which rises again and again as the legitimate occasion of (to paraphrase an old DM title) Interboogieology. At times it provides a provocative frame for an intriguing whole, and insists it is inside the flick as well.

Monk figures heavily in this collaboration because Monk was everywhere. Monk was Bop before Bird and used to say, as reported by Grachan Moncur III, "I hope none of them BeBoppers come in here tonight." A cold Monkish joke, but the essence was that Monk was no trend or surface formalism of pop manqué. Monk was the deepness of the whole number. From Duke on back through screaming fire engines (which Monk, as a child, used to sing duets with) and screaming church negroes thinking Christ was Elegba.

Monk, like Duke, and with Duke's commission, had drained Europe like a double bourbon and turned it into blood. That is, emotional reference past formal reference. There is no surrealism or dada or abstract expressionistic trope outer than T.S.M. Monk assumed he was as hip as the world, since he was hip to it.

What Murray and Fox are doing is using the Monkish paradigm to waste the clichéd separation of musical cultures and involve them into a single "vonz." (See Babs G.)

In "Song" there is the quiet cry that is almost his signature. The single rising call of David's kind of contemporary lyric. With something of the old soft poignant lyric feeling but a reaching, rising, calling, searching quality to it. Like there are cries always threatening to burst loose. As if the lyricism was a veil soon to be effortlessly swept aside, by quickly broadening darkening lamentations. The piano here ringing with sharpening urgency to retain its connection.

"Icarus," previously recorded on Murray's *MX*, another deep-reaching lyric. Don't hesitate to say ballad, it is, a dark one. Introspective, as if thinking itself a theme to encompass the unfolding power of the feeling. And that ballad, that story, of a slow rising, that tale, to fly, and at what cost. It ends he's still pondering, yet alive.

"Becca" has some Berg space, paramelodic, a simple statement, not clearly resolved, but re-presented. Another song that winds into a long swerving cry. The melody has a chordal voice, a bottom echo, the piano. What lyricism is harassed C. T.-like but Fox uncovering his own self. We will hear him again, there is no doubt.

Murray's "Picasso" presents the crossing outright, with Fox underneath the hood of the box, strumming, plucking, beating, tapping the wood. While David with his jump shuffle funks on into the Caribbean, which be the Spanish tinge of his Picasso reference. So Murray and Fox were the other two musicians of the famous flick, and Guernica was indeed funky from the bombs that blasted it. The taste of this, the criss crossed, blue funk to reggae/latino over Fox's double bypass on the box, is drama itself. It seems a curtain should be opening and something heavy eases into view.

Fox's "Ladders" is the most openly concertized. And there is a concerto aura to it, for piano and saxophone. But still it presents both a formal and psychological whole. Of where all of us have come from and how we gets along, inside and outside of each other.

Like the album itself is a point of reference and departure. For David Murray, it is simply another sign of his growing mastery, of every genre and style. For Donal Fox it is a sign that he is too hip to be typed or locked in with the dead peepas. He is singing for his own life and consciousness, from where he is on over to where he will be. Just like the rest of us.

8/95

CHAPTER 61

Tyrone Jefferson, *Connections*

Disapora Music.

It's good to hear this kind of set coming back. A wide-open swinging kind of jazz, seeking to combine all the different forms, historic and contemporary that characterize the whole music. Because "the music," like we say, comes from a lot of different places, a lot of different people, and a broad spectrum of experience.

We know (except for the lame and the insane) that Jazz (from the Bantu, Jism) is Afro-American. And to show how much work we got to do, many of our most famous jazz musicians resent the name because they think it got to do with somebody else naming it. Not understanding that the explosive spirituality of the music was called such because it was the creativity that life itself depended upon to continue.

But that's the way it is when you're in captivity. As the great Guinean revolutionary Amilcar Cabral said, only liberation can restore the oppressed back to their history. Slavery destroys our history and our memory, just as it destroys our human identity and lives.

So part of the task of conscious artists is to make cultural revolution, i.e., to use the arts to raise the consciousness. As Du Bois said, to create "true self-consciousness."

Tyrone Jefferson is on the case in this set, *Connections*. And that is just what he intends, to make those badly needed connections. To open our eyes. To ask enough "Why's?" so that we finally get Wise!

The connections he makes are geographical, from the West (where we are, and indeed, were born. Like, the music, Jazz, created in the West) to the East, where not only the life of our heritage and the beginning of history, but where all life was born.

Connections indeed. Tyrone, himself, is one of J. B.'s staunchest funk-ateers. So there's a bad connection, like they say, from "the hardest-working man in show business," James Brown. So we got to get that constant underpinning of hotness. It got to swing, otherwise like our Duke say, "it don't mean a thing." So it all swings. Gospel swing. Blues Swing. Swing Swing. Bop Swing. Plus to connect it correctly and like it is, he's got Native American swing, and hot and eerily hip as Crazy Horse must've seemed tricking them heathens. Latino swing, our family in the southwest, the islands, like Jamaica and Haiti, our Chicano, Cuban, Puerto Rican, Dominican family. Like that tomato sauce, "it's all in there!"

From the beginning we get Africa and the reminder that we are all from the same garden that brought life into the world. And from there, the music carries not only the animation of that life as rhythm and the spirit that goes back to the first eyes (I's) but without distraction carries a teaching and a preaching we need, particularly now the Heathens thinking about replaying slavery.

My man Abiodun, from the original original Last Poets, still at it. "We've got connections," he griots. And we've got to tighten up "our possessions." Make use of our senses and our tenses. The organs of I&I nations.

From the beginning as well, no matter the form or specific aspect of the music, whether gospel, or BeBop or African, Afro-Cuban, etc., Tyrone is on the scene. Playing his hip variations and admonitions. Adapting to the shifting forms like a world traveler. That's why we say, "I Am" and "Thou Art with Me."

There is also a skillful use of song and chorus, choir, soul-o. As in the cautionary tale "Who Are You?" A very good question, to get beyond what Du Bois called "the Double Consciousness." That is, seeing ourselves through the eyes of people that hate you. To get past seeing ourselves always with that sick mixture of amusement and con-tempt, like the present-day negroexploitation flicks.

Because once we know who we are, we can make more connections, and even further self-conscious development. Tyrone's music is very tuneful and soulful. A mixture of Jazz, blues, world beat, and even light fusion. Like James Brown funneled through a younger sophistica-tion toward the hip.

He comes on with Samba, and we hear echoes of Orfeo. Brazilian hip. Like "Samba Tswana," but even more in the beautiful ending piece "Bitter Sweet Liaison" with the lyrical reflective piano from under which comes the steadily rising drums, the "rap" of the ancient griots (actually *Djali* is the African word, *griot* is French, but we'll cop that too. So you can see how the *Djeli,* the plural, when we funking, becomes *Djeli ya,* is connected to *Jelly* as in *Jelly Roll* as *Jazz* is to *Jism.* Like Mr. B. said, Djeli Djeli Djeli!)

Another exceptional piece is "Cherokee," with its insinuating minor blues chant sleeking in. The connections being made. Where do you think we'd have to go when we fled the plantation? When bloods say they got indians in they family, they also mean they in the indians' family too. And it's true. Check that beautiful minor chant Tyrone runs against an overlay of Cherokee bells and drums. Until he runs it, bone first into a straight-out boppish Cherokee bridge and turn around back to the scatted chant over Afro-Indio drums. Connections like a mammy wammy.

We hear from South Africa in "Sisters." Mother Africa, Mother Earth, IsIs, the call from eternity to eternity. With the Zulu and Xhosa used as musical interludes for most of us, except we do understand Amandla! the cry for "Power," "Freedom," also the name of our granddaughter with her beautiful little two-year-old self.

Yes, that is a recurrent theme on this side. "Freedom" . . . "All I want is Freedom." It comes back as simple poignant narrative, it comes back in the sorrow song, the gospel, the hard bop scatted chorus, "Freedom."

Remember Max Roach's "Freedom Now: We Insist!" and "Tears for Johannesburg"? Sonny Rollins's "Freedom Suite"? Mingus's "Fables of Faubus," Trane's "Alabama"? Did you remember that the original name of Monk's "Evidence" was "Justice"? Duke's hundreds of "For My People," "Black, Brown and Beige," "Jump for Joy," etc., or Nina Simone's "Mississippi Goddamn." Or for that matter James Brown's "I'm Black & I'm Proud." etc. etc. The list is endless because we always put our consciousness into the music. Like Louis singing Fats's song, "What Did I Do to Be So Black and Blue?"

It's just that now that the whole society is rushing to the right, trying to replant slavery, and the big corpses got a stranglehold even on the young people's music. (Rap wasn't always about our mothers and wives and sisters being "B's" & "H's," it used to be about struggle.) But we got to get it back and get back on the revolutionary road. Tyrone Jefferson, with his pretty horn and advancing consciousness, is just trying to make us remember.

2/6/94

CHAPTER 62

James Moody*

BeBop was the righteous explosion of life and change that ushered in the second half of the 20th century in the U.S. and, by shattering influence, the world. It was the redemption of black music from the dead, the grim commercialism of what the corporations had mashed upon us as—no kidding—Swing! Not Duke Ellington and Count Basie, or Pres and Billie, but the sterile dummy bands of Kay Kaiser and Casa Loma, the covers of the Dorsey Brothers and the saccharine appropriations of Glenn Miller. The integrated copping of Benny Goodman.

All-American music, that's right. But the originals the creators languished under the continuing domain of chattel racial slavery, explained and repackaged, however, as segregation discrimination ignorance ghettoization. And wherever the black artists, the doers and creators of black culture, would erect their institutions of beauty, a consolidation of this beauty in real social life would always be kidnapped, musicnapped, soulnapped, rapnapped under the bleeding claws of the corporate slavemasters.

Greenwich Village was the first black community in New York, Hell's Kitchen the second, Harlem the third, and in each one the culture was so alive it created whole epics of artistic creation, and a commercial

---

*In July 2008 Moody was headliner, along with Grachan Moncur III, T. S. Monk, Smithsonian Ensemble playing a tribute to Johnny Hodges at the 3rd Annual Lincoln Park Coast Music Festival.

development that went with it, but when the monsters of profit saw, the beasts of white supremacy dug, they had to seize it, since the blacks had no defense, no politicized institutions to what they had developed.

Newark's Barbary Coast was such a place, a brawling swinging center of the industrial city. Where the Dukes, Willie the Lions, James P.'s rambled and dissembled, where they swung high philosophy straight out of the people's feelings and erected institutions of transcendent aesthetics only to see them torn down, and aggressive ugliness re-erected as progress. Segregation continued as new style. The music ate up or bowdlerized, put down as unserious, derivative, the ravings of illiterate niggers.

Ho, Hum, oh well, so much for the dying, the left behind, the money gods and their empty altars. But what of the creators the artists of our epoch. How do they continue and what is it they are continuing.

James Moody was one of the great figures of the explosion BeBop. It was my youngest consciousness to be sure. It was the reassurance, without it being known as that, that there was something more profound to life than radio and the U.S. social malaise, that segregation and discrimination were the sounds beasts make for humanity.

BeBop penetrated the mediocrity of high school, the reflection of dying culture trying to assure us there was nothing else but death and dullness. I heard Dizzy Gillespie, Bird, Monk, Miles, the BeBop boys and was hurled into a future of creation, a self-consciousness that was secret only because it was not commercial.

BeBop, for instance, raised improvisation as central to black music, again. That life was not on paper, that we might catch some of its nuance and stirring, with black dots on the page, be they the musical score or the poem or the novel or the social manifesto. But that life was alive, it was out there. And what one had to do was get in it, taste it, as it lived, as it coursed, as it was to be alive in us with us.

BeBop raised blues, that cultural matrix linking Africa with the West, that paean of deadly slave ships and the trade in black flesh, that classic holocaust, which is so menacing because it is a holocaust that is still going on. It raised the life of black people, from the inside out, it was the music of Americans who had never been allowed to be in America. It was a feeling that simmered throughout America, and was outlawed, said not to exist, or lynched when the opportunity presented itself, it could, however, never be dismissed, except by the cash registers of slavery which became cash registers of nazism and still staggers on in search of the world, all the world, as its final victim.

BeBop raised rhythm, the multirhythms of Africa, as central to the coming called jazz, that African word for orgasm, jism, become jasm, become jazz. The Ho House tip was like saying black literature was spawned by kitchens because Langston was a busboy, or slavery because Fred Douglass was a slave, or BeBop, cause I was a bopper from my young heart, it was new life being expressed, life instead of death, life instead of commercial soulicide.

When Moody played his solo on "Mood for Love," it was the arrival again of improvisation as focus, not the tired swing arrangement of the ipana troubadours. What Eddie Jefferson would do so hiply before he was squashed by the American nightmare, King Pleasure did with his lyrics and vocal what we all were doing in the street, what Lambert Hendricks and Ross would do, the hip quality of Sarah Vaughan and now the breathtaking beauty of Aminata Moseka (Abbey Lincoln) is to put that creative, live quality back into song. Billie's changed melodies are the improvisers' song, the new, the just born.

Moody with Gillespie's band was wondrous, because he was not only part of a wondrous age of creators and creation, but because the Gillespie band should still exist as an American Classical orchestra, just like Ecstine's. That is part of America that must be given institutional life, to reorganize us to the existent rather than the commercially persistent.

Whether on alto or tenor, Moody was himself, the southern existence replayed in the North, Moody was raised in Newark. I remember we used to mention Sarah and Moody and Hank Mobley as resident hipsters, on our strolls across our city, teenage bop fantasists creating a tomorrow in which we would be our real selves swinging.

For me, Moody and the BeBop era are still to be understood, they are still part of the unfathomed strength of American culture. The establishment still talks about English departments when George Washington won the war, that Attucks even got his ass blown away dealing with that. But this is not England. This is not Europe. This is America.

It is a multinational, multicultural society, multiracial. Though we know they keep the music lovers segregated so we can't compare experiences and come up with the truly grand truly realistic truly transforming American experience which would be all of us who are living and want to live, all of us who love life and like Mantan Moreland, don't dig death no way.

Moody is music of life. He is the urban, the blues, the improvisa-

tional, the hip, the meditating in the midst of chaos, the walker in
walkin, the cooker in cookin, the soul brother in the land of soul thieves
and soul murder. His story is his/story we/story, and it is the tale that
must be told and understood, deeply, emotionally, if we are to survive.

The stiff lying Coca Cola melody is what runs America and it is
a lie and aimed at destruction. There is no invention paid for by our
citizenship tax dollars worth as much as African American music, and
culture, none of their weapons is as profound, none of their inventions
will last as long as Moody's inventions on tenor or alto.

Duke Ellington, Bessie Smith, Billie Holiday, Louis Armstrong,
Thelonius Monk, Lester Young, Art Tatum, John Coltrane are great
names in the history of the world of ideas. There are few American
anythings, scientists or economists or social scientists or politicians,
that will be as likely to be remembered by future civilizations in which
exploitation and oppression are finally outlawed, and racists live in
zoos.

When you listen to James Moody understand you are listening to a
great philosopher artist create right from his living passion. Were you
alive in Beethoven's time when he improvised you might have got something like this. If you could hear Cheikh Diop speak about the history
of language and physics, you might. If you could dig Einstein laying it
down and out, you might. Perhaps one hour enrapt by Zora Neale's
living metaphors, or Brecht's *Jungle of Cities* or Ms. Holiday as she
turned on that stool, her diaphanous longing like blue love gathering us
into the meaning of what this all is. Like a history of night.

NO, the music is what will last, it has the profundity of the new, and
the history of what still is, it is carried by the sensitive, and passed to
us, as always, as songs.

You can blow now, if you want to. . . . We're Through. James
Moody!

4/89

CHAPTER 63

Barry Harris

In the Tradition

Barry Harris plays our complex feelings, like a heart/beating History—
No, it's *our* story Barry plays, 's'why it's BEBOP. Slaves still be trying
to sing in African! Trying to respeak our ancient souls, replace the sun
above our Mama's head. That's why Pops copped!

Barry Harris is one of those remarkable artists who understand the
great innovators and can bring them to us *whole!* Unlike the various
dissemblers who would play Monk's heads, for instance, then drift
immediately into tired clichés, diluting the Master's legacy.

When you hear Barry play the classics, the irresistible *swing* is the
result of his serious investigation of great music as well as his deep and
organic understanding. To play great music, part of you has to *be* great
music, not just music lessons!

There is in *the music* the heart, soul and memory of the African
American people. The fundamental expression of these is the blues.

Blues is the national consciousness, our western speech, the cultural
matrix—expressed in a myriad ways—music, dance, song, literature,
dress, plastic and graphic arts, even by Magic Johnson. The aesthetic
and tone of African America.

The world begins in black, its first humanity *blue*. Joe Lee Wilson
sings, "If it wasn't for the blues, wd'na been no jazz!"

Barry Harris confirms for me the premise—without blues there is no
sucha thing as Jazz. His music is blues's child, to paraphrase Langston.
BeBop was what blues called itself after it'd been in Harlem a few years,
and when by the '40s the big merchants operating under the traditional

skull and cross bones tried to hijack Black big band swing by nouning its verb into Gold! (As usual).

Such money delusion is tragic and illusory as those who thought they could dedark the world, since with the hearing of such jeering our spirits produced Birds and Monks and Undizzy "Dizzes," Roaches, and Buds—Klooks, young Miles to salvage human passion from the ravages of the Money Jungle.

Barry brings the tradition to us informed particularly by the revolutionary piano art innovated by Bud and Monk. He is among those undaunted by exploitive distortions and misuses of the music, the same as the exploitive misuse of musicians and most other people. He is one of those grand carriers of the message our advanced cultural innovators, music revolutionaries sent back from their hidden laboratories buried deep in the funk. Just before Glenn Miller was reported missing in action.

Barry is still prevailing against the attacks of the money addicts, who beat wonderful artists down as they beat the people down, in the name of ignorance, arrogance, and animal comfort. So both people and music, the black nations' culture itself, are still in slavery!

However, what BEBOP expressed and was, was the African Americans' more developed productive forces, not industrial northern garbage, as expressions whose existence confirmed Brer Rabbit had got in the wind by the time Elmer Fudd figured out where he usta was.

The imitation, the fake, the phony, the subjective wizardry of the mediocre, the antihuman, dilution freaks, are celebrated instead of towering artists like Barry Harris, because life itself in this society is largely prohibited for most of us.

Barry speaks constantly, infuses us, with life. New Life. But life includes passion, and passion is banned except twisted into pornography, because feeling is our first legacy—and the Intelligence contained therein raised throughout & understood through science is all that can free us from contemporary cave society. So the emphasis and constant reiteration of the safe dust of profits to suffocate the dangerous freedom sung constantly by these Black prophets of aesthetic and social transformation!

Barry Harris is part of our national strength, our evolving intelligence. He is a spirit messenger, upright forwarder of the history of Black life in America and, quiet as it's kept, America itself. That's why the music called "Jazz" is America's classical music. Plus, Barry can play like a muh'fuh!

6/22/87

CHAPTER 64

Pharoah Sanders, *Shukuru*

Evidence, 1981, EVI 22022.
Pharoah Sanders, sax (tenor); Leon Thomas, percussion/vocals;
Idris Muhammad, drums; William Henderson, synthesizer; Ray
Drummond, bass.

Any Pharoah Sanders album or club or concert appearance is going to
produce minimally very good music. More than likely, it will produce
a high percentage of *great* music. Because Pharoah at this point in his
career, and actually for at least the last decade and a half, has produced
some of the most significant and moving, beautiful music identified by
the name Jazz.

The whole general group of Theresa albums is at consistently awesome levels (*Rejoice, Journey to the One, Live,* etc.). Before that, when
Pharoah recorded for various labels, there were quite a few *classic*
works produced (*Thembi; Karma; Tauhid; Jewels of Thought; Deaf,
Dumb, Blind; Wisdom through Music,* etc.), including collaborations
with vocal innovator Leon Thomas (the magnificent "Creator Has a
Master Plan," for instance), who is heard here ("Beautiful Energy") in
a piece movingly reflective of those earlier efforts.

But as dazzling and historic as these earlier works remain, like the
greatest jazz artists, the most astonishing and emotionally transporting
performances have been those club dates in which Pharoah, his band,
the club atmosphere, and the audience have come together in something as close to a collective celebration of *life* itself as you are likely
ever to get in on. Sweet Basil, in the last period, and always the Village
Vanguard have been the usual venues, in NYC, where I have been party
to these transmutations of energy into spirit!

Another important factor to this high creative output has been the quality of Pharoah's groups. Players like John Hicks, Idris Muhammad, Ray Drummond, Billy Higgins, Lonnie Smith, Reggie Workman; discoveries like Greg Bandy and Joe Bonner, etc. Sanders has consistently had bands that not only could create a lyrical near-mystical Afro-Eastern *world* but sweat hot fire music in continuing display of the so-called "energy music" of the '6os. Plus, and this is its fundamental greatness, the music swang very very hard and was, yes, always extremely funky.

This is the legacy of Pharoah's association with Trane as Trane vaulted into an innovator's immortality as reflection of his artist's interpretation of the popular revolutionary spirit of that time. The "Freedom" the people called for was the same in essence as the jazz radicals who sought freedom from the stifling anti-emotional forms of commercial Tin Pan Alley America.

Pharoah has always taken that influence and association and apprenticeship to be serious and sacred. His approach to the music has been, as a result, as serious and meaningful. Any serious analysis of his work will quickly confirm this.

He has continued his innovations, both philosophically and technically, to sustain his demanding and powerful aesthetic. The sound of Sanders's horn is distinctive and completely his own. His sonship to Trane is always acknowledged, which is now the artist honoring tradition and acknowledging beauty. But Sanders himself has been, for quite a few years now, a Giant.

He has taken the use of circular breathing, in order to paint long tissues of sounded emotion, to levels of pure technical achievement that have seldom been duplicated. In fact, it is Sanders who has made circular breathing almost standard equipment for contemporary reed players.

The incredible palette of colors in the Sanders sound, his exquisite omni-timbred tone are his *exclusively*; ask all those who publicly covet them.

Indeed Pharoah has advanced the science of breathing so far that in recent appearances he can take the horn away from his mouth and the air he has filled up the horn with will continue to *play the horn,* and *move the keys,* for several seconds after he has removed the horn, holding it at arm's length, bemused at his own invention!

He said recently that he's been working on how to get "a cathedral sound" without being in a cathedral. The "round," as he implied, sound that is his, vibrating into the listener with rhythm fantastic. And the players Pharoah surrounds himself with can jump off Sanders's "exoticism" with the hard bop. The music is often a surge of emotional expression whose beauty is completed by the elaboration of Sanders's own development.

The whole musical persona of Pharoah Sanders is of a consciousness in conscious search of higher consciousness. So his Arkansas Blues was drawn to the high experimental school (Trane, Ornette, Ayler). Then the East and Africa. As consciousness, even of the currents of reality.

His music has always been superb yet *accessible*. His ideas have been movements. He is genuinely *popular,* even though a known inhabitant of the genuinely "way out." He makes people stomp, experience transcendental meditation, and think about revolution. Some, including Pharoah, even get to singing. Pharoah's big saxophone blues shouter bass is as funky as anything else he plays.

This is encouraging especially in this period of our losing giants like Duke, Count, Monk, Papa Joe, Philly Joe, Cootie, and others, an inestimable loss, and the challenge of development, evolution. A challenge to the great players of the music to re-state the tradition, yet take it on out!

For instance, Pharoah deals with strings on this album, apparently in the beautiful tradition of Bird and Clifford. But taking it a little further. How "fur" it is taken is revealed when we find out that both "voices" and "strings" are the product of a Kurzeil *Synthesizer!* (created by the same computer expert who has been working with Stevie Wonder).

Yet even so, the technology does not detract from the total musical product. The strings and voices not only make genuine musical statements but, as programmed and played by pianist William Henderson (another Sanders "discovery"), the music is quite thrilling. Pharoah even tries to come face to face with the often overwhelming legacy that Ellington has left in the use of the voice, the chorus, "vocalese," impressionist scene painting. The voices particularly are more aggressive here, more out front, than the classic efforts. Ellington's total *dramatic* creativity is what is being raised, which is still largely unexplored.

The fact that Pharoah is using a synthesizer to achieve this important music is consistent with Sanders's technical mastery as an integral part of his art. One reason Stevie is a Wonder!

These tunes are both familiar standards ("Too Young to Go Steady"), as well as the classic jazz performer's vehicle "Body & Soul," as well as, as always, something new. In this case, not only the synthesizer but the string-lit "Shukuru," complete with a Sanders vocal. It is a shimmeringly beautiful piece. But also "Precious Energy," demonstrating why Leon Thomas remains one of the most creative and innovative singers anywhere. There is also the swinging club favorite "Jitu" (named after Brooklyn political and cultural activist Jitu Weusi. *Jitu* means Giant in Swahili, *Weusi*, Black).

"Body & Soul" has been a measure of a Jazz soloist's stature for everyone from Bean's banner to Trane. Pharoah approaches this "monster" first by acknowledging tradition, but only as part of an overall spectacular demonstration of how the *new* got that way. And it would take a musician of Sanders's taste and creativity to make the old syrupy weeper "Too Young" stand up and be listened to anew, but that is Pharoah's work. Plus the spicy good carnival feelings of "Highlife," a constant Sanders incarnation. With this artist the listener runs the spectrum of feeling, from the transcendent technical mastery Sanders effortlessly achieves, e.g., the "tonal echo" that is his signature on many of his works, or the flying gutbucket of his contemporary blues. Whether with naked horn or with synthesizer Pharoah Sanders creates music of uncommon loveliness, depth, and strength. This is a small part of the measure of Sanders's musical stature and importance in the world. *Shukuru* is further evidence.

CHAPTER 65

Don Pullen–George Adams Quartet, *Breakthrough*

Blue Note Records, 1986, B21Y-46314.

Don Pullen appeared, mid-sixties, almost in full stride. He was part of the social and aesthetic eruption that lit up world skies during "the '60s."

The first meeting I had with Don was on the self-produced *Live at Yale University* album, co-created musically and business-wise with the incredibly powerful and innovative drummer Milford Graves. For a time, Pullen and Graves were one of the most awesome new groups in what was called "the Avant Garde" of the music.

What was clear, from the first, was that Pullen had absorbed the "post"–hard bop pianistic speech of the *new,* most often associated with the appearance of Cecil Taylor. But as Pullen developed and got heard, one clear contrast between Taylor and Pullen was that Don carried more thoroughly the *blues* voice, the day-to-day "funk" of our between-church self!

There is a searching bluesiness in Don which roots even his stunning pianistic runs and chromatics in the real, the *concretely blue.* For me, the pianistic pyrotechnics of Art Tatum and the crack-the-sound-barrier runs of Bud Powell are Pullen's obvious double-jointed Godfathers. Don says it was Ornette Coleman and Eric Dolphy, two new music classicists who were most influential on his playing. These are iconoclasts, one an innovator, the other a master of the new learning.

Pullen and the George Adams–Don Pullen group play, as drummer

Danny Richmond has said, "something for everybody," but at the same time it's obvious that they neither conform to dull musical conventions that are more useful to commerce than deep communication nor are of that boring school that thinks stylistic innovation must carry obscurity and abstraction as ends in themselves. Important innovation has to do with "making sense at higher and higher speeds," so to speak. But it is *more* information, broader, more sensuous registration, expression of a different or further emotion/"idea."

At times the band seems to play a music, especially Pullen, that is closer to some aspects of the concert hall than the barrelhouse. But Jazz is America's classical music, a profound artistic genre of African American invention. And as such it has yoked together, blended, absorbed every obvious musical trend since the Great Atlantic tour which brung us here.

So the Don Pullen–George Adams group demonstrates how at one point in American space East and West have already met, to great aesthetic advantage. The players (Pullen, Adams, Richmond, Brown) are "avant-garde" stars at the same time they are journeymen blues-soaked jazz players.

For all of their "outness," they have all come from musical backgrounds and continuing bread and butter supplying gigs that are decidedly "in." For instance Don was schooled in European concert classics, but also he has been schooled in the famous or infamous bar organ trio or quartet form which passes too frequently as an all-purpose musical panacea in Black urban communities. (This is not to be confused with Joe Papp's June 23, 1986, production of Pullen playing organ with a five-piece group and twelve pieces.)

George Adams, tenor, flute, vocals, met Don in an Atlanta club, the Royal Peacock. Pullen was gigging with Syl Austin in the late '60s, and Adams had come up from Covington, Georgia, to play with folks like Clyde McPhatter, Jimmy Reed, Little Walter. It was at Don's urging that Charlie Mingus hired Adams in 1973, after hiring Don the year before.

George, Don, and master drummer Danny Richmond all hooked up eventually in the Mingus band. Richmond, of course, was Mingus's alter ego. "Mingus wouldn't even play unless I was there." But all have musical backgrounds rooted in blues and rhythm and blues, "on the one," as the young black rock players call it. Yet Richmond, Adams, and Pullen also have extensive and very rich jazz experience as serious credentials in the ever developing "new."

When Mingus died in 1979, a Dutch promoter wanted to hook up the three as the nucleus of what he wanted to call "the Mingus Dynasty" and continue to bill them simply as carriers of Mingus's thing. They refused, though they did see the practicality of staying together, since the people seemed to dig it as much as they did. But as Adams confirms, "We'd been doing our own thing, even before Mingus, and we might have even injected some things into his music."

Adams has played with Gil Evans groups for ten years. Danny Richmond played with Mingus "on and off about twenty years." The Don Pullen–George Adams quartet has recorded eight albums previously, but ironically enough this is the first one in the U.S. Adams says, "It's why we call it *Breakthrough*, because we're finally getting an American recording."

Why this top-notch band with such heavy names should have had to wait so long to be recorded in the U.S. is anybody's guess, though obsession with quality has never been a fault of the American record companies. Be thankful there has been this *Breakthrough*.

The group sounds "fresh," accessible, and outward bound, all at the same time. Adams, whose searching tenor sound animates all these tunes with a moving heat, explains the group's tightness. "We have a common respect for music, a common pursuit, similar values. . . . I think what we got from Mingus was understanding his ways of communicating to the public and to the musicians, the mood swings. But love for the music was uppermost."

With bassist Cameron Brown, impulse with and at the same time in contrast to Richmond, unobtrusively carrying the whole group forward, at any tempo, with any stylistic face, almost effortlessly, these musicians complement each other and show each other off.

The Pullen-Adams band is a working band that's been together seven years. The compositions are Pullen's and Adams's, though Richmond is correct when he says, as drummer, he "leads the band." But their longevity means they've had time to digest the compositions and play them enough to get them tight and musical and swinging. Too often, especially in the new music, record sessions are thrown together, the players hoping their "outness" will carry the date. Unfortunately, what we often hear is just their lack of real organization. Not so this date.

Danny Richmond sums it up when asked about contrast and continuity of this present group and the Mingus bands. "Mingus set it up in the beginning—free music—Mingus was doing that in the '50s,

Expression that didn't have to stay in the bounds of what everybody else was doing. We've incorporated that into what we're doing.

"Lyrics, singing, hard passages. But the chemistry of this group is superb. . . . Bands don't usually stay together this long without no change of personnel."

This music comes from all the places these players have been, and some of the ones they're going. Don Pullen sounded like this when I first heard him, long before he went with Mingus, only now he has stretched out even further. He is one of the *major* soloists in the music. The Pullen-Adams group one of the most inventive and important groups on the scene.

On the album, Don and George have cooked up a seriously smoking, constantly intriguing, yet disarmingly accessible brew. Adams is represented by "A Time for Sobriety" and "Mr. Smoothie," Pullen by "Just Foolin' Around," "Song from the Old Country," "We've Been Here All the Time" (which sounds like the alternate title to the album), and "The Necessary Blues (or Thank You Very Much, Mr. Monk)," heard only on CD.

You have to cop to actually cop, but just for the "notes" side mention that "Smoothie" (the cool one despite the chaos, to paraphrase the composer) has a presence, musically, bright and straight-ahead, jazzically bluesy (no wonder!). It summons the classic continuum of the music, when most everyone who played what's called jazz knew it had to do with blues. There's even a hint of backbeat and a smidgen of Caribee, as it would have to be. The big Adams sound brings Don hoppin in it and on it, call this a flurrying funk.

"Just Foolin' Around," Pullen's piece, is all but that, no foolin. Like "The Necessary Blues (or Thank You)," there is a decidedly Monastic (as in *Monkish*) touch to this. "Foolin' Around" highlights Danny Richmond on machine guns, toms, and bass drum. You understand Mingus's feelings for Danny exactly.

"Song from the Old Country" begins like an insinuating ballad. What is insinuated is the funk to come. It is free, easy, old and "new" country, held with critical, mutually enfunkifying balance.

Don's "We've Been Here" is a blue anthem, the constant life pulse given with a descending happy line. It speaks to Don & Co.'s condition, what with this breakthrough, that these skilled, committed musicians have been here all the time, until the latest commercial fad went to fade.

Adams' "Sobriety," a quiet, soothing, yet mightily fortifying ballad. It is, like everything else on the album, very deeply satisfying. As Pullen commented, when asked what he was doing musically, "A variety of things. The direction depends on the composition. Sometimes blues feeling but no changes . . . definite blues rhythm but no changes. Sometimes freedom on the head, might put a little reggae in . . . so many things at our disposal." The whole music, and very tastily packaged. And about the breakthrough, it's about time.

CHAPTER 66

Von and Chico Freeman,
Freeman and Freeman

India Navigation, 1989. IN 1070.
Chico Freeman, tenor sax; Von Freeman, tenor sax; Kenny Barron,
piano; Muhal Richard Abrams, piano; Cecil McBee, bass; Jack
DeJohnette, drums.

Chicago was the largest early collecting point of Southern black
culture arrived North, from the late 19th century on. The southern
out-migration of African Americans in search of jobs, refuge from the
Klan, new life, post-slave America, etc., followed the Mississippi north
like the North Star's main highway.

So even today Chicago is the Blues Capital of Black America. The
city has maintained its aura of northern outpost for southern music
(white and black). For this reason there is always an outpouring of that
experience, from era to era. There are always very important musicians
using Chicago as their launching pad. From Louis Armstrong to Sun
Ra to the musicians of the AACM.

The musical Freeman family (Von, brothers George, guitar; Bruz,
drums; and Von's son, Chico) are such a Chicago phenomenon. They
are at all points the continuing expression of this African American/
American musical culture.

At the same time, New York City is obviously "the marketplace."
One must, from all directions, get to the "Apple" to display one's wares,
or pay the consequences. It is in NYC that one is "discovered" and
sometimes "covered" by big commerce. Where one's "distinctiveness"
can be lifted, cloned, exploited, while one struggles to eat. But also
where one's name can be bandied around until it is fairly well known in
some circles. You might even get the title "genius" but still be poor.

Von Freeman stayed in Chicago, like most of the city's residents.

Though he was and is, by the accounts of numerous great musicians, one of the most important players in the music.

Chico has been, in his comparatively short career (Von's been out there over forty years) more celebrated *(Kings of Mali, Young Lions)* and encouraged certainly, in contrast to his father. But then Chico did make the big trip Apple side.

Yet just as Chico is not possible biologically without Von, this is true musically as well. Quiet as it's kept, musically this is true for an entire contemporary expression of the jazz tenor saxophone tradition. This record should make this aggressively clear. What else we need to dig is that in the commercial shakeout of the music, many of the significant contributors to its development are "covered," neglected, or "lost."

So whatever happens with this record commercially, the music here is important now and will be. For not only are we being delighted but enlightened as well. It's what we used to call "inner attainment," not just entertainment. The performances themselves (recorded in NYC's Shakespeare Festival Public Theater) carry both an artistic heaviness and a historical revelation.

Von Freeman in many ways is as singular and signal in his appropriation and re-expression of the major tenor giants as Dexter Gordon. Hawk and Pres absorbed and reprojected as contemporary catalysts, now conjoined and expressed together!

And we hear in Chico this process almost seamlessly yet newly projected, adding Trane to the loving artifact on the way.

The ballad "I Can't Get Started" should be one clarifying example of what our "standard" jazz histories lack, i.e., the great influence of the relatively "unknown" masters like Von on a whole generation of players. The rush of energy, the dynamic conceptualizing phrases that state and at the same time "imply" a still greater mass of emotion beyond what's heard are something else. The big straight-ahead sound, but with the bends and interiorization of "telling" like the signifying President. The hauntingly personal intonation and matter-of-fact lyricism giving both heat and cool with effortless swing.

"Paying New York Dues" is a blowing session, Von on top, and the full-out swinging both establishes the Von/Chico connection and contrast. Von comes bigger and imposing. Chico is smoother, it seems, the timbre more rounded and Trane-like, but you feel the same inner dynamic reaching out. And both swing hard.

"Shadow" shows the casual hotness and invention of Von, to a tenderness when the rhythm lays out and it's like he wants to speak to us more directly. On "Lover Man" it is the odd intonation, the knotty solo phrases that intrigue and cause wonder.

"Undercurrent" is one of Chico's tunes. He featured it on an earlier LP, and it is still a moving work in its complex rhythmic movement, which provides him with a sleek vehicle for his driving solo and stream-lined post-Trane tone with its built-in cries and declamations. Chico rides the modal feeling of these rhythms, a kind of Afro-Latin groove, cool in the beginning but growing hotter and hotter with each turn of searching phrase. And please check especially Kenny Barron's essence of hip solo and the funky authority & direction McBee provides and DeJohnette confirms.

"I Remember You" is sweet, seemingly simply stated and running. But it is the emotional cargo that stops and touches us with the hearing and more with each rehearing. Again, without the rhythm the pure feeling in the horn reaches us with a burning clarity.

And this is to say nothing about the rhythm section, which is one of the best in the music today. Kenny Barron and Muhal Abrams are by now well-known piano innovators, and Abrams is the acknowledged "God Father" of the most recent Chicago AACM-inspired avant-garde, and a formidable composer. Jack DeJohnette is another proven and influential player and leader who has had several big jazz hits.

"Jug Ain't Gone" is a tribute to Gene Ammons, another Chicago tenor giant. It is a blowing blues for both horns, full of Jug's spirit, which is to say the spirit of the blues God (as Larry Neal would say). And here is a wonderful exchange between the horns, conversation, question and answer, point/counterpoint, all the way live feeling and funky as that city itself. Father and Son Freeman is no gimmick, but a long absent bit of musical intelligence. Two aspects, two generations, of the same marvelous tradition the history and the music passed from one to the other like a magical baton. You've got to check it.

8/89

CHAPTER 67

Alan Shorter, *Orgasm*

Polygram Records, 1998 (original release 1968), Boooo09DGH.
Side A: "Parabola," "Joseph," "Straits of Blagellan."
Side B: "Rapids," "Outeroids," "Orgasm."
Alan Shorter, flugelhorn; Muhammad Ali, drums; Leandro Barbieri, tenor; Charles Edward Haden, bass; Rashid Ali, drums; Reginald Johnson, bass.

I knew Alan Shorter and his, for the last few decades, more famous brother, Wayne, earliest in the city of Newark, where we all grew up. (See "Introducing Wayne Shorter," *Jazz Review.*) As teenagers, Wayne and Alan were active in Newark's emerging teenage BeBop scene. Wayne was famous, even then, as a widely predicted innovator and star to come, playing with Nat Phipps and Jackie Bland's widely hailed teenage big bands. Alan, though older and in some ways much like his younger brother . . . "the weird Shorter brothers" was the common wisdom, yet much less was known of Alan's music. He could be seen ubiquitously at all the spots and what-nots of first light BeBop Newark, always carrying his saxophone case, but we almost never saw him playing anywhere.

Alan and I got close at Howard University, "the capstone of Negro education," where we were students. And incidentally, both tossed, "blackballed" out of the Sphinx, the pledge club of the Alpha Phi Alpha fraternity, apparently for being ourselves at an early age. But when we ran into each other a few years later (I'd been exiled in the Air Force after getting tossed out of Howard), Alan was playing trumpet. Why? I never got that out of him, though I did ask a few times. But Alan *was* weird. And he would always tell me something contained in suddenly widening eyes and linguistic half-chuckle that resisted American speech. If you asked Wayne, he'd say something like, "Hey, man . . . !" with the same eyes.

I was a little surprised at this album, that it had resurfaced. I'd all but forgotten Alan had made any records. He'd brought a group and played at a few programs CAP had sponsored during the '70s, but I never got to the specifics of what he was doing musically.

But here is a legacy of this weird Shorter. And like Alan, it is weird, thorny, stylishly tenuous. "Parabola" is entrancing, like the march or marked stride of something portentous, even dangerous. The melodic line thrusting, but as if not quite focused, it could be this way, but then again . . . who knows.

Alan called this "new music," as we all did then. New, but related to what? New time, and place and conditions. A new generation. Aggressive and determined . . . to speak, to shout, to demand . . . yet—not altogether certain of what.

It is a music meant to shake, to stir, to arouse. To call for a "new dispensation," perhaps, of the whole order of things. Barbieri appears, twisting and calling, spreading a mystical frenzy across the proceedings, and that proclaims the music's focus . . . mood and emotion.

Shorter, with the muted flugelhorn, about the same time Miles began to use this horn. Miles, I think, because it presented his playing as "formally" cool, as well as hid the lovely earlier "fluffs" of his Bird period. I suspect Alan used this horn for the same reason . . . it was a cooler sound, plus you couldn't hear the clinkers. But there is an emotional quality to the timbre of this horn, as if it always had more to say and was about to burst out any minute.

Alan Shorter can be characterized by such an emotional stance. By this date, Shorter had been striving mightily to become not only a "heavy" player but an innovative one, a weird one, if you will. Having cast his tenor, which he had been playing since early teens, along with his brother, to the wind, knowing Alan, I imagine, did not want his path toward total "outness" blocked by Wayne's sudden immensity. So suddenly Alan was playing trumpet.

All the players on the date are young and full of the soon-to-be-confirmed promise of their apprenticeship in the music. They are all beginning to open into their own voices. Alan was gone before he could. But Leandro Barbieri ("Gato" in a minute) got to be known across the planet. He was playing with Don Cherry in Paris just before this. Charles Edward (you know, Charlie, was with Ornette) Haden. And the Alis, Muhammad and Rashid (went with Trane), all kept getting up. But even here, as an ensemble, they are striking. The total sound and conception and burning energy. There is a freshness to this music that makes you listen, here, on "Parabola," till the last eerie passage.

"Joseph" is another tale of "darkness," like they say. Of quest and search. From the arco bass opening then Shorter's questioning whole notes. The line slides from one horn to the next, with the hypnotic pacing of the bass beneath. It is like a warning, a short fearsome message, saying what?

"Blagellan" evokes an Ornette-like feeling, or at least what Ornette was doing then, pre-"rock," when he brought that first quartet to bum-rush New York City. Phrases, stop-go, tenuous, yet decisive in the over-all musical environment they set. But "Blagellan" suddenly unfolds into Barbieri's turbulent wailing and crying. Throwing the tempo with him and the whole ensemble, at once, into a jet stream of frantic perception, perhaps even proto-rational description.

Alan's solos are always implosions, even at the breakneck tempos of some of these pieces. He seems emotionally removed, as statement, from the whole. As if he is commenting on, rather than existing as part of, the whole. I believe this is because he had not yet found his full voice as a soloist, though these compositions are full of the unique "outness" that characterized the man.

"Rapids" with trumpet lead conjures Don Cherry, Ornette's Miles. A skittering flash of notes, never clearly stating a direction, preferring the sound to the statement. But again, the tone itself has a hipness to it that raises the musical level of the entire ensemble.

For instance, the bass-drum riff under all is much like Bird's "Big Foot," which Don Pullen used to such advantage on his own "Big Alice." The line has a droll freshness here in that it pretends at times to be an R&B "backbeat" but denies it and pretends to be a cool rubato, and is neither.

The music does owe quite a bit to Ornette's '60s scene-crashing approach, which captured the imagination of a whole generation. The new bop irregular pacing of the melodic line and the ensemble sound. Ali is clear, clean and swinging, no matter, making the brushes work like Max did.

"Outeroids," again, has an Ornette feeling. Part of the total state-ment of the times, but musically entrancing. Short startling phrases with sudden "bursts" of unison horns.

"Orgasm" uses a very spare line, almost the outline of a tune. That is, until Barbieri crashes through, full of dynamic fire. The ensemble itself is an expression of Rashid Ali and the thunderous swing he brought to the Trane groups he played in. There is a "zoooom" of increasing tension from what seems a tight bass field, widening until it provides

Barbieri a rising whirlwind of rhythm on which to rush, twisting and screaming for all he's worth. A short but brilliant passage.

When Shorter comes in, one finally digs that no matter what he has written, or the musical context with which he surrounds himself, Alan is still "cool." He's never left the old early Miles emotional worldview. The laid-back raconteur of "what it is." The world itself be crashing and screaming by, "but . . . ," like Oscar Brown sang, ". . . he was cool!"

Haden reinforces this seemingly aberrant coolness with his solo, but then we see that despite the "sound and fury" there is at the very center of Shorter's music a willful determination seemingly to resist the ultra-emotionalism that the music and perhaps the times have summoned.

As the head is reprised, with its spare melodic invention over a drum reduced almost to the slimness of a hand clap (one hand?), we are sure that even in *Orgasm* Alan Shorter remained, to the end, most cool!

12/97

CHAPTER 68

The Work Man

Reggie Workman

Reggie Workman Ensemble, live at Willisau Jazz Festival
Reggie Workman, bass; Gerry Hemingway, drums; John Purcell, reeds; Marilyn Crispell, piano; Jeanne Lee, vocals, narration; Jason Hwang, violin.

Opening with Reggie Workman's furious bowed lines. It is an aural pronouncement of the whole music. We know that this already almost legendary master bassist, still arguably un-old, has appeared for years with the greatest musicians in this music, Coltrane, Miles, Rollins, name them, list any group of "Top" . . . whatevers, as to number, of the greatest albums of the music, and the Work Man—as I have referred to him since the hottest part of the "new music" eruption during the '60s—Reggie Workman will be there. And we will hear, not only the high level of instrumental mastery, but the driving, pulsing, quickly identifiable musicality of the approach—very strong and consistent, yet as flexible as the melodic line. There is nothing sly about the Work Man, he is all over the music, in whatever precisely defined thematic "place."

Then there is the fact that Reggie Workman always brings a very challenging and distinct kind of music to us, whether of his own composition (as has for the last few years been his main focus) or as the solid flowing "song" upon which someone else's composition depends. Whatever, if the Work Man is present, there is going to be something hip, trust him.

On this date, Reggie has brought one of the most skillful and impressive multi- (or, perhaps, omni-) reed players on the set, John Purcell. I had the good fortune, a few years ago, to work with Purcell in one of my own "Boperas," *Primitive World*, in which he was a member of the

David Murray ensemble, playing and acting as the notorious "Ham," a reed-playing actor-chief executive of an unnamed but not too mythological country. Playing flute, clarinet, alto, and face, as front man for the "Money Gods" who ran the place.

I found out then about John's smooth facility, which carries, at the same time, an earnest reaching into intriguing emotional statement. Here, Purcell brings more of the same dazzling virtuosity set in stepping tableaux by Workman's ever powerful "walk," circumfunking Purcell and everything else. From the rather rushing abstract opening, the music made by this duo dances very early into Monkish Ba-Lue. This is one test, for me, of the recent music, that it bring the whole traditional "soul" of the music, no matter how "out" it means to take us. Workman is always clear about this.

The pianist here strikingly out of "C. T." for inspiration, the rolling arch arpeggios that characterize Taylor's approach, which has had a signal influence on jazz piano since his explosive emergence in the '60s. The identifying character of Workman's playing is given paradigm on No. 1 as he digs into the beat so it is rhythm, harmony, and melodic motion coalescing through its sharp persistence, the aggressive lunging of Crispell and Purcell's high style into a single timbre.

Workman speaks first on No. 2, a simple bluesy riff, urging the group, especially on violin, to elaborate an insistent minor "call." Which response is a seeming "whirling" by the others around the modal space. Reggie's songlike frame forces a whole minor motion on the other instruments. His "regularity" marks the melodic incarnations, and the rhythm's relentless focus allows the most "distant" as well as the totally congruent solo voices to move upon or around or "nearby" his life pulse.

It can't be news to those with ears who this Work Man is. One of the most celebrated bassists in the music. This group is not really modest musically, there is a depth to it that makes it very listenable and satisfying. There is a "newness" but as well, a refreshing maintenance of the "what it is" that makes this music such an incredible reflection of "Where are we?" Workman is a very fastidious and thorough band leader to work with, and his attention to the notes and the whole fabric of his compositions and arrangements is always evident. Working with all kinds of bands and playing across a broad spectrum of musical styles within a great variety of serious approaches and intentions.

Marilyn Crispell and Gerry Hemingway are names I know, which I have always associated with a more formal kind of Avant. But here they are as free and expressive as the whole, inventive and given to the fresh statement, rather than running the well-worn changes. Jeanne Lee is cast as a dreamy narrator of one genre of "WordMusic," as I am wont to call it. As a poet, certainly I am glad to hear the word begin to jump heavily into contemporary music. And then there are the wordless calls of Lee and Workman. From each to each and from each on out. If you been on the scene a minute you know the wordless chant/melody call is Ms. Lee's "thing," but, again, with the Work Man, this figure of style is given a "living" reference that enhances and animates it.

But the really impressive voice on this album, for me, with Workman, is John Purcell's vaulting, mood-wrenching intensity. He calls and summons, wails, cries, rises out of drum or bass, to go somewhere else. It is the human "longing" in Purcell's sound that touches you. In concert, Workman and Purcell can send shivers of question through you.

Reggie, all these years, is so respected by his peers because of the unrelenting strength and "swing" of his line. His musical capacity to dart from the background to the front at a stroke. For instance, from the opening number, the Hemingway is sharp. The music puts you in touch with the old "Third Stream" but it is more forceful. The drummer is up under Purcell and in nexus with Workman, they both constructing the mobile launch motion-site for the raging narrative John Purcell presents.

Workman holds the music to a focus and gets inside it to expand its impact. It is a challenging and "difficult" music, but like all Reggie's efforts, ultimately directly on the motive force of this expression. Free, yet rhythmically imposing—in a linear motion as well as circular. Appearing and disappearing, but always very much present. His deep-voiced pizzicato solo opens the piano response. He pulls at the soul of the instrument with his body of feeling and intelligence.

Purcell and Workman seem to hammer, tear, penetrate with such abandon the other instruments are response or call but complements, wherever the timbre of their own instruments. Hemingway is a study of perception and synthesis, directed with his own and the overall "rationale" of the music. With the piano, they are a "section" of individual voices, collectivized, on the run. Crispell carries the C.T. daring, though the lines are placed in Workman's music according to her own sensitivity, so it is nevertheless "fresh." So too, is Jason Hwang, one of the emerging group of Asian musicians (e.g., Fred Ho, Jon Jang) among "the cats," bringing another set of "where I beens" into the mix, which only serves to emphasize yet one more layer of what is "American" to the whole. Cause that's what the whole of American culture is, Native (Asian), African, and European, like that tomato sauce, "it's all in there." We are shaped by the absorption and perception of our experience, and what rationale we make and what ultimate *use*, which is principal.

Reggie Workman is known to have free, funky, and innovative musical units to fly with. This one is no exception. Recorded at the famous Willisau Festival in Switzerland. Where, unlike the "slave marches" that pass as U.S. jazz festivals (which might have Dick Tracy, Howard Stern, and Kenny G as headliners), Europe still takes the music more seriously, in presentation, criticism, and annotation. This is why the adventurous "round the corner" groups and music, like Workman and Purcell's, remain in Europe or marginalized into footnotes of not.

But in order for the music to continue to be more securely self-conscious, there has got to be more self-production and presentation by the musicians, such as Reggie Workman is committed to, and where possible more cooperation between the players, the producers, the critics and scholars, the various media, and the audience, to create new venues, here and internationally, new publications, new production groups as well as some reincarnation in those communities which spawned it and wider access to everyone who wants to dig it. You dig?

12/8/97

CHAPTER 69

Roscoe Mitchell and the Note Factory

Nine to Get Ready, ECM Records, 1999, ECM 1651, CD 539–725–2. Roscoe Mitchell, soprano, alto, tenor sax, flute, lead vocal; Hugh Ragin, trumpet; George Lewis, trombone; Matthew Shipp, Craig Taborn, pianos; Jaribu Shahid, bass and vocal; William Parker, bass; Tanni Tabbal, drums, jimbe, vocal; Gerald Cleaver, drums.

Roscoe Mitchell is most widely recognized as part of the innovative Art Ensemble of Chicago, which regularly lit up the ears of the Diggers in the '70s and '80s. An aggressively "avant-garde" group, whose logo, "Great Black Music from the Present to the Future," truthfully indicated their mission mind-set and broad musical resources.

Lester Bowie, Joseph Jarman, Malachi Favors, Famadou Don Moye, brought a tense and carefully worked-out tour of ancient jook joint wanderings as well as a contemporary redux of Trane, Ayler, Shepp, and also the purposeful forwarding of all that, developing as a unique ensemble and performance style.

Where are they now? Well, let's say, like the World Saxophone Quartet, and the other most forward of the "Blowers of the Now," they took a hit when the Big Dogs diverted and retroed the middle section of the music lovers and pumped various commercial cons on our suffering ears, Fusion, the biggest con, plus the rerouting of Rap from exciting social commentary to the tinseltown thuggery of much of 'Hip Hop," used Motown for cold cream TV ads, and foisted the shallow elevator concertos of everything from Boy George, the fake singers, right up to Kenny G (the good cop of the duo Kenny and Rudy G).

Roscoe was known as an exciting and experimental player even before Art Ensemble, ditto Jarman, as projections of the widely respected, musically important and willfully modern Association for the Advancement of Creative Music out of Chicago. I used to get on some of these players for what I perceived as a "Tail Europe" approach, i.e., not just utilizing the musical thread of European concert music, as, say, Duke did, but at times subverting what was fresh on this side, in order, it seemed to me, to be "respectably" "Out." Is this what the term *avant-garde* has to imply? Alas!

This CD suffers from some of the same tendencies. The first four tracks ("Leola," "Dream and Response," "For Lester B," "Jamaica Farewell") together are a tone poem, quiet, understated, without firm dimension, as if searching for direction. The fifth track ("Hop Hip Bip Bir Rap") feels like it is part of that same piece, but as a kind of summation, in contrasting sonic and tempo absolutes, removing itself from the "Lost Inside the Cathedral of the Awed" presence the first part set up. There is an energy and rhythmic focus, the frantic ensemble of collectively improvising instruments, that identified the Art Ensemble. So that we can hear the forceful rhythm, unmasked timbre, and ensemble groove of the whole. So we can be confronted by the "newness" of the group, without it being muffled by, it seems, a veil of composition.

"Nine to Get Ready" is a discursive undertone of conversation, between the instruments, winding around and around, as statement, with a subtle but moving and complex undertow of rhythm. Still searchingly muted and understated, but alive with a circling current of intent.

"Bertha" begins to stretch out, with more solo voices, and a percussion pumped into the lyrically bluesy vamp of the line that is warm, even danceable, in a cool Blakeyian fashion, i.e., solid and swinging. Hugh Ragin's fresh, brassy horn always brings the heat of syncopated feeling with it.

The musicians on the album are a formidable, highly skilled group. Trumpet, Hugh Ragin, is the next voice on that horn. From the Diz, Brownie, Woodie school of Back and Gone. Likewise, the powerful double bass set of William Parker and Jaribu Shahid, the former a relatively recent but wholly authoritative and powerful voice, Shahid the well-traveled Detroit bassist, a longtime Avant, whose strength is in his close listening and expert placing of elegant bounding chords, seems to be coming into his own or at least being heard more regularly in the last few ticks.

Matthew Shipp, like most of these musicians, has built his rep from outside Kafka's Castle, and this is all their strengths . . . to survive, and play, still strong, even while being generally Dissed by the Owners of the Money Jungle. Shipp is a "heard Cecil," can I say, Young, pianist, energetic with the will to be heard as a distinctive stylist and not just another co-signer of "comping" clichés. Together with Craig Taborn, whom I have not yet heard on his own album, they create an intriguing pianistic depth that, together with the bass duo's unrelenting force, gives the works a sonic gravity, a magnetizing deepness, that foregrounds the soloists and gives overall shape to the compositions.

Lewis is one of the most highly skilled musicians out here. He has a penchant for electronics and computer tech-based music, but American Ice Box trends aside, Lewis is able always to add a precise sector of sound, a full bottoming motion to the whole. His solo voice is always technically awesome.

Cleaver and Tabbal work out fully when the group unleashes its power and acumen. The inclusion of the jimbe adds always a spicy taste of pre-boat funk to the dimensions of the sound. The use of African instruments among the newer musicians is a welcome trend. (Dig David Murray's "Fo Deuk.")

The most important work on the side to this listener is the last, tongue in cheek though it seem, "Big Red Peaches." With a stirring, gut-churning bottom, reminiscent of New Orleans post-burial second-line vehicles.

This small but powerful work, pixilated by Rap, Full Chorus Singing, in the tradition, but stretching forward into fresh newly coined definition, is an oracle of what surely must develop in "the Music." The "true self-consciousness" Du Bois spoke of, that will allow American, particularly Afro-American, Artists to fully assimilate all the resources they actually have, across the broad spectrum of lives and cultures, in the West and throughout the world. But first, to understand, that there is nothing more "Out" than where they begin. And while it is unarguably true we must learn from everything and everyone, the music labeled Jazz, Blues, etc., began "Outside" and the multi-myriad elements that make up its history and total are endless revelations, were we but to pursue them.

Like the so-called "Self-Taught" Black southern painters I have written about in *Souls Grown Deep*, the wildest thing about these indigenous creators is that they are outer than the outest of the museum types. Like a blind sculptor in Tennessee who stores his works under the house, one, a hub cap with seven black rubber bands hanging from holes he made in the circumference of the cap, with a TV aerial stuck up through the center.

He said he began to make these sculptures because he needed something to scare the birds away who were eating his tomatoes. Blind almost from birth, I want to know who the critics will say he's been influenced by.

3/99

CHAPTER 70

Jimmy Scott, *But Beautiful*

Milestone, 2002, MST MILCD9321.

To listen to Jimmy Scott is to enter a ghostly corridor of unlikely romance. Romance in the older use, the fantasy of life expanded to include the possibility of desire. Jimmy Scott and I go back a ways, to the steel gray memorized reality of Newark, New Jersey, ca. the 1950s, when "Little Jimmy" was already a mythical quality of our lives to be conjured with. Growing up in this postage stamp proto-"hood," called then the Third Ward. The brick city Nathan Heard pulled his brilliant *Howard Street* from. Where we young selves could move and know already names like Sassy, Moody, Wayne, Babs, Grachan, who circled those same bricks, already paradigms of hip to us.

We used to turn the corner and see Jimmy handling that, part of a narrative for a life more glamorous than our own. But there, here, with us, leaning against a wall. We would later dig him at the Len & Lens, the Masonic Temple, the Key Club, as we got older. And that knife of deep feeling with which he shaped his songs was already part of our later hipness.

For years I used to talk about "Little Jimmy Scott" when I got to "the city" and only a very few had dug the extraordinary poetry of his creative presence or even heard of him.

So it was a grateful me that checked when his "new" emergence began a few years back. And some wonder that now there were miles of everybody who apparently had dug him, when?

Jimmy Scott is a troubadour in one sense, a *Djali* (Griot) of the sullen unsatisfied heart. His art is the emotional imagery of his telling and the story is shaped by whatever deep emotion the lyrics have told his feelings. So each word is some kind of sensuous perception to rationale, used to wrap us in his understanding of what these feelings mean.

Jimmy Scott's voice is near to dreamlike, haunting is something like it, but it is a haunting of something still alive and unnerved by its own passion. The classics, standards, anthems of feeling Jimmy does on this side are all reworked in the veins of his and our need. Did Billie Holiday dig Jimmy? Is night got stars in it?

Check "You Don't Know." Or if you are old as BeBop, "Darn That Dream" puts you with Miles's *Birth of the Cool,* plus another kind of heaviness. "It Had To Be You," "But Beautiful," "I'll Be Seeing You" repossessed and dragged against our knowing. "Blackbird" is miles away from Miles but at a deeper valence of longing. We wonder have we ever heard these songs before. Perhaps, but not like this!

Digging "Little Jimmy" is a unique learning, an acceptance of the wisdom of experiencing a stark reality. Warm with recognition, stark with truth. The real "awesome"!

5/2/02

CHAPTER 71

Malachi Thompson, *Talking Horns*

Delmark, 2001, DE 532 11.
With Hamiet Bluiett, baritone sax; Oliver Lake, alto; Willie Pickens, piano; Harrison Bankhead, bass; Reggie Nicholson, drums.

The new must be constantly renewed. So these fine musicians from one of the most recent traditions of the music, media-named "Jazz," are staying on the case of this great music's renewal. Malachi Thompson, Oliver Lake, Hamiet Bluiett, of the Chicago–St. Louis Connection, early cadre of St. Louis's Black Arts Group (BAG) and Chicago's venerable Association for the Advancement of Creative Music (AACM), have continued to "receive," create, and project perform the new, but continue to develop, sharpen, and rearm themselves with still more sophisticated yet more accessible excursions into the "Say what?" the "Did you dig that?" and the "That's some bad stuff right there!"

Because these three, in vital rapport, with Pickens's piano, Bankhead's solid bass, and Nicholson's drums—the piano and bass two of Thompson's musical comrades from Chicago and Reggie Nicholson a rising creative source whose name is being passed around—present us here a mixture of the known re-wrapped in fresh harmelodic vines, the recently "outrageous" now made familiar by these and other innovative musicians' relentless representation to the deepest diggers, but also there are some works still in the deliciously still-cooking stage.

Together, a package that should ingratiate a wider range of the serious, spread the good news across a broader front, and have the right-on Diggers hopping with joy.

The three main soloists, Thompson, Lake, and Bluiett, open and delight us with each track. The tunes, from all three, are by turn archly Neo-Boppist, On-Out-ish, Blue, Down and Funky. Lake's African-eared "Scope" is ancient and sweetly innovative at once. Minimalist yet seemingly filled with horns, percussion, voices. (And what is them dudes chanting under the groove?)

Hamiet Bluiett's surprisingly tender "Way Back . . ." posits lyrical ballad top over an insistent ostinato groove, with high, piercing stunting horn lines, singularly and in unison.

Malachi Thompson's "Circles in the Air" whirls in and out-of-the-recent avant, provides a percussive and shifting sonic carpet for Thompson and the rest to penetrate with ideophonic images. Shifting again into the frantic scatobopical vocal which send it whirling like a thoughtful "event" in space, Mr. Nicholson providing the turbulence and bumps of the passing comets. Something old, Something new, Something blue. Thoughtful and innovative.

2/27/02

CHAPTER 72

The Nexus Orchestra, *Seize the Time*

2 CDs, Splasch, 2001, CDH 841/842.2.

A big band is the most impressive of all music-making ensembles. And I admit I came to that relatively late, i.e., when I really dug Duke Ellington. The Symphonic arsenal, even the big swing bands, I could get too, and even appreciate. As who cannot dig Herr B's 3–7-9.

But the interior revelation that woke me when I actually heard "Koko," "Black Beauty," "Diminuendo," "Blood Count," etc., was, as Grachan M 3 used to say, Some Other Stuff.

Still, this raising reorganized my sensibility to dig a big, since from then I could peep more surgically into the offering, from wherever, and, I think, appreciate where it was coming from, why, and if and when it did all it desired, at least how I heard it.

The Nexus is a vast-sounding munition, which is its vaunt, the sound and the variousness of its forms. The thunderous drum-led force as melody and rhythm, the avant machinery it can turn into. Even a near-Debussyian whispering. All these, in and out, of whatever track the chart spins it.

Roswell Rudd seems a grand influence on this music, and by now should be on the nightly news, if that were about truth or beauty. He has been in the sound trenches of the "Next!" for so long and with such an internationally celebrated "sheet" of good doing. A powerful and dynamic musician, an instantly recognizable voice, yet with an accompanying drollery that always carries a chuckle in his aesthetic stash.

"Roz" is a composer artifacting a music that is very personal in its faithful reflection of his singular musicianship. So the compositions, which constantly transform the orchestra, speak with his unique sensibility and approach. With the same thoughtful, playful, deeply serious, innovating presence. And it is Rudd's "Numatik" that most intrigues and delights with its multi-formed dynamic. As well as the "Improvisations" that follow.

What is most hopeful about the orchestra is its fresh-sounding power. The feel that it can do anything it wants. The Orchestral improvisations—an opening with the language of percussion, like somewhere else calling. The blues-tinged moods of smeared horn (a Rudd i.d.) and cymbal, the use of the whole arsenal of the big, as intense pedestrians on a mysterious journey. The changes of mood and direction clearly in search of emotional impact (no. 3) for emotional revelation, the rudiment of all Art. And then to leap into a rushing alto-led collective improvisation, quizzical and meant to be transformational.

The most consistent criticism of the Avant is its self-absorption and thematic obscurity, as if every work had only a middle and neither beginning or end. Nexus is still solving this, mainly now through the dynamic of its diverse forms, the various "looks" of sports teams as a multiplicity of "hears"! And this is the key to its freshness and excitement, that it does not stay in one musical "place" or mode, but expresses a kind of "rascality" of musical intent. Here one minute, there, another, in and out, *P* then *F*, swarming with sound, then lyrical. Western symphonic for that expression, Caribbean, African (a thematic signing), American Swing, Boppish, wanting to be itself as a creative register and expression of the *every*.

There is always much talk, the most ignorant attempting to narrow the boundaries and create divisions in *the Music*, this 20th-century zephyr of Marx's dictum that it is "the Slaves Who Make History"! Nexus is further confirmation of the international valence, historic creative properties, and revolutionary potential of this music, in essence, the Afro-American Soul of American Classical Music. Clearly, the most positive and progressive import from the joint.

The Nexus makes me wonder when that soul-bound aesthetic network of human feeling can be created as an international social-political alliance of Humanity, a living pact of transforming consciousness, that will shape the world in the same truth and beauty as the music. The dialectic is, What is the politics of our Art, likewise what is the Art of our politics?

CHAPTER 73

Three Fresh Ticklers

The periodic disingenuous lamentations about the "demise" of the Music are regularly proven to be the ravings of dead people. Usually, like the old folks said, they "ghoses," without feet, so they got to wait till a good wind blow em 'way.

The emergence of D. D. Jackson, Rodney Kendrick, and Vijay Iyer is the good wind, so we trust the feetless mouthpieces for commercial despair will shortly repair to the boneyard, where they can be judged by Louis, Duke, Sun Ra, & them.

But, jubilation is in order, intrepid lovers of the Music! These three young men, all pianists, hence the renovation of the old-time name for the hippest of the box-cookers is in order, "Ticklers," they called em back in Willie "the Lion" and James P.'s day. When Newark's *Coast*, the Apple's *Hell's Kitchen*, Chicago's *Levee* and S.F.'s *Barbary Coast* were the places the most advanced of the players would work out of.

There was a distinctive aura to the name *Tickler*, that such artists could tickle the keys until they laughed or cried or shouted or wailed, whatever the mode. What it meant is that there was heavy Music goin' on. Advanced technique and high-level Funkistry.

Jackson, Kendrick, and Iyer are such players. New pianists bringing their own arch-lyricism, awesome technique, and most importantly, their own touch and content, coming from elder and recent tradition, learning from a myriad diverse inposts of outery. Playing themselves in such a distinctive and ear-opening way that any serious listener has to stop, check, and dig.

Jackson's *So Far* (RCA) is a deliberately lyrical offering in its deepness, but at all times wailing, running, thundering, singing, reaching into the listener with the heavy yet tender paths of feeling.

Kendrick's two albums I've heard, *Last Chance for Common Sense* and *We Don't Die We Multiply*, are revelation. We hear a player steeped in both, it seems, a Caribbean mode of blue antic very tuneful irony, at the same time one of Monk's "interns," already turning out something lovely and hip.

Dig both these CDs and give yourself a musical rush that must renovate your enthusiasm for the music's future, especially if you've been over-drugged by the spate of recent sophistry from the well-paid sophists of big-time newspapers and journals hawking up that sad combination of aesthetic boobery and chauvinism.

Iyer, born in the U.S. of Indian parents, part of the broad multinational, multicultural spectrum that is the authentic U.S. culture, is subtle, signifying, technically capable of going anywhere in any direction of expression, is another joyful grace entering and expressing the continuous newness within the deep essence of the music.

That all three are pianists is significant to me because, at bottom, the "Ticklers" (after de *Oom Boom Ba Boom* of the drum) set the harmonic and melodic shape of what it is that's coming into being. Both Iyer and Kendrick consistently bring an "Eastern" aura and feeling. India, frequently, as specific reference, from there and from Kendrick's Trinidadian origins. Fresh tempos and cadences, Fives, Sevens, rhythms we have probably heard before, now integrated seamlessly as blues or whatever lyrical musing, or the happy "getdowns" of the straight-ahead wailosonic zoom.

Jackson is an incredibly lyrical, grand *auteur*. He exhibits his awesome technique not as dreary display but as a means to get inside us with his story. Kendrick is the funkiest, his *Hot* as casual as Monk's tongue-in-cheek array of boppish Outness. The music is right here wiggling, yet the laughter you feel, like his paradigm, is that he is all the time stretching your ears.

Jackson and Kendrick are also very *tuneful*, melodic, and clearly narrative. Iyer is more abstruse and subtle, but the overform of his *trips* are tight and musically direct enough so we are touched by his lovely, diverse, & memorable *mise en scenes* of feeling. The newest CD, *Architextures,* with a Trio and Octet, is an intriguing introduction to Iyer, and of course *Memorophilia* (AIR 0023), which is a first hearing.

Kendrick's two albums I've heard: *Last Chance for Common Sense* (Gitanes) features Kiane Zawadi, euphonium, trombones; Tim "Bone" Williams, trombone; Rodney Kendrick, piano; Tarus Mateen, bass; Taru Alexander, drums; Chi Sharpe, percussion; Daniel Moreno, percussion; Badal Roy, tablas, vocals; Ali Jackson, additional percussion. The title track is all the way out of sight, but then pick up on the multi-rhythmic bass, piano, ensemble . . . the vamp a deep hook of "frantic lyricism" of "Rodney's Rhythms," a funk from the East, but so is the album an impressive trip on the transfunkamental downway. But what about the straight-out Monkish "the Nac," which adds Graham Haynes, cornet; Justin Robinson, alto; Eric Wyatt, tenor. Like just when you thought it was safe to bring in Kenny G, etc., Kendrick (likewise Iyer and Jackson) whip out the really new like the dude wasting vampires with the cross. The whole album a "must cop." Ditto *Multiply*.

Jackson's *So Far* is a solo presentation. But with his focused virtuosity, a consistently intriguing and exciting debut. Another "must cop"!

CHAPTER 74

Rodney Kendrick, *Last Chance for Common Sense*

Polygram, 1996.
Ali Muhammed Jackson, percussion; Badal Roy, tabla, vocals: Chi Sharp, percussion; Daniel Moreno, percussion; Dewey Redman, sax (tenor), musette; Eric Wyatt, sax (tenor).

Rodney Kendrick is something else. He is coming from Monk, but also Trinidad and James Brown. Plus, he was Abbey's pianist for a minute. So Kendrick carries a variety of hips, funks, and finesse. He is a Monkish player, with that antic rhythmic and harmonic spontaneity, and with a very lovely melodic sense that gives his music a "hook," like they say, which brings you very quickly further into the music and all its further emerging deepness.

It is a songful, quirky, charmingly rhythmic music Kendrick makes. I am always taken by a player's rhythmic sense. The Music, "Jazz," etc., is, for me, a fundamentally rhythmic revelation, even in harmony and melody. Louis, Monk, Duke, Trane, Billie, Bird, Abbey, Miles, come out of the very bottom of the music, from its heartbeat. And Rodney Kendrick is hip to that.

Max Roach says, the music changes when the rhythm changes. Too many players, imitating the whatevers of not, wander around making melodic and harmonic feints, but without "that Swing," as the Duke of the Omniverse has remonstrated. And without that fundamental funk, the rest is silence.

Not only the standard fours, Kendrick deals with rhythmic diversity. As in the title piece, "Last Chance," the quirky meter gives the melody a singable buoyance, nevertheless, funky. The Trinidad tip is very much in evidence. In quite a few of his works, Kendrick uses the tabla and steel drum. There is a heavy East Indian influence in Trinidad, and in the Caribbean generally. Kendrick uses both Indian-derived timbre and rhythm and the throbbing fleshy underpinning of the classical Indian tabla, first introduced widely in the U.S. by tabla drummers. This part of his ensemble, not a marginal exoticism. Rodney Kendrick is also a composer arranger who can make his musical presence even more impacting as his music is played by other players. This album is much like a long, suitelike work, the ensemble restating the rhythmic restatement of Kendrick's unique Afro-Asian syncopation, as *motion* heard. As intro to "Sun Ray" or "Nac" or the other sweet memorable pieces.

Kendrick is a ferocious first listen. Like they say, Infectious and thoughtful, with the depth that goes with that. Find this album and start following Rodney Kendrick. Heavy stuff!

11/98

CHAPTER 75

Jazz Times Review, Multiple Artists

Polygram, 1996.
Dennis Charles, *Captain of the Deep*, Eremite, 1991, MTE09.
Julius Hemphill, *Blue Boyé*, 2 CDs, Screwgun, 2003 (original release date 1977), SCREWU 70008.
Von Freeman and Ed Peterson, *Von and Ed*, Delmark, 1999, DE-508.
Sabir Mateen, *Divine Mad Love*, Eremite, 1997, MTE011.
One World Ensemble, *Breathing Together*, Freedom, 1998, FF5.CD001.
Roscoe Mitchell, *In Walked Buckner*, Delmark, 1999, DE-510.
Cecil Payne, *Payne's Window*, Delmark, 1999, DE-509.

Mitchell's music is an eloquent paradigm for Du Bois's "Double Consciousness," the Afro-American "twoness," the contradiction, between being Americans or Black, though they are both.

This record swings between warmly acrid, BeBopish grooves, and a pastiche of Berg, Webern. "Off Shore" is a few kilometers out. "In Walked Buckner" straight ahead, tuneful . . . Roscoe's baritone, lovely . . . the music too. "Squeaky," back off-shore, contemplating . . .

These CDs express the contradictory currents in contemporary music, either near us or "offshore." The experimentation and "Outness" of the sixties has become, in many cases, *academic*. An "anti-academy" academy, academy nonetheless. What began as deeply emotional, psychological, intellectual search, rejecting the "given" (the commercial, the clichéd), became a broad international trend, its material base actual rebellion, revolution, resistance, struggle in the real world. Proliferated Acts and Ideas producing a genuine "avant-garde." The "New Music," "the new thing," "Out" versus mainstream "In."

"Free Jazz," "Freedom Now," "Freedom Suite" reflected attempts to break out the Tin Pan Alley Penitentiary where creativity is imprisoned by money. Trane, Archie, Ayler, Cecil, Ornette, Sun Ra, Pharaoh, Milford Graves, Pullen were some of the best-known escapees, their music authentic departure and resistance.

The academic tip here is ubiquitous except for "old heads," Von Freeman, Cecil Payne, the post-bop mainstream, backbone of the music. Polished instrumentalists wearing musical hearts out front and funkily blue. Freeman does elegant things to Trane's "P.C.," Miles's "Four," Diz's "Tunisia," from the Hipster's Canon. Peterson is contrasting, but less than organic. Payne's sweet relaxing persona, from that same "holy book," e.g., "Delilah," "Tune Up," "Lover Man."

All these musicians can play, though the "Outs" flaunt mastery of technique much more aggressively than they tell their stories. Pres said, the music, if transforming and revelatory, tells "a story." "Beyond Notes," said Ayler. What does the music tell us, where does it take us, what ideas, emotions does it impart. Music communicates its feelings, ideas, direction, what it loves, what it hates, what it thinks beautiful, what ugly.

The screaming, wailing, keening, attack mode of the '60s outbreak was warlike, assaulting, hostile, tone and expression, the innovators also played penetrating beauty, thoughtful introspection. Both aspects a reflection of the period's most cogent ideas or at least the most co-signed by that trend's fellow travelers.

Today, many musicians play "Outness" ONLY as *a Style*, any revolutionary departure, at best, metaphor, without a genuinely incendiary or transformative image of the world. Some claim innovation and experiment, yet the music is neither, and often so predictable and stylized it resembles mood music, but for another crowd.

Where Trane, Ra, Pharaoh went to the East, India, Africa for their inspiration, many self-proclaimed "Keepers of the Flame" go to Europe for theirs . . . the height of irony, since often it was Europe as an actual or symbolic figure of stultification and cultural aggression that many of the advanced players were in rebellion against.

Blue Boyé Hemphill produced on Mbari. Ditto *Dogon A.D.*, which struck a definite note of freshness, thoughtfulness, most impressive for the subtlety of its variations and inventive compositional logic. Hemphill sparkled with the World Saxophone Quartet (David Murray, Oliver Lake, and Hamiet Bluiett) a post-'60s watershed. Hemphill's playing, self-consciously cerebral, sometimes to a fault, the tart, incisive tone, the richness and whimsicality of his improvisation, give a cutting edge of excitement to his work. In retrospect, it is easy to see how influential, for the good and the opposite, Hemphill's work remains, certainly as a model for many of the "off shore" avants.

I've been hip to Dennis Charles, since "Introducing" him in the *Jazz Review* in 1961 as Cecil Taylor's drummer. His recent departure is tragic, just as he was getting his life together, and his music, his delightfully spare, "old-timey" traditional approach (put you in the mind of Eddie Blackwell), he is taken.

Captain of the Deep suffers from an over-discursiveness and seeming randomness of non-thematic blowing. Jemeel Moondoc, an exciting player, is not given enough direction by leader, Charles, who remains the beating heart of the set. Yet behind Ayler-blunt melodies, straight-ahead timbre, the unique daring simplicity of Charles's rhythmic motive force, *Deep* has lovely moments. Dennis's solos, hip, self-contained, quirky links and carriers of the whole. (Check "We Don't" and "Rob.")

One World Ensemble was recorded "down the street." Inspirational, if you know this "Brick City." Wilber Morris's sensitive musicality pins our ears and the other players' with his intelligent "Listening." The overarching focus of the musicians gathered was to play a wholly improvised, spontaneously created series of works, demonstrating the fertility and expressiveness of free and collective creativity.

We are enthralled and fascinated by the process as invention from accretion and accumulation, yet too often we hear a great deal of "aiming," which fixes the music, with the ironic dialectic of its method, as somewhat "aimless." Improvisation is the heart of the Music, expressing variations on some thematic focus, which then links them as a "symmetrical" or logical (aesthetic, not geometric) whole. Without this contrast and resulting "tension," the "wholly" spontaneous coheres as overly formal, or unconnected and meandering.

The biggest drag about sides like these attempts at "Outness," the insistence on playing only their own compositions; the most profound elements of the music, including the great works of its giants, are left "in the box."

Verbal homage to "the Masters" doesn't guarantee actual Use of their works and thought, which express the grand aesthetic Continuum of the music. Ask many of the folks styling themselves "Out," do they know Duke's Suites, or Monk's amazing array, or for that matter Trane's engines, Tadd Dameron's gorgeous confections, Dizzy's wonderful compositions, or Sun Ra's cosmic messages, and they grimace in embarrassment. The world is very old, it is only we who are "new."

3/99

CHAPTER 76

More Young Bloods
to the Rescue!

Abraham Burton Eric McPherson Quartet, *Cause and Effect,* Enja,
1998, ENJ-93772.
Abraham Burton, tenor; Eric McPherson, drums; James Hurt, piano;
Yosuke Inoue, bass.

Rescue? Who? From What? Well, first from the old deadhead saw that
the Music "is daid"! Next, and more formidable, perhaps, is the swash
of nonplaying commercial catatonics and call-persons the corporations
have set loose upon us to make money by lying that they are dealing
with American Classical music, which they smuggle in under the, now,
almost meaningless rubric of "JAZZ!" What's worse, these corporate
corsairs put out the term *contemporary jazz* for their various ugly
forays into fusion and worse, so that the unsuspecting "marks" can be
made to think that what the masters created was some old stuff, but,
Hey! Eureka, Dig, Kenny G.

But as I note recently about three young pianists, Vijay Iyer, Rodney
Kendrick, D. D. Jackson, Thank Blues! It seems a whole young army of
folks have come swiftly to the rescue. A-Funk! But the truth is, with the
appearance of musicians like this Abraham Burton–Eric McPherson
Quartet, along with those other folks I mentioned and an expanding number of others, e.g., Ravi Coltrane, Malachi Thompson, Hugh
Ragin, the hip zone gets larger and larger. A-Funk!

This Burton-McPherson side is another "must cop" number. From
the very first sounds on the CD, the music is nearby exquisite. And if
that sounds too "tinkly," that's because we associate it with the tin-
klers. What I mean is that not only is the playing all the way live, even
commanding, but the overall conceptualization or way into the music is
often stunning. The musicians themselves are right on it, as well, from

jump. The "conception" their own voice undistracted, thank Blue, by the myriad onerous distractions of commerce or the hypnotic gestures of the dead, like so many who want to sound "Heavy" at the expense of their own deepest experience.

For instance, *all* the tunes on the CD are worth listening to again and again. From the opener, pianist James Hurt's brooding indigo "Nebulai," which grows on you with each hearing. Somber, its lyrically crystalline line broad enough to carry some living breath of rhythm and continuously mounting excitement, augmented by the pianist himself, with his distinctive "trills" under the line and sweeping solo.

Burton's "Dad," so sweet and narratively tuneful. One of the things I most admire about this group is the *tunefulness*. Re-emergence of the melodic line! In recent times, the '60s legacy of all-out frenzy and *sturm und drang* made many of the players and composers feel melody was somehow reactionary. But Thank Blues! Burton-McPherson leave no doubt that melody is back!

Drummer Eric McPherson, who naturally carries the whole proceeding on his "western industrial machine," is also harmonically and melodically always in evidence. Plus, his "Cause and Effect," the title piece, is a marvelous thing. This group favors slowly mounting statements, gaining weight, funk, and gravity as the various pieces move forward cohering in some diversely hip ways. "Cause" begins like some call, call, call, of mounting mystery but then, over McPherson's rumbling wings, breaks into the broadest kind of swinging. And when Burton comes in Hurt leading he got the response, lightning fast, with his warm distinctive sensuous tenor sound.

We must also mention bassist Yosuke Inoue, who is tasteful yet aggressively musical in his "laying." Hear him create a echo chamber of mystery on "Cause . . ." with Hurt's thematic insistence. Inoue's tight melodic lowway and pianist James Hurt's skillful "concomitance" with the whole, as soloist or comping, the group comes off very tight very focused as a unified expression.

Likewise, the beautiful "Lullaby Punta" of Burton's barely whispers when arriving yet it logically with great aesthetic balance transforms itself into a variation of the "Canto Jondo" of the Flamenco. "Cause and Effect," "Nebulai," "Lullaby . . ." are obvious winners. But, like I said, each piece carries a rapture of its own. Burton's "Forbidden Fruit," again, that building sensuous insinuating line, quick to zig or zag into another mood and theme. Its openness and lyric melodic grace, never sacrificing the basic ritmos of the groove, Thank Blues!

All this is to say it is very refreshing to hear this new wave of *Down-sters* getting down, *swinging* so authoritatively and boldly. When I read that both Burton and McPherson come out of the Rap generation, that their first groove was the Hip and the Hop, it was no surprise, as I've said a buncha times, when the most conscious of the players get to the gate of limitations of any form they'll look for what is the most unlimited and advanced.

Hip pianist Rodney Kendrick was with James Brown for a minute. These young players come out of the living heart of the music, the *rhythm*, from all else flows. I would imagine there will be more rap survivors coming into the music, I know I used to be down with the Orioles, Ravens, Big Jay McNeeley, etc., when I was coming up . . . the straight out, stomp down, like they say, hope to die, BaLues! In all its funky majesty. In fact we called it *Rhythm & Blues*, Well! And no matter where the music coming from or where it went, what was it Duke said, "It Don't Mean a thing . . . et cetera, et cetera. . . ." Right On, Burton-McPherson!

12/99

CHAPTER 77

Vijay Iyer, *Memorophilia*

Asian Improv Records, 2005, AIR 00233.
Vijay Iyer, piano; Steve Coleman, alto; George Lewis, trombone;
Francis Wong, tenor; Kash Killion, cello; Jeff Bilmes, electric bass;
Jeff Brock, acoustic bass; Liberty Ellman, guitar; Brad Hargreaves,
drums; Eliot Humberto Kayee, drums.

Iyer is an oncoming phenomenon, already up to his fingers in the most
advanced music of this wildly contradictory age, where we have got to
since a whole couple of generations of giants have swooped. Imagine,
just a few years ago, you could stand and discuss Who of the masters you wanted to dig on any particular evening. Duke, Count, Sassy,
Monk, Miles, Brownie . . . a few blocks apart on our best nights. Now
we're in another place time where a gross commercialism has seized the
center stage of U.S. culture. But, Lo! another promising crop is rising,
so don't get terminally depressed, and much of it is hip, despite the
Caesars telling us Kenny G is where it's at!

Iyer is one of that crop, still young and in motion. Born in the U.S.
of Indian parents, early violin lessons ran him into the Music, and he
entered its availing depths with his mind and feelings.

You dig this side you can feel his motion, his rising spectrum of
sensuous Communication, still unveiling, but already formidable. The
music called JAZZ, no matter that word is just, as Max says, a generic
brand name wherein the mind bandits can insert any mediocre would-
be imitator of what, finally, cannot be imitated, and say, "SEE, Here
'Tis . . . JAZZ!" Matter of fact, there is an "On Air Personality" on
our local station who says that word, "JAZZ," in a way turn you off
forever. You can hear, in his saying, a frivolous unserious funny-hat
conglomeration you would back off from.

But poison commercial culture aside, what is so encouraging about young folks like Iyer is that not only has he got the overall what-it-is together, but he has brought some of his own stuff to add to the huge treasure chest of the Music. Proving again, as my wife, Amina, is always saying, "How can they say Fusion, the music is already fused with everything on the planet!"

What Iyer brings, together with an immediately recognizable advanced bag of pianistic skills, announcing from his first chord, that he knows what's happening, is a rhythmic concept apparent throughout the album that makes use of classic Indian Tabla rhythms and traditional Indian cadences. So that as part of the drive and funk of his music's movement is the 5, 7, 9 of a Shankar, against the overall 4 of the piece. Even in a ballad like "Stars over Mars" or "Spellbound" the 5 or 7 creates a flowing spice that gives the music an uncommonness that removes it immediately from sodden narrowness of contemporary funk clichés.

Iyer's innovative use of these classic rhythms puts you in mind of some of the things pianist Rodney Kendricks does (Dig *Last Chance for Common Sense* or *We Don't Die We Multiply*), reflecting his Trinidadian background. Trinidad has a large Indian population, so there is a somewhat similar creative use of some of the same cadences.

Another indication of somebody on the road to the real is Iyer's choice of musicians. Consistently advanced performers like alto saxophonist Steve Coleman (of M-Base) and trombonist George Lewis, who has to be one of the articulate voices now working on that instrument, both add a depth of thoughtfulness and heat to the proceedings. The opening piece, "Relativist's Waltz," features Coleman's incisive lyricism not only shaping the work with his presence but giving it the sound of some hip group we have heard before, but the newness of the work gives recognition that, NO, it is just a well-organized ensemble playing some very hip music.

Iyer is already able to shift cadences, tempos, touch, with an expressive cache of influences, Monk, the post-McCoy saunter, but his use of block chords, at times, huge blocks of sound in the run of the whole, again gives his playing, already, an entrance that is impressive, and should lead to an even more expressive music. But make no mistake, Iyer is already in the mix, thoroughly and for the listener, very rewardingly. It's just that, like everybody who's got something ultimately heavy to say, when you first hear them, you hear what they're doing, but also intimations of what they intend. All the compositions are Iyer's, way past interesting, there is an emotional and intellectual depth to them that declares their composer definitely "into something" ("March" and "Epilogue," etc.).

Iyer brings a sensuous (i.e., reaching the senses) sensitivity to the instrument and a clearly stated intellectual aesthetic that seeks to organically link the infinite microtonics of Eastern music, not as a musical passport but with a precise congruence that flows into really lush harmonic constructions. A very stimulating and thoughtful presentation.

7/99

CHAPTER 78

TriFactor, *If You Believe*

8th Harmonic Breakdown, 2002, 8THHB 80004.
Kahil El'Zabar, vocals, hand drums; Billy Bang, violin; Hamiet
Bluiett, baritone sax.

An impressive breakthrough, in many ways, because it projects a
much-needed "new wave" (one hopes) in the Music. A refreshing trend
that can be said to include David Murray's *Fo Deuk* and *Speaking in
Tongues*, Olu Dara's *In the World,* and several other recent releases.

It is, stated perhaps reductively, a return to the fundamental and
traditional aesthetic psycho-cultural and social elements that have ac-
creted historically to identify the classic presence of the genre as it has
existed in its broadest expression. A wily thrust toward reassertion of
that oldest form and content.

The projection of what seems the most ancient Afro-American
ground burning blues and the always concomitant underpinning of
rhythm. Since, for the African, and early American slaves, the drum
could literally *speak*, so Kahil, Bluiett, and Bang give a consistent
vocalization to their playing, and Kahil sings, moans, chants, using
voice and drum to dimension the ensemble as a harmonically and
rhythmically constructed voice.

Simple indeed, but for the last few years, we have seen a rise to faux
hegemony of a largely corporate-directed mediocrity of the grossest
commercial dross, cynically and ingeniously touted as "art," or whatever. One of these disrevelational directions has been what I've called
the "Tail Europe" malignance where bourgeois European insipidity is
"shot up" into what's called *new music to* produce an ossified anti-
funk which is supposed to prove its intellectual grandeur.

Another, as insidious, is the ersatz grooves of "fusion" mixing a mechanical "bump" of pretend R&B as bottom, with a diaphanous meta-melodic "hook." And voila! we get "cheap furniture," the grossest, e.g., being Kenny, who wants the world *to be an elevator.*

Then there are the constipated (alas) would-be heirs of the '60s "new music" who slander Albert, Trane, Ornette, Pharaoh, etc., by abandoning both beginning and end of their solos for a high-energy seemingly endless "middle" of symmetrically boring *Yawping,* much like the staged "orgasm" of a dissembling sexual partner. All in the name of "avant-garde"!

So we are near awed to hear from players like these, Olu Dara, David Murray, we shd add Rodney Kendricks various cd's, the young Abraham Burton–Eric McPherson beauty, *Cause & Effect,* intriguing melodic and dynamic rhythmic grounding in the most basic aspects of the music made fresh by the innovative harmonic and timbral and tonal instrumental creativity.

"If You Believe," for instance, is as old as "cullut peepas'" *hereness,* an old-time sanctified church chant. Its repetition of lyrics and harmelodic line in a diverse timbral prosody is deeply moving. The entrance, departures and continuous "ancestral" groove of Kahil's conceptually fresh percussion, Bang's wonderful violin, arco, pizzicato counter-melodies, tense, dreamy, sudden, harmonizing and Bluiett, as always, with the ear-waking baritone, sounding anyway he wants it to sound, are singularly, in unison, harmonically placed, intriguing, entrancing throughout.

The entire album is similar in approach, but never unemotionally repetitious. Plus, it all swings, swings, gets all the way *down.* Kahlil's hand-drumming is the motor and the dimensioning character that gives overall aesthetic coherence to the whole. Where we get a simple blue chant, the free imagination of the players blows it till the impacting presence of the music is raised emotionally, aesthetically, philosophically so we are confronted by something quite "new." Though, ironically, but to the point, the collaboration, especially where the baritone takes on the role of the pre-bass tuba of the *very old,* reminds one of the classic Angola Prison *Origins of Jazz* album, spare, muscular and past hip.

On "Sequence of Our Hearts," again, the percussion, the set this time, posits the motion and dimensioning depth, Kahil humming a relentless drone . . . then Billy Bang entering a romantic lyricism, Bluiett edging the line broader, sharper, together creating a graceful procession of awesome beauty. Check it!

All the pieces work off a similar, but ever re-structured re-sounded combining, at times quiet and lovely, yet as quickly biting, penetrating raw and questioning! The contrasting timbre of the instruments, the voice, the direct Blue rhythmic "hooks," from church to cabaret, are an elixir of skillfully organized sound, we calls it great music. This trio needs to be reassembled as many times as they wants.

"Dark Silhouette," with its hypnotic minor lament, the harmonic space of instrumental placement sweet yet acrid at the same time. "Ahhh, Ahh," we say, "Ahhh." Bang searching above the wheels of steadily patient percussion, modulated by Bluiett's "tuba" or his uniquely discursive sweeping interventions. All these, appearing and re-emerging in a spectrum of varied tonal, harmonic, rhythmic colors, together create a much-needed antidote to the doldrums of commercial prankery. More power to this kind of groove, we say. Much more power and much more ubiquity!

10/26/01

CHAPTER 79

Live Lessons

Amiri Baraka has been getting in the groove again during the past year, though as he says to those who wonder why he's "back on the music," "I never did go nowhere. Somewhere just runned away from the boy . . . "

That is to say, when JazzTimes fired the Crouch named Stanley, (and if we know, as well, that there is no major publication in the Colonies with a Black writer on what's called Jazz), then what's Baron is not Kenny nor Charles but born of a willful chauvinism. (Is that too complicated? I guess so!)

Here are reports on sounds of the cities by Mr. B.*

CHARLES TOLLIVER BIG BAND

One thing we can treasure and if we cannot it means the "Yet" of this ain't borned where we can dig it.

We thought by leaving the house (Newark) at 6:00 we'd be at the Jazz Standard (East 27th Street, NYC) in plenty of time to see the Tolliver set. But we found we were actually "late," people were crowded in the place already, so we had to sit in a sideways corner, though close, digging the musicians from the side and rear.

No matter, Jimmy, this is some of the best music we've heard in a long minute! Tolliver and I go back to *The New Wave in Jazz*, an LP

---

*This review originally appeared on www.firstofthemonth.org.

I produced as a benefit for the Black Arts Repertory Theater School, which myself and some other self-determining minded Black artists opened in Harlem, on West 130th Street a month after Malcolm X was murdered.

Tolliver was then a hottening but streaky "Hard Bop/erator" from Brooklyn, one of the knowledgeable graduate students of Professor Blakey's Funkiversity. Tolliver came through Max Roach, Sonny Rollins, with groups that featured John Hicks, Stanley Cowell. And did a year or so with Gerald Wilson's California Big Band.

I'd just about forgotten, in the torrent of the Unhip and the submissive that clouds the scene these days at the bottom of the Sisyphus Syndrome where the rock has been rolled so far back down the mountain of human progress it has almost disappeared into the Bushes ... that Charles Tolliver and Cowell, in those heavy days ('71) when the idea of Black Self- Determination was a mass expression, founded their own record company, Strata-East!

Part of what was so refreshing this night was that you could hear in the music, the compositions and solos, of this Tolliver-led band the fire of the Blakey/Jazz Messenger CHARGE! type heat, but with an obvious finesse and consummate orchestration of the parts and the smooth yet ever forceful sonic dynamism of the whole. You hear what the leader learned not only from the Blakey hard bop Classicism, but also the orchestral teachings of Wilson, and check it out, what Diz exploded into being with his big bands shot straight out of Gillespie's marvelously wild yet impeccably well-ordered compositions, likewise his overall still much undervalued orchestral conceptualization! Usually, Diz the sonic stylist and even his hip comedic antics overshadow the genuine grandeur of John Birks Gillespie, the truly great innovative artist! But none of this is lost on Charles Tolliver, himself one of Diz's freshest and most skilled progeny in all aspects, compositionally, orchestration, conducting, he even wanna crack some jokes.

After not seeing Tolliver in quite a few years, what we witnessed was a source of deep excitement and gratification. Tolliver stood the music up on tiptoe, Dizzy Gillespie Brass-First style, and it was deep down thrilling! Not just the unpreventable nostalgia such magic carries with it, but to hear again such music, such an approach, such charts, such solos, such ideas, played so well, was utterly transforming!

The band, I suspected it, checking the notice, was most likely a squad of skilled veterans, old enough to be funky and conscious, shaped psychologically and socially by "the tradition" to be awesome musical raconteurs of its wonders. And so it was, James Spaulding and Bill Saxton, tenors; Jimmy Owens, trumpet; Howard Johnson (the great tuba player), baritone; Cecil McBee, bass; Ralph Peterson, drums, just to name some of the biggest names, though believe me, there was some young'ns and some veterans who will come to me who carried much heavy in the set. But just from the names I mentioned, experienced, highly skilled, hope-to-die funky operatives, who have actually heard the masters of our late Golden Age, the Birds, Dizzys, Dukes, Fats, Tranes, Mileses, J.J.'s, Carters, Sassys, Billies, Prez's, who have actually heard the wonderful Dizzy Gillespie and Billy Eckstine big bands, who carry Ellington & Basie in the amulets of their hearts!

So the incredible precision, the unchallengeable swing, Yeh, that, at undecipherable speeds, spraying visions of grand classicism, yet possessing us, themselves and the place, with the newness of the right now.

A wonderful evening, fully Gillespie-like, but with its own excellence and excitement. The loud thrashing riffs (Check "Things to Come," "Emanon," etc.), the sudden lightning of solos or key changes, all calling on whatever was in charge of the joint to challenge the heat of this truth, this beauty (whew!).

Just before the set, as musicians came trooping over to our table, a couple in front said, "Whooh, you're too popular" and moved so they would not have to be stepped over.

It was a re-unioning of sorts, the musicians to some acolytes, us both and all to the grand BeBoppers of our finest sessions. So dig, next time you see Charles Tolliver Big Band some where (he's got a refinery, I'm told, at the New School) don't blow, pick up and go! You'll love me for telling you.

THE HEATH BROTHERS

Recently my wife, Amina, and I have started to come out for the Music, with encouraging though, of course, mixed returns. One night, we journeyed up to just below the golden trestle that connects upper and lower Park Ave to the Kitano (a new very polished joint), trying to dig John Hicks. But the man in the lobby said, in impeccable whatever it was, "No Jazz tonight."

So we went back downtown to more familiar turf, and lo and behold the Heath Brothers were at the Village Vanguard. Only Percy, hospitalized after an operation, was missing. Jimmy with his paradigmatic tenor and Tootie of the energizing smile and energetic tubs held the fort in what must be one of the smoothest bands extant.

What it is, Jimmy's approach seems still to pay tribute to the President of the Tenor, easy, flawless, sensuous, but swinging relentlessly. Tootie, like they say, always tasty, a little salty, down with the commas, apostrophes, exclamation points that make the "straight ahead" the constantly sought-after refreshment in the midst of whatever the "Dangs" is pushing in the contemporary mix of commerce uber feeling.

Plus, the band's got a new "wunderkind" on the piano, a student of Jimmy's & Sir Roland Hanna's, a young (white) pianist, Jeb Patton, who can play, even though one day he will make a squillion dollars. Add bassist Paul West, who has cruised through Dinah Washington, Carmen McRae, Dizzy Gillespie, which layers a bunch of priceless experience, and you have the content and contour of a very easy to dig contemporary package, combining much history, virtuosity, and musical hip.

Plus Jimmy Heath, as always the fastidious funkmeister, subtly shaping the whole ensemble, breezing through the most familiar charts, Monk, Trane, Miles, etc., reminding us why these are some of our favorites, and why and how the Heath Brothers have pleased the real Diggers for so long.

SPIRIT OF LIFE ENSEMBLE

One night we went to Newark's Priory, which is, like the big dude said, "a chancy job," us taking a chance that, as the flyer said, they would feature Joe Lee Wilson, who's been living "unexiled" says he, in England, near the White Cliffs.

Unfortunately, this night was not much Joe Lee, though the group who was, in truth, given the most ink, Spirit of Life Ensemble, Daoud Williams's Jersey City–shaped confection, did hold forth with enviable energy. The group changes personnel so much, though, it's hard to get a fix on where they're coming from musically.

This night they were into a big Latino sound, which at times was on it but sometimes rather confusing. Like when the trombone player who seemed to be the leader gave us a lengthy example of arch trombonery sonics and then had one of his little girl students in duet on one of the tinkle tinkles. We was not impressed and were so distressed we made loud unsophisticated noises as to how we had come to hear Joe Lee Wilson. And I herewith apologize for the raucousness of my conduct but not the spirit.

But that is one problem generally with the Priory, that too many of their acts ain't acting all that tough, especially those from out of the boondockery of church properties now given to neatly reemerging as polite "funk" joints. Though Spirit of Life has been on the scene for a couple decades, for which they should be celebrated, too many of the Priory's offerings are unengaging mysteries. Especially when there are so many great musicians out here not working regular, you know?

JOE LEE WILSON

The next night we went over to Bro Wm's lair in Jersey City, specifically the Miller Branch of the Jersey City Public Library, where he has held forth for many moons. Sure enough, though, our late sallying forth from Newark brought us into the second set. But here, Joe Lee could get heavy with his marvelous style and voice.

What I dig about Joe Lee Wilson is that he is able to take the vocal pyrotechnics of the hippest jazz singing and root it so deep in the blues that it all rings like an epoch. I mean like history being explained in a song phrase.

We missed the great "Where or When," which he uses, he told me as I pouted, as his opener. A wild arrangement Joe Lee hinges on a kind of native American–like rhythmic emphasis, zooming the old words high up and smoking across their bow! But what about "Pink Champagne," which brought back the Terrace Ballroom in Newark in the '50s, or "The Blues Ain't Nuthn," one of Joe Lee's signature pieces.

What remains a large drag is why a singer of Joe Lee Wilson's unique innovative quality can only be seen in the marginalia of New Jersey while commercial still lifes masquerading as singers crowd into the big well-advertised venues. But the arts reflect the social and political life of a society. So that when there is a political upsurge, you can be sure the most sensitive artists will reflect it. We should understand that we are in the downward roll of the huge boulder of struggle for equality and self-determination, Sisyphus style, then the answer to that last question should be plain as Kenny G.

DAVID MURRAY AND THE GWO-KA DRUM MASTERS

We went to see David Murray during the so-called JVC Jazz Festival, the commercial George Wienie roast, characterized by a few hits and a buncha misses. At the same time, the JVC operation puffs itself up by tagging whatever clubs have something (anything) theoretically going as part of the Festival. As far as I know the sole connection is a little white JVC flag strung up somewhere on the premises.

Happily one of those expansion venues, the Jazz Standard, had really exciting music in the latest reappearance in the U.S. of saxophone innovator David Murray, this time with his Gwo-Ka Drum Masters group.

My wife, Amina, and I came early this time, since the last time we showed up On Time to see Charles Tolliver's wonderful big band, the joint was already packed. But this time, our reward for coming early is that we met David coming out of the club, just as we were about to enter.

This was serendipity, because David and I go back over twenty years, when he, Steve McCall, & I worked together for several years as a poetry jazz trio (see *New Music-New Poetry*, India Navigation).

But the music David brought back this time was of a high order, what you'd call International Funk. The Gwo-Ka drummers are part of a socio-cultural and partially religious drumming organization that features the most ancient musical traditions of Guadeloupe. Murray has spent a lot of time in Guadeloupe and a lot of other places since booking out of the States a few years ago to live in Paris. And although he is heavy in European gigs, he has been a world traveler on the real side for the past decade. Though, fortunately for the U.S. faithful, he comes back home regularly, NYC and the coast definitely.

David Murray has also been doing a great deal of earnest work broadening his musical palette. A big band gig in Cuba, the CD *Creole* also utilized musicians from Guadeloupe. The marvelous CD *Fo Deuk* combined the great Senegalese sabar drummer Doudou N'Diaye Rose and a phalanx of Senegalese drummers and Wolof-speaking rappers, plus a high-powered funk component including drummer J.T. Lewis, Electric Miles's keyboardist, Robert Irving, and the incomparable electric bassist Jamaaladeen Tacuma. (Am I saying all this because I was on that album as well? Dig that!)

The latest outcarnation of Murray's PanAfrofunkistry carries another part of that international presence, the likewise African-derived Black culture of Guadeloupe. So that the Black North American & the Black South American embrace as a hemispheric reinvention of the Ancient Mother Tongue. From the mix at the bottom, the southerners still funky with the hand drum, and the northerners with their eloquent "boom a loom" machine derived from the post U.S. slavery one-man bands.

What David Murray has envisioned, just as he showed on *Fo Deuk*, was that the combining of the old and new vonze would be as he projected it earlier as an Interboogieology. What I conceived a few years before in an essay called "The Changing Same" (in *Black Music*): "Let the new people take care of some practical bi-ness and the R&B peepa take care of some new bi-ness and the unity musick, the people-leap, can begin in earnest."

So that is my take on Gwo-Ka, as in *Creole* and *Fo Deuk*, Murray is in deep construction of such a Unity Music. Here with recent Guadeloupe constants Klod Kiave (ka drums and vocal), Francois Ladrezeau (boula drum, lead vocal), plus the veteran new music bassist Jaribu Shahid, a young omni-musical guitarist, Herve Sambe, from Senegal. Omni, because he can deal with "the one" as well as the more complex next, i.e., the funk and the new.

Pieces like "Gwotet," "Ouagadougou," "Ovwa," have the percussive passion of the ancient, motorized with the north slick industrial rumble, which cushions, projects, provides the blast-off for Murray's still incredible saxophone pyrotechnics, or the subtly rapaphonic toning of his bass clarinet. The young guitarist was a perfect textural foil, whether in screaming contrast or echoing melodically. That is the feeling, the African, the Caribbean, the Afro-American neoning North, "The Black Music which is jazz and blues, religious and secular. Which is New Thing and Rhythm and Blues" (op. cit., "The Changing Same"), i.e., the Unity Music.

The Standard appearance coincides with an album with the Gwotet on Justin Time in association with Murray's own 3-D Family, called *David Murray & the Gwo-Ka Masters*, which also includes another master, Pharoah Sanders, taking the Gwo-tet even further up up and away.

12/05

CHAPTER 80

New York Art Quintet

We never really know where we're going. Though we can usually give an answer. Reflects us then, where we are, where we think we are. In 1963, as it turned out, the end and beginning as always transiting through the present.

We had been raising the Loft sets and alternative space gigs because the merchants had yet to understand what had already come. Unlike "Abstract Expressionism," which had emerged at first anathema, or Duchamp's Toilet Bowls in the Paris exhibition, we were never that IN because too often what seems ALL THE WAY OUT, as, say, to disconnect from the Real Next, is actually not OUT but IN as too far "Left" cruises into Right. Dig? (Why the same AE that the "Establishment" denigrated found later that, like Brecht said, it is better to have non-representational Red rather than the Red of actuality, e.g., blood from a slain worker's chest . . . because then you have to take sides. And the toilet bowl, it is now a most valuable and sacred e.g. of Surrealist Resistance to the "Establishment," though it can be viewed at MOMA, etc., anytime.

The point . . . that if what one proffers as NEW is really that, i.e., actually some vital ReNewing of the Deep, the On, the Gone, the truly Out, is authentic transportation up up up to Digging (*Digitaria*, the Dogon named it, the star one had to peep in order to dig the furthermost star in the Universe, SERIOUS! Yeh). The really new (so afterwards you really knew) cannot be mere title and titillation (no matter how well

intentioned). The genuinely or profoundly new remains a portal of revelation whose wisdomic essence and value can be assayed and accessed
into the way off. Ultimately more difficult to be completely co-opted,
"copped" we say, or "covered" (like Jackie, etc., by Elvis, etc).

So in the early sixties, after Trane was called Insane and Sonny
started playing "funny" and C.T. had transformed the Five Spot from
a Bowery hangout for poverty-stricken millionaires to an avant-garde
beer garden, and Pharaoh and Archie and Eric had arrived and Ornette
with his yellow plastic axe and new-style BeBop, and Sun Ra was
sighted as he landed with his crew, and in a minute Albert Ayler would
appear . . . .you see the music had Re-Be'd, at another outer level, and
the few places there ever were to play were filled usually by what the
merchants thought would pay. Them.

So the Diggers, of whom I am was will, we thought we better seek
alternative, cause these natives would not do. And this thinking is still
important. We thought, well why not go out in the world as well, out of
the clubs if they gonna claim lame as they game. That's how the Lofts
and Coffee Shops began to be venues for the New Music. (See "Loft &
Coffee Shop Jazz, 1963," in *Black Music,* LeRoi Jones).

This move to alternate sites was not just logistical, it was philosophical and psychological and filled with aesthetic potential. The lack of
the strict and most backward commercial packaging that the Clubs
imposed provided a Freedom of Thought, a Creative Unbinding which
allowed many of the young players to at least try to carry out what they
were feeling, to express what they were thinking, to play the way they
wanted to.

The New York Art Quintet appears during this period of vigorous
aesthetic and social renewal. Remember, from 55 on the Emmett Till
horror, the Montgomery Bus Boycott, Rosa Parks and Dr. King's emergence and SCLC, Robert Williams ambushing the Klan, the Mau Mau
in Kenya, Fidel Castro liberating Cuba, Malcolm X exploding out of
our TVs, SNCC, all over the world like rising blood pressure the call
would be "Revolution Is the Main Trend in the World Today!"

So that NYAQ was part of that whole, where the world was going and
where the art, a reflection in whoever's mind, was going in reflection of
the world. Monk and Trane would make the great Breakthrough at the
now formally avant-garde Five Spot, opening the door for Ornette and
some indication of what was flowing loose and ubiquitous in people's
sensibilities and the streets.

What was being brought by the world gestalt was an aggressive

Openness as a historical continuum of mass desire given intellectual and artistic articulation, to get away from the dead peepas and what they "give" as reality. Just as the most progressive people across the world were rejecting the world they Knew, struggling to create the world as New. So the New Music rejected emotionally and intellectually the Tin Pan Alley Musicians' Penitentiary. Aesthetically this was confirmed by a willful and continuous needs to Experiment, to change up, to find, as Grachan Moncur III says, "some other stuff." An Openness of many times not knowing completely where we were yet feeling a path to the next realness inside ourselves which only confirmed what we had experienced in the world which demanded we express it.

But we were trying to get Realer not leap from the box of was into the box of not. The ubiquitous calling of Free, e.g., Free Jazz, Freedom Suite, Freedom Now: We Insist! Let Freedom Ring, Freedom Jazz Dance, Free, all speak to the feeling the attempt at playing and being. And that is not a trend but a recurring profile of the soul of American Classical Music. Because the living humanity of the culture that created that music and all who really dig it understand that FREE/FREEDOM was is and will be the philosophy, aesthetic and social center of the Afro-American people and any people else who understands they ain't. Taken directly from our historical material life, as DuBois said, "Many have suffered as much as we . . . but none of them was Real Estate."

So that Freedom, to be, to be human, to find our road not be one . . . that has animated the great American Classical Music from the vector of its Afro-American Soul, which is not mystical, simply culturally specific, but accessible from Digitaria. John Tchikai from Denmark . . . and that is not fully known that Ham was there before Hamlet. Tchikai with his Bird imagined Johnny Hodges's "metal poem" (I said then) . . . incisive, insinuating, penetrating, slicing, with narrative invoking improvisational style. Roswell who haunts the present with its own memory . . . that big percussively aggressive sound, the mechanism of its creation shaping it from the inside. Yet as tender as touching as searching as it is brash and open.

Reggie Workman, everybody claiming some information about the music must know. (He took over the bass from Louis Worrell.) The Workman, whose history is as illustrious as the last few decades of the music itself. Whose strings have been, literally, the wings of any claiming to be players in the grand trad of deep feeling deep meaning new understanding.

For me, Milford has always projected the vision of our self-willed invincibility. I remember when he and Don Pullen (a marvelous expressionist, now tragically gone, like too many of us). Their entrance on the scene was as heavy as the whole, like the new kept coming. Pullen had taken even the new and made it newer while Milford actually frightened folks. The energy of transformation is awesome, and with Milford he brought such power and force to the set it spoke discursively, as music, but about the changes society was going through itself.

The new CD is necessary today as facts and food, in this world dominated almost completely by corporate commercial culture. If we are not being conned with fusion we are offered trash for cash crap for rap. Look at the Literary or Music or Film or Video Best Seller Lists. And remember there was a time when we could stand on the corner and decide whether we were going to see Monk & Trane, or Duke or Billie or Sassy or Miles, or for that matter Albert or Eric or Sun Ra. The new CD carries some of that feeling of what we Knew as the revelationally New.

8/99
Newark

CHAPTER 81

Peter Brötzmann, *Nipples,* and Joe McPhee, *Nation Time*

Peter Brötzmann Sextet & Quartet, *Nipples,* Atavistic Records,
2000, UMS/ALP205CSD.
Peter Brötzmann, tenor; Evan Parker, tenor; Derek Bailey, guitar; Fred
Van Hove, piano; Busch Niebergal, bass; Han Bennink, drums.
Side A: "Nipples" (Brötzmann). Side B: "Tell a Green Man"
(Brötzmann) (No times given).
Joe McPhee, *Nation Time,* Atavistic Records, 2000, CJR-2.
Joe McPhee, tenor, trumpet; Mike Kull, piano, electric piano; Tyrone
Crabb, bass, electric bass, trumpet; Bruce Thompson, Ernest Bostic,
percussion.

Two CDs reflecting the impact, influence of ideas and techniques
most dynamic in "the '60s" "new music." In each case, the impact
of the ubiquitously proclaimed "Freedom" which shaped that period,
as social political or aesthetic focus. Here, specifically, this thesis is
demonstrated through the arts.

This is a general phenomenon, historically confirmed, that the most
influential political, intellectual, and artistic ideas and trends of any
period, whether as a positive confirmation or as a theoretical and ideological rejection of them, will dominate the period. But that influence,
depending on the consciousness and ideological character of those
influenced, will be expressed in very diverse ways.

There are also a host of other contesting influences at all times,
which might tend to dilution, superficiality, marginalization of important aspects of the original source. Overemphasis of marginal aspects
of the source, etc. The difference between innovation, popularization,
dilution or outright vulgarization.

Brötzmann, here, obsesses with the initial explosiveness of the original form's emergence. The form being the incredible dynamism of the '60s "Free Jazz" outburst usually identified with Trane, Pharoah, Archie. He particularizes, it seems, a kind of homage to Albert Ayler or Frank Wright. He is absorbed by this form qua form, projecting it as a complete aesthetic construct, thereby minimalizing its deeper philosophical and creative Use as musical innovation. So that he apotheosizes the blunt power and raw timbre of the original, but strips the paradigm of its deeper compositional and improvisational expressiveness.

What Brötzmann seems oblivious to is that the explosion was an introduction to new ways into the music, entrance into newer forms of a total expression. By one-sidedly emphasizing only one aspect of the new, Brötzmann transforms the music into a kind of still life, reducing it to a *style*, without concomitant creative substance. In fact, if we judge as well, by titles like this CD, *Nipples,* or the name of one of his touring ensembles, *Die Like a Dog,* we can believe that the emotional presence of the music not only disconnects "style" from substance but replaces it with a one-sided, flat snapshot of the form as path, but is unable to conceive of where that path leads.

Ayler, e.g., "Spirits Awake," "Witches and Devils," "The Truth Is Marching In," "Ghosts," etc., narrates a world of struggle against diverse negative forces, material, psychological, emotional, as Albert conceives it, raising good, destroying evil. Brötzmann seems to think that only the "destruction" is important and so makes repetitious hyperbole without understanding that this music reflected and was a *living* being, an opening not a closing, a beginning not an end. When the emotional content of this music is missing, as it is here and from a depressing number of other players of "the new music," it becomes formalist and academic. A one-sidedness that makes it superficial and drains the music of real life.

It reminds me of a Swiss saxophonist I did a gig with several years ago, who, when I laid out the Monk, Duke, Trane, etc., pieces I wanted his group to play with my poetry, told me, "I don't play tunes." A self-aggrandizing elitism that could only produce a predictably empty art.

McPhee is often in danger of being the other pole of what happens to influence without depth, impact without complete understanding of WHY the paradigmatic expression emerged in the first place. It is ironic that the title of the CD and the first piece carry a phrase that this writer first introduced, as a political statement animated by the Black Liberation Movement, most visible as projected by the 1972 National

Black Political Convention in Gary, Indiana, and subsequently as the title of a Word-Music album.

McPhee, past the cry of "Nation Time," tries to stretch his essentially rhythm and blues shaped mainstream musical approach into the frenzy and force he identifies with that first call. His blunt funkiness and insistent tunefulness do save him from the still life of Brotzmann and the other neo-academic "Outs" I mentioned, but finally the whole of the music is limited by a confused and incomplete *use* of his materials. And behind this settles overall into a restatement of funk clichés hoisted occasionally by flashes of "the new." So that despite the Call for the New, R&B cliches obstruct the shaping of something really new. Still when he blue screams our old Call "What Time Is It?" which was to be answered by the album's title, it does put one in mind of more dynamic times, would that they were more completely expressed in this music.

CHAPTER 82

Jon Jang and David Murray, *River of Life*

Asian Improv, 2000, AIR 0062.
Jon Jang (piano) and David Murray (tenor sax).

This is very fine music, a CD of exceptional sensitivity, intellectual depth, and artistic excellence. David Murray is, of course, for those just got to the planet, the "State of the Art" on the tenor saxophone, an innovative soloist, exciting composer, and one of the most imaginative arrangers and band leaders on the set.

One contributing factor of David's importance to the music is the diversity of his concerns and the striking ensembles he puts together, the musicians and the instrumentation, to play them.

When I first heard David, I thought of Albert Ayler, the broad, powerful, sharply aggressive sound and swaggering path of tone and timbre. Since then, Murray has developed and broadened his musical palette, consistently creative zooming ark of rhythm-based harmelodic narrative, that characterize his solos. The historically enhanced aesthetic of his choices. David Murray is at once an authentically daring and advanced player, with a musical persona shaped by the Was the Is and the Will Be.

Jon Jang is relatively recent, though he has played with some of the most respected names in the music. Emerging, it seems, fully matured, from the vineyard of the historically hip and the contemporarily creative. Jang also brings the East Wind of international digging up front. He is yet another important voice reflecting the multicultural multinational nature of any actual "America." Like D. D. Jackson, from Canada, or Vijay Iyer, whose parents are from India, or Rodney Kendricks, originally from Trinidad, or the ubiquitous dazzling presence of "the Latin Tinge," via David Sanchez, Jerry Gonzalez, Hilton Ruiz, and the Puentes, Bauzas, Bobos, Mongos, Palmieris, y todos los otros. The confluence and interfunkistry of the world inside the real U.S.

Murray and Jang are actually very contrasting players in many ways. Jang, an almost tender lyricist, who spreads the funk like petals of light when he rushes across the keys. But he can also be Largo, Staccato, powerful as the classic Chinese "Boxer."

Murray, of course, carries the huge timbre of the blue wailing night, the explosive cries of the middle passage, the low down out of the gone. Both are very skilled players, whose imagination and taste are their only musical parameters.

But for all their oppositeness, like everything else, they form a dialectic that is constructed of both contradiction and identity. So that at times, even though superficial presumption might give them no chance to connect, on the contrary they are as connected and mutually enhancing, blowing together as this picture in front of me showing Mao and Dr. Du Bois laughing together in Tiananmen Square.

And the nature of the dialectical process, sometimes, they become each other. David, with his upper-register lyricism, Jon hammering the box with a percussive emotional depth. So that the opposites like the polarities of Ancient Africa, the Ying and Yang of Ancient China, are *sonideographed* through us, as if we are hearing such aesthetic completion for the first time.

What is further intriguing about the CD is that it is a Duo, two marvelous artists creating at the top of their knowing. From the Outset, "Moon Reflected over the Lake" by Hua Yan-Jun, a sweet imagist ballad that reminds one of the Odes, the Classic Anthology of Chinese Lyrics, the expert rendering of which Confucius said was the test of a Wise Man. An indication of historical knowledge and appreciation of beauty and tradition. Jang's exquisitely expressive opening, blues inside with David Murray's undering it into *Djeli ya* reflective Afro-Asian tale, a ballad of meditation and tender memory which grows more animated as it is recalled.

The names of the works convey the intellectual depth and social grasp of these musicians very clearly. Sometimes with delight, at times with humor, but, by the results, always seriously. "Two Portraits of Capital Punishment: If You Don't Have the Capital, Then You Get Punished" and "Two Portraits of Capital Punishment: If You Do Have the Capital, Then You Don't Get Punished," which reflect what Mao called for from Progressive Artists, to create that which is Artistically Powerful and Politically Revolutionary.

Dig this, the statement comes open with the sound and rhythm of the Native Peoples, whose purloined land has been transformed into capital, near-genocide has been their punishment.

The striking relevance of these concerns, e.g., "Free Mumia Now," screams at us every day, especially in a world where a Bushman governor has killed more people on his watch than all the other states combined. Or the Grisly headlines the title "Eleanor Bumpurs" recalls of the elderly black woman murdered by New York's fiendish. Here retold as a slowly twisting swallowing, tragic yet forthright musical drama. The horn searches for description, the piano elaborating, rumbling, running, dramatizing the horror, together, as provocative and inspiring as our will to live. "Mumia" is anthem and call . . . colored by the sadness and madness of this place. Moving adventurous music. Advanced social ideas contexted and projected by advanced artistic concepts. As it should be.

I am especially flattered by the naming of a few of these tunes after poems of mine. A few years ago, in homage to the long reading of the Japanese Haiku form, I came up with an Afro-American tribute form, the *Low Coup*. No fixed amount of syllables like the classic, just short and sharp.

Jang and Murray use two of the first, one called "Lowcoup," which essence is Truth is in the Act, the other, "The Heir of the Dog," re: American middle-class concern about animals more than humans. The Lowcoup, featuring Murray on Bass Clarinet, an instrument to which he has brought much distinction, and Jang laying amplifying chords under the rhythmic pop of the horn producing what has to be a new dance step . . . humorous and lilting, but funky. Finally, "Lift Every Voice and Sing," called in my youth the Negro National Anthem, James Weldon and Rosamund Johnson's Harlem Renaissance example of artistic and cultural Self-Determination, which our own Word Music ensemble, Blue Ark, finished our historical work, Funk Lore, as the denouement, over which Amina Baraka read her moving "Ode to Malcolm." Jon and David render it at full lyric and narrative power, creating an anthem, a penetrating "sorrow song" and another hymn of revolutionary democratic consciousness, like another movement of the Internationale, to demonstrate the changing conditions that had Lenin change Marx's classic "Workers Unite" to "Workers and Oppressed Peoples Unite."

CHAPTER 83

Trio Three, *Encounter*

Passin Thru, 2001, UPC: 687317121224.
Reggie Workman, Andrew Cyrille, Oliver Lake.

These are three formidable musicians. Each with uniquely identifiable sounds and approaches to the music. The seriousness and commitment are never in doubt, especially if you have listened across the last decade or so, you understand that they will move us, involve us, as motif, theme, or where the melodic line and the harmonic path of its whole musical movement is itself a rhythmic paradigm. We calls it syncopation.

Bobby Bradford's "Crooked Blues" is Crooked, as in "Monkish," Oliver Lake threads the seemingly asymmetrical line serving as introduction to the unclichéd, the heaviness, of its lightness. Like that smile at the bottom of the world, the Bodhidarma tip, the laughter of revelation! So hip it's happy!

The understanding is the exchange the movement—self to selves. So Reggie wants to see outside the out or where it lead from the place in sonic space, between be and at, where Oliver passed off. Andrew, with Reggie, collect till Oliver returns to report Bradford's Monkish Outstructions, as a philosophisonic map of how to reach Gone.

The change is the exchange, the relations of production, the changes. What is spontaneous is not the same as improvised. The improvised is a practice, like Billy the Kid shooting a hole for his nephew's whistle in a reed without seeming to aim. He say, "I'm always aiming!"

Adegoke's "Leaving East" brings the east as mystery, anticipation of the wonderful, sensuous and moody, Oliver leading over Reggie's underflecting darkness and signifying . . . , like where is we, Jim? Near Java, Andrew announces Cymballically. The coming of the Whatnot!

Music like this unbuttons our image-making instruments, the sound makes pictures, words. So Andrew's singing cymbals shake this first impression loose to dig whatever deeper "else" we can.

Syncopation is a form, itself, of communication. Since the soi-disant Christians brung us here, and wrung our drum loose from our speech. Without the traditional Dun Dun (talking drum) the run and stop, leap and hold, of the music's whole funkistry, means to tell, to relate, report, analyze. Reggie running off disappearing from the East . . . running, Oliver raised to airspeed by Workman's velocity and drive, reporting, now, from above the land and people- scapes. An *Encounter*, winding and twisting overhead, the earth rumbling in motion below. Soon, everything is in flight, the new penetrating the before. Andrew . . . bow, bam, sladoouummm . . . to Gone.

Not just the abstraction of sound, but a tale. They tell a story, experience, beginning with history and the environmental paint of the music's whole. Africa, America, blows what it knows. This is a complete deepening music, i.e., it never just leaves, the lingering is what ideas emotion carries. Feeling, thought, memory, rationale, doing . . . Reggie at the end, still flying through the where, Oliver looking back, near gone, toward out.

Lake's "Reminds Me" lyric, the "statement," with Workman's chordal reflections, like the vibes of memory. *Reminds* . . . .of what . . . the winds of whens . . . the who . . . the where, a dimension of reflection, searching for the whatever of this moment's realness. Never static, gone gone gone, return . . .

To get such music, like drama, there has to be the script, on the page, out the head and run of feeling. The musicians, like these Triple hip three, capable of blowing life dimensions from where they got them over to us, complex yet simply delivered, And the relationships, the known discovering the Un. Music like a metaphor of what it was inside them. Connected by the intensity of their collective expression.

. . . The "Ode" is a triumphant celebration. Andrew hammering meaning from the earth itself, like melodic singing of the march-dance-rah rah-rah . . . the living tree, The flow and beat of life as celebration-ing-ing.

Workman's "Suite," like all this music, begins with a declared deepness. Sweet yet digging, Lake's flute singing a melody hearingly suspended, a gentle narrative, well seasoned with parenthetically flashing asides. Lake is out front Cyrille and Workman are his whole self, the three together one spectrum of the We.

As on the super-hip "Nicodemus," what we calls a droll blue stroll, like my man, coming downtown to get some sun. Dig Andrew's digging how the dude move, and Workman the inside ring of what vibes he/we brings. This is music at the edge of the next . . . underknown only because of Square Rule.

4/00
Newark

CHAPTER 84

Jackie Mc—Coming and Going

Amina & I were at Jackie McLean's Funeral. He went "home," to Abyssinia (Baptist Church), to be funeralized. Rev. Butts said to us all, particularly the musicians, "You need to come home. Where somebody knows you. And don't wait till this time, because you know, we all going to go through this sometime. But come before that, just drop in, so we know you. So you know us."

That was, it seemed, heartfelt. Especially in a place teeming with the creators of music. Jackie's son, whom we hugged out on the sidewalk, for once coming early, Rene, is already, himself, a formidable voice on all the bent horns. Having been readied and guided by his old man from way back.

Rene's wife was there, Thanteweh, the South African ambassador to Portugal. Later, during the service, she gave a stirring ambassadorial narrative, citing her meeting Rene when he went to Africa to play with Hugh Masekela, how they got married, and how she came back to the states to become part of a truly Pan-African family. How the music itself, this improvised Afro-American, American Classical music, was like their romantic hookup, full of the sensuous depths of flesh and feeling, memory and history.

We also embraced Jackie's wife, Dolly, whom we knew when all three of us were running nearly amuck on the Lower East Side, furiously making art and almost suiciding ourselves in the process. Elvin Jones, Hank Mobley, the painters Bob Thompson and William White were also part of that mad junket that orbited unsteadily around the planet Slugs, which was a high musical way station on the Low East Apple full of the grim laughter of those promised until death. Those who are allowed to hear wonderful, even miraculous, things before they pass into the where ever. Lee Morgan actually got wasted on a bar stool in Slug's by his wife. But I had stopped going there before that. I think Jackie and Dolly had gravitated to Hartford by then and began building their Artists Cooperative, Jackie also gave musical depth to Hartford University's Hart School of Music, which now has Jackie's name added to it to make it officially hip.

At the funeral, Gil Noble gave a riveting description of his and Jackie Mc's childhood friendship, which lasted until Jackie turned completely spiritual on us. The two of them growing up in the Sugar Hill section of an earlier sweeter Harlem. Back when DuBois and Duke Ellington lived not too far away, when the genius of great artists, like Langston and Zora and them and great thinkers, like W.E.B, Garvey, Bumpy J, and them, was as liable to be its identity, from the Harlem Renaissance on, not just poverty crime and murder.

And as Gil talked about he and Jackie Mc, he could not fail to bring up how it was in Harlem that he was first touched by Dr. King, which opened his eyes to what he was not, and then how he reluctantly, and even after initially digging, resisted once he had stumbled into the assault on his consciousness made by a man who had just got rid of his street name "Big Red" and took on the warrior sobriquet Malcolm X.

So Gil was hipping us to what it was like to be in Harlem then, the late '50s, and how he and Jackie had grown up through that. After having their brains lit up a little earlier by Bird, Charlie Parker and the message of Bop, which made us think of things we had never thought of before.

But that is the mixture my generation grew up in and when I first heard that Jackie Mc had passed, in some sad addlebrained displacement I thought, "Well, Jackie's generation is getting out of here." But then, a split second later, when I read that Jackie McLean was 73 (I was tempted to write "only 73") I knew what I had known before trying to make believe I didn't know, that Jackie and I are of the same generation, me about to be 72 by the time this comes out.

Newark has never been "Sugar Hill," though we have some measured sweetness in our rough travail, and Sassy (Sarah Vaughan) and Wayne (Shorter) called this place home, Babs helped invent BeBop Language, and "Humphrey" (Walter Davis) and the immigrant Hank Mobley were actually in the Messengers, i.e., the University of Buhaina

Art Blakey's Jazz Messengers) just like Jackie Mc. But they all had to make the pilgrimage to said Apple anyway. Almost everybody does.

I remember the first time I heard Jackie Mc, it was in the early '50s with Miles, on those bad sides that burned the super swinging mixture of first- and second-generation Boppers into our persons. Dig, no title really to the album, *Miles Davis,* volume 1 (Blue Note) its only nomenclature, the names Jay Jay Johnson, Jackie McLean, Art Blakey, Kenny Clarke across the top, hip Miles and J.J. on the cover.

Or check *Trumpet Giants* (Prestige New Jazz), where Miles shares the album with Fats Navarro, Dizzy Gillespie, and the list of sidemen, including the young Jackie Mc, reads like the hall of fame, Sonny Rollins, Walter Bishop Jr., Tommy Potter, Art Blakey. You should be listening to "My Old Flame" or "Conception" right now, as I am about to, to re-dig the what it is of the what it was.

So from then on through his *Capuchin Swing, Bluesnik* (we was close), *Jackie's Bag,* through the Messengers to those hip sides he made with Grachan Moncur III.

Tony Williams, Bobby Hutcherson, and Wayne Shorter in the middle '60s Jackie was always one of my main men. In fact, if there is any musician whose very sound, the brusque timbre of his instrument itself, conjured "the City," which is New York stripped down to its anonymous exactness of is and ain't, and what it is ain't no piece of fruit!

And that is part of my précis, that from the glories of Sugar Hill's ethnic emotional loving, the nurturing that would come from having a father, John, a guitarist with Tiny Bradshaw, an uncle who played in the local church, being surrounded by a common funkiness of the uptown masses, among whom moved actual giants, who could perceive, rationalize, and use as various kinds of expression such reflections of material life.

From there and that, like the most sensitive of us, congeal it all deep inside us, but always on the ready, Billy the Kid style. Because all of our experience is in there. To the question asked by his little nephew, "How can you hit that without aiming?" Billy replies, "I'm always aiming!"

So what does this mean right now? I'm sitting in the Abyssinia Baptist Church listening to Jimmy Heath play Monk's "Round Midnight." Hilton Ruiz and Grachan Moncur III and Mickey Bass, and Bill Saxton and Jayne Cortez and Mel Edwards and Les Payne and Tom Porter and Rashidah Ismaili and Larry Ridley among a thousand are there. Musicians and Poets and Sculptors and Journalists and a horde of the actual diggers of the sounds without whom the world itself could not exist.

And my mind wanders, digging Monk thinking about Jackie Mc thinking about all the lives touched by this music and this way of being and feeling and I remember one of Jackie's greatest sides. Actually it came to me when Jackie's daughter introduced herself before the service started. She said, "My name is Melonae." To which I answered, "Yeh, I know you." And she laughed at the irony, knowing I must have meant the song her father wrote for her many years before, when she was little, "Little Melonae," on an album called *Let Freedom Ring.*

It was in 1963, the movement was at full tilt, Lumumba had been murdered the year before, and I had met artists like Roland Snellings (Askia Toure) and Larry Neal in the demonstrations, one which led to folks, including Maya Angelou and Abbey Lincoln, rushing into the United Nations and embarrassing Ralph Bunche for being so meekly Black.

The album *Let Freedom Ring* would come out in the hottening motion of our growing objective mobilization to fight for Equal Rights and Self-Determination. Though Jackie was specifically referring to the fact that Ornette Coleman and others had swooped onto the New York scene, to be followed by or at the same time as folks like Archie Shepp, Pharoah Sanders, Albert Ayler, and given John Coltrane's majestic leadership of the whole from the launching pad of Miles and Monk, into glorious "outness," it made Jackie Mc more thoughtful as to what he wanted to do with his life and his horn. The liner notes, which Jackie wrote, speak specifically to this new mission. It is a paean to the new masters who had moved onto the scene. It was clearly a musical declaration, but at the same time what can be separate in the world, since what we pick up is shaped most obviously by time, place, and condition.

What Jackie Mc said himself, "Getting away from the conventional and much overused chord changes was my personal dilemma. . . . These changes do not fit the personality of the tune. . . . Today . . . I use sections of scales and modes. I try to write each thing with its own personality. . . . I am going through a big change compositionwise, and improvising. Ornette Coleman has made me stop and think. . . . The new breed has inspired me all over again. The search is on. Let Freedom ring."

The very term of the most "avant" of the new music, "Free Jazz," speaks from the ground, from the zeitgeist of the world itself, reflecting and still invoking that time when Mao said, "Countries want Independence, Nations Want Liberation, People Want Revolution!"

When, as he added, "Revolution Is the Main Trend in the World Today!" Alas, it is no more today, which is why the superpowers run amuck throughout the world and Greenwich Village looks like Coney Island and hip Soho resembles nothing so much as Tiffany's garden.

When *Let Freedom Ring* came out, the world was rocking to an anti-imperialist antiracist beat, though John Kennedy would be murdered by that November and Malcolm X a couple years later to try to turn the beat around. In other words it was not possible merely to talk about the music, the world itself was included.

So when I walked into this Eighth Street record shop and asked for the record *Let Freedom Ring*, this bald-headed clerk who did not actually look like Otto Preminger, however it suits me to metaphorize the incident with this image, stiffened and snatched the record from my hand, "Why don't you people learn when you want to make music it's not the same as making a speech?"

"Silly Motherfucker!" was the only rational response. I still have the side!

4/10/06

Text:	10/13 Sabon
Display:	Sabon
Compositor:	BookMatters, Berkeley
Printer and Binder:	Maple-Vail Book Manufacturing Group